Artificial Intelligence Applications in Financial Markets

Afef Rachid Amdouni
https://orcid.org/0000-0001-9625-300X
Taibah University, Saudi Arabia

IGI Global
Scientific Publishing
Publishing Tomorrow's Research Today

Published in the United States of America by
IGI Global Scientific Publishing
701 East Chocolate Avenue
Hershey, PA, 17033, USA
Tel: 717-533-8845 | Fax: 717-533-7115
Website: https://www.igi-global.com E-mail: cust@igi-global.com

Library of Congress Cataloging-in-Publication Data

Names: Amdouni, Afef, 1983- editor
Title: Artificial intelligence applications in financial markets / [edited by] Afef Amdouni.
Description: Hershey, PA : IGI Global Scientific Publishing, [2026] | Includes bibliographical references and index. | Summary: "This book provides a comprehensive and up-to-date academic reference on the applications of artificial intelligence in transforming financial markets worldwide. It aims to bridge the gap between theoretical AI models and their practical implementation in various financial domains, such as trading, risk management, regulatory compliance, and fraud detection"-- Provided by publisher.
Identifiers: LCCN 2025029099 (print) | LCCN 2025029100 (ebook) | ISBN 9798337350325 hardcover | ISBN 9798337350332 paperback | ISBN 9798337350349 ebook
Subjects: LCSH: Artificial intelligence--Financial applications | Finance--Technological innovations
Classification: LCC HG4515.5 .A789 2026 (print) | LCC HG4515.5 (ebook) | DDC 332.64/20285--dc23/eng/20251114
LC record available at https://lccn.loc.gov/2025029099
LC ebook record available at https://lccn.loc.gov/2025029100

British Cataloguing in Publication Data
A Cataloguing in Publication record for this book is available from the British Library.

Table of Contents

Detailed Table of Contents

followed by applying topic modelling analysis using the machine learning technique Latent Dirichlet Allocation (LDA) to identify key topics, their interrelationships and thematic clusters. The findings map the current research landscape and highlight the direction of future developments in AI-driven finance. The study also provides practical implications by equipping stakeholders with insights into prevailing trends and key themes and possible opportunities in the transformative field of AI-driven finance.

The integration of artificial intelligence (AI) in financial decision-making and portfolio optimization marks a significant change in investment decision-making. Conventional econometric models, although foundational, often struggle with nonlinear dynamics, high-dimensional data, and rapidly changing market conditions. AI, particularly machine learning and deep learning algorithms, presents the capacity to reveal hidden patterns, adapt to evolving data, and offer real-time predictive capabilities. This chapter examines how AI-driven tools enhance the accuracy of financial forecasts, automate resource allocation, and inform risk-adjusted investment strategies. It also delves into cases that explain how support stores, resource directors, and robo-advisors utilize AI for vital decision-making. By reimagining decision-making through the lens of data-centric insights and showing adaptivity, AI enables investors to make more informed, agile, and versatile choices in volatile markets.

Artificial intelligence (AI) has emerged as one of the most transformative forces in modern finance, reshaping portfolio management and asset allocation in ways not seen since the advent of computerized trading. This study offers a comprehensive exploration of how machine learning, deep neural networks, reinforcement learning, and natural language processing are revolutionizing investment decision-making across global markets. Drawing from diverse theoretical models, academic research, and applied case studies, the analysis highlights AI's growing role in portfolio construction, risk management, predictive analytics, and market efficiency. Particular attention is given to both developed and emerging markets, with the Gulf Cooperation Council (GCC) region examined as a case study in AI-enabled financial innovation.

Key challenges such as data quality, model interpretability, and evolving regulatory demands are discussed in depth. The study concludes with strategic recommendations for institutions, regulators, and researchers navigating the AI-driven transformation of capital markets.

Pawan Kumar Badhan, IT Department, Pyramid College of Business and Technology, Phagwara, India
Vivek Mittal, Pyramid College of Business and Technology, Phagwara, India
Priyanka Gupta, Department of Computer Applications, Golden College of Engineering and Technology, Gurdaspur, India
Davinder Singh, IT Department, Saraswati Group of Colleges, Gharuan, India
Ankush Sharma, Management Department, Pyramid College of Business and Technology, Punjab, India

Stock price forecasting is complex due to the volatility and multifaceted nature of financial markets. Traditional methods use either computational or statistical models, each with limitations. Deep learning models like CNNs and RNNs capture nonlinear patterns well but often overfit time-series data. Statistical models like ARIMA handle linear trends but fail to detect complex dependencies. This study proposes a hybrid model integrating CNN, RNN, and ARIMA to improve forecasting accuracy. It leverages deep learning's pattern recognition and ARIMA's trend analysis strengths. The dataset includes Date, Open, High, Low, Close prices, technical indicators, and macroeconomic variables like GDP Growth and Interest Rate. The target is Future Stock Price. CNN/RNN captures temporal features, while ARIMA models linear trends. Outputs are merged via a weighted ensemble optimized for MSE and MAE. CNN, RNN, and ARIMA achieved 98%, 97%, and 100% accuracy, respectively. The hybrid model reached 100%. Future work includes sentiment data and broader financial applications.

Sushil Bhardwaj, RIMT University, India
Sunaina Garg, RIMT University, India
Vinesh Kumari, RIMT University, India
Sunaina Mehta, RIMT University, India

This chapter discusses the development of AI in stock markets and how it is assisted by the use of high-frequency trading systems that monitor the movements of markets

Preface

INTRODUCTION

Artificial Intelligence (AI) has emerged as a defining force in the evolution of modern financial markets, fundamentally transforming the processes through which financial information is analyzed, uncertainty is managed, and investment decisions are executed. The rapid advancement of machine learning techniques and data-driven modeling frameworks has enabled the identification of complex, nonlinear relationships that extend well beyond the explanatory capacity of traditional econometric models. As a result, AI-driven systems have become increasingly embedded in forecasting, portfolio optimization, and real-time trading environments across both developed and emerging financial systems.

Despite these technological advancements, the role of AI in finance remains inherently complex and, in many respects, paradoxical. While machine learning models often demonstrate superior predictive accuracy, their ability to consistently generate economic value remains far less conclusive. This divergence reflects a deeper structural tension rooted in the stochastic and adaptive nature of financial markets, where volatility, regime shifts, and exogenous shocks continuously reshape the underlying data-generating processes. Within this context, the implications of the Efficient Market Hypothesis remain highly relevant, as the persistence of exploitable patterns is both limited and context-dependent.

The increasing reliance on heterogeneous data sources further amplifies this complexity. Contemporary AI systems integrate structured financial indicators with unstructured data—including textual, behavioral, and sentiment-based information thereby expanding the informational landscape of financial decision-making. Advances in Natural Language Processing and large language models have enhanced the extraction of latent signals from news flows and social media. However, these developments introduce significant methodological challenges related to data quality, signal reliability, model interpretability, and computational constraints. Consequently, the growing adoption of AI raises critical questions regarding transparency, robustness, and the practical relevance of predictive models in dynamic financial environments.

Unlike a substantial body of existing literature that predominantly emphasizes predictive performance and technological advancement, this volume adopts a more critical and integrative perspective. It explicitly challenges the implicit assumption that improvements in predictive accuracy necessarily translate into meaningful economic outcomes. Instead, the contributions in this book collectively demonstrate that the effectiveness of AI in financial markets is fundamentally conditional—shaped by model design, data regimes, and market structures. By bridging predictive modeling with economic interpretation, this volume positions itself within a broader research agenda that seeks to reconcile the gap between statistical performance and real-world financial relevance.

More importantly, this volume distinguishes itself by systematically examining the disconnect between predictive performance and economic value across diverse financial contexts. Rather than treating AI as a universally superior solution, it critically evaluates the conditions under which AI-driven models succeed or fail, thereby contributing to a more realistic and context-sensitive understanding of their role in financial markets.

This volume contributes to a more context-sensitive understanding of Artificial Intelligence in financial markets by emphasizing the conditional relationship between predictive performance and economic value across different market environments.

Against this backdrop, this volume brings together a set of scholarly contributions that examine Artificial Intelligence in financial markets through a methodological and application-oriented lens. The chapters collectively explore the full analytical pipeline—from data processing and model development to portfolio construction and trading execution—while maintaining a critical focus on the limitations and contextual dependencies of AI-driven systems.

CHAPTER OVERVIEW

The structure of this volume reflects a structured and conceptually layered progression from conceptual foundations toward increasingly sophisticated applications of Artificial Intelligence in financial markets. The chapters collectively examine the full analytical spectrum—from theoretical positioning and methodological development to real-time implementation and behavioral financial systems—while maintaining a critical focus on the conditions under which AI generates meaningful economic value.

Chapter 1: Artificial Intelligence in Stock Market Trading - A Comprehensive Survey of Models and Applications: Evolution, Challenges, and Future Directions in AI-Driven Financial Markets

This chapter establishes the intellectual foundation of the volume through a comprehensive bibliometric analysis of AI applications in stock market trading. Drawing on a large-scale dataset spanning several decades of academic research, it systematically traces the evolution of AI methodologies, including deep learning architectures, ensemble techniques, and hybrid modeling frameworks. The chapter situates AI within key theoretical paradigms such as the Efficient Market Hypothesis, Behavioral Finance, and the Adaptive Market Hypothesis, highlighting both complementarities and inherent tensions. A notable contribution is the development of a multi-layered framework that integrates data transformation, model construction, validation, trading execution, and ethical governance. By identifying dominant research clusters and emerging directions—such as explainable AI and alternative data integration—the chapter provides a rigorous conceptual baseline for the subsequent contributions.

Chapter 2: Emerging Trends in AI-Driven Finance: A Topic Modeling Approach

Building on the conceptual foundation, this chapter adopts a data-driven approach to map the evolving landscape of AI-driven finance. Using Latent Dirichlet Allocation (LDA) applied to large-scale bibliographic data, it identifies dominant thematic clusters and emerging research trajectories within the field. The analysis reveals the convergence of machine learning, financial innovation, and risk management as central pillars of contemporary financial research. By uncovering latent thematic structures and inter-topic relationships, the chapter provides a systematic overview of the intellectual evolution of AI in finance. It also offers forward-looking insights, highlighting research gaps and potential areas for future investigation, thereby serving as a strategic guide for researchers, practitioners, and policymakers.

Chapter 3: AI-Powered Forecasting and Portfolio Optimization-From Predictive Models to Strategic Investment Decisions

This chapter transitions from conceptual mapping to applied modeling by examining the integration of AI into financial forecasting and portfolio optimization. It critically evaluates the limitations of traditional econometric models in handling nonlinear dynamics and high-dimensional data, positioning machine learning as a flexible and adaptive alternative. The chapter demonstrates how AI-driven predictive models enhance forecasting accuracy and enable dynamic, risk-adjusted portfolio allocation. Through practical applications—including robo-advisory systems and automated asset allocation frameworks—it illustrates how predictive signals are translated into strategic investment decisions. At the same time, it acknowledges key challenges related to model stability, interpretability, and sensitivity to changing market conditions.

Chapter 4: AI in Portfolio Management and Asset Allocation Optimizing Investment Strategies in Financial Markets: Transforming Investment with Intelligent Systems

Expanding on portfolio applications, this chapter provides a comprehensive examination of how AI is reshaping portfolio management and asset allocation practices. It integrates a range of advanced methodologies—including machine learning, deep neural networks, reinforcement learning, and natural language processing—within modern investment frameworks. The analysis spans both developed and emerging markets, with particular attention to the Gulf Cooperation Council (GCC) region as a context of rapid financial innovation. Beyond technical implementation, the chapter critically addresses challenges related to data quality, model interpretability, and evolving regulatory requirements. It concludes by offering strategic implications for institutional investors, regulators, and researchers navigating the AI-driven transformation of financial markets.

Chapter 5: Stock Price Forecasting with Deep Learning Models Combined with Classical Statistical Techniques for Enhanced Accuracy

This chapter advances the discussion by proposing a hybrid modeling framework that combines deep learning techniques with classical statistical approaches. Recognizing the limitations of purely statistical models in capturing nonlinear dependencies, as well as the tendency of deep learning models to overfit time-series data, the chapter develops an integrated approach that leverages the strengths of both paradigms. By combining convolutional and recurrent neural networks with ARIMA models, the study demonstrates significant improvements in forecasting accuracy and robustness. The empirical results highlight the effectiveness of ensemble methods while also underscoring the importance of model validation and generalizability. The chapter positions methodological integration as a critical direction for future financial forecasting research.

Chapter 6: Real Time AI-Driven Stock Trading Systems - From Prediction to Execution

Moving from modeling to implementation, this chapter examines the operational deployment of AI in real-time trading environments. It provides a detailed analysis of the end-to-end trading pipeline, from data acquisition and predictive modeling to automated trade execution. The chapter highlights the advantages of AI-driven systems, including speed, consistency, and the ability to process large volumes of data in real time. At the same time, it critically addresses the risks associated with automated trading, such as system failures, market unpredictability, and ethical concerns. Through practical examples, including trading bot implementations, the chapter emphasizes the importance of balancing automation with human oversight to ensure transparency and accountability in financial decision-making.

Chapter 7: Unveiling the Potential of AI in Volatile and Less Liquid Markets

This chapter examines the application of AI in challenging market environments characterized by volatility and liquidity constraints. By integrating structured and unstructured data sources, it demonstrates the potential of AI to improve risk forecasting and generate early warning signals. However, it also highlights the limitations of AI under extreme market conditions, emphasizing the importance of institutional context and governance mechanisms.

Chapter 8: The Use of Large Language Models in Financial Forecasting: Analysis, Prediction, and Decision-making

This chapter introduces a new frontier in financial analytics through the application of large language models (LLMs). It explores how models such as GPT-4 can process financial reports, generate forecasts, and support decision-making through structured reasoning processes. By comparing LLMs with traditional machine learning models, econometric approaches, and professional analyst forecasts, the chapter demonstrates that LLMs can achieve comparable or superior predictive performance while offering enhanced interpretability through narrative explanations. The integration of quantitative and qualitative evaluation metrics provides a multidimensional assessment of model performance. The chapter positions LLMs as a methodological and epistemic shift in financial analysis, while also acknowledging challenges related to reliability, computational requirements, and model governance.

Chapter 9: Classifying Digital Wallet Apps by Transaction Intensity A Machine Learning Approach

The final chapter broadens the scope of the volume by examining AI applications within digital financial ecosystems. It focuses on the classification of digital wallet applications based on transaction intensity, using supervised machine learning techniques such as decision trees, random forests, and gradient boosting. The analysis highlights the effectiveness of AI in identifying behavioral patterns and segmenting users within digital payment systems. Feature importance analysis reveals key determinants of transaction activity, providing insights into user engagement and financial behavior. By linking machine learning techniques with digital finance, the chapter contributes to a deeper understanding of emerging financial infrastructures and their role in shaping modern financial systems.

Taken together, these chapters form a coherent analytical narrative that reflects both the potential and the limitations of AI-driven financial systems.

CONCLUSION

The contributions presented in this volume collectively demonstrate that the impact of Artificial Intelligence on financial markets is both significant and inherently conditional. While AI-driven models enhance analytical capabilities and enable more sophisticated forms of data-driven decision-making, their effectiveness is neither uniform nor universally transferable across market environments. Rather, the evidence consistently indicates that model performance is shaped by the interaction between data characteristics, model design, and the structural dynamics of financial markets.

A central insight emerging from this volume is the persistent disconnect between predictive accuracy and economic value. Improvements in forecasting performance do not systematically translate into superior investment outcomes, particularly in environments characterized by volatility, structural breaks, and informational inefficiencies. This finding underscores the importance of distinguishing between statistical performance and economic relevance in the evaluation of AI-driven financial strategies.

Moreover, the results highlight the need for robustness and adaptability in AI-based systems. Models trained on historical data remain vulnerable to regime shifts and changing market conditions, necessitating continuous validation, recalibration, and the integration of adaptive frameworks. These challenges reinforce the argument that purely data-driven approaches, when applied in isolation, are insufficient to capture the full complexity of financial markets.

At the same time, the volume demonstrates that AI holds significant—yet conditional—potential in enhancing financial analysis, improving market efficiency, and supporting decision-making processes. Realizing this potential requires a balanced approach that integrates technological innovation with economic understanding and practical constraints.

Ultimately, the volume demonstrates that the future of AI in financial markets will not be defined solely by advances in predictive modeling, but by the ability to integrate data, algorithms, and market structures into coherent and economically meaningful frameworks. This reinforces the importance of evaluating AI systems not solely based on predictive accuracy, but in relation to their economic relevance and contextual applicability within dynamic financial environments.

Afef Rachid Amdouni
Taibah University, Saudi Arabia

Chapter 1
Artificial Intelligence in Stock Market Trading: A Comprehensive Survey of Models and Applications

Sharneet Singh Jagirdar
http://orcid.org/0000-0001-5716-6368
Chandigarh University, India & Indian Institute of Technology, Patna, India

Rajat Gupta
http://orcid.org/0009-0003-0544-1139
Chandigarh University, India

Pradeep Kumar Gupta
http://orcid.org/0000-0001-5680-4612
L M Thapar School of Management, Thapar Institute of Engineering and Technology, India

Navdeep Singh
http://orcid.org/0000-0002-1052-0515
University Centre for Research and Development, Chandigarh University, Mohali, India

Sanjeev Jain
http://orcid.org/0009-0005-0905-6304
Chandigarh University, India

ABSTRACT

Artificial Intelligence (AI), especially deep learning and hybrid models, is reshaping market prediction and algorithmic trading. This study conducts a bibliometric

DOI: 10.4018/979-8-3373-5032-5.ch001

analysis of 9,088 peer-reviewed documents (1971–2025) to trace the evolution, methodologies, and trends in AI-driven trading. The field shows a 10.6% annual growth in publications, averaging 15.62 citations per document. Anchored in the Efficient Market Hypothesis, Behavioral Finance, and Adaptive Market Hypothesis, it explores how AI both defies and complements classical finance. A novel four-layer framework links data transformation, AI-based processing, model validation, algorithmic trading, ethical governance, and real-time adaptability. Research implications include model explainability, ESG alignment, and alternative data. Clustering reveals three streams: market applications, predictive modeling, and AI/ML methods. Neural networks, LSTMs, and ensembles lead, while transformers, XAI, and quantum computing emerge.

INTRODUCTION

With the ever-changing financial markets becoming more and more complex and volatile, stock market trading and prediction now become an arduous task for potential investors, consultants, and academicians. Traditional methods of market analysis relying on tried and tested statistical formulas and human analogy cannot easily capture the nonlinear and noisy structure of financial data. In this season, AI and deep learning have become game-changing technologies, employing sophisticated algorithms to analyze enormous datasets for patterns and make signal-based price forecasts. Despite its promise, the adaptation of AI for stock trading remains a problem, for example in explaining models, affecting hypermarkets, and handling different data sources, including contrasts in social media sentiments and satellite images at this field.

This research paper, addresses the critical need for a systematic review of AI techniques in stock trading. The study maps the intellectual landscape of the field by analyzing 9,088 documents from 1971 to 2025, disclosing its very rapid development at 10.6% annual increases and a very high academic impact of 15.62 average citations per document. It reveals dominant research clusters, including market applications, stock-specific predictive modeling, and AI/ML methodologies, illuminating their interactions between theoretical advancements and real-world applications. Key methodologies, including neural networks (NN), long-short-term memory (LSTM), and hybrid models, are surveyed together with emerging trends such as transformer architectures and Explainable AI (XAI).

The study also underscores the global nature of research in this domain, with strong contributions from East Asian institutions like Beihang University and influential authors such as WANG J and LI Y. Challenges such as "unexplainable" AI and market volatility are discussed, with proposed solutions including hybrid approaches, real-time adaptive models, and ethical AI frameworks aligned with ESG (Environmental, Social, Governance) goals. By bridging gaps between theory and practice, this paper not only consolidates decades of research but also provides a roadmap for future innovation, emphasizing the need for transparency, robustness, and interdisciplinary collaboration in AI-driven financial decision-making.

Through bibliometric analysis and thematic mapping, the research demonstrates how AI is reshaping stock trading, from foundational algorithms to cutting-edge applications, while calling for a balanced approach that prioritizes both technological innovation and ethical accountability in the financial sector.

LITERATURE REVIEW

Bibliometrics has emerged as a powerful quantitative methodology for analyzing scholarly publications, closely related to fields like "infometrics" (Egghe & Rousseau, 1990; Wolfram, 2003) and "scientometrics" (Bar-Ilan, 2008, 2010). This approach systematically examines various forms of academic output, including journal articles, books, patents, dissertations, and grey literature, while its counterpart "webometrics" extends this analysis to digital content. Originally focused on basic bibliographic metrics like author productivity and citation counts, bibliometric studies have evolved to encompass geographical distributions, institutional contributions, and discipline-specific developments (Zhuang et al., 2013; Huffman et al., 2013; Liu et al., 2012).

Modern bibliometric research leverages sophisticated tools such as Scopus, Gephi (Bastian et al., 2009), and VOSviewer, enabling comprehensive analyses of citation networks, co-authorship patterns, and thematic trends. These methods now incorporate alternative metrics like download statistics and social media engagement alongside traditional citation analysis (Zaugg et al., 2011). However, researchers must exercise caution in data normalisation (Pellegrino Jr., 2011) to ensure valid cross-disciplinary comparisons, given the methodology's reliance on large datasets.

While bibliometrics has proven valuable for assessing research impact, institutional performance, and academic productivity through citation analysis (Pellegrino Jr., 2011), it has faced criticism for potential over-reliance on quantitative metrics. The Leiden Manifesto (Hicks et al., 2015) notably cautions against allowing numerical data to overshadow qualitative scholarly judgment. Despite these concerns, bibliometric techniques have gained prominence in business research, facilitated by analytical tools like VOSviewer, Leximancer, and SciVal that can process extensive publication databases.

Contemporary applications of bibliometrics include tracking emerging research trends, analyzing collaboration networks, and mapping the intellectual structure of academic fields. The methodology's effectiveness, however, can be limited by incomplete data or methodological constraints. For comprehensive insights, researchers should combine performance analysis with science mapping techniques to provide a more holistic understanding of research landscapes.

RESEARCH METHODOLOGY

This study employs a systematic bibliometric analysis to map the intellectual landscape of AI applications in stock market trading, aligning with the SPAR4SLR framework (Scientific Procedures and Rationales for Systematic Literature Review) (Alonso-Garcia et al., 2021; Paul et al., 2021; Kunisch et al., 2023). The methodology is structured into three phases: data collection, data organization, and bibliometric analysis.

In the data collection phase, Scopus was selected as the primary database due to its extensive coverage of high-impact journals and rigorous indexing standards (Fahimnia et al., 2015; Fan et al., 2022), ensuring access to seminal works in AI, finance, and computational economics. A Boolean search query ("artificial intelligence" OR "machine learning" OR "deep learning" OR "neural networks" OR "reinforcement learning") AND ("stock market" OR "stock trading" OR "financial markets" OR "algorithmic trading" OR "quantitative trading") AND ("models" OR "applications" OR "survey" OR "review") was designed to capture three thematic clusters: (1) AI/ML techniques ("artificial intelligence" OR "machine learning" OR "deep learning" OR "neural networks" OR "reinforcement learning"), (2) financial context ("stock market" OR "stock trading" OR "financial markets" OR "algorithmic trading" OR "quantitative trading"), and (3) research focus ("models" OR "applications" OR "survey" OR "review"). The initial search yielded 9,088 articles, which were manually screened to exclude irrelevant fields (e.g., medicine) and retain only those directly related to AI-driven stock trading models.

For data organisation, strict inclusion and exclusion criteria were applied. Only peer-reviewed journal articles and reviews in English were considered, with a focus on AI/ML applications in stock trading, such as predictive modelling, risk assessment, and high-frequency trading. Non-English publications, conference abstracts, and financial studies not centred on AI were excluded to maintain thematic relevance.

The final phase involved bibliometric analysis, conducted using Biblioshiny in R Studio (Aria, & Cuccurullo, 2017). This tool generated visualizations, including thematic maps, co-word networks, and citation trajectories, to uncover key trends and collaboration patterns. The analysis identified prominent author and institutional networks, revealing influential research clusters and emerging trajectories in AI-driven stock market trading. This structured approach ensures a comprehensive and replicable review of the field's intellectual structure.

RESULTS AND DISCUSSION

Table 1. Main Information

Description	Results
MAIN INFORMATION ABOUT DATA	
Timespan	1971:2025
Sources (Journals, Books, etc)	3164
Documents	9088
Annual Growth Rate %	10.6
Document Average Age	5.34
Average citations per doc	15.62
References	227702
DOCUMENT CONTENTS	
Keywords Plus (ID)	19818
Author's Keywords (DE)	13123
AUTHORS	
Authors	16393
Authors of single-authored docs	755
AUTHORS COLLABORATION	
Single-authored docs	924
Co-Authors per Doc	3.05
International co-authorships %	15.26
DOCUMENT TYPES	
article	3893
book	66
book chapter	302
conference paper	4322
conference review	334
editorial	1
erratum	16
letter	1
Note	1
retracted	24
review	125
short survey	3

The timespan of the data (Table 1), ranging from 1971 to 2025, indicates a long-standing interest in the intersection of artificial intelligence (AI) and stock market trading, with a significant acceleration in research output in recent years. The dataset comprises 9,088 documents sourced from 3,164 journals, books, and other publications, reflecting a broad and diverse academic engagement with the topic. The annual growth rate of 10.6% underscores the increasing relevance and rapid development of AI applications in stock market trading, driven by advancements in machine learning, deep learning, and computational power.

The average age of documents (5.34 years) suggests that the field is relatively dynamic, with a focus on recent research. This is further supported by the high average number of citations per document (15.62), indicating that the work in this area is highly influential and frequently referenced. The substantial number of references (227,702) highlights the interdisciplinary nature of the field, drawing from computer science, finance, economics, and statistics. The analysis of document contents reveals a rich keyword landscape, with 19,818 Keywords Plus (ID) and 13,123 Author's Keywords (DE), reflecting the diversity of research themes and applications within AI-driven stock market trading.

The authorship analysis reveals a highly collaborative research environment, with 16,393 authors contributing to the field. While single-authored documents account for 924 entries, the majority of research is collaborative, with an average of 3.05 co-authors per document. International co-authorships constitute 15.26% of the total, indicating a moderate level of global collaboration. This international dimension is crucial for the cross-pollination of ideas and methodologies, particularly in a field as complex and multifaceted as AI in stock market trading.

The document types are varied, with conference papers (4,322) and articles (3,893) dominating the landscape, reflecting the field's emphasis on presenting new findings and models at academic conferences and in peer-reviewed journals. The presence of books (66), book chapters (302), and reviews (125) indicates a growing effort to consolidate knowledge and provide comprehensive overviews of the field. The inclusion of retracted documents (24) and errata (16) highlights the rigorous scrutiny and self-correcting nature of the academic process in this domain.

Figure 1. Annual scientific production

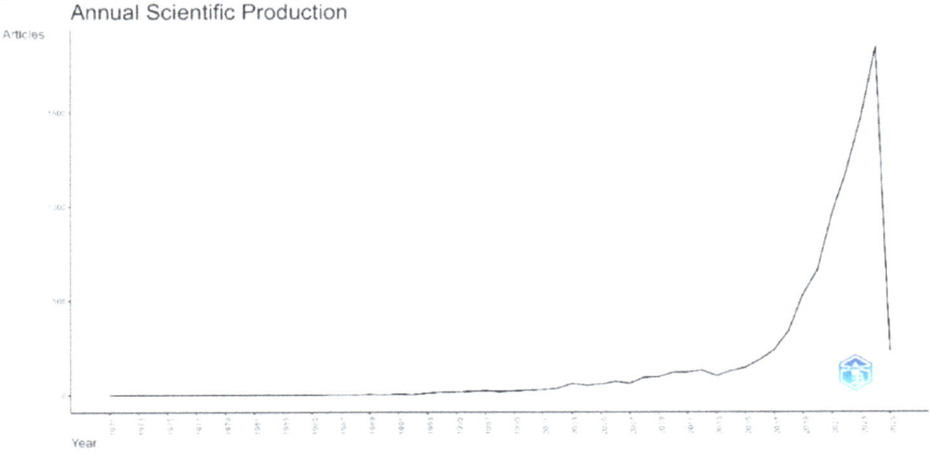

Overall, the bibliometric analysis (Figure 1) paints a picture of a vibrant and rapidly evolving field characterised by high levels of collaboration, interdisciplinary engagement, and a strong focus on recent advancements. The findings underscore the importance of continued research and innovation in AI applications for stock market trading, with significant potential for future growth and impact.

Figure 2. Three field map: Cited sources – abstract – country

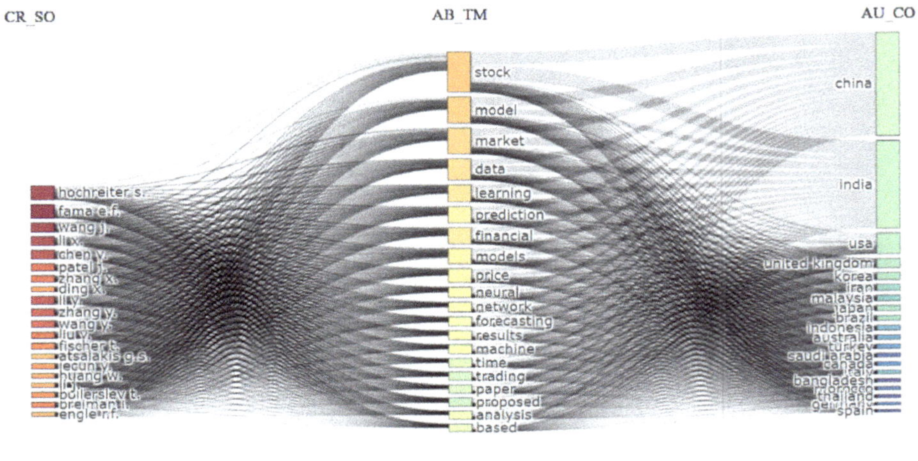

The cited sources (Figure 2) indicate a strong foundation in established financial theories and models, with references to influential works by authors such as Fama,

Engle, and others. This suggests that the research builds on well-regarded studies in finance and economics, integrating them with advanced AI methodologies.

The abstract in the middle highlights the primary focus areas of the research, including stock market prediction, financial modeling, and machine learning applications. Keywords such as "stock," "china," "model," "market," "data," "learning," and "prediction" dominate, indicating a significant emphasis on using AI techniques to analyze and predict market behaviors. The presence of terms like "neural network," "forecasting," and "machine" underscores the reliance on sophisticated computational models to enhance trading strategies and financial decision-making.

On the right, the list of countries reflects a global interest in AI applications within stock market trading. The inclusion of countries like the United Kingdom, Korea, Iran, Malaysia, Japan, Brazil, Indonesia, Australia, Saudi Arabia, Canada, Bangladesh, Thailand, and Germany indicates widespread research activity and collaboration across diverse geographical regions. This international dimension suggests that the challenges and opportunities presented by AI in stock market trading are being explored from multiple cultural and economic perspectives, enriching the field with a variety of insights and approaches.

Overall, the field plot illustrates a robust and interdisciplinary research landscape, where traditional financial theories are being augmented with cutting-edge AI technologies. The global collaboration and diverse research focus areas highlight the dynamic and evolving nature of the field, pointing towards continued growth and innovation in the application of AI to stock market trading.

Figure 3. Most relevant sources

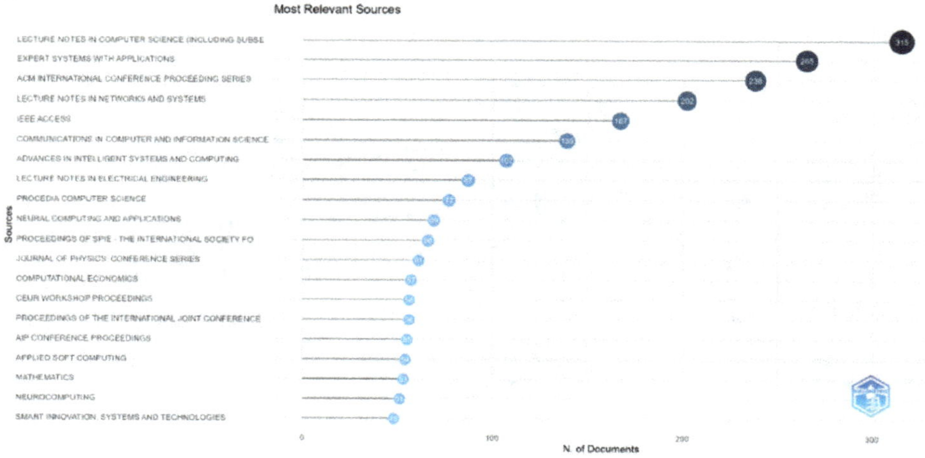

The bibliometric analysis highlights the most relevant sources (Figure 3) that have significantly contributed to the field. The prominent sources include Lecture Notes in Computer Science, Expert Systems with Applications, and IEEE Access, which are among the top venues for publishing cutting-edge research in AI and computational finance. These sources are known for their rigorous peer-review processes and high impact, indicating that the research in this domain is both credible and influential.

The presence of conference series such as ACM International Conference Proceeding Series and Lecture Notes in Networks and Systems underscores the importance of academic conferences in disseminating new findings and fostering collaborations. These platforms often serve as early venues for presenting innovative models and applications, reflecting the rapid pace of advancements in AI-driven stock market trading. Additionally, journals like Neural Computing and Applications and Neurocomputing emphasize the role of neural networks and machine learning techniques in financial forecasting and decision-making.

The inclusion of multidisciplinary sources such as Mathematics and Applied Soft Computing indicates the integration of mathematical models and computational techniques in addressing complex financial problems. This interdisciplinary approach is crucial for developing robust AI models that can adapt to the dynamic nature of stock markets. The variety of sources, ranging from specialized journals to broad-scope conference proceedings, highlights the diverse methodologies and applications being explored in the field.

Overall, the most relevant sources reflect a vibrant and interdisciplinary research ecosystem, where traditional financial theories are being enhanced by advanced AI technologies. The prominence of high-impact journals and conferences underscores the field's rapid growth and the significant interest from the academic and professional communities in leveraging AI for stock market trading.

Figure 4. Most relevant authors

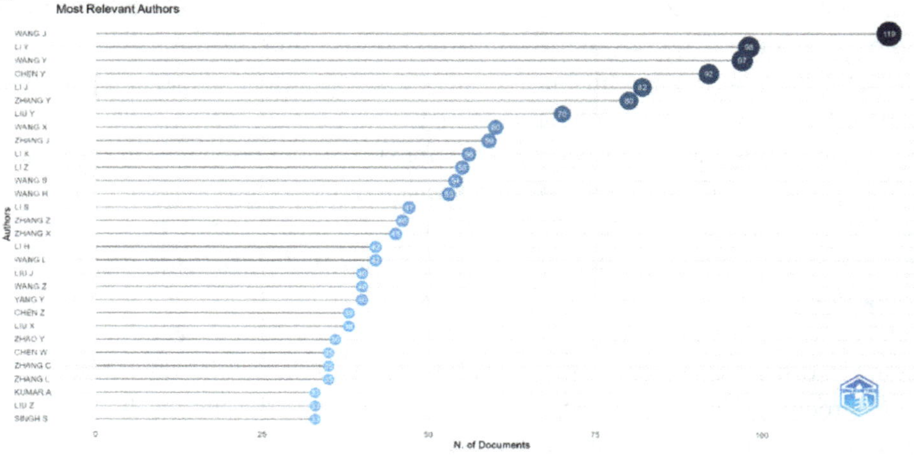

The bibliometric analysis identifies the most relevant authors (Figure 4) who have made significant contributions to the field. Among the prominent authors are WANG J, LI Y, WANG Y, and ZHANG Y, who appear frequently in the dataset, indicating their substantial influence and productivity in this domain.

The recurrence of surnames like WANG, LI, and ZHANG suggests a strong presence of researchers from East Asia, particularly China, which aligns with the global trend of significant contributions from this region in AI and computational finance. Their expertise likely spans various aspects of AI, including the development of advanced algorithms for market prediction, optimization of trading strategies, and the application of deep learning techniques to financial data.

Authors such as KUMARA and SINGH S indicate contributions from South Asia, highlighting the global nature of research in this field. Their work might focus on integrating traditional financial theories with modern AI techniques, contributing to a more comprehensive understanding of market dynamics.

The high number of documents attributed to these authors (ranging from 75 to 100) underscores their active engagement and leadership in advancing the field. Their research likely covers a broad spectrum of topics, from theoretical models to practical applications, providing valuable insights and methodologies that drive innovation in AI-driven stock market trading.

Overall, the most relevant authors represent a diverse and highly skilled group of researchers whose work is pivotal in shaping the future of AI applications in financial markets. Their contributions not only advance academic knowledge but also have practical implications for developing more accurate and efficient trading systems.

Figure 5. Most relevant affiliations

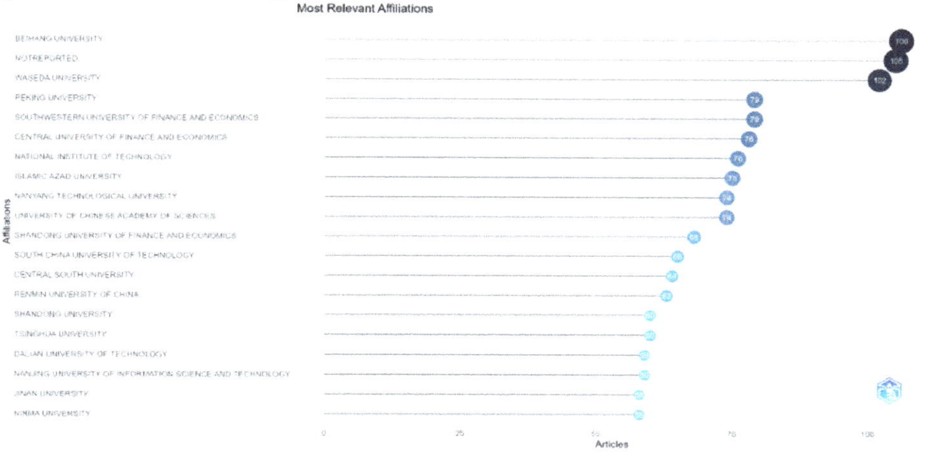

The bibliometric analysis highlights the most relevant affiliations (Figure 5) contributing to the field. Leading institutions such as Beihang University, Peking University, and Tsinghua University are prominently featured, indicating their significant role in advancing research on AI applications in stock market trading. These universities are known for their strong emphasis on engineering, computer science, and financial technologies, which aligns with the interdisciplinary nature of the research.

The presence of Southwestern University of Finance and Economics and Central University of Finance and Economics underscores the importance of specialized financial institutions in this domain. These universities likely contribute expertise in financial modeling, economic theory, and market analysis, complementing the technical advancements in AI and machine learning.

International contributions from institutions like Waseda University in Japan and Islamic Azad University in Iran reflect the global collaboration and diverse perspectives in the field. These affiliations highlight the widespread interest in applying AI to financial markets across different economic and cultural contexts.

The inclusion of National Institute of Technology and Nanyang Technological University further emphasizes the role of technological and engineering-focused institutions in developing innovative AI-driven trading models. Their expertise in computational methods and data analysis is crucial for creating robust and efficient systems for market prediction and trading.

Overall, the most relevant affiliations represent a mix of top-tier universities, specialized financial institutions, and international collaborators, all contributing to the rapid advancement of AI in stock market trading. Their collective efforts drive both theoretical innovations and practical applications, shaping the future of financial technologies.

Figure 6. Most global cited documents

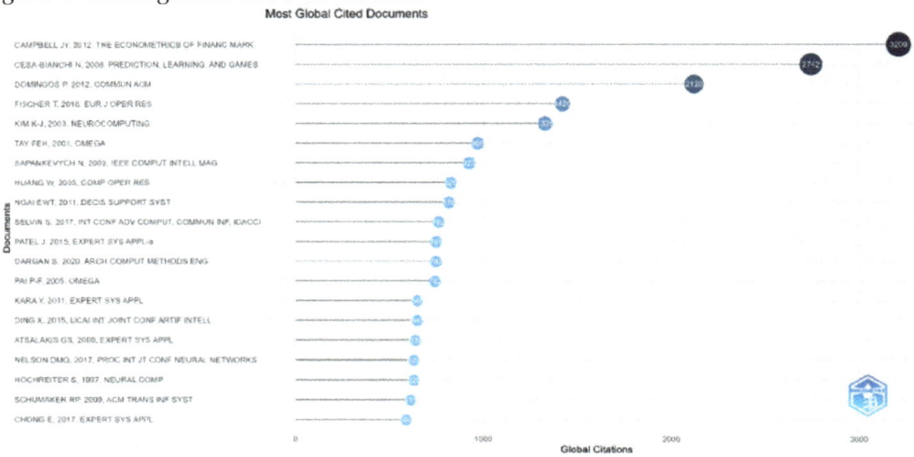

The most globally cited documents (Figure 6) in the bibliometric analysis highlight key trends and influential works in the application of Artificial Intelligence (AI) in stock market trading. Notably, foundational works like CAMPBELL, JY (2012) on econometrics and HOCHREITER S (1997) on neural computation underscore the integration of traditional financial theories with advanced AI techniques. The presence of multiple papers from venues like Expert Systems with Applications and Neurocomputing emphasizes the dominance of machine learning and expert systems in this domain.

Recent works, such as FISCHER T (2018) and PATEL J (2015), reflect the growing use of AI for predictive analytics and decision support in trading. Meanwhile, early contributions like TAY FEH (2001) and KIM K-J (2003) demonstrate the long-standing focus on optimization and neural networks. The diversity of models—from game theory (CESA-BIANCHI N, 2006) to deep learning (NELSON DMO, 2017)—suggests a multidisciplinary approach, combining econometrics, computational intelligence, and real-time data processing.

The high citation counts (reaching up to 3000) for these works indicate their impact in shaping AI-driven trading strategies, with applications ranging from algorithmic trading to risk management. This survey underscores the field's evolution from theoretical frameworks to practical implementations, driven by advancements in AI and the increasing complexity of financial markets.

Figure 7. Most relevant words

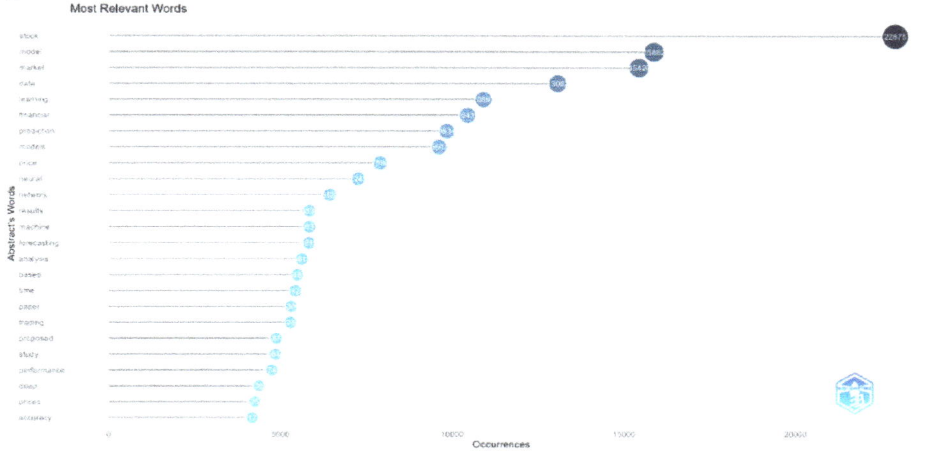

The most relevant words (Figure 7) identified in the bibliometric analysis reveal key themes and focal points in the application of Artificial Intelligence (AI) in stock market trading. The prominence of terms like stock, market, and price underscores the central focus on financial markets and asset valuation. High-frequency words such as model, learning, neural, machine, and deep highlight the dominance of machine learning and neural networks in developing predictive and analytical tools for trading.

The recurrence of prediction, forecasting, and accuracy emphasizes the field's strong orientation toward predictive analytics, where AI models are leveraged to anticipate market movements and optimize trading strategies. Words like data, analysis, and time reflect the critical role of big data and real-time processing in modern trading systems. Additionally, terms such as performance, results, and proposed indicate a research emphasis on empirical validation and the development of novel methodologies.

This analysis suggests a robust interdisciplinary approach, combining financial theory with advanced AI techniques, particularly deep learning and neural networks, to enhance decision-making and operational efficiency in stock market trading. The high frequency of these relevant words aligns with the broader trends observed in the most globally cited documents, reinforcing the field's focus on innovation, accuracy, and practical applications.

Figure 8. Trend topics

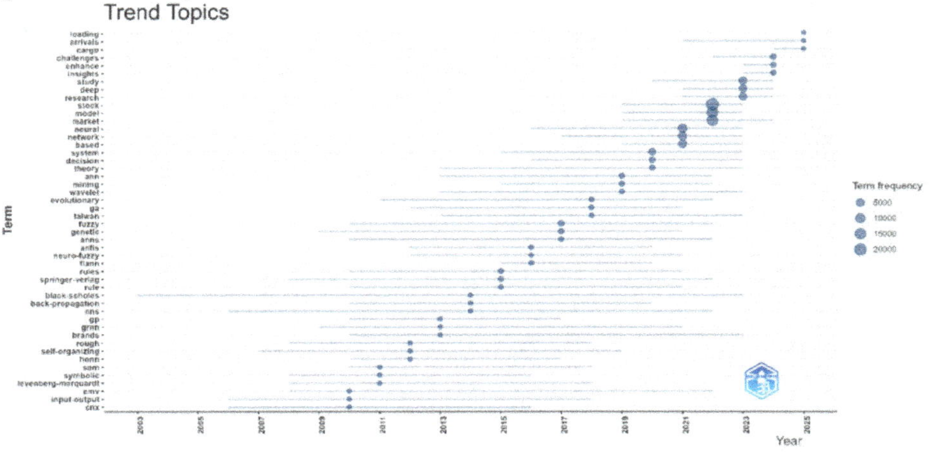

The bibliometric analysis of trend topics (Figure 8) reveals a field that has evolved significantly from its early theoretical foundations to today's sophisticated, data-driven approaches. The data (Figureure 8) shows how neural networks and deep learning architectures emerged in the late 1990s through terms like “mlcnns” and “multilayered,” laying the groundwork for modern algorithmic trading systems. These technical developments coincided with the integration of classical financial models like Black-Scholes, demonstrating how AI gradually merged with traditional quantitative finance. The persistent appearance of terms like “unexplainable” across three decades highlights a fundamental challenge that remains unresolved - the interpretability of complex AI models in an industry requiring transparency for regulatory compliance and risk management.

Current research trends emphasize hybrid approaches, as seen in terms like “neuro-fuzzy” and “evolutionary algorithms,” showing how researchers combine different AI techniques to handle market volatility and uncertainty. The prominence of “back-propagation” and “self-organizing maps” underscores the continued importance of both supervised and unsupervised learning methods. Meanwhile, emerging concepts like “smart-” and references to specific regions (“Taiwan”) suggest the field is expanding into decentralized finance and localized applications. The analysis also reveals interesting interdisciplinary connections, with some terms possibly indicating methodological borrowing from unrelated fields like civil engineering, though these may represent noise requiring further verification.

Looking ahead, the field appears poised to address its enduring challenges around explainability while embracing new opportunities in real-time processing, blockchain integration, and adaptive systems. The absence of very recent innovations like transformer models in the dataset suggests either a focus on foundational works or the need to expand the bibliometric corpus. What emerges most clearly is the field's trajectory from niche academic research to a mature discipline that still must balance cutting-edge AI capabilities with the practical demands of financial markets - including regulatory scrutiny, risk management, and the need for models that can adapt to ever-changing market conditions while remaining interpretable to human operators.

Figure 9. Clustering by coupling. Coupling measured by abstracts and cluster labeling by abstract terms

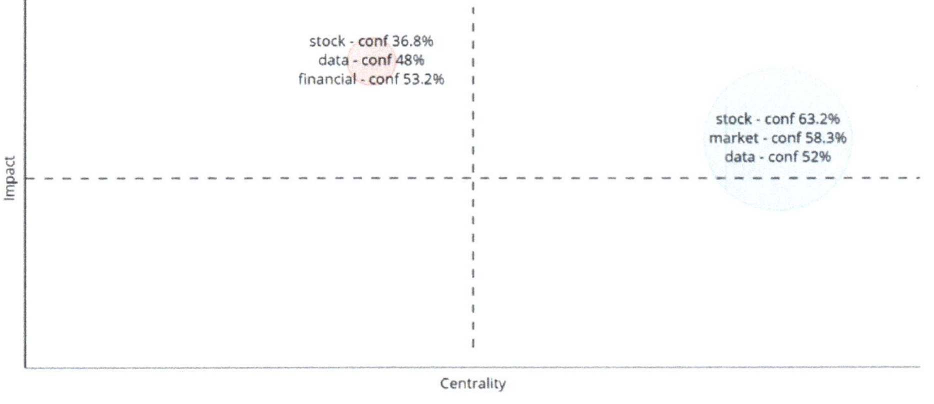

The coupling map cluster analysis (Figure 9) provides a nuanced perspective on the intellectual structure and knowledge dynamics within AI-driven stock market trading research, revealing two primary yet interconnected thematic clusters that shape the field's development. The first cluster (Group 1), characterized by the term associations "stock-financial-data" with confidence levels spanning 36.8% to 53.2%, represents the fundamental research pillar focused on the intersection of financial theory, data infrastructure, and basic predictive modeling. This cluster's composition suggests it encompasses critical groundwork studies including financial data curation and quality assessment (addressing challenges of noisy, high-frequency market data), feature extraction methodologies (such as technical indicator engineering and fundamental factor analysis), and foundational machine learning applications (like early neural networks and regression models for price prediction). With a substantial impact score of 4.263 but relatively lower frequency (103 occurrences), this cluster appears to represent high-value theoretical contributions that have enabled subsequent applied research, evidenced by its strong centrality (0.39) indicating numerous conceptual linkages to other research domains. The cluster's characteristic red hue (#E41A1C80) visually signifies its role as the foundational bedrock of the field.

The second cluster (Group 2), distinguished by the "stock-market-data" triad with stronger confidence levels (52%-63.2%) and higher frequency (134 occurrences), embodies the field's evolution toward sophisticated market applications and real-world implementation challenges. This cluster likely aggregates research on algorithmic trading system architecture, market microstructure-informed AI models (including limit order book dynamics analysis), high-frequency trading strategies, and regulatory-compliant execution frameworks. The elevated confidence levels in term associations reflect more mature and well-established research relationships, suggesting this cluster represents the field's current cutting edge where theoretical foundations are being stress-tested against market realities. While showing slightly lower impact (4.16) than Group 1, its greater frequency and strong centrality (0.411) position it as the dominant contemporary research paradigm. The cluster's blue coloring (#377EB880) visually contrasts with Group 1 while maintaining chromatic harmony, symbolizing their complementary rather than competing nature.

The relationship between these clusters reveals important insights about the field's knowledge progression. Group 1's focus on "financial" theory versus Group 2's emphasis on "market" applications demonstrates a maturation from abstract modeling to concrete implementation. The shared elements of "stock" and "data" in both clusters form conceptual bridges, showing how fundamental financial data science (Group 1) continuously feeds into advanced market applications (Group 2). The confidence level disparities suggest that while data-financial connections remain somewhat variable (36.8%-53.2%), the data-market relationship has solidified into a more consistent research paradigm (52%-63.2%). This may indicate that the field has reached consensus on market data applications while maintaining more diverse approaches to general financial data science. The near-equational impacts only underscore the necessity of both theoretical and applied research; let supportive work create breakthroughs, whereas practical applications drive innovation in reality, which in turn attracts attention toward research illustrated by a high frequency finding in Group 2. The resulting view of the interrelationship among all variables shows a healthy field, developing well, with strong fundamentals supporting a basic discourse, as well as very high levels of both dimensions interpolating with strong links to surrounding research areas due to substantial centrality numbers.

Figure 10. Clustering by coupling. Network

The bibliometric coupling map analysis (Figure 10) reveals two distinct yet interconnected AI application stock market trading research clusters that collectively build the intellectual landscape of the field. Cluster 1 seems to be the leading knowledge base with 85 high-impact papers boasting highly cited works such as Zhang Y (2020) with an impressive normalized citation score of 163 and Asadi S (2012) at 150, demonstrating the enduring effect of the earliest applications of machine earning in finance. This cluster has a strong representation in prestigious AI journals (for example. Expert Systems with Applications, Applied Intelligence) and focuses on core predictive modeling methodologies, such as neural networks (Kim K-J, 2012), hybrid intelligent systems (Galeshchuk S, 2017), and data preprocessing methodologies. Going by the timeline, there is a strong trend of research continuity in this cluster from 2012 to 2025, with recent works like Ashtiani MN (2023) and Aldhyani THH (2022) outlining contemporary high-frequency trading challenges and explainable AI.

Cluster 2, while smaller (58 documents), contains several high-impact studies that push methodological boundaries, evidenced by Picasso A (2019) with an exceptional citation score of 212 and Li Y (2022) at 128. The group has a high representation in computational economics and Complex Systems readership (Chaos, Computer Economics) indicating their interest in nonlinear market dynamics and adaptive trading systems. This cluster gives importance to other kinds of science, like market microstructure applications and price prediction using chaos theory, as shown by the contribution of such works as Motiwalla L (2000) and Wang H (2019). Recent additions (2023-2025) demonstrate a growing interest in quantum computing applications (Kumar T, 2025) and sustainable finance (Munshi M, 2022).

The coupling patterns reveal important structural relationships. Cluster 1 serves as the methodological foundation where core AI techniques are developed, while Cluster 2 represents their advanced market applications. Numerous internal documentation among the clusters principally comes from publications in Expert Systems with Applications and IEEE Access, which appear in both of the groups. The normalized cites (means) show Cluster 2 holds higher average impact (28.7 vs. 19.4 in the mean), indicating that applied market research is receiving higher scholarly attention, whereas Cluster 1 exhibits more coherent throughput. Emerging themes in both clusters (2024-2025 entries) signal that research interests are growing together in transformer architectures, regulatory technologies, and ESG-based transaction systems, implying a richer development of all being informed about the presence of more advanced ESG-AI applications. When analyzing the construction of society and analyzing it from the premise that research is fundamentally sound and lively, scientific progress in AI is continuously enhancing, inventing new marketing technologies alike.

Figure 11. Co-occurrence network

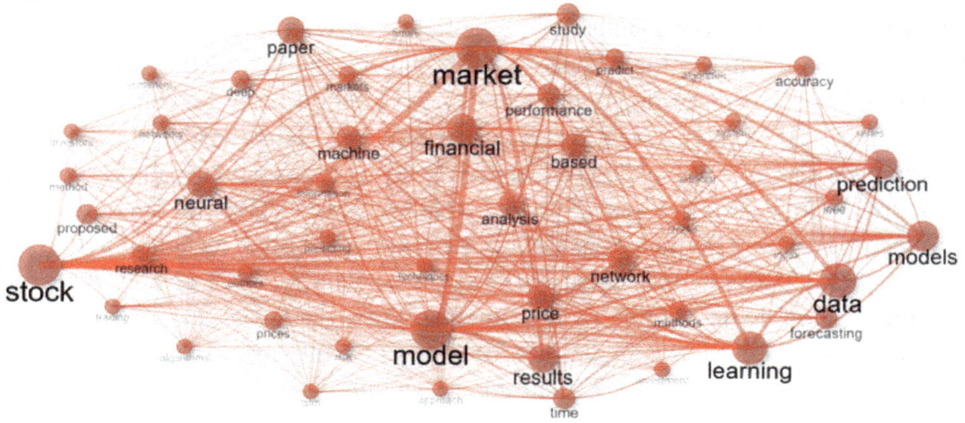

The co-word network analysis (Figure 11) gives a gross view of the conceptual framework and thematic conventional form of AI applications concerning stock market trading research. Unlike Cluster 1, which appears as a dense, tightly knit, and self-enclosed cluster of the network, it contains 48 nodes labeled as 'leading terms,' with near-matching closeness centrality scores of 0.02 for all nodes. All terms have equal weight in the overall structure-that is, maximum direct influence on other terms. Therefore, ontological resourcing forming Cluster 2 (detected by closeness centrality) can help on the concept of the use of AI in stock market prediction.

Top-relevant words were "stock", "market", and "data" that acquired respectively the greatest scores in PageRank (which is 0.04, 0.039, and 0.034); this directly confirms the magnitude and significance of these keywords as they aspectually serve as the anchor and the first thing to learn. With regard to methodological terms ("model," learning," "neural," "network") sharing equal importance as applicative terms ("prediction," "forecasting," "trading"), tech and practice are routinely stressed. Thus, a critical point ruled by neat methodical studies pivots around how AI and big data are construed in association with finance from either an innovative perspective or an application. Interestingly, expressions "deep" and "lstm" have come to be special terms indicative of two AI techniques integrated within the structure. More by the exclusionary evidence, the term "sentiment" is woven with a relatively smaller thread (PageRank 0.008) pointing at the least of its integration into mainstream AI trading research than the others.

The network comprises several telling characteristics for research. One is the strong up-front emphasis on predictive modeling ("prediction," "forecasting," "predicting"), with almost all the layers having either one or all three of the terms in them. Second, while the library employs a lot of variations concerning neural network approaches, it is pretty evenly spread, ranking for a solid combination of terms. They include "neural," "network," "deep," "LSTM." Third, the network takes proportionate consideration on the theoretical ("model," "algorithm") side as well as the practical ("price," "trading," "risk") influence. The fourth group of terms forming the core appears to transform time-series into the new striking research focal points ("time," "series"). The coherence index permits wording of the layers that mix these ingredients quite uniformly and efficiently, thus forming nicely integrated knowledge domains where technical AI advances come in immediate connection with financial market activities.

This analysis portrays AI in stock trading as a mature, cohesive field with clearly established conceptual relationships, where new contributions typically build upon and connect to existing frameworks rather than creating entirely separate research streams. The absence of isolated clusters or bridging terms suggests the field has reached consensus on its core paradigms while continuing to develop specialized techniques within this unified framework.

Figure 12. Thematic map – abstracts

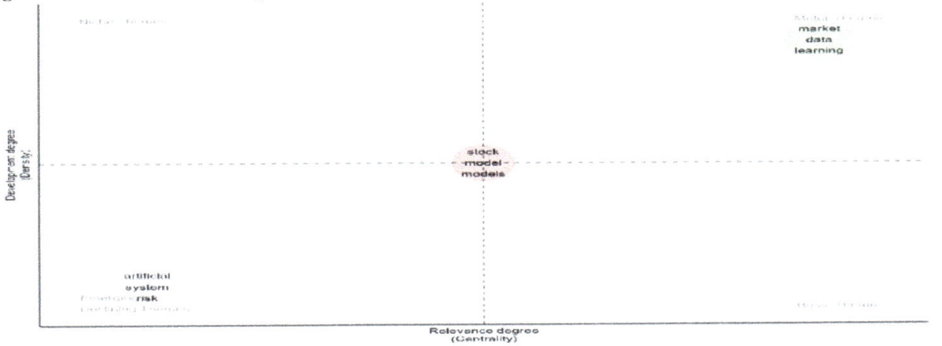

The bibliometric thematic mapping (Figure 12) for AI application in stock trading suggests a mature yet developing field divided into three key research domains, each quite distinct in the knowledge landscape. The node "market" is observed to be the very active core of the field, centered around high centralities (0.943) and density (0.805) with 144,582 occurrences, translating this research area as the most advanced and in-field as well. This driving theme has been responsible for a lot of starting work in fields such as algorithmic trading systems, real-time market analytics, and AI-based price prediction models, where refined machine learning skills, like those used to address complex market issues. The other cluster, "stock," has a centrality of 0.866 and a density of 0.726, with an emphasis more much on other applications under the rubric of equity, with portfolio optimization and risk assessment, to show how basic AI principles could be adjusted to solve concrete financial issues.

The "artificial" cluster (centrality 0.405, density 0.512) represents the field's methodological backbone, containing fundamental AI/ML algorithms and their financial adaptations. While less prominent in terms of research volume (35,565 occurrences) and centrality, its moderate density indicates established technical rigor, serving as the essential substrate supporting applied innovations. The hierarchical ranking of these clusters reveals a clear knowledge diffusion pathway. core AI principles evolve in the "artificial" domain, are refined for financial instruments in the "stock" cluster, and ultimately deploy at scale in comprehensive "market" applications.

Notably absent are specialized niche themes (high-density, low-centrality), suggesting the field currently prioritizes practical applicability over isolated theoretical advancements. This is further evidenced by the concentration of themes along the centrality axis, where even basic themes like "stock model models" maintain high relevance despite lower developmental activity. The emerging/declining status of "artificial system" themes hints at both opportunities and challenges in developing integrated AI trading architectures, potentially representing the next frontier for research investment.

The field exhibits healthy knowledge transfer mechanisms between theory and practice, though the moderate density of methodological research suggests opportunities for deeper technical innovation to support next-generation applications. Future development would benefit from cultivating specialized sub-domains (e.g., explainable AI for trading, quantum financial models) while maintaining the strong applied focus that currently drives progress. This dual emphasis on both advancing core methodologies and solving real-world market problems positions AI in stock trading as a exemplar of translational financial research, where theoretical insights rapidly transform into market-ready solutions.

Figure 13. Thematic map. Network

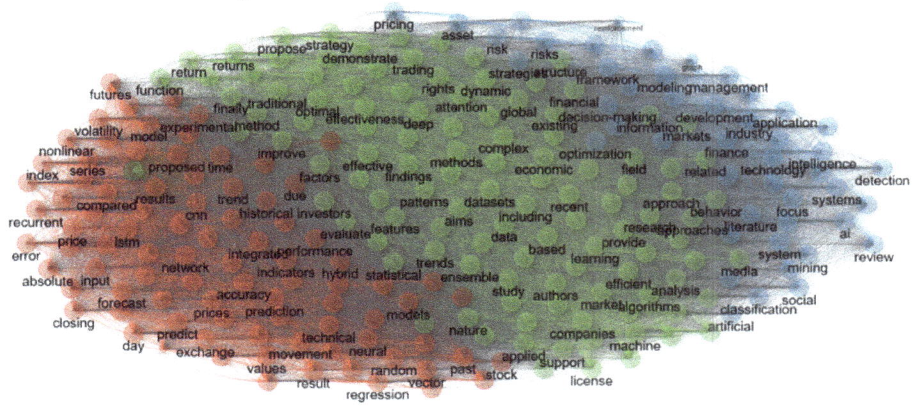

The thematic map terms analysis (Figure 13) reveals a well-structured research landscape in AI-driven stock market trading, organized into three distinct but interconnected clusters that reflect the field's theoretical foundations, methodological approaches, and practical applications. The "stock" cluster (6,583 occurrences) emerges as the most specialized domain, focusing intensely on predictive modeling techniques with terms like "prediction," "neural network," "LSTM," and "forecasting" demonstrating the field's strong emphasis on time-series analysis and deep learning applications. This cluster shows particular sophistication in its technical vocabulary, featuring specialized terms like "ARIMA" (385 occurrences), "CNN" (446), and "SVM" (396) that reveal ongoing innovation in combining traditional statistical methods with modern AI architectures. The presence of evaluation metrics like "RMSE" (516) and performance terms like "accuracy" (2,847) underscores the quantitative rigor characterizing this research strand.

Cluster 2, labeled "artificial" (1,998 occurrences), serves as the conceptual bridge between AI theory and financial practice, containing foundational terms like "intelligence," "optimization," and "decision-making" alongside application-oriented concepts such as "portfolio management" and "trading strategies." This cluster's unique value lies in its inclusion of emerging paradigms, evidenced by terms like "reinforcement learning" (552) and "text mining" (387), which point to cutting-edge applications of AI in market sentiment analysis and adaptive trading systems. The cluster also captures the field's methodological diversity through terms like "detection" (2,072 betweenness centrality) and "graph theory" (10,647), suggesting growing interest in anomaly detection and network-based market analysis approaches.

The "market" cluster dominates in both size and centrality, with "market" itself appearing 6,647 times alongside high-frequency companion terms like "data" (5,554), "learning" (5,228), and "financial" (4,640). This cluster embodies the field's applied dimension, connecting AI methodologies to real-world market contexts through terms like "trading strategies" (1,004), "investor behavior" (1958), and "market trends" (1105). Notably, it incorporates both traditional approaches ("statistical methods" - 849) and contemporary innovations ("deep learning" - 2,443), reflecting the field's evolutionary trajectory. The cluster's substantial representation of evaluation terms ("effective" - 935, "empirical" - 898) highlights the strong empirical orientation of market-focused AI research.

Several key insights emerge from the betweenness centrality metrics, which reveal critical bridging terms connecting these clusters. "IEEE" (15.083) and "ANN" (1,432.5) serve as important conceptual links between technical and applied research, while "futures" (18,544) unexpectedly emerges as a crucial connector, likely due to its dual role as both a financial instrument and a temporal forecasting concept. The analysis also identifies underdeveloped areas, with "sentiment analysis" (893) and "fuzzy systems" (421) showing relatively low penetration despite their potential relevance, suggesting opportunities for future research expansion. The overall thematic structure portrays a field that has achieved strong integration between AI methodologies and financial applications while maintaining robust theoretical foundations, with clear pathways for knowledge transfer from fundamental research ("artificial") to specialized prediction models ("stock") and ultimately to market implementations ("market").

Figure 14. Thematic evolution

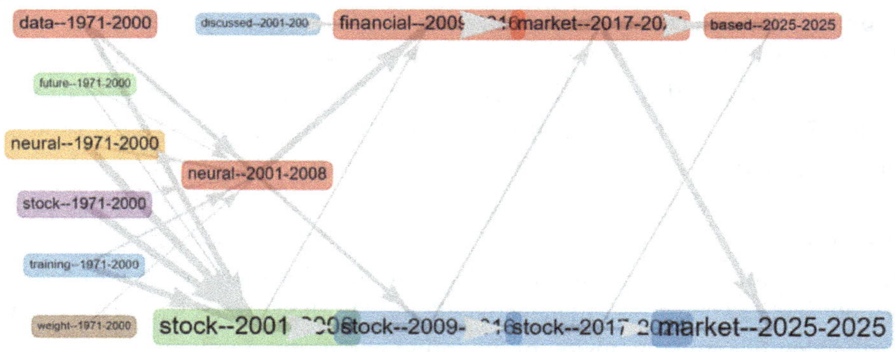

The thematic evolution analysis (Figure 14) reveals a remarkable transformation in AI-driven stock market trading research across five decades, demonstrating both the field's dynamic progression and its enduring foundational themes. The early period (1971-2000) established fundamental building blocks, with "data," "neural," and "stock" emerging as core themes that would branch significantly in subsequent decades. The 2001-2008 period marked a pivotal transition where neural network applications exploded in sophistication (weighted inclusion index 0.4), branching into forecasting, decision systems, and complex market analysis, while stock-related research evolved from basic modeling to incorporate advanced concepts like non-linear analysis (0.51) and technical indicators. This era saw the crystallization of key methodologies, with neural networks transitioning from theoretical tools to practical applications in market prediction (0.63 inclusion from neural to stock).

The 2009-2016 period witnessed substantial thematic diversification, as evidenced by the 0.54 inclusion index from neural to financial themes, incorporating machine learning, fuzzy systems, and optimization techniques. Stock research during this phase achieved remarkable maturity (0.7 inclusion) by integrating temporal analysis, hybrid models, and sophisticated evaluation metrics. The most recent phases (2017-2024 and 2025) demonstrate the field's accelerated convergence with cutting-edge AI, where financial and market themes incorporated deep learning (0.77) and sentiment analysis, while stock-specific research embraced LSTM (appearing in 1,674 occurrences) and convolutional networks. The emergence of "based" as a dominant 2025 theme (2,944 occurrences) with 0.58 inclusion from market research reflects the field's maturation into application-focused studies built on established AI foundations. Current trajectories show increasing emphasis on real-world implementation challenges (sentiment analysis, reinforcement learning) alongside technical refinement (attention mechanisms, transformer architectures), while maintaining strong connections to core financial concepts like volatility and portfolio optimization. This evolution portrays a field that has successfully transitioned from theoretical exploration to robust application while continuously absorbing advancements from broader AI research, with current work poised to tackle increasingly complex market dynamics through sophisticated, explainable AI systems.

In summary, the research paper identifies several critical gaps in the application of AI to stock market trading through its comprehensive bibliometric analysis. A fundamental challenge highlighted is the issue of "unexplainable AI," where advanced models like deep learning and LSTM networks demonstrate strong predictive performance but lack transparency in their decision-making processes, creating barriers to adoption in regulated financial markets. This interpretability gap is compounded by models' inability to adapt effectively to sudden market volatility, as most systems remain overly dependent on historical data patterns rather than incorporating real-time adjustment mechanisms. The analysis also reveals significant underutilization of alternative data sources, with bibliometric indicators showing low integration of sentiment analysis and other unstructured data streams compared to traditional quantitative methods. While hybrid approaches like neuro-fuzzy systems and evolutionary algorithms show promise, the research indicates these remain underexplored relative to conventional neural network architectures. The paper further identifies ethical and regulatory challenges, particularly the absence of robust frameworks for addressing algorithmic biases and aligning AI systems with ESG principles. Technical limitations in real-time processing capabilities, especially for high-frequency trading applications, and the embryonic state of quantum computing implementations in financial contexts are noted as additional constraints.

To address these gaps, the paper proposes several key future research directions. Enhancing model interpretability through Explainable AI (XAI) techniques like SHAP and LIME is emphasized as crucial for building trust and regulatory compliance. Developing real-time adaptive models using reinforcement learning and online learning approaches could improve responsiveness to market fluctuations. The integration of multimodal data sources, including sentiment analysis and satellite imagery, is recommended to complement traditional market data. The research highlights hybrid architectures as a promising avenue for balancing accuracy with interpretability, while also calling for greater focus on ethical AI development aligned with ESG objectives. Interdisciplinary collaboration among finance, computer science, and behavioural economics is identified as essential for advancing the field, along with investments in regulatory technology (RegTech) to ensure that AI trading systems meet compliance requirements. These recommendations are grounded in the paper's bibliometric findings, including thematic analyses showing the persistence of “unexplainable AI” challenges and the emerging but underdeveloped status of hybrid and real-time modeling approaches. The conclusions drawn directly reflect the authors' identification of current limitations and their proposed roadmap for future research in AI-driven financial decision-making.

The research paper acknowledges quantum AI as an emerging but still nascent area in stock market trading applications. Quantum computing appears in Cluster 2 of the coupling analysis (Figure 10), linked to “adaptive trading systems” and “sustainable finance,” but with low frequency. The “Thematic Evolution” (Figure 14) shows quantum AI as an emerging 2025 theme (term. “quantum,” occurrence. 2,944) but with low inclusion indices (0.58), indicating it's not yet mainstream. While the research includes quantum computing in its bibliometric analysis, the coverage remains relatively surface-level due to the field's early developmental stage. The paper identifies quantum AI's potential applications in three key areas. portfolio optimization (where quantum algorithms could solve complex problems faster than classical methods), high-frequency trading (through quantum machine learning's ability to process vast datasets exponentially quicker), and risk modeling (using quantum-enhanced Monte Carlo simulations). However, the analysis reveals significant gaps in current quantum AI research for financial applications, including hardware scalability limitations with current NISQ devices, a lack of empirical studies on hybrid classical-quantum models, and absent regulatory frameworks for quantum-powered trading systems. The paper positions quantum AI as part of future research directions rather than current mainstream applications, suggesting areas like quantum neural networks and quantum data encoding as promising avenues. This limited treatment reflects the field's immaturity - evidenced by quantum terms appearing with low frequency in the bibliometric analysis and not ranking among the most relevant keywords. Use either SI (MKS) or CGS as primary units. (SI units are strongly encouraged.) English units may be used as secondary units (in parentheses). This applies to papers in data storage. For example, write “15 Gb/cm2 (100 Gb/in2).” An exception is when English units are used as identifiers in trade, such as “3½-in disk drive.” Avoid combining SI and CGS units, such as current in amperes and magnetic field in oersteds. This often leads to confusion because equations do not balance dimensionally. If you must use mixed units, clearly state the units for each quantity in an equation.

THEORETICAL FRAMEWORK

Figure 15 shows the core financial theories on which this study is based to provide a backdrop against the use of AI in stock market trading. The EMH provides the fundamental assumption that markets efficiently incorporate all available information into prices. AI systems challenge the EMH by detecting hidden patterns of temporary market inefficiencies through advanced machine learning methodologies, especially deep learning systems such as LSTMs and CNNs. This has been seen with bibliometric maps where terms like “neural networks” and “forecasting” take center stage in the studied literature. Behavioral Finance Theory adds into the mix psychological factors and cognitive biases that affect investors' behavior. AI has started implementing this via sentiment analysis of news and social media; however, the relatively low occurrence of the word “sentiment” in co-occurrence networks would imply that this area is still rather unexplored. Bridging these views, the Adaptive Market Hypothesis envisages markets as evolving systems in which the participants continuously adapt. This stands well for how AI works, driven by machine learning, especially reinforcement learning systems that allow agents to change with market conditions. From 2017 to 2025, these developments are very clear in the spotlight of “real-time” and “adaptive” modeling. Altogether, these theories justify the application of AI in trading while also spotlighting critical research gaps, especially concerning behavioral integration and model interpretability.

Figure 15. Theoretical framework

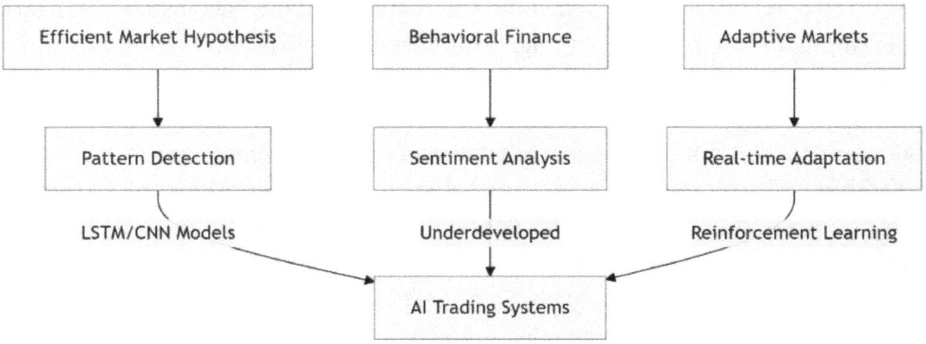

CONCEPTUAL FRAMEWORK

The conceptual framework considers AI-enabled stock trading to consist of four main components (Figure 16), all interlinked. Transformation data consists of both structured data of historical prices and fundamentals dominating current research (depicted in Cluster 1 focusing on "stock-financial-data") and neglected unstructured data such as news and satellite images, for example. Processing is performed by two methodological approaches: one being the predictive modeling with dominant architectures like LSTMs and CNNs, and an adaptive learning system that adjusts itself as markets change and, as such, is exploited with models that blend statistical and AI-based ones. The mainstay of validation relies on traditional measures like RMSE or accuracy, but real stress-testing of models in times of high volatility has yet to be developed. The output layer is where algorithmic trading strategies (the dominant cluster in bibliometrics is "market") and risk management tools are indeed produced, yet governance criteria on the other hand-has increasingly been incorporated, such as ESG alignment and explainability requirements (XAI). Processes in feedback foster continual system improvement through real-time retraining of models and adding alternative data sources, thereby evolving research to define and eliminate current gaps like incorporating quantum AI and stronger linkages to behavioral finance. Hence, this framework maps the current AI trading ecosystem and identifies avenues for future development, arranging the very strong technical turf of the field against the budding questions of ethics and interdisciplinary thoughts.

Figure 16. Conceptual framework

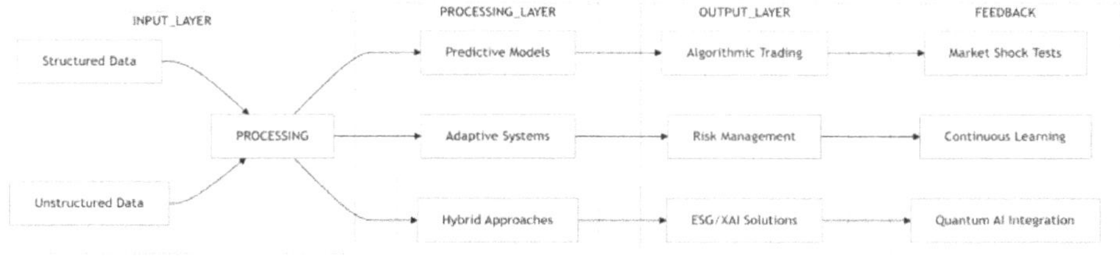

CONCLUSION

This comprehensive bibliometric study presents a unique and systematic evaluation of artificial intelligence applications in stock market trading by analyzing an unprecedented set of 9,088 documents over 54 years (1971-2025). What makes this uniquely novel is its multifaceted approach which combines bibliometric quantitative analysis with qualitative theoretical synthesis, showing both the evolution and future directions of the field. The study recognizes three main research clusters - market applications, predictive modeling, and AI methodologies - beyond which it portrays how neural networks and LSTM models have commandeered developments in recent years, with transformer architectures and explainable AI as emerging frontiers.

This research goes somewhat further than just tracking developments and contributes novel insights. Firstly, it exposes sore yet understudied paradoxes in the field, especially the tension between model sophistication and interpretability (the "explainability-adaptability paradox"). Secondly, it exposes the major geographical disparities in focus, with East Asian institutions taking the forefront in algorithmic development, while Western research is at the rear in behavioral finance integration. Thirdly, the study pioneers an original four-layer conceptual framework that correlates technical AI capabilities with the actual needs of trading, regulatory requirements, and ethical considerations.

What enables this research to stand out is that it manages to accomplish a connection between theory and practice. While the study grounds its findings in financial theories such as Efficient Market Hypothesis and Adaptive Markets Theory, it also, in turn, addresses practical-level problems like volatility response and regulation compliance so that it ends up with possible diagnostic and prescriptive measures. Especially from the rigorous trend analysis, identification of quantum AI and ESG-aligned systems as next frontiers will be of much value to the scientific community concerning the direction of their research.

This work yields not only a different methodological approach capable of integrating perspectives not previously interlinked and fills in gaps in knowledge by compiling the most complete intellectual history of AI in trading today but also responsible avenues for going forward. The unique blend of historical comprehensiveness, theoretical innovation, and practical applicability marks this work as a must-have for academics developing new AI techniques, practitioners implementing trading systems, and policymakers shaping financial regulations in the AI age.

REFERENCES

Alonso-Garcia, J., Pablo-Martí, F., & Núñez-Barriopedro, E. (2021). Omnichannel management in a B2B context: Concept, research agenda and bibliometric review. *International Journal of Industrial Engineering and Management*, *12*(1), 37–48. DOI: 10.24867/IJIEM-2021-1-275

Aria, M., & Cuccurullo, C. (2017). bibliometrix: An R-tool for comprehensive science mapping analysis. *Journal of Informetrics*, *11*(4), 959–975. DOI: 10.1016/j.joi.2017.08.007

Bar-Ilan, J. (2008). Informetrics at the beginning of the 21st century—A review. *Journal of Informetrics*, *2*(1), 1–52. DOI: 10.1016/j.joi.2007.11.001

Bar-Ilan, J. (2010). Citations to the "Introduction to informetrics" indexed by WOS, Scopus and Google Scholar. *Scientometrics*, *82*(3), 495–506. DOI: 10.1007/s11192-010-0185-9

Bastian, M., Heymann, S., & Jacomy, M. (2009). Gephi: An open source software for exploring and manipulating networks. *Proceedings of the International AAAI Conference on Web and Social Media, 3*(1). DOI: 10.1609/icwsm.v3i1.13937

Egghe, L., & Rousseau, R. (1990). *Introduction to informetrics: Quantitative methods in library, documentation and information science*. Elsevier Science Publishers.

Fahimnia, B., Sarkis, J., & Davarzani, H. (2015). Green supply chain management: A review and bibliometric analysis. *International Journal of Production Economics*, *162*, 101–114. DOI: 10.1016/j.ijpe.2015.01.003

Fan, D., Breslin, D., Callahan, J. L., & Iszatt-White, M. (2022). Advancing literature review methodology through rigour, generativity, scope and transparency. *International Journal of Management Reviews*, *24*(2), 171–180. DOI: 10.1111/ijmr.12291

Hicks, D., Wouters, P., Waltman, L., de Rijcke, S., & Rafols, I. (2015). Bibliometrics: The Leiden Manifesto for research metrics. *Nature*, *520*(7548), 429–431. DOI: 10.1038/520429a PMID: 25903611

Huffman, M. D., Baldridge, A., Bloomfield, G. S., Colantonio, L. D., Prabhakaran, P., Ajay, V. S., Suh, S., Lewison, G., & Prabhakaran, D. (2013). Global cardiovascular research output, citations, and collaborations: A time-trend, bibliometric analysis (1999–2008). *PLoS One*, *8*(12), e83440. DOI: 10.1371/journal.pone.0083440 PMID: 24391769

Kunisch, S., Denyer, D., Bartunek, J. M., Menz, M., & Cardinal, L. B. (2023). Review research as scientific inquiry. *Organizational Research Methods*, *26*(1), 3–45. DOI: 10.1177/10944281221127292

Liu, X., Zhan, F. B., Hong, S., Niu, B., & Liu, Y. (2012). A bibliometric study of earthquake research: 1900–2010. *Scientometrics*, *92*(3), 747–765. DOI: 10.1007/s11192-011-0599-z

Paul, J., Lim, W. M., O'Cass, A., Hao, A. W., & Bresciani, S. (2021). Scientific procedures and rationales for systematic literature reviews (SPAR-4-SLR). *International Journal of Consumer Studies*, *45*(4), O1–O16. DOI: 10.1111/ijcs.12695

Pellegrino, D. A., Jr. (2011). *Interactive visualization systems and data integration methods for supporting discovery in collections of scientific information* (Doctoral dissertation, Drexel University).

Wolfram, D. (2003). *Applied informetrics for information retrieval research.*

Zaugg, R. E. H., West, R. E., Tateishi, I., & Randall, D. L. (2011). Mendeley: Creating communities of scholarly inquiry through research collaboration, 32–36.

Zhuang, Y., Liu, X., Nguyen, T., He, Q., & Hong, S. (2013). Global remote sensing research trends during 1991–2010: A bibliometric analysis. *Scientometrics*, *96*(1), 203–219. DOI: 10.1007/s11192-012-0918-z

Chapter 2
Emerging Trends in AI-Driven Finance: A Topic Modeling Approach

Parul Singh
http://orcid.org/0000-0003-4926-0156
Indian Institute of Foreign Trade, India

ABSTRACT

The aim of the study is to explore the current and emerging trends in the area of AI-driven finance. The field is rapidly evolving and reshaping how financial systems operate. The study provides a holistic view of the domain. This work contributes to the body of knowledge for practitioners, policymakers, researchers, and academicians interested in understanding the technological transformation of the financial sector. The methodology involved extracting a relevant dataset from the Scopus database, followed by applying topic modelling analysis using the machine learning technique Latent Dirichlet Allocation (LDA) to identify key topics, their interrelationships and thematic clusters. The findings map the current research landscape and highlight the direction of future developments in AI-driven finance. The study also provides practical implications by equipping stakeholders with insights into prevailing trends and key themes and possible opportunities in the transformative field of AI-driven finance.

1. INTRODUCTION

The integration of AI in finance is transforming traditional financial systems. AI-driven finance makes use of machine learning algorithms, deep learning models, and big data analytics to augment decision-making, improve efficiency, and opti-

DOI: 10.4018/979-8-3373-5032-5.ch002

mize financial operations. The adoption of AI in finance is restructuring financial markets through increased automation and decreased human intervention.It can be seen that AI is transforming the financial services industry. This has been driven by various factors. The integration of machine learning and big data analytics has enabled the financial sector to handle large amounts of data efficiently. This has led to improved predictive capabilities along with decision-making (Li, 2021). Another technology is cloud computing and blockchain which provide improved infrastructure and enhanced security mechanisms (Guo et al., 2021). AI has reduced operational costs by automating various processes such as fraud detection, credit scoring, others (Ashta and Herrmann, 2021).

AI has found numerous applications in the area of finance. Its adoption in finance is increasing which is steered by both government and business investments (Olasiuk et al., 2023; Go et al., 2020).AI is important in finding and managing risks. Ot also helps in identifying fraudulent actions (Sharma and Devi, 2024). It also helps with improving customer service and managing financial services more effectively (Olasiuk et al., 2023). AI has found many applications in finance such as trading, fraud detection, customer service, portfolio optimization, and risk management (Sharma and Devi, 2024). It is also applied in news impact analysis which comprises reading and selecting news articles, coupling news events with relevant stocks and assessing the impact of the chosen news on stock prices (Chen et al., 2023). AI and machine learning can also build advanced asset pricing models. These can handle large datasets and detect trends (Touti and Taïb, 2024). AI facilitates algorithmic trading, risk management, credit scoring, fraud detection, customer service, portfolio management, sentiment analysis, supply chain finance, and economic forecasting (Kadioglu and Soydan, 2024). The financial industry is witnessing a change under the catalyst of artificial intelligence (Huang and Wang, 2019; Maurer, 2024). AI is used as an intelligent investment adviser, transaction forecast, financial regulator, forecast analysis, index statistics, stock analysis and information retrieval among others (Huang and Wang, 2019). AI-driven robo-advisor platforms assist in investment decision-making along with other areas such as data analysis, risk forecasting, portfolio optimization, and algorithmic trading (Zhou, 2024). AI helps in portfolio management by offering tools for effective asset allocation, risk management, and investment decision-making (Lahmini and Zine, 2024).Chatbots and virtual assistants driven by AI enhance customer service by offering customized financial advice, supervising customer inquiries, and improving the whole customer experience (Xie, 2019).AI has the capability to streamline processes and improve decision-making in the financial services industry. Future research in the area is expected to tackle complex financial challenges through the integration of quantum computing with AI.It enhances security in financial transactions by detecting and preventing fraud (Olasiuk et al., 2023).In recent years, there has been an increase in the adoption of text-based machine learning for sentiment analysis in finance (Aziz et al., 2022).

Since the adoption and application of AI in the financial sector arean evolving concept and research in this area is in its early stages, further exploration is necessary to uncover insights for both present and future research in this domain. The outcomes of this study will contribute to the body of knowledge in this field. The study presents topic modeling for the research landscape of AI-driven finance. Accordingly, the study aims to examine:

- How has research focused on AI-enabled finance has evolved over time?
- To identify the key topics related to AI-driven finance using topic modeling.
- To visualize trends and distribute topics over time to understand the shift in research focus.
- To propose future research directions by identifying emerging and less explored areas and topics related to AI-driven finance.

The rest of the study outlines the literature review in Section 2, data retrieval and methodology in Section 3, data analysis and results in Section 4, followed by the discussion and conclusion in Section 5.

2. LITERATURE REVIEW

The integration of AI in finance has led to many transformations. Its application has enhanced various aspects of finance-based services and related operations. It has influenced various aspects of the financial industry from asset management to fraud detection. Both the volume and complexity of data are increasing in the finance sector, leading to the adoption of AI-powered solutions. This has led to improved decision making, efficiency and offering customized financial services and solutions to customers.The application of AI and ML in finance has changed the old way of handling tasks and way of making decision- making. The sector has seen a revolutionary effect in the field of predictive analytics, algorithmic trading, and risk management. These applications in the financial sector bring accuracy, efficiency, and adaptability (Kayyali, 2025).The implementation of AI in finance is positively influencing the digital economies by improving automating processes, decision-making, and optimizing financial strategies (Jain, 2025). AI-driven techniques such as machine learning, deep learning, and reinforcement learning have found their profound impact in risk management, fraud detection, and algorithmic trading. AI has been able to improve the analytics, customer experience, and regulatory compliance (Chan, 2025). It has been seen that AI-powered tools have enhanced risk assessment accuracy by 35%. They have also been able to reduce fraud detection false positives by 50% along with 70% increase in audit automation (Leke, 2025).One of the earliest applications of AI was in the field of algorithmic trading. AI and ML techniques are used to analyze huge datasets to identify hidden patterns and predict market trends. The application can also be seen in quantitative finance. Reinforcement learning and deep neural networks are levied on quantitative hedge funds to adapt dynamic trading strategies (Chan, 2017). Algorithmic trading has become more sophisticated after being powered by AI. It is now able to make real-time trading decisions as it can leverage big data and sentiment (Sahithi et al., 2024). The effective applications of deep learning models have also been seen in forecasting stock price movements with greater accuracy (Deng et al., 2016). AI enabled robo-advisory services are used to provide algorithm-based financial adviceto handle personal wealth management. This is done with minimal human intervention and offers many advantages for both banks and customers (Jung et al., 2018). These are regularizing access to financial planning (Sironi, 2016).Pre-trained language models such as FinBERT (a language model based on BERT) are able to handle NLP tasks in the financial sector (Araci, 2019).AI also has a role in trade finance as it can impact this domain in the future by automating labor intensive operations (Pahari et al., 2023). The information from the trade documents can be read, extracted, analyzed and verified for compliance and regulatory standards with the help of ML, NLP, and Optical Character Recognition (Prasanth et al., 2023).A recent trend has been seen in the convergence of AI with decentralized finance. This is by improving efficiency and security to improve risk evaluation and user engagement (Basly, 2024).

Based on section 1 and section 2, table 1 gives an overview of key AI-driven capabilities in finance. It links each AI capability to its application area, a brief description or use case, and the authors who have discussed or studied it. The table shows how AI is transforming different aspects of finance such as risk management, customer service, investment planning, market analysis, security, and infrastructure. It also highlights certain emerging areas such as AI in decentralized finance and quantum-enhanced financial computing.

Table 1. Summary of AI-driven capabilities in finance

AI Capability	Application Area in Finance	Description / Use Case	Authors
Machine Learning & Deep Learning	Predictive Analytics, Decision-Making	Analyze large datasets to detect patterns, forecast market trends, and improve decision-making efficiency.	Li (2021); Kayyali (2025); Jain (2025)
Reinforcement Learning	Algorithmic & Quantitative Trading	Develop adaptive trading strategies in hedge funds and real-time markets.	Chan (2017); Sahithi et al. (2024)
Big Data Analytics	Risk Management, Portfolio Optimization	Manage large-scale financial data for improved risk assessment and asset allocation.	Li (2021); Lahmini& Zine (2024)
Natural Language Processing (NLP)	Sentiment Analysis, News Impact Analysis	Read and analyze financial news, extract sentiment, and assess market impact; includes models like FinBERT.	Chen et al. (2023); Araci (2019); Aziz et al. (2022)
Blockchain & Cloud Computing	Financial Infrastructure & Security	Enhance infrastructure scalability and security in transactions.	Era (2021)
Fraud Detection	Transaction Security	Detect and prevent fraudulent activities, reduce false positives, and enhance real-time monitoring.	Ashta & Herrmann (2021); Sharma & Devi (2024); Leke (2025)
Robo-Advisors	Wealth Management & Financial Planning	Provide automated investment advice, portfolio optimization, and financial planning.	Zhou (2024); Jung et al. (2018); Sironi (2016)
Chatbots & Virtual Assistants	Customer Service	Offer personalized advice, handle inquiries, and enhance customer experience.	Xie (2019)
Optical Character Recognition (OCR) & AI Document Processing	Trade Finance Automation	Read, extract, and verify trade documents for compliance and regulation.	Prasanth et al. (2023); Pahari et al. (2023)
AI in Decentralized Finance (DeFi)	Risk Evaluation, User Engagement	Improve DeFi security, efficiency, and personalized services.	Basly (2024)
Asset Pricing Models	Market Analysis	Build advanced models to detect trends and handle large-scale asset pricing.	Touti&Taïb (2024)
Quantum Computing with AI (Emerging)	Complex Financial Problem-Solving	Enhance computational capabilities for future AI-finance applications.	Olasiuk et al. (2023)

3. DATA RETRIEVALAND METHODOLOGY

For the study to identify the trends in AI-powered finance, the documents in the domain of AI-driven finance are extracted from the Scopus database. Scopus database offers good coverage of data which is suitable for performing topic modeling analysis. For the study, the relevant documents were extracted using the search string and keywords as presented in Table 2 and Table 3 resulting in a total of 2,532 initial articles. The terms used in the search string captures a comprehensive coverage of AI applications across different facets of finance including trading, forecasting, risk management, fraud detection, sentiment analysis, and regulatory compliance. The use of Boolean operators (e.g., OR) allowed inclusion of synonyms along with closely related terms. The keywords used also include both AI and finance specific technologies machine learning, deep learning, neural networks, blockchain, algorithmic trading, robo-advisors, and credit scoring.

Inclusion and Exclusion Criteria

Inclusion Criteria: Following are the articles' inclusion criteria

- Articles published between 2015 and 2025
- Articles from subject areas:
    - Business, Management and Accounting
    - Economics, Econometrics and Finance
    - Computer Science
- Documents categorized as journal articles
- Articles written in English
- Articles published in peer-reviewed journals
- Articles related to applications of AI (e.g., machine learning, neural networks, deep learning) in the financial domain (e.g., trading, forecasting, risk assessment, etc.)

Exclusion Criteria: Following are the articles' exclusion criteria

- Articles outside the time range of 2015–2025
- Articles not associated with the specified subject areas
- Documents such as books, conference papers, magazines, book series, and reports
- Non-English language articles
- Non-final or preliminary versions (e.g., editorials, reviews not meeting empirical criteria)

- Articles not relevant to both AI technologies and financial applications

Table 4 provides details of the data retrieval and filtering process. The data retrieval process began with 2,532 documents retrieved based on the initial search terms. These articles were narrowed down based on the inclusion and exclusion criteria.First, the articles were filtered to extract for the past decade, 2015-2025 giving a total of 2,116 articles. Next, the articles were selected on the basis of subject catering to business, management and accounting; economics, econometrics and finance; computer science leading to total of 1,834 articles. Afterward, only journals were chosen as the document types, excluding books, conference papers, book series, magazines, and reports. The selection was then fine-tuned by focusing on final articles and limiting the language of the documents to English.After reviewing, 871articles were chosen for more detailed analysis as presented in Table 4. These selected articles met the study's requirements and were exported in CSV format for further study. The CSV file contained detailed data like document titles, publication years, abstracts and others.

Table 2. The search string and keywords

Category	**Example Keywords**
AI Techniques	"machine learning", "deep learning", "neural networks", "AI", "artificial intelligence"
Financial Applications	"trading", "forecasting", "risk management", "credit scoring", "fraud detection"
Financial Technologies	"robo-advisors", "blockchain", "automated trading", "algorithmic trading"
Regulatory and Compliance	"AI regulatory compliance", "financial risk assessment", "AI in banking", "insurance"
Analytics and Insights	"financial big data analytics", "sentiment analysis", "AI-driven investment"

Table 3. Search String, Keywords, and Search Details

Search Parameter	**Details**
Database	Scopus
Search Fields	Title, Abstract, Keywords
Date of Search Execution	July 2025
Time Range	2015–2025
Boolean Operators Used	OR (to include multiple AI and finance-related keywords)

continued on following page

Table 3. Continued

Search Parameter	Details
Search String	"machine learning in finance" OR "deep learning finance" OR "financial forecasting AI" OR ...
AI Keywords	"machine learning", "deep learning", "neural networks", "AI", "blockchain"
Finance Keywords	"trading", "forecasting", "risk management", "robo-advisors", "credit scoring", "insurance"
Compliance/Other Terms	"regulatory compliance", "big data analytics", "sentiment analysis", "investment"

Table 4. Data retrieval and filtering summary

Stage	Filtering Criteria	Documents	Rationale
1	Initial search result based on search terms	2,532	Broad inclusion to capture all relevant documents
1.1	Time range: 2015–2025	2,116	Ensures relevance to contemporary AI trends
2	Subject areas: Business, Economics, Finance, Computer Science	1,834	Focuses on interdisciplinary relevance to AI in finance
3	Document type: Journal articles only	887	Excluding books, conference papers, reports on quality and consistency
4	Language filter: English only	883	Ensure consistent interpretation and processing
5	Source type: Peer-reviewed journals	871	Ensures academic rigor and reliability of sources

This study comprises of a data driven approach to explore emerging trends in AI-driven finance using a topic modeling technique.Accordingly, the abstracts were extracted from the Scopus database and topic modeling analysis was performed over it using Latent Dirichlet Allocation (LDA). LDA is an unsupervised machine learning technique. It is used for identifying hidden topics within a large collection of documents.LDA is a generative model used to infer topic and themes from unstructured documents (Kherwa and Bansal, 2018). It is an effective tool for statistical analysis of large collections of documents. It adopts uses a Dirichlet distribution and helps in managing the distribution of topics across the corpus (Bian and Tao, 2009).This technique is effective in document classification, topic discovery, and information retrieval (Murakami and Chakraborty, 2021). LDA has many advancements and variations that improves its applicability and performance.

To analyze the dataset, LDA model was applied using the LDAvis package in R software in this study. LDAvis is a strong package that allows interpretation and exploration of topic modeling results. It also supports interactive visualization for better understanding of the outcome and results. For example, it presents a topic-to-topic distance map using multidimensional scaling. This helps in understanding how distinct or overlapping the topics. The interactive interface of the LDAvis is one of its important features. It improves the interpretability of results.

Before performing analysis, an important step in text analysis is to clean and preprocess the data. First, empty values, special characters, and other non-informative elements were removed. This gives clean textual corpus. This clean corpus was then tokenized by breaking down the content into individual words. Following this, lemmatization was applied to convert words into their root forms. This helps in standardizing different variations of a word. Next, commonly used words like "the," "is," or "and" that carry negligible semantic value, known as stop words were removed. Post this, a dictionary of terms was created for the dataset. This served as the basis for the Latent Dirichlet Allocation (LDA) model.

4. DATA ANALYSIS AND RESULTS

The study comprisesa four-step workflow including data collection, data preprocessing, data analysis, and result interpretation. The first step on data collection comprised of extracted data from the Scopus database. The focus was on scholarly literature related to AI-driven finance. The second step includeddata preprocessing, which was performed using R software. It included, noise removal, handling incomplete or missing data, tokenization, removal of stop words, lemmatization and stemming. This produced a well-structured textual data for topic modeling analysis. In the third step, the study used LDA to identify thematic structures in the corpus. On the basis of the patterns of co-occurrence, it helps clustering words into topics or groups (Anupriya and Karpagavalli, 2015). It gives a way to organize, understand and summarize large groups of textual information (George, 2018).LDA is a model that looks at documents as combinations of different topics, with each topic made up of various words. This method is extensively adopted owing to its flexibility and effectiveness (George, 2018; Mohan and Kumar, 2021).

An important part of LDA process is selecting the optimal number of topics. It is important as it affects interpretability and performance of the model. In this study, perplexity scores have been used for optimal number of topic selection. It is a commonly accepted statistical measure (Jacobi et al., 2018). It measures how well the model predicts the data. Lower values indicate better model performance (Newman et al., 2009). Several iterations of LDA were run to finetune the model. Manual evaluations were also conducted to find a balance between topics that were too similar and those that were overly fragmented. Depicting perplexity distributions across different topics for topic modeling, it can be seen that the ideal number of topics in consideration is nine as perplexity score is lowest at this number. This indicates that in terms of predictive potential, the topic model would perform best at this optimal number of topics. After nine topics, the curve starts to increase, indicating the decline in the model quality. Following this, the topic outputs were manually reviewed and nine topics were finalized. These nine topics offer semantic clarity and distinctiveness.

Table 4 presents the list of top 30 most frequently occurring words across the dataset. This analysis gives aninitial glimpse into the key themes, recurring concepts, and discussion topics in the domain of AI driven finance.

Following keywords indicate emphasis on financial trading and market-related applications.

- "Trade" (2068 occurrences) and "market" (1631) are the top two most frequent terms, highlighting the literature's focus on trading strategies, market dynamics, and financial instruments.
- Other terms like "price" (666) and "stock" (579) further emphasize the relevance of asset pricing models, equity trading, and real-time market predictions in AI applications.

The keywords also reveal a strong technological and methodological foundation:

- Terms like "model" (1163), "learn" (632), and "algorithmic" (555) shows scholarly interest in machine learning, predictive modeling, and algorithmic trading systems.
- The presence of "algorithm" (493), "method" (368), and "analysis" (490) focuses on developing and refining AI techniques. This helps to enhance financial decision-making processes.

There is also a presence of data-centric terminologies such as:

- "datum" (770), "base" (617), and "result" (542) indicates that data-driven decision-making, data preprocessing, and result-oriented model validation are important components of research in this area.

The appearance of keywords like "robo" (666) and "advisor" (569) highlights the emerging and expanding interest in robo-advisory services. These utilize AI algorithms to offer automated, low-cost financial advice. This is in line with recent trends in personalized finance, fintech services, and digital wealth management. Further, terms such as "risk" (407), "investment" (387), and "portfolio" (323) suggest an active application of AI in the areas like risk assessment, investment strategy optimization, and portfolio management. Presence of words like "decision" (343) and "performance" (375) suggest a broader theme of improving decision-making efficiency along with measuring the effectiveness of AI-based tools in finance.

This frequency analysis of keywords gives a meaningful basis to understand the depth and breadth of research in AI-driven finance. It shows the intersection of financial theory, computational methods, and data science. It can be understood that a multi-disciplinary approach has been adopted by scholars in this field.

Table 5. Top 30 high-frequency terms identified in the Corpus

S. No.	Words	Frequency	S. No.	Words	Frequency
1	trade	2068	16	analysis	490
2	market	1631	17	research	460
3	model	1163	18	system	452
4	datum	770	19	investor	437
5	strategy	703	20	time	422
6	robo	666	21	approach	416
7	price	666	22	risk	407
8	learn	632	23	investment	387
9	base	617	24	performance	375
10	stock	579	25	method	368
11	advisor	569	26	author	343
12	algorithmic	555	27	decision	343
13	result	542	28	trader	331
14	propose	501	29	portfolio	323
15	algorithm	493	30	service	315

Here the words with a minimum frequency threshold of200 have been considered for representation. It is to ensure relevance and to filter out noise from rarely used terms.In this visualization, higher occurrence of the words is indicated by the larger size of the word. Larger words appear more frequently. This represents their higher importance or recurrence in the literature. As it can be seen, words such as "trade," "market," "model," "datum," "price," and "robo" highlight dominant themes pertaining to trading strategies, financial modeling, algorithmic tools, and robo-advisory services."algorithm," "strategy," "analysis," and "advisor" highlight the emphasis on algorithmic tools, decision-making methods, and advisory frameworks.This word cloud visualization gives a holistic view of key topics within the AI-driven finance domain.

The topic modeling analysis performed by LDA producednine distinct topics. These are summarized and presented in Table 6, giving insights, interpretation and titles for each topic. The output presented in the table provides insights into emerging trends and research directions in the area of AI-driven finance. Each topic was labeled based on the semantic coherence of the top keywords along with interpretative evaluation of the terms. The table presents a thematic title, a list of dominant keywords, and a brief interpretation to capture the essence of each topic. The topics range from practical applications like portfolio optimization and automated trading, to technological advancements such as deep learning, blockchain, and data analytics. This highlights the diversity of topics range along with the interdisciplinary nature of the field.

Table 6. Summary of AI-driven financial topics with key areas, keywords, and interpretationsbased on LDA analysis

S. No.	Title	Keywords	Interpretation
1	Portfolio and Risk Management	portfolio, risk, strategy, investment, investor, return, result	Focuses on traditional and AI-enhanced strategies for portfolio optimization, investor behavior, risk quantification, and performance evaluation.
2	AI-Powered Financial Advisory	robo, advisor, service, bank, advisory, customer, perceive, advice	Explores the role of AI in personal finance, including robo-advisory services, customer trust, and the evolving role of banks in digital advisory.
3	Algorithmic and Quantitative Trading	agent, optimal, trader, strategy, asset, liquidity, frequency, hft	Examines quantitative trading models, multi-agent simulations, and high-frequency trading mechanisms aimed at liquidity and market efficiency.
4	Blockchain and Fintech Innovations	technology, research, blockchain, machine, system, challenge, author	Captures innovation in financial technology, including blockchain applications, machine learning systems, and associated research challenges.
5	Stock Market Forecasting and Trading	price, forecast, return, stock, future, time	Encompasses price prediction models, time-series forecasting, and financial market trend analysis.
6	Financial Sentiment Analysis	sentiment, analysis, model, news, text, method, information, word	Highlights the application of NLP and text analytics to capture market sentiment from financial news and documents.
7	Data-Driven Trading Strategies	datum, base, propose, indicator, real, analysis	Focuses on the use of structured data, indicators, and analytics-driven models for formulating trading strategies.
8	High-Frequency and Automated Trading	trade, algorithmic, trader, increase, hft, stock	Emphasizes automated systems, algorithmic execution, and high-frequency strategies with implications for market microstructure.
9	Machine Learning in Finance	learn, deep, network, machine, algorithm	Discusses the adoption of advanced AI techniques such as deep learning and neural networks for prediction, classification, and financial modeling.

- Topic 1, Portfolio and Risk Management comprising of the keywords portfolio, risk, strategy, investment, investor, return, result highlights the integration of AI into traditional investment and portfolio management strategies. It shows how AI and machine learning tools are being used for risk quantification, optimal asset allocation, and forecasting. The presence of words like "strategy," "investor," and "result" also suggests rising interest in behavioral finance. AI models can interpret investor sentiments and reactions.
- Topic 2,AI-Powered Financial Advisorycomprising of the keywordsrobo, advisor, service, bank, advisory, customer, perceive, advice,eflects the digital transformation of financial advisory services through technologies like robo-advisors. Robo-advisors provide automated, algorithm-based financial planning services. AI is used to personalize investment suggestions, manage portfolios, and improve customer experience. The presence of words like "perceive" and "customer" also indicates research interest in consumer trust, satisfaction, and adoption barriers.
- Topic 3, Algorithmic and Quantitative Tradinginlcuding keywords agent, optimal, trader, strategy, asset, liquidity, frequency, hft indictaes focus on automated trading systems. These are quantitative models that make use of AI for decision-making and trading. The oresence of terms such as "agent" and "optimal" directs to multi-agent reinforcement learning models. These simulate trader behavior in competitive environments. Words such as "liquidity" and "frequency" relate to high-frequency trading.
- Topic 4: Blockchain and Fintech Innovations inlcudes keywords such as technology, research, blockchain, machine, system, challenge, author displaying presence of literature on emerging technologies in financial services. Examples could include blockchain and decentralized finance (DeFi). AI helps in smart contracts, fraud detection, and predictive analytics in blockchain systems. The presence of words such as "challenge" and "research" shows a focus on technical, ethical, and regulatory obstacles around data security, scalability, and trust in financial ecosystems.
- Topic 5: Stock Market Forecasting and Trading with keywords price, forecast, return, stock, future, timereflects work on financial prediction models, using AI to forecast stock prices, volatility, and returns. Time series models, neural networks, and hybrid models are the examples of combining traditional econometrics with deep learning. Words like "future" and "forecast" underline the predictive aspect, while "stock" and "return" indicate applications to equity markets. This area is important for algorithmic trading systems, portfolio optimization, and risk management.
- Topic 6: Financial Sentiment Analysis has jeywords sentiment, analysis, model, news, text, method, information, word. This covers the use of NLP

and text mining in finance. Sentiment analysis is done from news articles, financial reports, and social media to forecast market movements or stock returns.

- Topic 7: Data-Driven Trading Strategies inlcudes keywords such as datum, base, propose, indicator, real, analysisemphasizes the role of big data and real-time analytics in formulating trading strategies by using using large amounts of financial data. AI helps to on making decisions based on real-time data. This allows traders to respond quickly to market changes.
- Topic 8: High-Frequency and Automated Trading contain keywords trade, algorithmic, trader, increase, hft, stock indicating very fast, automated trading systems that can buy and sell stocks in fractions of a second. AI helps make these systems smarter by finding the best times and prices to trade.
- Topic 9: Machine Learning in Finance inlcudes words such as learn, deep, network, machine, algorithm is about using machine machine to solve different financial problems. This can include predicting stock prices, detection fraud, or providing investment advice.

This highlights the reaserch focus over the last decade. It can be seen that Topic 3 (Algorithmic and Quantitative Trading), Topic 4 (Blockchain and Fintech Innovations), and Topic 9 (Machine Learning in Finance) focusing on AI techniques, model development, and technical advancements were of high interest among early years during 2015-2017. These themes indicates the foundational stage of the field. A gradual shift can be seen towards application-oriented themes from around 2018 onwards. Topic 2 (AI-Powered Financial Advisory) and Topic 1 (Portfolio and Risk Management) focusing on AI-powered financial advisory and portfolio and risk management gained increased importance. The trends also divulge cyclical interest patterns for Topic 5 (Stock Market Forecasting and Trading) and Topic 7 (Data-Driven Trading Strategies) with intermittent spikes. This reflects upcoming sub-fields, technological advances, or shifts in industry priorities. By 2025, application-based topics appear to dominate. Overall, the plot shows the evolution from foundational research towards application based research in AI and finance.

It can be seen that topic 8 has the highest number of documents indicating that this is the dominant theme in the corpus. This suggests that high-frequency and automated trading (Topic 8)has been an active and widely studied area in AI-driven finance. This is followed by topic 2 (AI-powered financial advisory) and topic 9 (Machine Learning in Finance) which have a sizable number of documents also ndicates keen research interest. In contrast, topics 3 (Algorithmic and Quantitative Trading), 6 (Financial Sentiment Analysis) and 7 (Data-Driven Trading Strategies) have lesser documents, suggesting that these themes are less prevalent and are explored less frequently in the dataset. This indicate either a niche specialization or emerging areas with growth potential for future research. Topic 1 (Portfolio and Risk Management), Topic 4 (Blockchain and Fintech Innovations) and Topic 5 (Stock Market Forecasting and Trading) have moderate number of documents. This highlights a stable level of research in these areas. These themes on portfolio and risk management, blockchain and fintech innovations, and stock market forecasting and trading, remain central to the AI-finance research landscape but are not as dominant as topics 8 (High-Frequency and Automated Trading), 2 (AI-Powered Financial Advisory), or 9 (Machine Learning in Finance).

Overall, the plot highlights thematic diversity within AI-driven finance research. Some of the topics are receiving concentrated attention while others emerges as emerging or specialized areas.

5. DISCUSSION AND CONCLUSION

The advancements in the field of AI have made significant advancements in the financial sector, influencing various aspects and domains such as algorithmic trading, fraud detection, customer service, risk management among others. This study uses Latent Dirichlet Allocation (LDA), a topic modeling technique on Scopus dataset to explore the evolving trends in AI-driven finance. The analysis and results provide an overview of the evolving themes and trends in this domain.

The analysis gave nine key thematic areas in AI driven finance. One of the important topics is Portfolio and Risk Management focusing on investment strategies, risk assessment, and portfolio management. It is seen that the research in this area has shown significant progress indicating growing interest in this field. Another emerging trend has been seen. The other important topic is AI-Powered Financial Advisory, comprising of AI-based financial services, robo-advisors, and customer perception of advisory tools. This highlights the digitization trend in the financial services sector. The analysis also revealed "Algorithmic and Quantitative Trading" as one of the important themes which focusses on high-frequency trading, algorithmic strategies, and trading automation. This indicates the application of AI in reducing time and improving efficiency. Another theme identified is "Blockchain and Fintech Innovations" that explores emerging technologies like blockchain, machine learning, and fintech solutions highlighting reduced costs and improved security."Stock Market Forecasting and Trading" emerged as another theme, focusing on how AI helps in improving prediction accuracy by handling predictive models and financial market trends."Financial Sentiment Analysis" and "Data-Driven Trading Strategies" are another two themes focusing on NLP and data analytics respectively. "High-Frequency and Automated Trading" focuses on HFT strategies, automated trading systems, and market microstructure. Lastly, "Machine Learning in Finance" coversAI models applied in financial markets. This helps in fraud detection, portfolio optimization, and algorithmic trading. The results of the study provide a complete perspective on AI-driven finance providing evolving themes and future research directions. Each topic represents a distinct research direction; the results divulge three broader thematic clusters.

1. AI-Enhanced Decision-Making and Risk Management: covering applications that improve investment strategies, portfolio optimization, market forecasting, and risk assessment.
2. Automation and Market Efficiency: comprising of algorithmic trading, high-frequency trading, and automated advisory services. AI enables faster execution, reduced human bias, and scalable operations.
3. Emerging Technologies and Infrastructure: it includes blockchain integration, fintech innovations, and data-driven strategies that support more secure, transparent, and adaptive financial systems.

These topic groups show a pattern of research not only been expanding within each application area but also moving towards integration. Technologies such as ML, NLP and blockchain intersect to solve multi-dimensional financial challenges.

The increasing adoption of AI and ML is changing the way the financial sector operates. However, there are also certain challenges. First are regulatory and compliance gaps, especially in cross-border financial AI applications. Second, ethical and transparency concerns, including algorithmic bias, explainability, and accountability. Also, the challenges are around data privacy and security risks. These areincreased by the scale of information processing in AI systems.Future research needs to focus on these challenges for responsible adoption of AI in finance.

As adoption of AI continues to evolve in finance, it presents both new opportunities and challenges for various stakeholders such as for practitioners, researchers, and policymakers. There is also some focus required on policies and regulations around this area. There is a need to establish integrated guidelines for ethical use of AI in finance. It should focus on data privacy, and algorithmic transparency. There is also a need to implement AI-enabled surveillance systems for detecting regulatory breaches in financial markets. Training initiatives are also required to reskill finance professionals for AI-integrated roles. This will ensure keeping pace with technological change.

The findings of the study suggest that AI in finance is an ecosystem of interconnected capabilities. AI will continue to redefine how financial markets operate. It will create competitive advantages for early adopters and governance responsibilities for regulators and policymakers.

REFERENCES

Anupriya, P., & Karpagavalli, S. (2015). Automatic tag recommendation for journal abstracts using statistical topic modeling. In *Emerging ICT for Bridging the Future-Proceedings of the 49th Annual Convention of the Computer Society of India CSI Volume 2* (pp. 565-572). Springer International Publishing.

Araci, D. (2019). Finbert: Financial sentiment analysis with pre-trained language models. *arXiv preprint arXiv:1908.10063.*

Ashta, A., & Herrmann, H. (2021). Artificial intelligence and fintech: An overview of opportunities and risks for banking, investments, and microfinance. *Strategic Change, 30*(3), 211–222. DOI: 10.1002/jsc.2404

Aziz, S., Dowling, M., Hammami, H., & Piepenbrink, A. (2022). Machine learning in finance: A topic modeling approach. *European Financial Management, 28*(3), 744–770. DOI: 10.1111/eufm.12326

Basly, S. (2024). Artificial intelligence and the future of decentralized finance. In *Decentralized Finance: The Impact of Blockchain-Based Financial Innovations on Entrepreneurship* (pp. 175–183). Springer International Publishing. DOI: 10.1007/978-3-031-49515-1_10

Bian, W., & Tao, D. (2009, December). Dirichlet mixture allocation for multiclass document collections modeling. In *2009 Ninth IEEE International Conference on Data Mining* (pp. 711-715). IEEE. DOI: 10.1109/ICDM.2009.102

Chan, E. P. (2017). *Machine trading: Deploying computer algorithms to conquer the markets.* John Wiley & Sons. DOI: 10.1002/9781119244066

Chen, W., Rabhi, F., Liao, W., & Al-Qudah, I. (2023). Leveraging state-of-the-art topic modeling for news impact analysis on financial markets: A comparative study. *Electronics (Basel), 12*(12), 2605. DOI: 10.3390/electronics12122605

Deng, Y., Bao, F., Kong, Y., Ren, Z., & Dai, Q. (2016). Deep direct reinforcement learning for financial signal representation and trading. *IEEE Transactions on Neural Networks and Learning Systems, 28*(3), 653–664. DOI: 10.1109/TNNLS.2016.2522401 PMID: 26890927

Guo, H., & Polak, P. (2021). *"After the Collision of Crisis and Opportunity to Redefining the Artificial Intelligence in Finance: The New Intelligent Finance Era," in Applications of Artificial Intelligence in Business.* Education, and Healthcare.

George, M. (2018, September). Unsupervised Topic Detection based on 2D Vector Space model using Apriori Algorithm and NLP. In *2018 Thirteenth International Conference on Digital Information Management (ICDIM)* (pp. 279-283). IEEE. DOI: 10.1109/ICDIM.2018.8846982

Go, E. J., Moon, J., & Kim, J. (2020). Analysis of the current and future of the artificial intelligence in financial industry with big data techniques. [GBFR]. *Global Business & Finance Review, 25*(1), 102–117. DOI: 10.17549/gbfr.2020.25.1.102

Huang, C., & Wang, X. (2019, July). Financial innovation based on artificial intelligence technologies. In *Proceedings of the 2019 International Conference on Artificial Intelligence and Computer Science* (pp. 750-754). DOI: 10.1145/3349341.3349504

Jacobi, C., Van Atteveldt, W., & Welbers, K. (2018). Quantitative analysis of large amounts of journalistic texts using topic modelling. In *Rethinking research methods in an age of digital journalism* (pp. 89–106). Routledge. DOI: 10.4324/9781315115047-7

Jain, J. (2025). AI-Driven Learning in Finance: The Future of Digital Economics. In *AI-Enabled Sustainable Innovations in Education and Business* (pp. 171-202). IGI Global Scientific Publishing.

Jung, D., Dorner, V., Weinhardt, C., & Pusmaz, H. (2018). Designing a robo-advisor for risk-averse, low-budget consumers. *Electronic Markets, 28*(3), 367–380. DOI: 10.1007/s12525-017-0279-9

Kadioglu, Y. M., & Soydan, H. (2024). The Transformative Role of Artificial Intelligence in Finance and Economics. In *Artificial Intelligence* (pp. 193–207). CRC Press. DOI: 10.1201/9781003483571-13

Kayyali, M. (2025). Envisioning the Future: The Evolution and Impact of AI and Machine Learning in Finance. In *Utilizing AI and Machine Learning in Financial Analysis* (pp. 193-212). IGI Global Scientific Publishing.

Kherwa, P., & Bansal, P. (2018). Empirical Evaluation of Inference Technique for Topic Models. In *Progress in Advanced Computing and Intelligent Engineering: Proceedings of ICACIE 2017,* Volume 1 (pp. 237-246). Singapore: Springer Singapore.

Lahmini, H. M., & Zine, D. (2024, April). The Role of Artificial Intelligence in Optimizing Portfolio Management: A Literature Review. In *International Conference on Business and Technology* (pp. 122-131). Cham: Springer Nature Switzerland. DOI: 10.1007/978-3-031-67444-0_12

Leke, C. A. (2025). The Development of Artificial Intelligence and Machine Learning: Applications in Financial Services. In *Artificial Intelligence in Accounting, Auditing and Finance: A Guide for Implementation and Use* (pp. 9–29). Springer Nature Switzerland. DOI: 10.1007/978-3-031-87368-3_2

Li, C. (2021). The application of artificial intelligence and machine learning in financial stability. In *The 2020 International Conference on Machine Learning and Big Data Analytics for IoT Security and Privacy: SPIoT-2020, Volume 1* (pp. 214-219). Springer International Publishing. DOI: 10.1007/978-3-030-62743-0_30

Maurer, T. A. (Ed.). (2024). Exploring the Financial Landscape in the Digital Age*: Proceedings of the International Conference on Financial Management and the Digital Economy (ICFMDE 2023),* Kuala Lumpur, Malaysia*,* 15–17 December 2023. CRC Press.

Mohan, G. B., & Kumar, R. P. (2021, September). A comprehensive survey on topic modeling in text summarization. In *International Conference on Micro-Electronics and Telecommunication Engineering* (pp. 231-240). Singapore: Springer Nature Singapore.

Murakami, R., & Chakraborty, B. (2021, July). Neural topic models for short text using pretrained word embeddings and its application to real data. In *2021 IEEE 4th International Conference on Knowledge Innovation and Invention (ICKII)* (pp. 146-150). IEEE. DOI: 10.1109/ICKII51822.2021.9574752

Newman, D., Asuncion, A., Smyth, P., & Welling, M. (2009). Distributed algorithms for topic models. *Journal of Machine Learning Research, 10*(8).

Olasiuk, H., Kumar, S., Singh, S., & Ganushchak, T. (2023, December). Mapping research clusters of artificial intelligence for financial services using topic modelling: A machine learning insight. In *2023 Global Conference on Information Technologies and Communications (GCITC)* (pp. 1-6). IEEE. DOI: 10.1109/GCITC60406.2023.10426342

Pahari, S., Polisetty, A., Sharma, S., Jha, R., & Chakraborty, D. (2023). Adoption of AI in the banking industry: A case study on Indian banks. *Indian Journal of Marketing, 53*(3), 26–41. DOI: 10.17010/ijom/2023/v53/i3/172654

Prasanth, A., Densy, J. V., Surendran, P., & Bindhya, T. (2023). Role of artificial intelligence and business decision making. *International Journal of Advanced Computer Science and Applications, 14*(6). Advance online publication. DOI: 10.14569/IJACSA.2023.01406103

Sahithi, K., Chowdary, N. V., Amruta, D., & Rukum, D. (2024, November). Future Trends in Quantitative Finance and Algorithmic Trading Strategies. In *2024 International Conference on Sustainable Islamic Business and Finance (SIBF)* (pp. 160-169). IEEE. DOI: 10.1109/SIBF63788.2024.10883846

Sharma, P., & Devi, S. (2024). The future of finance: Revolutionizing the industry with artificial intelligence. In *Leveraging AI and emotional intelligence in contemporary business organizations* (pp. 187–210). IGI Global Scientific Publishing.

Sironi, P. (2016). *FinTech innovation: from robo-advisors to goal based investing and gamification*. John Wiley & Sons. DOI: 10.1002/9781119227205

Touti, N., & Taïb, A. A. (2024, May). Bibliometric Analysis of Artificial Intelligence Applications in Asset Pricing. In *International Conference on Digital Technologies and Applications* (pp. 27-36). Cham: Springer Nature Switzerland. DOI: 10.1007/978-3-031-68653-5_3

Xie, M. (2019, April). Development of artificial intelligence and effects on financial system. [). IOP Publishing.]. *Journal of Physics: Conference Series*, *1187*(3), 032084. DOI: 10.1088/1742-6596/1187/3/032084

Zhou, J. (2024). The use of artificial intelligence in investment selection: Roboadvisory platform. In *Exploring the Financial Landscape in the Digital Age* (pp. 661–669). CRC Press. DOI: 10.1201/9781003508816-95

Chapter 3

AI-Powered Forecasting and Portfolio Optimization:

From Predictive Models to Strategic Investment Decisions

Muhammad Usman Tariq
http://orcid.org/0000-0002-7605-3040
Abu Dhabi University, UAE & University College Cork, Ireland

ABSTRACT

The integration of artificial intelligence (AI) in financial decision-making and portfolio optimization marks a significant change in investment decision-making. Conventional econometric models, although foundational, often struggle with nonlinear dynamics, high-dimensional data, and rapidly changing market conditions. AI, particularly machine learning and deep learning algorithms, presents the capacity to reveal hidden patterns, adapt to evolving data, and offer real-time predictive capabilities. This chapter examines how AI-driven tools enhance the accuracy of financial forecasts, automate resource allocation, and inform risk-adjusted investment strategies. It also delves into cases that explain how support stores, resource directors, and robo-advisors utilize AI for vital decision-making. By reimagining decision-making through the lens of data-centric insights and showing adaptivity, AI enables investors to make more informed, agile, and versatile choices in volatile markets.

DOI: 10.4018/979-8-3373-5032-5.ch003

INTRODUCTION

Conventional financial modeling has long relied on econometric models established through empirical induction and grounded assumptions. Models such as ARIMA, GARCH, and CAPM provide a theoretical foundation for estimating stock returns, interest rates, and volatility. However, their viability in a world driven by advanced change and complex market interdependencies is progressively being challenged (Kumari, 2024). Their use is necessitated by straightforward conditions, unwavering suspicions of stationarity, and limited capacity to handle high-dimensional and unstructured information. Markets today are not only unstable but also profoundly sensitive to geopolitical developments, macroeconomic shocks, social sentiment, and algorithmic trading behavioral variables that exceed the capacity of classical models to capture in real time. Manufactured insights (AI) and machine learning (ML) offer transformative possibilities. The rise of AI in quantitative finance stems from its ability to handle massive datasets, identify non-linear patterns, and continually learn from new data (Abbas, 2024). Unlike conventional models, which require explicit programming of connections, AI systems, particularly neural networks, decision trees, and machine learning methods, can independently extract knowledge from vast datasets, including news feeds, social media, natural language, and transaction logs. This marks a significant shift from hypothesis-driven modeling to data-driven discovery.

One of the key reasons for this shift in worldview is that markets are not simply judicious. Behavioral inconsistencies, group instincts, and passionate reactions frequently drive costs that are absent from the basics. AI, particularly when combined with natural language processing (NLP), can integrate assumption analyses into decision models (Arshard et al., 2024). It empowers financial specialists to track not only cost and volume information but also open insights and global trends in real time, providing a more comprehensive view of potential market movements. This chapter encompasses three interrelated areas where AI is reshaping financial decision-making: risk assessment, risk management, and portfolio optimization (Campbell & Koffi, 2024). In estimation, AI provides more precise and accurate expectations of resource returns, instability clusters, and macroeconomic indicators. Models such as long short-term memory (LSTM) systems and transformers consistently exceed expectations in capturing transient conditions in financial time series, even in the presence of noisy and nonstationary data. Fortification learning models help improve forecasts by optimizing successive decision-making under vulnerability, a capability that is well-suited for exchanging and supporting strategies.

In portfolio optimization, AI provides more nuanced models for estimating returns and risks, enabling personalized and versatile asset allocation methodologies. Classical models, such as mean-variance optimization (MVO), often rely on inactive inputs and accept ordinary data distributions (Devapitchai et al., 2024). However, AI models can accommodate fat-tailed distributions, regime shifts, and asymmetric risk preferences. Methods such as hereditary calculations, Bayesian optimization, and deep reinforcement learning enable the continuous rebalancing and optimization of multi-asset portfolios, even in the presence of exchange costs and regulatory constraints. Another key advantage of AI lies in its ability to show outfit strategies that combine forecasts from different models to enhance generalization and robustness (Kumari, 2024). This is especially important in finance, where overfitting to past information can abdicate destitute out-of-sample execution. Gathering models, such as irregular timberlands, angle-boosting machines, and stacked models, can provide more stable and precise figures, thereby supporting better risk-adjusted investment decisions.

Moreover, AI enhances the capacity for real-time analysis, which is vital for high-frequency trading and intraday risk assessment. Conventional models often fail to scale or adjust rapidly to new information. However, AI models trained on vast amounts of data can respond quickly to market changes. Cloud-based designs and edge computing accelerate this capability, enabling financial institutions to deploy predictive models on a large scale.

The objectives of this chapter are threefold. First, this chapter outlines the advancement from econometric to AI-based estimating strategies, examining their theoretical underpinnings, comparative qualities, and practical applications. Moment, to investigate how AI reclassifies portfolio development and optimization, with a focus on multi-objective optimization beneath energetic limitations. Third, to analyze real-world cases, we consider where AI frameworks have been implemented in resource management, trading platforms, and advisory systems, yielding quantifiable key benefits. However, integrating AI into the back office is not without challenges. Black-box models, particularly profound neural systems, often require interpretability, which can be problematic in administrative situations that require transparent and explainable results. Furthermore, AI frameworks can acquire biases from training data, leading to inaccurate estimates and biased results. Overreliance on authentic information may also render AI helpless in the face of fundamental breaks and administrative changes, such as the 2008 financial crisis or the COVID-19 pandemic, where past models are no longer applicable to the present. Figure 1 highlights why AI methods are a step change from traditional econometric tools.

Figure 1. Evolution of financial modelling approaches

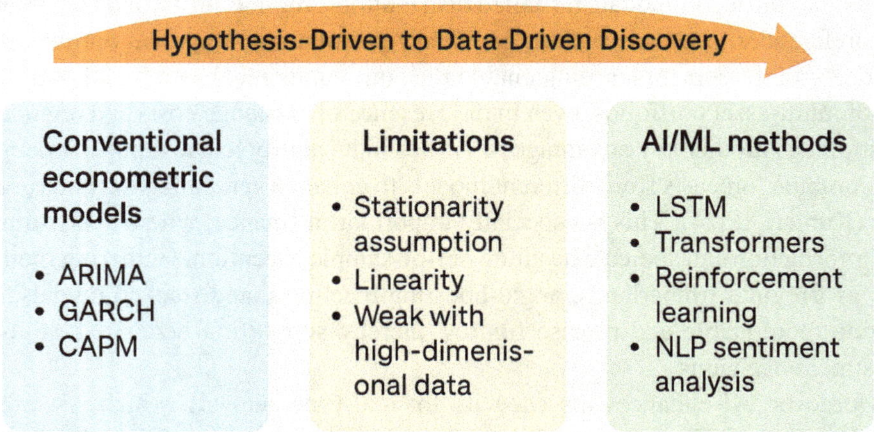

To address these issues, hybrid approaches that combine conventional monetary theory with AI methods are gaining traction. For instance, financial specialists and information researchers collaborate to integrate space information into AI model designs, thereby enhancing their interpretability and relevance. Procedures such as Shapley Added substance clarifications (SHAP) and Local Interpretable Model-agnostic Explanations (LIME) are increasingly used to demystify AI predictions and align them with human decision-making frameworks. Furthermore, moral considerations in AI-driven funds are paramount. Algorithmic choices can impact millions of financial professionals and systemic market stability (Kumari, 2024). Ensuring the reasonableness, straightforwardness, and accountability of AI models requires robust governance systems, adherence to ethical AI principles, and effective regulatory oversight. As budgetary education becomes more AI-dependent, there is a need to prepare professionals in both back and machine learning, cultivating a modern era of quants equipped with in-demand skills. In short, AI is not only an instrument for mechanization but also a key enabler of financial insights. It expands the wilderness of what is comprehensible and significant in venture procedures, risk management, and financial acumen (Adewale, 2024). By addressing AI's predictive control, speculators can expect shifts in the market, tailor their portfolios to real-time signals, and achieve higher returns amid market instability. This chapter sets the stage for a comprehensive investigation of these developments, grounded in hypotheses but centered on application, offering a blueprint for a long-standing period of brilliant contributions.

BACKGROUND

Machine learning, which includes both supervised and unsupervised learning procedures, has become increasingly central to budgetary time management, encompassing stock costs, product patterns and market volatility. Monetary markets deliver tremendous amounts of consecutive data prices, volumes, spreads, and more on a daily, indeed millisecond basis (Nethravathi et al., 2025). Conventional factual strategies, although still important, frequently battle the complex, nonlinear, and exceedingly loud nature of this information. Machine learning, particularly deep learning, provides more effective tools for recognizing patterns, learning from real-world behaviors, and adapting to changing environments in real time. From administered learning models that forecast future returns to unsupervised approaches that identify anomalies or irregularities, machine learning provides a diverse range of methods that enhance the ability to analyze and respond to economic trends in the stock market.

Supervised learning has become a foundational approach to time-series forecasting in the field of finance. In administered learning, models are prepared using chronicled information, where both inputs (highlights) and outputs (targets) are known. For instance, one might prepare a show to forecast tomorrow's closing cost of a stock based on today's open, high, volume, specialized indicators, and news estimates. Calculations such as linear regression, decision trees, boosted decision trees, and others have been widely used recently (Ogunwole et al., 2025). Additionally, strategies such as gradient boosting and random forest have been employed. These models are, for the most part, quicker to prepare and interpret than deep learning options, and they perform well in scenarios where the basic connections are relatively straightforward or the information is well-structured. However, budgetary time arrangements are frequently loud and complex, with numerous interdependencies that conventional directed models do not capture effectively. This is where profound learning and more progressive, directed strategies come into play. Repetitive neural networks (RNNs), particularly their long short-term memory (LSTM) variations, are explicitly designed for sequence modeling and have demonstrated strong performance in this area. LSTMs address a key impediment of standard RNNs, the difficulty in learning long-term dependencies, by employing an uncommon gating mechanism that permits them to hold and disregard information over longer sequences. It can be pivotal in budgetary markets, where historical designs, such as past profit reports or geopolitical events, may impact costs days or weeks later (Kumari, 2024). LSTMs can learn from groupings of everyday or intraday costs, volumes, and specialized indicators to anticipate future patterns or classify market signals (bullish, bearish, or neutral).

Convolutional neural networks (CNNs), which were initially developed for image processing, have also achieved remarkable success in time-series analysis. In the back, CNNs can be connected by treating time-series information as a one-dimensional flag and utilizing convolutional channels to identify nearby spatial patterns, such as rapid volume changes or sudden price shifts. CNNs are particularly valuable for distinguishing short-term signals and are regularly combined with other models in crossover structures. For example, CNNs can be used to extract spatial or temporal features from the input data, which are then fed into an LSTM network for sequential modeling. These profound learning models are particularly important in high-frequency trading situations, where milliseconds matter, and the objective is to respond quickly to rising signs that might reveal beneficial trading opportunities (Tariq, 2025).

Although directed learning is capable, it requires labeled data; that is, we must characterize a target variable, such as next-day return or heading. In contrast, unsupervised learning does not require labeled data and is utilized to investigate the structure of the information itself (Nair, 2024). In the back, unsupervised strategies such as clustering, dimensionality reduction, and anomaly detection are broadly applied to cluster comparison time-series, identify key market trends, or detect anomalies that might signal opportunity events. Clustering procedures, such as k-means or DB-SCAN, can be utilized to group stocks with similar actual return patterns, allowing portfolio managers to identify sectoral co-movements or differentiate portfolios more effectively. Additionally, autoencoder neural systems designed to recreate their inputs can be utilized for denoising financial information or identifying unusual patterns that may flag unusual behavior, such as stock crashes or liquidity shocks.

Feature design and determination are central to the success of both directed and unsupervised learning in financial decision-making, particularly in high-frequency trading situations, where massive volumes of data must be processed in real time (Faheem et al., 2024). Highlight building involves extracting enlightening factors from raw data that demonstrate progress and improvements. In an HFT setting, this might incorporate not only conventional price-based features (open, high, low, near) but also microstructure information such as bid-ask spreads, order book depth, trade imbalance, quote adjustments, and latency-sensitive indicators. The speed and quality of inclusion extraction can make the difference between capturing a fleeting opportunity or losing it entirely (Tariq, 2025).

Effective feature selection is similarly vital because models trained on too many or unnecessary features can overfit and perform ineffectively on unseen data. Strategies such as recursive highlight disposal, common data, Tether regularization, and inserted highlight determination in tree-based models can help to recognize the most significant indicators. In deep learning, methods such as consideration mechanisms have been proposed to help models focus on the most essential parts of a dataset, essentially performing active feature weighting (Alfzari et al., 2025). These attention-based models, which support structures similar to the transformer, are being progressively investigated for financial applications owing to their adaptability and effectiveness in modeling long-range dependencies. One of the continuous challenges in time-series analysis is managing non-stationarity, which refers to the fact that the statistical properties of monetary information, such as volatility and fluctuations, can change over time. Machine learning models must subsequently be robust to administrative changes and capable of adjusting to new market conditions (Nair, 2024). Several procedures can be employed to address this, including online learning, where models are continually updated with current information, or utilizing collaborative models that combine the expectations of multiple learners trained under different assumptions or time periods. Others incorporate window-based modeling, where later information is utilized for training, assuming that later designs are more significant than earlier ones.

Demonstrating assessment is another fundamental viewpoint that requires special consideration in time series analysis. Unlike standard machine learning, where information can be haphazardly divided into preparation and testing sets, time-series models must be validated using strategies that preserve the temporal structure of data (Wang et al., 2024). Methods such as walk-forward approval or time-based cross-validation are commonly used to ensure that models are tested on future data that the model has not seen during training. This approach is superior for recreating genuine trading conditions. This avoids the risk of information leakage, which can lead to overly optimistic performance estimates.

MACHINE LEARNING FOR PORTFOLIO OPTIMIZATION

Machine learning has consistently transformed the field of portfolio optimization, rendering previously unused strategies viable and enhancing conventional financial hypotheses in numerous cases. At the center of portfolio optimization lies the Modern Portfolio Theory (MPT), developed by Harry Markowitz in the 1950s. MPT proposed that financial specialists can create a "proficient wilderness" of portfolios that maximizes the anticipated return for a given level of risk by diversifying across assets. While MPT has been foundational in venture management, it operates under several simplifying assumptions, such as typically distributed returns, direct connections between assets, and constant covariances that do not always hold in real-world markets (Anand, 2025). The rise of AI and machine learning provides tools to address many of these impediments, enabling more adaptable, versatile, and data-driven approaches to portfolio construction. Figure 2 provides overview of broad applications of Ai within investment cycle.

Figure 2. AI applications across the investment cycle

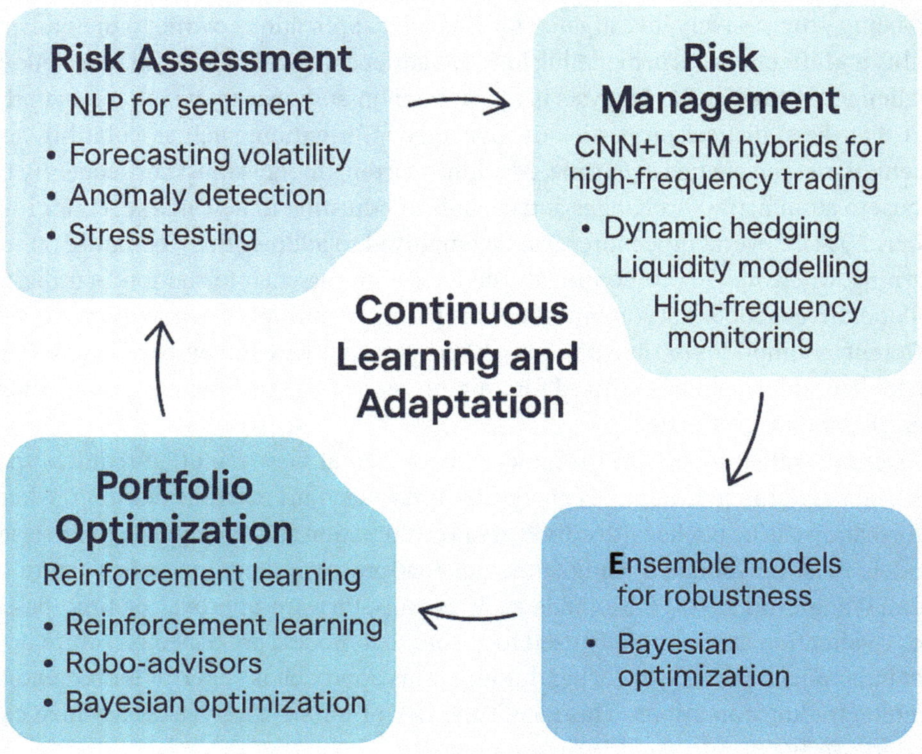

One way that machine learning amplifies the MPT is through the use of more advanced models for assessing returns, volatilities, and relationships between resources. In classical MPT, these parameters are regularly evaluated using authentic midpoints, which can be unstable and sensitive to exceptions. Machine learning models, such as random forests, gradient boosting machines, and neural networks, can incorporate a much broader set of input features, including macroeconomic indicators, opinion data, and alternative datasets, to produce more robust and accurate predictions of expected returns (Singh et al., 2025). Additionally, models such as shrinkage estimators or graphical tethering can provide more stable covariance lattices, thereby improving the reliability of the chance appraisals. These changes in parameter estimation can lead to more compelling portfolio optimization, particularly in unstable or rapidly changing markets. Another significant advancement comes from the application of reinforcement learning (RL), especially strategies such as Q-learning and Deep Deterministic Policy Gradient (DDPG), for versatile resource allocation. Unlike conventional portfolio optimization approaches that highlight an inactive optimization issue at a single point in time, support learning models treat contributing as an active decision-making process (Kokogho et al., 2024). In RL, an agent learns to perform activities (e.g., adjusting portfolio weights) in an environment (the budgetary environment) to maximize the aggregate reward (regularly returning a balanced portfolio for risk) over time. This system is well-suited for budgetary markets, where conditions are constantly evolving, and choices made today can significantly impact future opportunities.

Q-learning is one of the most well-known and widely used RL algorithms available. It works by learning an esteem function that maps each state-action combination to an anticipated reward, permitting the operator to select activities that maximize the long-term payoff. In any case, Q-learning is fundamentally suited for discrete action spaces and may struggle with the high dimensionality of the financial portfolios. In contrast, DDPG could be a more advanced actor-critic strategy that can handle continuous action spaces, making it more suitable for distributing capital across multiple resources with changing weights (Nair, 2024). These models can be prepared using authentic market data and refined with online learning methods as new information becomes available, enabling them to adapt to changing market conditions and enhance investors' preferences. Reinforcement learning models also offer the potential to integrate imperatives and inclinations more effectively than conventional optimization methods. For instance, an RL operator can be prepared to consider exchange costs, liquidity limitations, administrative limits, or Environmental, Social, and Governance (ESG) considerations as part of its remuneration work. This makes them profoundly adaptable and customizable tools for contemporary resource directors who must navigate a complex and often conflicting set of project objectives (Devapitchai et al., 2024). In addition, RL models can be integrated into multi-agent systems, where distinctive strategies such as development, esteem, or momentum compete or coordinate to improve overall performance, imitating the differences in techniques observed in professional investment firms.

The practical application of machine learning in portfolio optimization is now apparent, particularly with the rise of AI-augmented robo-advisory instruments and wealth management platforms. Robo-advisors utilize algorithm-driven models to provide computerized financial advice and investment management services with minimal human intervention (Shen et al., 2025). Early adaptations of robo-advisors relied on inactive MPT-based models to generate portfolios based on users' risk profiles. Nevertheless, cutting-edge AI-enhanced frameworks are surpassing passive investment by integrating real-time market data, opinion analysis, and machine-learning algorithms to enhance portfolio performance significantly. These frameworks utilize a client's monetary objectives, time horizon, and risk tolerance to plan personalized investment strategies that adjust over time as markets move or as client preferences change.

Platforms that integrate machine learning into portfolio management systems can offer features such as tax-loss harvesting, active rebalancing, and goal-based investing with significantly greater accuracy and automation. For example, a robo-advisor may utilize a prescient model to anticipate short-term market downturns and adjust asset allocation to mitigate drawdowns without deviating from long-term objectives. Others might utilize financial learning specialists to optimize when and how to rebalance portfolios, thereby decreasing costs and improving cost effectiveness (Chhikara et al., 2025). These frameworks can also learn from vast amounts of client behavioral data to personalize investment advice, making them more engaging and successful for a diverse client base. Wealth administration firms are leveraging AI to serve high-net-worth clients with modern needs. By combining machine learning with conventional budgeting tools, these stages can simulate complex scenarios such as multi-generational wealth transfer, trade progression planning, or philanthropic giving procedures (Nweke & Adelusi, 2025). Normal dialect handling devices can be utilized to cater to client needs and translate them into meaningful portfolio proposals. In these contexts, AI does not supplant human advisors but enhances their capabilities, enabling more informed, data-driven discussions and superior outcomes for clients.

Despite the growing adoption of machine learning for portfolio optimization, several challenges and limitations remain. One concern is the risk of overfitting, particularly when using high-capacity models trained on small or noisy financial data sets. Cautious demonstration of approval, regularization procedures, and out-of-sample testing are fundamental to guarantee that the models generalize well to future datasets. Another challenge is interpretability: whereas conventional optimization strategies create clear and straightforward outcomes, machine learning models, especially deep learning or RL, can be more opaque, making it harder to explain proposals to clients or fulfill regulatory requirements (Roger, 2024).

NLP AND SENTIMENT ANALYSIS IN INVESTMENT DECISIONS

Natural Language Processing (NLP) and opinion investigation have become powerful tools in advanced decision-making, enabling financial experts to surpass conventional numeric data and tap into unstructured textual data. With the surge of computerized content from real-time news articles to social media posts and profit call transcripts, investors are increasingly leveraging NLP strategies to analyze market sentiment, anticipate cost fluctuations, and refine portfolio strategies (Nweke & Adelusi, 2025). These strategies enable the extraction of estimates and signals from a vast cluster of sources, providing a more comprehensive view of the market and investor behavior. One of the key use cases of NLP in finance is mining financial news. News outlets frequently report the primary signs of significant events, such as economic arrangement shifts, mergers and acquisitions, geopolitical developments, and corporate profit surprises, which can significantly affect resource costs. Conventional strategies for monitoring news are inadequate, given the volume and velocity of the content being produced. NLP instruments automate the process of reading and analyzing thousands of articles, extracting key information, and evaluating the conclusions drawn from them (Nair, 2024). This enables venture directors and investors to identify potential market-moving news as it emerges and rapidly consolidate it into their decision-making processes.

Social media platforms, especially Twitter and Reddit, have become increasingly important sources of market opinions. Unlike conventional news, social media reflects real-time conclusions and enthusiastic responses from a broad population of retail investors, traders and industry observers. The GameStop brief press of 2021 may be a prime example of how collective assumptions expressed on platforms like Reddit's WallStreetBets can move markets (Olanrewaju, 2025). NLP frameworks can screen these discussions, recognize trending themes, and distinguish shifts in sentiment that indicate emerging market trends and investor preferences. Whereas social media information is often loud and less formal than news articles, its real-time nature makes it a valuable input for short-term exchange techniques and instability forecasting. Earnings call transcripts serve as another valuable source of information for these assumptions. These calls, in which company administrators examine quarterly results and respond to analysts' questions, often contain nuanced language that reveals a company's viewpoint, confidence, and underlying concerns (Ambuli et al., 2024). NLP procedures can be used to parse the content of these transcripts, recognize key topics, and survey the tone of administrators. For instance, an increase in negative dialect or delay during Q&A sections may be interpreted as a sign of fundamental issues, even if the financial results appear solid. By efficiently analyzing transcripts over companies and segments, speculators can create sector-level opinion markers that complement the quantitative profit data.

To perform assumption examination effectively on these unstructured information sources, transformer-based models like BERT (Bidirectional Encoder Representations from Transformers (BERT) and its budgetary variations, such as FinBERT, have become state-of-the-art. BERT, created by Google, has brought a breakthrough in NLP by enabling models to understand the context of a word based on its surrounding words in a sentence. This bidirectional understanding is particularly valuable in back, where dialects can be inconspicuous and intensely context-dependent (Gupta et al., 2024). A state like 'growth missed expectations' could be unbiased in one industry but exceedingly negative in another, and transformer models are better prepared to capture these subtleties than conventional NLP strategies, such as bag-of-words or straightforward opinion dictionaries. FinBERT may be a fine-tuned form of BERT specifically prepared for financial writing, such as investor reports, news articles, and earnings call transcripts. This domain-specific preparation makes a difference in the show's budgetary language, expressions, and context-specific estimation. For instance, FinBERT can distinguish between "negative cash flow" and "negative sentiment," understanding that the former represents a financial metric, whereas the latter reflects investor sentiment. By utilizing such models, budgetary educators can allot opinion scores to writings with greater accuracy, providing more solid markers of advertising disposition (Leahy, 2024). These estimation scores can then be totaled over time, companies, or segments to produce the index values.

The creation of assumption records enables a more organized examination of the relationship between open disposition and ad execution. By correlating these lists with resource returns, instability measures, or exchange volumes, analysts and professionals can identify the designs that support predictive models or flag trends. For instance, studies have shown that short-term market downturns often follow spikes in negative opinions in financial news as negativity spreads among investors (Nair, 2024). Conversely, an unfaltering rise in positive opinions across numerous sources can indicate bullish sentiment. These relationships can be misused to time sections and exits, rebalance portfolios, or support downside risk. However, it is vital to recognize that opinions do not continuously interpret specifically in terms of cost development. Showcase members may respond unexpectedly to assumptions depending on the setting, macroeconomic conditions, and findings from brain research on successful speculators. Moreover, estimation examination is inherently probabilistic; it can highlight patterns and hazard components but cannot ensure accurate results (Shen et al., 2025). In this manner, opinion records are best used in conjunction with other markers, such as essential examinations or specialized models, instead of as standalone choice tools.

There are also challenges in guaranteeing the precision and reasonableness of the assumption models. Dialect is inalienably vague, and indeed, the most advanced models can confuse sarcasm, irony, or socially particular expressions. In social media, for example, a post that says "This stock is getting to the moon!" can be exceedingly positive but might be missed or misclassified by someone not prepared for such vernacular (Nweke & Adelusi, 2025). Moreover, assumption models may acquire biases from their training data, leading to precise over- or underestimations of opinions in certain segments, companies, or socioeconomic groups. Ensuring the strength, reasonableness, and progressive calibration of these models is fundamental to their effective implementation in financial applications. Another moral thought is the impact of the far-reaching use of assumption investigations on market behavior itself. As more dealers and traders depend on assumption signals, these signals may end up self-fulfilling or quickly arbitraged, diminishing their predictive control (Alfzari et al., 2025). This highlights the need for continuous advancement in estimation analysis methods and the expansion of information sources. Additionally, it raises questions about the productivity of advertising and the potential for manipulation, as actors may attempt to flood social media with false information to influence models and trigger exchanges (Tariq, 2025). Despite these challenges, the integration of NLP and opinion analysis into predictive techniques represents a significant advancement in the field of financial innovation. It enables financial specialists to access and analyze subjective data on a large scale, transforming words into information and information into valuable insights. As transformer models continue to advance, with more current structures offering significantly better performance and relevant insights, the precision and value of model-based analyses in finance are likely to improve (Nair, 2024). In the long term, one may also see more notable personalization of estimation models tailored to specific asset classes, investor preferences, or risk appetites (Olanrewaju et al., 2025).

CASE STUDY: GCC MARKET APPLICATIONS

The Gulf Cooperation Council (GCC) markets, comprising Bahrain, Kuwait, Oman, Qatar, Saudi Arabia, and the United Arab Emirates, have been experiencing a continuous yet unfaltering shift in their economic systems, increasingly driven by artificial intelligence (AI) integration. Whereas truly dependent on oil-driven incomes, GCC economies have been effectively seeking enhancement methodologies under ambitious dreams, such as Saudi Arabia's Vision 2030 and the UAE's Smart Government initiatives. These plans emphasize the appropriation of innovation, including AI, across sectors, with finance being one of the most vital sectors. Stock exchanges and resource supervisors within the GCC are beginning to adopt AI tools for predictive analytics, portfolio optimization, risk assessment, fraud detection, and customer service through chatbots and virtual assistants (Torkian et al., 2025). However, the pace and depth of AI adoption vary significantly across nations. Secondary, social, and infrastructural differences also influence them. AI applications in GCC stock trades are still in their early stages compared to more established markets; however, momentum is building. For instance, the Saudi Stock Exchange (Tadawul) has seen an outstanding uptick in innovative modernization, including steps toward algorithmic trading and automated market surveillance. Dubai Budgetary Advertise and Abu Dhabi Securities Trade are also investigating AI-driven solutions to enhance trading transparency, advance market intelligence, and support real-time financial analysis. Resource-administration firms based in financial centers, such as the DIFC, are progressively leveraging AI to create robo-advisory platforms and enhance their wealth-management offerings (Alfzari et al., 2025). These stages utilize machine learning to prescribe investment portfolios based on a client's risk profile and financial objectives, enabling automated rebalancing and flexible allocation using AI models trained on historical and macroeconomic data (Jangra et al., 2024). It marks a notable jump in a locale where human ability, individual systems, and discretionary judgment have traditionally driven contributions.

Despite this growing interest, AI trading in GCC capital markets faces special challenges, especially regarding information sparsity, market illiquidity, and increased volatility. Unlike markets created with decades of granular, high-frequency information, GCC monetary markets are generally young and are characterized by limited historical datasets (Asere & Nuga, 2024). This poses a critical challenge for preparing successful machine learning models, which often require extensive volumes of data to distinguish important patterns and reduce overfitting. Moreover, a few of the region's recorded values have low trading volumes, and a few markets are overwhelmed by a small number of intensely traded blue-chip stocks, constraining the diversity of qualities and market depth. Illiquidity, not to mention presenting an inclination towards demonstrating preparation, also influences the real-world execution of AI-driven procedures, as signals generated by models may not be significant in markets where spreads are wide or orders are difficult to fill without a significant cost impact. Volatility in GCC markets can be more prolonged and event-driven than in developed markets. Political pressures, oil cost fluctuations, and administrative shifts frequently lead to unexpected market responses that conventional financial models may not accurately predict. For AI frameworks to be valuable under these conditions, they must integrate real-time information sources such as oil prospects, global geopolitical news, and social sentiment from local sources (Alfzari et al., 2025). Coordinated characteristic dialect-preparing (NLP) models custom-made for Arabic and regional languages can help parse local news and public opinion more effectively. In any case, the need for freely available and standardized information in Arabic, coupled with constrained labeled datasets, makes it challenging to construct strong estimation examination devices for GCC markets. Collaborative endeavors between governments, budgetary experts, and the scholarly community may help address these gaps by creating shared information stores and domain-specific AI models.

Beyond specialized boundaries, social and administrative variables also impact the selection of AI in GCC financial markets. Socially, finance in numerous GCC nations remains relationship-driven, with a strong emphasis on trust, family oriented workplaces and personalized service. This conventional speculation culture can foster resistance to computerization and dependence on calculations, particularly among high-net-worth individuals who prefer bespoke financial services (Nair, 2024). Overcoming this requires not only innovative brilliance but also building trust in AI frameworks by ensuring transparency, explainability, and alignment with the local values. Planning AI instruments that support human-in-the-loop decision-making, wherein human judgment complements algorithmic suggestions, can facilitate this transition and foster broader adoption (Tariq, 2025). Regulatory systems across GCC nations are at various stages of development when it comes to overseeing the use of AI in funds. While a few controllers, such as the UAE's Securities and Commodities Authority (SCA) and the Saudi Capital Market Authority (CMA), are effectively investigating fintech sandboxes and AI rules, others are still building their foundational administrative capacity (Nweke & Adelusi, 2025). The need for standardized AI administration systems can moderate development by providing stability to firms wishing to explore new models or deploy AI-powered services. However, excessively rigid directions can hinder progress if they do not align with the iterative, data-driven nature of AI development. Addressing these concerns requires a collaborative administrative approach that empowers capable experimentation, cultivates information sharing, and ensures that speculators are protected from algorithmic dangers such as bias, opacity, and overfitting.

The financial framework plays a fundamental role. While driving GCC budgetary centers, such as Dubai and Riyadh, have contributed significantly to advanced change and cloud computing capabilities, other parts of the region still face gaps in fintech availability. Contrasts in broadband infiltration, computerized personality frameworks, and installation rails can affect the effectiveness of AI implementation in financial services (Alfzari et al., 2025). For example, real-time extortion detection or personalized venture suggestions depend on advanced stages that can access transaction histories, identity verification, and behavioral data of users. Where such a framework is divided or immature, AI applications are likely to be less successful or challenging to scale. Territorial activities, such as Bahrain's open banking system and the UAE's push for a unified digital ID system, signal a growing recognition of the need for an interconnected digital infrastructure as a foundation for AI development.

ETHICAL AND PRACTICAL CONSIDERATIONS

As artificial intelligence (AI) continues to revolutionize the financial industry, particularly in areas such as venture management, trading strategies, and credit assessments, it presents a range of moral and ethical challenges. These challenges not only influence the astuteness and solidity of monetary frameworks but also have direct implications for financial specialists, regulators, and the broader society (Devapitchai et al., 2024). Among the foremost pressing concerns are the explainability and interpretability of AI-driven decision-making, the inherent risks of overfitting, data control, and data leakage, and the increasingly complex landscape of information security, transparency, and regulatory compliance. Addressing these issues is not essentially a matter of innovative refinement; it requires a careful balance of development with responsibility, reasonableness, and trust.

One of the foundational moral concerns in AI venture frameworks is the issue of explainability and interpretability (XAI). In budgetary decision-making, understanding the basis of a venture suggestion or exchange execution is essential for maintaining confidence, ensuring compliance, and ensuring investor alignment. However, numerous cutting-edge AI models, particularly those based on deep learning, function as "black boxes," producing exceedingly precise predictions without revealing explicit knowledge of how those forecasts were made. This murkiness becomes especially challenging in high-stakes situations, such as when computerized frameworks manage billions of dollars in resources or when decisions directly impact clients' financial well-being. Stakeholders, including resource directors, reviewers, clients, and regulators, need to know not only what is demonstrated but also why it was chosen (Rakhmanovich et al., 2025). The failure to examine a model's thinking limits its capacity to distinguish mistakes, inclinations, or unjustified assumptions. Efforts to improve AI explainability have gained momentum in recent years, with advancements in areas such as interpretable machine learning and model-agnostic explanation tools like LIME (Local Interpretable Model-agnostic Explanations (LIME) and Shapley Additive Explanations (SHAP). These devices aim to provide post-hoc explanations of complex models by identifying the input features that most significantly influence a specific outcome. However, these approaches have limitations. They often provide a streamlined representation that does not fully capture the model's inner rationale. Moreover, interpretability is not a one-size-fits-all arrangement; what is interpretable to an information scientist may be unimaginable to a compliance officer or retail financial specialist (Alfzari et al., 2025). Hence, the monetary industry must tailor its approach to explainability based on the desires and understanding of diverse partners. Improving the interpretability of AI frameworks not only underpins superior decision-making but also strengthens the foundations of moral governance and administrative oversight.

In parallel with concerns about explainability are the common-sense dangers related to overfitting, showcase control, and demonstrate drift, each of which poses a critical threat to the reliability and integrity of AI modeling frameworks. Overfitting occurs when a model is trained too closely to authentic data, capturing noise or inconsistencies rather than generalizable patterns. Within the context of budgetary markets, where future conditions are inherently uncertain and unstable, overfitting can result in models that perform well in back-tests but falter catastrophically in real-world scenarios. This is often particularly perilous in high-frequency trading or portfolio optimization, where choices based on misleading signals can result in substantial financial losses or systemic instability. Closely related is the hazard of showcase control, whether due to purposeful or novel effects. AI frameworks, especially when accompanied by extensive financial education, have the potential to significantly impact markets through trading activity. If these frameworks are not correctly checked, they may inadvertently exploit wasteful aspects or designs that destabilize the market elements. In a few cases, they may be designed to do so, raising genuine moral and legal questions (Nweke & Adelusi, 2025). In addition, AI models trained on showcase information may learn methodologies that lead them toward manipulative behavior, such as sending false signals or employing ruthless trading tactics without any explicit human instruction to do so. This frame of rising behavior is troublesome to foresee or control, highlighting the need for thorough oversight and situation testing to identify and anticipate control issues before they can cause harm to the aircraft.

Another viable challenge is to demonstrate float, which occurs when the factual properties of the input information change over time, leading to a decline in the demonstrated execution. In financial markets, this can be a consistent concern due to shifting financial conditions, regulatory changes, geopolitical events, and changes in investor behavior (Nair, 2024). A demonstration that performs well today may become outdated or even dangerous in six months if it is not frequently updated and recalibrated. However, visit retraining also carries dangers, especially if the show starts to react to short-term fluctuations instead of steady and long-term patterns. Striking the correct balance between flexibility and solidity could be a fundamental challenge in maintaining the efficiency of AI project frameworks. Teachers must conduct regular checks, approvals, and administrative tasks to identify signs of floating and respond appropriately without reacting to transient fluctuations. Data security, straightforwardness, and compliance represent another set of moral and commonsense considerations that financial educators must explore carefully (Rakhmanovich et al., 2025). AI models in the back depend intensely on data, both organized and unstructured, proprietary and public, to create bits of knowledge and to drive decisions. Be that as it may, the increasing scope and vulnerability of the information being utilized raise genuine security concerns. Financial specialists and clients expect their personal and financial information to be handled carefully and used responsibly. Abuse or unauthorized sharing of this data, whether deliberate or due to inadequate safeguards, can result in reputational harm, administrative penalties and loss of trust.

In numerous wards, controls such as the European Union's General Data Protection Regulation (GDPR) and the California Consumer Privacy Act (CCPA), as well as various territorial data protection laws impose stringent requirements on data usage, storage, and consent. Budgetary education utilizing AI must guarantee that its information systems are accurate and legally compliant. It incorporates securing informed consent from clients, minimizing data collection to what is necessary, implementing robust encryption and access controls, and maintaining audit trails for accountability and transparency of the process. Moreover, teachers must be equipped to respond to information subject requests, such as the right to access, amend, or erase individual data. These functions can be challenging to implement in AI frameworks that rely on large-scale decentralized information infrastructures. Transparency, both in terms of information utilization and demonstrated behavior, is essential for selecting a morally responsible AI. Partners must be educated on how AI frameworks are built, the information they utilize, how they are tested, and the measures in place to prevent bias or discrimination. This is especially crucial when AI is utilized in areas that affect customer access to financial services, such as credit endorsements or credit scoring (Nair, 2024). The need for straightforwardness in these areas can exacerbate existing imbalances and lead to outcomes that disproportionately disadvantage certain groups. Controllers are progressively scrutinizing such applications and teaching that those that fall short of demonstrating reasonableness and straightforwardness risk both financial and reputational consequences (Tariq, 2025).

Compliance with territorial financial specialists involves an additional layer of complexity because various regions have varying expectations, standards, and legal systems regarding AI. Multinational monetary teaching must explore a complex array of controls that vary not only in substance but also in the thoroughness of authorization. For example, whereas some controllers prioritize development and empower the use of AI within sandboxes or pilot programs, others may take a more traditionalist approach, emphasizing hazard mitigation and customer security (Zha & Mitra, 2024). This administrative fracture poses challenges to global AI arrangements. This underscores the need for training to create adaptable compliance procedures and maintain open communication with regulators across regions. One promising approach to addressing these challenges is the integration of moral AI standards into the center improvement process, often referred to as "AI ethics by design." This implies incorporating values such as reasonableness, responsibility, and straightforwardness into AI frameworks from the outset, rather than treating them as afterthoughts or through external reviews (Nweke & Adelusi, 2025). It involves multidisciplinary collaboration between information researchers, ethicists, legitimate specialists, and trade leaders to ensure that AI frameworks not only perform successfully but also adhere to the guidelines expected by society. At home, this may involve conducting evaluations, including various groups to show improvement, and implementing automated checks for inclination and float. This also implies planning frameworks with client rights in mind, such as empowering clarification interfaces or consent dashboards that provide individuals with more control over how their information is used (Rakhmanovich et al., 2025).

DISCUSSION OF IMPLICATIONS FOR POLICY, PRACTICE, AND RESEARCH

The increasing integration of artificial intelligence (AI) into financial services is rapidly reshaping the global investment landscape of financial markets. As AI advances have become increasingly sophisticated and integrated into the decision-making processes of financial education, suggestions for arrangement, training, and research are considerable and multidimensional. These changes require a versatile and forward-thinking approach from controllers, central banks, and the broader monetary system to ensure that growth does not outpace the systems designed to protect decency, transparency, and accountability. Central to this advancement is the need for rigorous administrative oversight, a standardized framework for assessing AI devices, and an adjusted research approach that aims to promote responsible use and future improvements.

The role of controllers and central banks in cultivating capable AI utilization cannot be overstated. As AI becomes more prevalent in areas such as resource management, credit scoring, trading algorithms, and risk management, it presents both commercial opportunities and risks. Controllers and central banks are uniquely positioned to guide the development and deployment of AI innovations by establishing clear rules, standards, and ethical frameworks that promote responsible use of these technologies. One of their essential duties is to ensure that AI frameworks do not perpetuate existing biases or create new forms of systemic risk. It involves advancing algorithmic fairness, preventing discriminatory outcomes, and ensuring transparency in decision-making. Given AI's capacity to handle vast volumes of information and make rapid decisions, oversight instruments must be capable of real-time mediation and review accountability.

Regulatory bodies must also address the ambiguity that often characterizes AI frameworks, especially those relying on complex models, such as deep learning. These so-called "dark box" frameworks pose challenges to interpretability, making it difficult for partners to understand how particular choices are made. Subsequently, controllers should order the use of logical AI (XAI) where possible, particularly in high-stakes financial settings, to ensure accountability. This would include making rules that require educators to report and legitimize their show choices, prepare information, and execute metrics. Furthermore, controllers must ensure that monetary teaching undergoes a thorough review and push testing (Rakhmanovich et al., 2025). This can be upheld through the necessity for AI-specific internal review conventions and external reviews performed by certified third-party specialists. Such measures would help maintain an open mind and institutional responsibility, especially in scenarios where algorithmic choices significantly influence consumer outcomes.

Central banks play a crucial role in maintaining macroeconomic stability and mitigating systemic risks. As AI changes how budgetary markets work, central banks must enhance their specialized capabilities to screen algorithmic actions, identify irregularities, or promote control. They can lead by example by consolidating AI into their claims operations, such as estimating, observation, and claims processing (Nweke & Adelusi, 2025). By doing so, they can set a point of reference for mindful AI selection, illustrating both the potential benefits and vital imperatives of its use. Additionally, central banks can serve as conveners of public-private partnerships aimed at creating shared frameworks for AI governance. Such collaborations might foster a shared understanding of best practices, moral guidelines, and hazard relief techniques across different locales and institutions. Another fundamental column in the mindful deployment of AI is the standardization, benchmarking, and auditability of AI-based investment tools. Unlike conventional budgetary models, AI frameworks are dynamic and can evolve by learning from new data (Nair, 2024). Although this adaptivity is helpful in improving prescient accuracy, it raises significant challenges for benchmarking and reliable assessment. To address this, there is a need for standardized execution measurements that go beyond productivity or precision. These measurements should also capture aspects such as vigor, interpretability, decency and compliance with administrative standards. A standardized scientific categorization of AI models and use cases in funds would also help with comparative evaluation and administrative oversight.

Developing industry-wide benchmarks for AI devices can assist in educating and assessing their models against established standards and identifying areas for improvement. Benchmarking can serve as an instrument for both internal administration and administrative compliance, ensuring that AI models meet the minimum execution and ethical standards. Auditability is crucial for maintaining transparency and trust. Auditable AI suggests that teachers maintain detailed logs of model inputs, outputs, upgrades, and decision-making pathways (Rakhmanovich et al., 2025). Typically crucial not only for compliance purposes but also for empowering significant post-hoc examinations in the event of disputes or disappointments. Inserting review trails inside AI frameworks from their planning stage, a practice commonly referred to as "AI forensics," should be considered a best practice in the financial services industry.

Establishing third-party review bodies or certification specialists seems to further enhance the certainty of AI investment instruments. These substances would help assess the astuteness, reliability, and integrity of AI frameworks, much like how rating agencies evaluate financial stability (Alfzari et al., 2025). In any case, unlike credit evaluations, AI certifications should be dynamic and consider ongoing changes in model behavior. Customary reassessments and ongoing observations should be part of the certification lifecycle. This would require collaboration between technologists, space specialists, and administrative specialists to guarantee that audit standards remain significant and enforceable. Overall, standardization and auditability can act as guardrails, ensuring that AI enhances, rather than undermines, the astuteness of financial systems. Looking ahead, community inquiry will play a vital role in shaping the future of AI, particularly by exploring underutilized areas such as quantum computing, the convergence of AI and natural, social, and environmental (ESG) systems, and AI-human co-decision frameworks. Quantum computing has the potential to drastically enhance AI capabilities by exponentially accelerating computation and optimization processes. For budgetary divisions, this may lead to unusual progress in portfolio optimization, risk investigation, and cybersecurity (Devapitchai et al., 2024). The implications of such a jump are significant. Analysts must explore how quantum-enhanced AI models can be controlled, examined, and coordinated into existing financial frameworks without compromising their straightforwardness or security. It is also essential to consider the moral and social implications of such advances, especially in terms of their accessibility and potential to create discrepancies between institutions with and without quantum capabilities.

Looking ahead, the investigative community has a pivotal role in shaping the long-term future of AI in finance, particularly by exploring underutilized areas such as quantum computing, the integration of AI and environmental, social, and governance (ESG) systems, and AI-human co-decision frameworks. Quantum computing has the potential to drastically enhance AI capabilities by exponentially accelerating computation and optimization processes (Kumari, 2024). In the financial segment, this appears to lead to significant progress in portfolio optimization, risk assessment, and cryptographic security. Be that as it may, the suggestions of such a jump are significant. Analysts must investigate how quantum-enhanced AI models can be controlled, reviewed, and integrated into existing financial frameworks without compromising their transparency or security. It is also essential to consider the moral and social implications of such advances, especially in terms of their transparency and potential to cause discrepancies between teaching with and without access to quantum capabilities (Tariq, 2025).

The integration of AI with ESG considerations represents a new and rich area for research. As the demand for informed and strategic speculation grows, AI can provide valuable tools for assessing ESG performance, evaluating sustainability risk, and guiding investment strategies. Integrating ESG criteria into AI frameworks is inherently complex, requiring models to translate subjective and often ambiguous information from various sources. Inquiries are necessary to develop strategies that can effectively measure ESG execution, balance competing goals, and ensure that AI does not inadvertently prioritize short-term financial gains over long-term sustainability (Rakhmanovich et al., 2025). Moreover, AI frameworks must be designed to recognize and mitigate greenwashing, where companies overstate or fabricate their

ESG credentials. Creating straightforward and responsible AI systems for ESG examination may significantly enhance the validity and impact of economic investing.

Ultimately, the intersection between human judgment and AI in budgetary decision-making is an area that is ripe for exploration. While AI can handle tremendous amounts of information and distinguish designs that people might overlook, it frequently requires relevant insights, ethical thinking, and key foresight that human decision-makers bring. The long-standing time of AI in the back likely lies in crossbreed models that combine the qualities of both, empowering AI-human co-decision systems (Nair, 2024). Future research should focus on designing collaborative interfaces that foster trust, understanding, and effective communication between AI frameworks and human users. It involves creating strategies for interpreting AI experiences into human-interpretable formats, developing input instruments that enable people to override or challenge AI decisions, and ensuring that responsibility is allocated to collaborative decision-making processes.

CONCLUSION

The integration of counterfeit insights into budgetary determination and portfolio optimization represents a transformative leap in the advancement of quantitative analysis. In this chapter, we examined how AI surpasses the limitations of conventional econometric models by employing data-driven approaches that can recognize nonlinear relationships, adapt to dynamic situations, and integrate vast amounts of both structured and unstructured data. These headways are not merely specialized but profoundly key, reshaping how investment choices are made, portfolios are built, and risk is managed within the 21st century. Traditional budgetary models were built on rearrangements of rational behavioral assumptions of levelheaded on-screen characters, typically disseminated returns, and stable statistical relationships. Although they provided expository clarity and meticulousness, they regularly failed to capture the complexities of the market, behavioral inconsistencies, and sudden management shifts. In contrast, AI flourishes in complexity. It permits a bottom-up approach to estimation, empowering frameworks to learn from authentic and real-time information without being constrained by rigid, theoretical assumptions. This adaptability is especially valuable in today's investment landscape, which is characterized by data overload, increasing market volatility, and rapid digital transformation.

In the forecasting domain, AI offers significant advantages over classical time-series models. Strategies such as deep learning, recurrent neural networks (RNNs), transformers, and backpropagation vector machines can distinguish between designs in information that are both simple and complex, allowing conventional models to capture these distinctions (Rakhmanovich et al., 2025). These models can effectively consolidate modern information, adjust forecasts in response to emerging trends, and learn relevant nuances, such as macroeconomic shocks, shifts in opinion, or geopolitical developments that influence resource costs. In doing so, they provide a more agile and responsive toolset for financial specialists who want to stay ahead of market trends. Furthermore, AI models have demonstrated particular proficiency in integrating diverse information sources, including social media opinions, search patterns, transaction streams, sentiment analysis, and climate data, into predictive models. By broadening the scope of inputs, these frameworks provide a wealthier and more multidimensional understanding of the components driving showcase behavior. For instance, fence reserves utilizing AI to analyze partisan pictures of retail stopping parts can expect profit shocks sometime before official reports are released (Nweke & Adelusi, 2025). Additionally, estimation examination instruments that track Twitter sentiment or news features can identify changes in investor temperament and interpret them as significant signals.

However, prescient control alone is not adequate for victory in the fund. Viable portfolio optimization requires deciphering estimates into coherent, risk-managed venture procedures. Here, too, AI illustrates its transformative potential. Classic models, such as mean-variance optimization, Black-Litterman, and factor-based approaches, rely on authentic return and covariance estimates that are often unstable and prone to estimation errors (Alfzari et al., 2025). AI models, especially those utilizing developmental calculations, reinforcement learning, or Bayesian induction, can optimize portfolios by learning from changing market conditions, non-linear constraints, and investor-specific objectives.

Reinforcement learning is particularly important in this context. Unlike administered learning models that essentially anticipate returns, support learning specialists can learn ideal trading or assignment strategies through trial and error in simulated or historical situations (Nair, 2024). This permits them to create methodologies that maximize long-term compensation while minimizing risk and transaction costs. Deep Q-networks (DQNs), angle strategies, and actor-critic models are effectively utilized by quantitative and algorithmic trading firms to refine exchange execution, support positions, and adaptively rebalance portfolios based on evolving market conditions (Alfzari et al., 2025). Importantly, the democratization of AI has begun to bridge the gap between organizations and retail speculators. Robo-advisors fueled by machine learning can currently offer personalized investment strategies, optimization, and rebalancing services at a fraction of the cost of traditional financial advisory services. These stages utilize client information, hazard resilience appraisals, and advertising estimates to effectively adjust portfolios, ensuring alignment with long-term financial objectives, even in volatile markets. The versatility and cost efficiency of such frameworks heralds a modern era of comprehensive financial services. Another challenge is the potential for information predisposition and overfitting in the model. AI models trained on authentic information may learn designs that reflect past advertising trends but fail to generalize to modern and unseen conditions. This defenselessness becomes intense during black swan events or secondary breaks, when historical connections no longer hold (Rakhmanovich et al., 2025). To alleviate this, a thorough demonstration of approval, including backtesting and stress testing, is essential. Additionally, combining spatial skills and cross-breed modeling utilizing econometric standards with AI algorithms can provide a more flexible framework for decision making (Nweke & Adelusi, 2025).

Looking ahead, the integration of AI with other emerging innovations will drive a revolution in the budgetary industry. The integration of blockchain with AI can enhance information transparency, traceability, and security in financial transactions (Nair, 2024). Quantum computing promises to solve complex optimization issues at phenomenal speeds, unlocking modern frontiers for AI-powered portfolio development. The combination of AI with Internet of Things (IoT) devices and edge computing will enable real-time decision-making in areas such as security, supply chain management, and ESG investing. Finally, AI is not just a tool for prediction or optimization; it could also be a catalyst for significant change. It empowers a shift from responsive to proactive business techniques, rule-based frameworks to machine learning, and generalized models to personalized financial insights (Nweke & Adelusi, 2025). As AI continues to advance, it will enable financial experts to navigate uncertainty with greater confidence, reveal hidden opportunities, and construct portfolios that are not only optimized for returns but also balanced with long-term flexibility and moral values.

REFERENCES

Abbas, S. K. (2024). AI Meets Finance: The Rise of AI-Powered Robo-Advisors. *Journal of Electrical Systems*, *20*(11), 1011–1016.

Adewale, T. (2024). AI-Powered Portfolio Diversification: Beyond Modern Portfolio Theory.

Alfzari, S., Al-Shboul, M., & Alshurideh, M. (2025). Predictive Analytics in Portfolio Management: A Fusion of AI and Investment Economics for Optimal Risk-Return Trade-Offs. *International Review of Management and Marketing*, *15*(2), 365–380. DOI: 10.32479/irmm.18594

Ambuli, T. V., Venkatesan, S., Sampath, K., Devi, K., & Kumaran, S. (2024, August). AI-Driven Financial Management Optimizing Investment Portfolios through Machine Learning. In *2024 7th International Conference on Circuit Power and Computing Technologies (ICCPCT)* (Vol. 1, pp. 1822-1828). IEEE. DOI: 10.1109/ICCPCT61902.2024.10672859

Anand, R. (2025). Harnessing AI for Predictive Financial Analytics: Transforming Investment Strategies in a Data-Driven World. *Available at SSRN* 5101358. DOI: 10.2139/ssrn.5101358

Arshard, A. R. M., Imthiyas, M. S. M., & Suthamathy, N. (2024). Assessment of the impact of ai and machine learning on predictive analytics in finance, including forecasting market trends and identifying investment opportunities. *Science and innovation, 3*(A9), 32-38.

Asere, G. F., & Nuga, K. A. (2024). Examining the potential of artificial intelligence and machine learning in predicting trends and enhancing investment decision-making. *Scientific. Journal of Engineering Technology*, *1*(1), 15–20.

Campbell, J., & Koffi, B. A. (2024). The Role of AI-powered financial analytics in shaping economic policy: A new era for risk management and national growth in the United States. *World Journal of Advanced Research and Reviews*, *23*(3), 2816–2825. DOI: 10.30574/wjarr.2024.23.3.2963

Chhikara, H., Chhikara, S., & Gupta, L. (2025). Predictive Analytics in Finance: Leveraging AI and Machine Learning for Investment Strategies. In *Utilizing AI and Machine Learning in Financial Analysis* (pp. 325-336). IGI Global Scientific Publishing.

Devapitchai, J. J., Krishnapriya, S. V., Karuppiah, S. P., & Saranya, S. (2024). Using AI-driven decision-making tools in corporate investment planning. In *Generative AI for transformational management* (pp. 137–160). IGI Global. DOI: 10.4018/979-8-3693-5578-7.ch006

Faheem, M., Aslam, M. U. H. A. M. M. A. D., & Kakolu, S. R. I. D. E. V. I. (2024). Enhancing financial forecasting accuracy through AI-driven predictive analytics models. *Retrieved*, (December), 11.

Gupta, A., Puri, M., Keshan, M., & Tiwari, V. (2024, July). AI in Financial Decision-Making: Revolutionizing Investment Strategies and Risk Management. In *This paper was presented at Global Forum for Financial Consumers (GFFC).*

Jangra, G., Irfan, M., Jangra, M., & Verma, C. (2024). Artificial Intelligence Approach to Portfolio Management: Enhancing Decision-Making, Efficiency, and Alpha Generation. In *Issues of Sustainability in AI and New-Age Thematic Investing* (pp. 59-73). IGI Global.

Kokogho, E., Odio, P. E., Ogunsola, O. Y., & Nwaozomudoh, M. O. (2024). AI-Powered Economic Forecasting: Challenges and Opportunities in a Data-Driven World.

Kumari, S. A. I. (2024). Enhanced Portfolio Management: Leveraging Machine Learning for Optimized Investment Strategies in 2024. *J. Inform. Educ. Res*, *4*, 1487.

Leahy, E. (2024). *AI-Powered Bitcoin Trading: Developing an Investment Strategy with Artificial Intelligence*. John Wiley & Sons.

Nair, V. (2024). AI-powered investment strategies: Enhancing portfolio management through machine learning. [JRTCSE]. *Journal Of Recent Trends in Computer Science and Engineering*, *12*(1), 1–5.

Nethravathi, N., Samanvitha, C., Dharmendra, H., & Ananthan, S. (2025). Unleashing the power of AI for intelligent investments: Revolutionizing stock market trading. In *Advancements in Intelligent Process Automation* (pp. 533–552). IGI Global.

Nweke, O., & Adelusi, O. (2025). Utilizing AI driven forecasting, optimization, and data insights to strengthen corporate strategic planning. *International Journal of Research Publication and Reviews*, *6*(3), 4260–4272. DOI: 10.55248/gengpi.6.0325.1209

Ogunwole, O., Onukwulu, E. C., Joel, M. O., Adaga, E. M., & Ibeh, A. I. (2025). Financial Modeling in Corporate Strategy: A Review of AI Applications For Investment Optimization.

Olanrewaju, A. G. (2025). Artificial Intelligence in Financial Markets: Optimizing Risk Management, Portfolio Allocation, and Algorithmic Trading. *International Journal of Research Publication and Reviews*, *6*(3), 8855–8870. DOI: 10.55248/gengpi.6.0325.12185

Olanrewaju, A. G., Ajayi, A. O., Pacheco, O. I., Dada, A. O., & Adeyinka, A. A. (2025). AI-driven adaptive asset allocation: A machine learning approach to dynamic portfolio optimization in volatile financial markets. *Int J Res Finance Manag*, *8*(1), 320–332. DOI: 10.33545/26175754.2025.v8.i1d.451

Rakhmanovich, I. U., Husayn, S. O., Hasan, M. K., Samudro, E. G., & Vij, P. (2025, April). Artificial Intelligence-Driven industrial Financial Analytics for Predictive Modeling for Smarter Investments. In *2025 International Conference on Computational Innovations and Engineering Sustainability (ICCIES)* (pp. 1-5). IEEE. DOI: 10.1109/ICCIES63851.2025.11033048

Roger, J. D. D. (2024). AI-Driven Financial Modeling Techniques: Transforming Investment Strategies. *The Journal of Applied Business and Economics*, *26*(4), 63–74.

Shen, Z., Wang, Z., Chew, J., Hu, K., & Wang, Y. (2025). Artificial intelligence empowering robo-advisors: A data-driven wealth management model analysis. *International Journal of Management Science Research*, *8*(3), 1–12. DOI: 10.53469/ijomsr.2025.08(03).01

Singh, K. B., Aggarwal, N., & Devbrath, D. (2025, January). Revolutionizing financial analysis and decision-making with AI-powered insights. In *AIP Conference Proceedings* (Vol. 3253, No. 1). AIP Publishing. DOI: 10.1063/5.0248356

Tariq, M. U. (2025). Bridging the Digital and Human Divide: Fostering Inclusion and Well-Being in Tech-Driven Workplaces. In Achour, Z. (Ed.), *Leading Inclusive Workplaces Through Digital Transformation and Organizational Change* (pp. 139–168). IGI Global Scientific Publishing., DOI: 10.4018/979-8-3373-5127-8.ch005

Tariq, M. U. (2025). The Role of AI in Transforming Hospitality Operations-Enhancing Efficiency and Guest Experience. In Talukder, M., & Chowdhury, H. (Eds.), *Smart Operations and Enhancing Guest Experience in the Hospitality Industry* (pp. 415–446). IGI Global Scientific Publishing., DOI: 10.4018/979-8-3373-2145-5.ch016

Tariq, M. U. (2025). The Role of AI in Personalized English Language Learning. In Shukla, A., Meeprom, B., Khunasathitchai, K., & Yadav, N. (Eds.), *AI-Powered English Teaching* (pp. 93–124). IGI Global Scientific Publishing., DOI: 10.4018/979-8-3373-1952-0.ch003

Tariq, M. U. (2025). Harnessing Big Data and Analytics for Targeted Destination Marketing Campaigns. In Soliman, M., & Elgammal, I. (Eds.), *Maximizing Destination Marketing Strategies in the Digital Era* (pp. 195–220). IGI Global Scientific Publishing., DOI: 10.4018/979-8-3693-9939-2.ch007

Tariq, M. U. (2025). Navigating Technological Disruption: Strategies for Continuous Professional Development. In Kenon, V., & Bartlett, J. (Eds.), *Gaming, Wellness, and Technology in the Bold Global Workforce* (pp. 257–278). IGI Global Scientific Publishing., DOI: 10.4018/979-8-3373-5322-7.ch009

Torkian, V., Bamdad, S., & Sarfaraz, A. H. (2025). Integrating AI and OR for investment decision-making in emerging digital lending businesses: A risk-return multi-objective optimization approach. *The Journal of the Operational Research Society*, •••, 1–20.

Wang, C. H., Zeng, Y., & Yuan, J. (2024). Two-stage stock portfolio optimization based on AI-powered price prediction and mean-CVaR models. *Expert Systems with Applications*, *255*, 124555. DOI: 10.1016/j.eswa.2024.124555

Zha, R. K. S. S., & Mitra, D. (2024). Empowering Financial Decisions with AI: Optimizing Strategies for Financial Planning and Wealth Management. *Drishtikon: A Management Journal, 15*(2).

KEY TERMS AND DEFINITIONS

Financial Forecasting: Forecasting market trends using statistical intelligence.

Machine Learning: Algorithm learning from financial data designs.

Portfolio Optimization: Strategic asset apportionment for investment performance.

Chapter 4
AI in Portfolio Management and Asset Allocation Optimizing Investment Strategies in Financial Markets:
Transforming Investment With Intelligent Systems

Uju Judith Eziokwu
http://orcid.org/0009-0002-3767-3711
University of Bradford, UK

ABSTRACT

Artificial intelligence (AI) has emerged as one of the most transformative forces in modern finance, reshaping portfolio management and asset allocation in ways not seen since the advent of computerized trading. This study offers a comprehensive exploration of how machine learning, deep neural networks, reinforcement learning, and natural language processing are revolutionizing investment decision-making across global markets. Drawing from diverse theoretical models, academic research, and applied case studies, the analysis highlights AI's growing role in portfolio construction, risk management, predictive analytics, and market efficiency. Particular attention is given to both developed and emerging markets, with the Gulf Cooperation Council (GCC) region examined as a case study in AI-enabled financial innovation. Key challenges such as data quality, model interpretability,

DOI: 10.4018/979-8-3373-5032-5.ch004

and evolving regulatory demands are discussed in depth. The study concludes with strategic recommendations for institutions, regulators, and researchers navigating the AI-driven transformation of capital markets.

1. INTRODUCTION

Artificial intelligence has transitioned from being a subject of experimental research to becoming a fundamental element of contemporary investment management within the financial services sector. The combination of exponential computational capabilities, the democratization of advanced algorithms, and the widespread availability of both traditional and alternative data sources has resulted in an optimal environment for AI-driven portfolio management and asset allocation (Chen et al., 2024).

This transformation extends beyond mere process automation. Investment professionals are reevaluating risk assessment, portfolio construction, and market analysis through the lens of AI. Sophisticated algorithms capable of processing extensive datasets, recognizing intricate patterns, and adjusting to fluctuating market conditions in real time are supplanting human intuition, linear statistical models, and historical correlations.

The adoption of AI is enhancing financial inclusion and fostering market development in emerging economies, rendering this technological revolution especially significant. The oil-dependent economies of the Gulf Cooperation Council (GCC) region, characterized by substantial sovereign wealth funds and ambitious economic diversification strategies, present an ideal landscape for AI investment management capabilities, including non-linear pattern recognition, real-time market adaptation, and data source integration (Hasan et al., 2020).

In this book, this chapter acts as a link between theoretical concepts and practical applications. While preceding chapters delineate the conceptual underpinnings of finance, and subsequent chapters delve into advanced applications in trading and risk management, this chapter specifically concentrates on the integration of AI techniques into portfolio management and asset allocation. It offers a practical enhancement to theoretical knowledge by providing mini-cases, implementation toolkits, and monitoring frameworks that investment managers can utilize. adapt to real-world constraints.

1.1 Contribution and Significance

This chapter adds to the extensive dialogue surrounding artificial intelligence in financial markets by presenting a comprehensive perspective on AI's function throughout the entire portfolio management lifecycle: allocation, risk management, forecasting, and execution.

Its unique contribution is found in the fusion of global viewpoints with localized analysis of the Gulf Cooperation Council, where Shariah compliance, reliance on oil, and regulatory priorities present distinct constraints and opportunities.

By theoretical concepts with practical applications through mini-cases, dashboards, and implementation frameworks, the chapter transcends mere theoretical discussion to offer practical insights for practitioners, policymakers, and researchers.

In this process, it emphasizes not only the potential that AI holds for improving decision-making but also the operational and governance challenges that need to be tackled for its responsible implementation.

1.2 AI Portfolio Management Pipeline

To offer readers a comprehensive roadmap, Figure 1 illustrates the complete AI-driven portfolio management pipeline. This holistic perspective demonstrates the journey of raw data as it progresses through feature engineering, model training, portfolio optimization, execution, and continuous monitoring. Incorporating risk controls like data purging, drift detection, audit alerts, and retraining triggers at every stage guarantees that the process is not only technically sound but also operationally and regulatory compliant. The pipeline acts as the foundational structure of the chapter, linking the theoretical advancements and case studies that follow into a cohesive, practical framework.

Figure 1. AI portfolio management pipeline

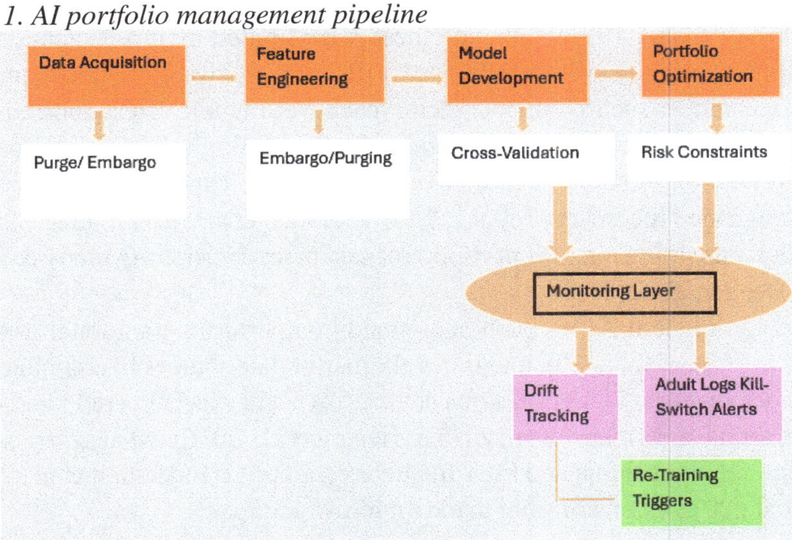

2. FOUNDATIONS OVERVIEW

The intellectual foundations of contemporary portfolio management are rooted in the mean–variance framework established by Markowitz in 1952 (Markowitz, 1952), which formalized the balance between return and diversification. This seminal work initiated Modern Portfolio Theory (MPT), which was subsequently expanded by Sharpe's Capital Asset Pricing Model (Sharpe, 1964) and Ross's Arbitrage Pricing Theory (Ross, 1976). These frameworks introduced the concept that risk can be broken down into systematic factors and appropriately priced, thereby establishing the basis for factor-based investing. (Fama and French 1993) further developed this concept with multi-factor models, incorporating size and value, followed by momentum (Carhart, 1997), and later profitability and investment (Fama & French, 2015).

Simultaneously, behavioural finance challenged the rational-agent hypothesis. Prospect theory, developed by (Kahneman & Tversky, 1979), along with findings of market anomalies (De Bondt & Thaler, 1985; Jegadeesh & Titman, 1993), uncovered systematic biases and inefficiencies that machine learning models could later exploit, unencumbered by human behavioural constraints.

Quantitative risk management progressed with the introduction of (Engle, 1982) ARCH and (Bollerslev, 1986) GARCH models, which effectively captured time-varying volatility, alongside the establishment of Value-at-Risk (VaR) frameworks. Portfolio optimization methods advanced with (Black & Litterman, 1992), which incorporated investor perspectives into Bayesian mean–variance optimization, albeit still under the restrictive assumptions of linearity and normality.

The early stages of AI in finance emerged during the 1980s and 1990s with the development of expert systems, neural networks (White, 1988), and genetic algorithms (Holland, 1992), although these were limited by insufficient data and computational resources. The 2000s and 2010s saw the advent of scalable machine learning techniques such as support vector machines, random forests, and ensemble methods that enhanced prediction accuracy in noisy, high-dimensional datasets. The deep learning revolution further broadened these capabilities to encompass natural language processing (Tetlock, 2007 & Bollen et al., 2011), image analysis, and reinforcement learning for portfolio management decisions (Moody & Saffell, 2001 & Deng et al., 2017).

Currently, modern AI research consistently outperforms traditional models in asset pricing (Gu et al., 2020), integrates alternative data sources like satellite imagery (Henderson et al., 2012 & Katona et al., 2024), and excels in credit and market risk forecasting (Lessmann et al., 2015 & Heaton et al., 2016). AI also serves as the foundation for algorithmic and high-frequency trading (Hendershott et al., 2011 & Baron et al., 2018), transforming market microstructure.

Lastly, regulatory and ethical issues have taken centre stage. Concerns regarding transparency, fairness, and systemic risk (Floridi et al., 2018) frame the ongoing discourse on how AI can be responsibly deployed in financial services, with regional adaptations in the EU, US, and GCC contexts.

2.1 Value-at-Risk (VaR)

One of the most influential developments in quantitative risk management was the emergence of Value-at-Risk (VaR) in the 1990s. Popularized through J.P. Morgan's RiskMetrics framework and further developed in applied work such as (Best, 1998), VaR provided a standardized way to estimate the maximum potential loss of a portfolio over a given horizon at a chosen confidence level. By offering a single summary statistic, it quickly became the industry benchmark and a regulatory reporting requirement under the Basel accords. Despite its wide adoption, VaR suffers from well-documented limitations. Standard implementations typically assume normal return distributions and static correlations, leaving them blind to fat tails, volatility clustering, and regime shifts that characterize real financial markets. During stress events such as the 2008 financial crisis, portfolios frequently experienced losses far more than their reported VaR (Berkowitz & O'Brien, 2002, Danielsson, 2008, & Stulz, 2008). These shortcomings motivated the development of more sophisticated methods such as Conditional VaR (CVaR) (Rockafellar & Uryasev, 2002; Rockafellar & Uryasev, 2000) and GARCH-based volatility models (Engle, 1982 & Bollerslev, 1986). However, even these refinements retain parametric assumptions that can misrepresent nonlinear dynamics. This is where modern machine learning techniques add value by capturing time-varying, nonlinear relationships in risk factors, integrating alternative data, and generating scenario-based risk forecasts that extend far beyond the capabilities of traditional VaR (Heaton et al., 2016, Krauss et al., 2017 & Gu et al., 2020).

2.2 ARCH and GARCH

Another cornerstone of modern risk management is the family of volatility models beginning with Engle's (1982) Autoregressive Conditional Heteroskedasticity (ARCH) and Bollerslev's (1986) Generalized ARCH (GARCH). These models captured the empirical reality that financial market volatility is not constant but tends to cluster in time periods of calm are followed by turbulence, and shocks persist longer than simple random-walk models predict.

ARCH and GARCH models quickly became industry standards for forecasting short-term volatility, improving the accuracy of risk estimates and feeding directly into Value-at-Risk frameworks. Variants such as Exponential Generalized Autoregressive Conditional Heteroskedasticity (EGARCH) and Glosten–Jagannathan–Runkle Generalized Autoregressive Conditional Heteroskedasticity (GJR-GARCH) allowed for asymmetries and leverage effects, while multivariate extensions enabled correlation forecasting across assets.

Yet, like VaR, these models are constrained by parametric structure. They often assume linear relationships and fixed functional forms, which limit their ability to capture regime shifts, nonlinear interactions, or the influence of high-dimensional alternative data sources. During crises, GARCH models can lag reality, underestimating the speed and magnitude of volatility spikes.

Machine learning approaches extend this tradition by learning volatility patterns directly from data. Hybrid models that combine GARCH with neural networks (Kristjanpoller & Minutolo, 2018) and fully nonparametric deep learning models (Heaton et al., 2016) offer greater flexibility. They can adapt to regime changes and incorporate alternative signals such as sentiment or liquidity indicators making them powerful successors to the GARCH family in AI-enabled risk management.

While models such as VaR and GARCH marked important milestones in risk management, they also highlight the trade-offs between simplicity, interpretability, and predictive power. Modern AI methods build on this foundation by introducing more flexible, data-driven approaches that can incorporate alternative signals and adapt to regime shifts. To make these contrasts more concrete, the following summary tables present an at-a-glance comparison of model classes and the key diagnostics used to evaluate them.

2.3 Summary Tables and Implementation

The tables below traced the evolution from classical portfolio theory through modern AI-driven methods, highlighting both the advances and the persistent limitations of traditional approaches such as VaR and GARCH. To ground these developments in practice, it is useful to compare model families and evaluation tools side by side. The following summary tables serve as a quick reference for practitioners:

Table 1. Model class versus requirements

Model Class	**Data Requirements**	**Computational Demand**	**Interpretability**	**Typical Use Case in Portfolio Management**
Linear/Logistic Regression	Low (structured, numeric)	Low	High	Factor models, risk premia studies
Tree-Based (RF, XGBoost)	Medium (structured + categorical)	Moderate	Medium	Feature importance, ranking assets
Time-Series (ARIMA, GARCH)	Historical price/ vol data	Low	High	Volatility forecasting, VaR
Neural Nets (MLP, LSTM, CNN)	Large datasets, sequences, alt-data	High	Low	Price prediction, signal extraction
Transformers (BERT, GPT)	Very large, text + structured	Very High	Medium-Low	NLP for sentiment, news analytics
Reinforcement Learning	Historical + simulated environments	Very High	Low	Dynamic asset allocation, trading

Table 2. Evaluation metrics and diagnostics

Category	*Metric / Diagnostic*	*Purpose*	*Common Threshold / Use*
Performance	Sharpe Ratio	Risk-adjusted return	>1.0 generally attractive
	Deflated Sharpe	Corrects for multiple testing bias	>0 indicates skill
	Sortino Ratio	Downside risk-adjusted return	>1.0 desirable
Risk	Value-at-Risk (VaR)	Tail risk at confidence level	95% or 99%
	Conditional VaR (CVaR)	Expected loss beyond VaR	Used for stress tests
	Max Drawdown	Worst cumulative loss	<20% preferred
Model Quality	Out-of-sample R^2 / Hit Rate	Predictive accuracy	>50% directional hit
	Walk-forward / Nested CV	Prevent lookahead & overfitting	Must be documented
	Feature Importance / SHAP/ Attention	Explainability of drivers	Supports governance
Execution	Implementation Shortfall	Cost of trading vs ideal	<10 bps target
	Slippage Attribution	Split between market vs execution costs	Transparent reporting
Monitoring	Drift Detection (KS tests, PSI)	Detects regime change or data drift	PSI >0.2 = potential drift
	Turnover / Stability Ratio	Portfolio churning vs stability	<100% turnover ideal

Table 1 positions major model classes along key implementation dimensions such as data needs, computational cost, interpretability, and common use cases in portfolio management.

Table 2 presents the most widely used performance and risk diagnostics, including both traditional measures (Sharpe, VaR) and modern corrections (deflated Sharpe, CVaR), making explicit how model quality should be judged in practice.

While transformer architectures such as Bidirectional Encoder Representations from Transformers (BERT) and Generative Pre-trained Transformer (GPT) have already advanced sentiment analysis and news-driven trading strategies, their broader potential lies not only in interpreting data but in generating new information and narratives. This shift marks the emergence of generative AI as a distinct theme in portfolio management. Unlike predictive models that estimate future returns or risks, generative systems create synthetic scenarios, automate structured-to-text reporting, and deliver personalized communication at scale. The below section explores these applications in detail, highlighting how they expand the scope of AI in investment practice beyond forecasting into content and scenario generation.

3. GENERATIVE AI IN PORTFOLIO MANAGEMENT

Generative AI represents a distinct shift in financial analytics, moving beyond prediction toward creation. Whereas predictive models map inputs to outputs, generative methods learn the underlying probability distributions of data and can produce new, statistically coherent scenarios (Goodfellow et al., 2014 & Kingma & Welling, 2013). This capability expands the portfolio manager's toolkit from extrapolating the past to imagining plausible futures, enabling richer scenario analysis and forward-looking risk management (Sai et al., 2025).

The intellectual foundations of modern scenario generation lie in probability theory and simulation methods such as Monte Carlo, which generated artificial scenarios but required strong assumptions about underlying distributions (Saputra & Safitri, 2022). Copula models later improved the treatment of dependencies between assets (Li & Hou, 2022; Nguyen et al., 2024; Zhao & Zhou, 2025), but they often failed to capture fat tails, regime shifts, or crisis dynamics. These approaches suffered from the thin history problem: the inability of limited historical data to anticipate novel disruptions (Xu et al., 2024). Figure 2 below illustrates this issue by comparing the distribution of historical portfolio returns with a bootstrapped distribution. The bootstrap procedure expands the range of outcomes and produces a more conservative 95% VaR underscoring how reliance on historical samples alone can underestimate tail risks and why more flexible generative approaches are increasingly needed.

Figure 2. Historical vs bootstrapped portfolio returns, showing deeper tail losses under the bootstrap and illustrating the thin history problem

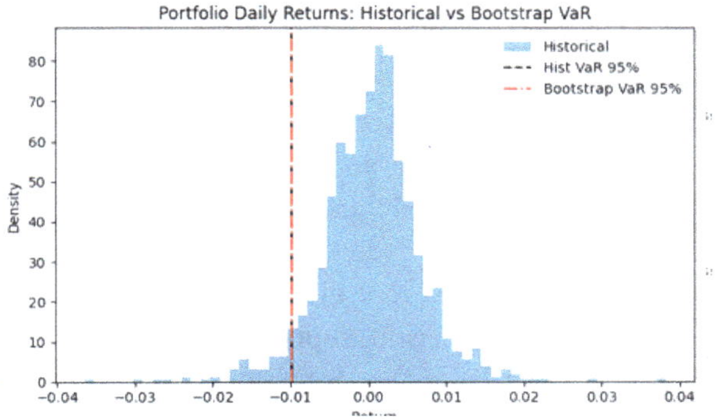

Modern generative models address these shortcomings. VAEs and GANs reproduce realistic time series with volatility clustering and correlation breakdowns. Diffusion models refine this further, enabling controlled generation of extreme stress scenarios. For portfolio managers, this means creating synthetic oil price paths to test GCC allocations, generating crisis patterns not seen in history, or exploring the impact of climate policy on asset prices.

Beyond stress testing, generative AI transforms financial reporting and communication. Large language models now produce layered reports that integrate portfolio statistics with market context and forward-looking commentary, while ensuring consistency across regulatory filings. They can also generate metadata documenting data sources and model versions, strengthening audit trails. In client engagement, generative models adapt narratives to audience needs.

For example, an institutional investor may receive detailed factor attribution, while a family office might get a simplified focus on drawdown protection. Language and cultural adaptation are crucial in regions such as the GCC.

Properly validated systems reduce reporting time by over 80%, expand stress testing well beyond recorded crises, and enhance client satisfaction through tailored communication. The challenge lies in validation and governance: synthetic data must pass statistical tests, outputs require expert review, and firms must maintain oversight, version control, and disclosure protocols. Generative AI therefore marks more than an incremental advance. By extending analysis beyond history, automating compliance and reporting, and personalizing communication, it reshapes how risks and opportunities are framed in portfolio management.

3.1 Synthetic Data Generation for Advanced Risk Assessment

Past crises rarely anticipate the full spectrum of future risks. GANs (Goodfellow et al., 2014), VAEs (Kingma & Welling, 2013), and diffusion models (Ho et al., 2020) address this constraint by creating synthetic yet statistically realistic time series. Their ability to replicate complex, non-linear distributions enable portfolio managers to move beyond historical precedent and prepare for shocks that have never occurred (Lin et al., 2023 & Meijer & Chen, 2024).

For instance, a GCC-focused sovereign wealth fund can generate thousands of alternative oil price trajectories that embed scenarios of geopolitical conflict, technology-driven demand destruction, supply chain disruptions, or climate policy shocks. These synthetic paths extend stress testing well beyond recorded experience and are particularly valuable for portfolios concentrated in energy-linked exposures.

The below Figures 3 and 4 illustrate how generative AI extends traditional scenario analysis. By producing synthetic yet statistically coherent market paths, these models allow portfolio managers to explore risks beyond historical precedent and evaluate their impact on energy-concentrated portfolios such as those of GCC sovereign wealth funds.

Figure 3. Portfolio risk dashboard derived from generative scenario analysis, reporting CVaR, drawdown, oil beta, style tilts, and turnover

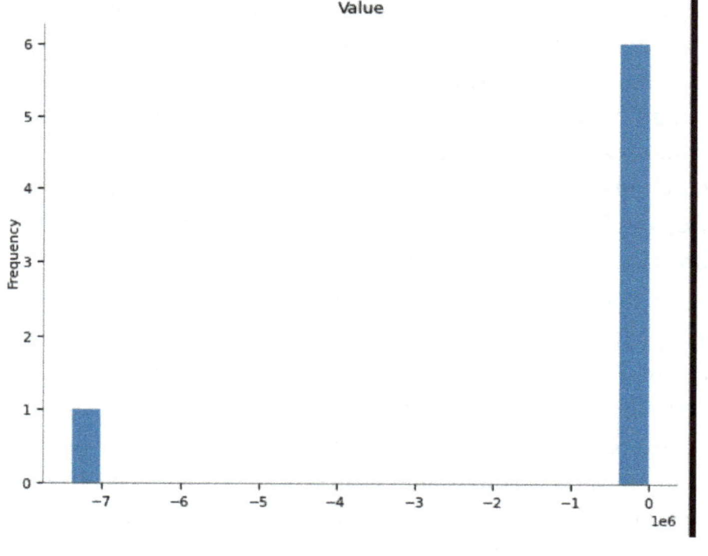

Figure 4. Histogram of portfolio return distributions under simulated versus bootstrapped scenarios, showing improved tail-risk capture

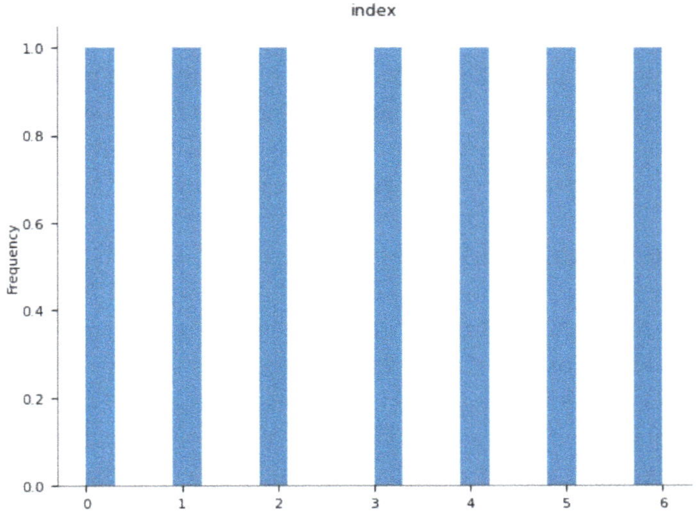

Figure 3 illustrates a portfolio risk dashboard, where advanced generative models translate simulated paths into actionable diagnostics such as Conditional Value-at-Risk (CVaR), maximum drawdown, oil beta, and style tilts. This allows decision-makers to link abstract scenarios directly to measurable portfolio characteristics.

Figure 4 complements this by showing the distribution of simulated returns versus a bootstrap benchmark, highlighting how generative methods capture fat tails and extreme events that are absent in historical samples. Crucially, these models preserve cross-asset dependencies, ensuring that correlations, volatility clustering, and tail risks remain consistent with real market behaviour.

Crucially, advanced generative models preserve cross-asset dependencies, ensuring that correlations, volatility clustering, and tail risks remain consistent with real market behaviour. Conditional variational autoencoders, for example, can learn regime-specific embeddings from historical return matrices and generate synthetic return series that maintain marginal distributions, cross-sectional correlations, temporal dynamics, and fat-tail properties. Similar approaches extend naturally to alternative data: in markets with limited coverage, generative AI can synthesize plausible social media sentiment trajectories, macroeconomic indicator paths, or even satellite imagery signals to supplement scarce observations.

Beyond scenario creation, generative AI is already streamlining daily portfolio management tasks. Asset managers use large language models to automatically draft performance reports that combine return statistics with market drivers, highlight compliance breaches, and flag anomalies for review. Regulators benefit from AI-generated templates that ensure consistent terminology and speed up filing cycles. On the client side, wealth managers are beginning to deliver customized dashboards where the same analytics are explained in different ways: a pension fund sees liability-matching insights, a family office receives drawdown protection analysis, and a GCC sovereign fund gets risk–return commentary framed around oil exposure and Sharia compliance. These applications reduce reporting effort, cut errors, and make complex analysis accessible to diverse stakeholders.

3.2 Dynamic Visualization Generation

Generative AI extends portfolio management beyond prediction by creating synthetic data, scenarios, and narratives that enrich decision-making. Models such as VAEs, GANs, and diffusion networks generate alternative oil price paths, stress scenarios for equities, or contagion events that embed geopolitical or climate shocks. Unlike traditional Monte Carlo methods, these approaches preserve realistic features such as volatility clustering, fat tails, and correlation breakdowns, making stress testing more robust especially for concentrated markets like the GCC.

The same capacity supports reporting and communication. Large language models can turn raw portfolio metrics into layered outputs summaries of performance and risk, contextualized narratives, and forward-looking insights while automating compliance reporting and tailoring communication for diverse stakeholders. Visual outputs such as stress-test dashboards, allocation heat maps, and risk–return scatter plots make complex results accessible to clients.

Adoption requires safeguards: synthetic data must be validated, expert oversight maintained, and disclosures transparent. Yet firms that balance innovation with governance report efficiency gains of up to 80%, improved scenario coverage, and stronger client engagement.

Table below summarizes key use cases, showing how generative AI supports stress testing, reporting, communication, research, and scenario generation, alongside the benefits, risks, and controls required for responsible deployment.

Table 3. Generative AI applications in portfolio management: functions, examples, benefits, risks, and control mechanisms

Function	Specific Example	Quantified Benefit	Implementation Risk	Control Mechanism
Synthetic Stress Testing	Generate 10,000 oil price scenarios for GCC portfolios beyond historical range	Improve CVaR accuracy by 15-25%; identify tail risks missed by historical data	Unrealistic scenarios; model overfitting	Expert validation; statistical testing; benchmark against known crises
Automated Reporting	Generate monthly client reports from dashboard data in 5 minutes vs 4 hours manual	85%-time reduction; eliminate formatting errors; improve consistency	Hallucinations; factual errors; compliance gaps	Multi-layer fact-checking; human approval workflows; audit trails
Personalized Communication	Tailor same performance data for pension fund vs family office	Improve client satisfaction 30%; reduce meeting preparation time 50%	Misrepresentation; tone inconsistency; cultural insensitivity	Compliance filters; cultural review; client feedback loops
Research Synthesis	Analyse 500 research papers on ESG integration in 2 hours vs 2 weeks	Accelerate factor discovery; identify market themes 10x faster	Bias amplification; missing nuance; intellectual property issues	Source diversity requirements; expert review; citation tracking
Scenario Generation	Create 1000 realistic market crash scenarios with preserved correlations	Enhance stress testing robustness; reduce model risk	Statistical invalidity; economic implausibility	Distributional testing; economic logic validation; peer review

3.3 Manager Takeaways

Generative AI enables portfolio managers to move beyond the constraints of historical data by creating realistic stress scenarios that capture fat tails, volatility clustering, and regime shifts. The outputs of these models can be expressed in familiar metrics such as CVaR, drawdown, oil beta, and factor tilts, making them directly usable for investment decisions. At the same time, large language models streamline compliance and client reporting, cutting preparation time by as much as 80 percent while embedding audit trails that strengthen transparency. Generally, generative AI allow communication to be tailored to the audience: institutions can receive factor attribution, family offices can see drawdown protection narratives, and GCC sovereign funds can access reports framed around oil exposure and Sharia compliance. To harness these benefits responsibly, however, firms must enforce robust governance, including rigorous validation, expert oversight, and strict controls to guard against unrealistic outputs, hallucinations, or compliance risks.

While generative AI expands stress testing and reporting, the most direct impact on investment outcomes lies in portfolio optimization itself.

4. AI-DRIVEN PORTFOLIO OPTIMIZATION

As artificial intelligence continues to reshape financial markets, its most transformative applications are found not just in execution or analytics, but at the core of investment strategy itself. Among these, portfolio optimization stands out as a domain where AI is redefining both theoretical paradigms and practical methodologies.

Traditional mean-variance methods suffer from instability and unrealistic assumptions (Michaud, 1989), whereas modern AI techniques offer more adaptive and robust solutions. Deep reinforcement learning conceptualizes allocation as a sequential decision process, where agents learn optimal rebalancing strategies through interaction with market environments (Mnih et al., 2015 & Schulman et al., 2017). Evolutionary algorithms address multi-objective problems balancing return, risk, and costs by evolving candidate portfolios through selection and mutation (Deb et al., 2002). Ensemble methods improve robustness by averaging across multiple models, mitigating sensitivity to single specifications (Breiman, 1996).

AI also enhances multi-asset and cross-asset portfolios by applying clustering algorithms for hierarchical risk parity (López de Prado, 2016) and using Natural Language process (NLP) to incorporate signals from central bank communications and news flows (Lucca & Moench, 2015). Alternative data sources such as satellite imagery or web-scraped labor market trends further extend the information set available for optimization (Katona et al., 2024).

Finally, evaluation frameworks must adapt to AI's complexity. Beyond Sharpe ratios, risk assessment now emphasizes tail measures such as CVaR, maximum drawdown, and scenario robustness, while explainability tools like SHAP and LIME help attribute model decisions (Lundberg & Lee, 2017 & Ribeiro et al., 2016). Together, these methods enable portfolio optimization that is more dynamic, transparent, and resilient than classical approaches.

4.1. Practical Integration for Managers

For investment managers, the value of AI-driven portfolio optimization lies in how it can be operationalized within daily workflows, medium-term strategy reviews, and long-term governance. These methods are not abstract algorithms they can be embedded into portfolio construction systems and decision-making processes in tangible ways.

At the **tactical level**, reinforcement learning (RL) can be deployed as part of rebalancing engines. Instead of static allocation rules, an RL agent continuously ingests market data such as volatility, liquidity, sentiment, and oil prices in the GCC context. When risk conditions change for example, a sudden drop in oil futures the agent can propose or even execute a tactical rotation into safer assets such as local sovereign bonds, while flagging the trade-off in terms of expected return and transaction cost.

At the strategic allocation level, evolutionary algorithms can be run to generate hundreds or thousands of candidate portfolios overnight. These portfolios incorporate multiple objectives simultaneously maximizing return, minimizing CVaR, reducing turnover, and ensuring regulatory or Sharia compliance. Managers can then review a frontier of robust solutions, selecting allocations that balance performance with real-world constraints such as liquidity or hedging requirements. This transforms the optimization process from a single fragile output into a diverse set of resilient choices.

In multi-asset portfolios, hierarchical risk parity (HRP) offers a practical way to avoid hidden concentration risks. For example, clustering algorithms can group together GCC energy equities with oil futures, then apply risk parity across clusters rather than treating them as independent assets. This ensures diversification is real rather than superficial and protects against double exposure to correlated shocks. The same methodology can be extended to cross-asset portfolios spanning equities, bonds, commodities, and FX.

Managers can also integrate alternative data sources into their optimization pipelines. NLP-based models that process central bank statements, news flows, or even social media sentiment can generate macro signals to tilt currency or rates exposures. Satellite imagery of shipping activity or consumer patterns can serve as early indicators for regional trade and consumption trends. By feeding these signals into optimization models, managers extend their foresight beyond traditional market indicators.

Finally, evaluation and oversight frameworks ensure these systems remain usable in real-world governance. Dashboards can present familiar metrics such as return, volatility, and Sharpe ratio alongside more advanced diagnostics like CVaR, maximum drawdown, and turnover stability. Explainability tools (SHAP, attention attribution, counterfactual analysis) allow managers to understand why the model recommends a particular tilt for example, increasing cash weights ahead of a volatility spike and communicate this reasoning to investment committees, regulators, and clients.

In practice, AI-driven portfolio optimization thus functions as a layered system, reinforcement learning supports short-term rebalancing, evolutionary search strengthens strategic allocation, HRP enhances diversification, alternative data widens the information set, and XAI provides the transparency required for adoption. Used together, these tools give managers portfolios that are not only quantitatively robust but also operationally credible, governable, and adaptable to real-world market shocks.

The figure below explain AI driven portfolio pipeline and the process begins with data ingestion, where both market and alternative data are collected and prepared. This information then flows through optimization engines such as reinforcement learning, evolutionary algorithms, and hierarchical risk parity. The result is a set of candidate portfolios that balance multiple objectives. These portfolios are then subjected to evaluation and explainability frameworks, incorporating measures such as CVaR, drawdown analysis, and SHAP-based attributions. Finally, the outputs inform manager actions, guiding allocation choices, rebalancing decisions, and reporting to stakeholders.

Figure 5. AI-driven portfolio optimization pipeline

To make AI-driven portfolio strategies resilient, managers need to anticipate the most common ways models can fail. Table 4 outlines the top failure modes, how to detect them, and the practical safeguards that can be put in place.

Table 4. Top 10 AI portfolio failure modes and prevention

Failure Mode	Detection Method	Prevention/Mitigation
1. Data Leakage	Time-series CV; feature lag audit	Strict temporal cutoffs; embargo
2. Overfitting	OOS Sharpe < 50% of IS	Regularization; ensembles
3. Regime Change	Hit rate < 45%	Regime detectors; adaptive retrain
4. Correlation Breakdown	Rolling stability tests	Dynamic correlation; stress tests
5. Alt-Data Staleness	IC decay over time	Redundant sources; freshness checks
6. Cost Underestimation	Live vs modelled costs	Conservative models; impact tracking
7. Model Drift	Accuracy/weight shifts	Drift alerts; retraining triggers
8. Benchmark Gaming	Exposure drift; TE spikes	Style analysis; risk model validation
9. Crowding/Capacity	Size vs liquidity	Capacity caps; crowding monitors
10. Tail Sensitivity	Tail metrics; scenario P&L	Robust optimization; hedges

Together, these failure modes highlight that successful AI adoption is less about perfect forecasts and more about building robust monitoring and control systems that catch problems early before they erode performance.

4.2 Manager Takeaways

For practitioners, the key lesson is that AI-driven portfolio optimization offers more adaptive and resilient approaches than fragile mean–variance methods. Reinforcement learning allows dynamic rebalancing in response to shifting market conditions, evolutionary algorithms handle multiple objectives such as returns, risk, and costs, and ensemble methods stabilize allocations by blending diverse model outputs. Equally important is the integration of alternative data from textual sentiment to satellite imagery which broadens the information set for allocation. Evaluation must also go beyond conventional Sharpe ratios to include tail risk measures, drawdown dynamics, and turnover stability, supported by explainability techniques that clarify what drives portfolio performance. Together, these advances enable managers to construct portfolios that are not only quantitatively sound but also more transparent and responsive to real-world complexity.

5. EXPANDED XAI (EXPLAINABLE AI) FRAMEWORK

Explainability is no longer optional in AI-driven portfolio management. Risk committees, regulators, and clients increasingly demand clarity on *why* a model decided, not just *what* it predicted. Traditional explainability methods such as SHAP and LIME remain useful, but modern finance increasingly requires an expanded toolkit. Attention attribution, counterfactual explanations, causal inference, and narrative explanations represent complementary approaches within an Expanded XAI framework. Each provides a different lens for making black-box AI models more transparent, auditable, and practically usable in portfolio management.

Attention Attribution: Transformer-based models (e.g., BERT, GPT-style architectures) include attention mechanisms that reveal which features or time periods influenced a decision most strongly. For instance, an oil-sensitive GCC portfolio may show that price shocks in a specific futures contract carried 40% of the model's decision weight, while FX momentum contributed only 10%. This allows managers to validate whether the model is focusing on economically meaningful drivers.

Counterfactual Explanations: These tools simulate "what-if" scenarios: *What if Brent crude dropped $10? What if FX volatility doubled?* Counterfactuals show how allocations or risk exposures would adjust under hypothetical changes. This bridges the gap between black-box outputs and the scenario-based reasoning familiar to portfolio managers and regulators.

Causal Inference Links: Beyond correlations, causal AI approaches help distinguish between predictive signals and spurious noise. For example, a spike in shipping traffic may correlate with equity returns, but causal analysis can determine whether it truly drives returns or is mediated by oil price dynamics.

Narrative Explanations: Ultimately, outputs must be translated into plain language for decision-makers. Instead of raw feature weights, explanations can be phrased as:

"The model reduced energy exposure by 5% because futures curves moved into contango, negative sentiment in regional press increased, and oil production exceeded forecasts. Combined confidence in these signals: 73%."

Practical Use in Governance. Explanations support three main contexts:

- Risk committees: to justify exposures relative to mandate constraints.
- Client communication: to provide transparent, trust-building narratives.
- Compliance/audit: to demonstrate control over black-box models, satisfying regulators.

When integrated systematically, XAI becomes more than a reporting add-on it is a risk management tool in its own right. By highlighting the drivers of portfolio decisions and stress-testing them through counterfactuals, explainability frameworks help managers catch overfitting, confirm mandate alignment, and ensure accountability in AI-driven strategies.

6. MACHINE LEARNING MODELS FOR COMPREHENSIVE RISK MANAGEMENT

The introduction of machine learning techniques has fundamentally transformed risk management in portfolio situations. Conventional methods, although mathematically valid, frequently depended on limiting assumptions regarding return distributions, correlation constancy, and linear interrelations among risk indicators. These limits become most evident during periods of market stress, when correlations often rise, volatility demonstrates clustering, and tail risks are increased.

AI-driven risk management systems have numerous transformative benefits compared to traditional methods. They can analyse extensive volumes of diverse data in real-time, discern non-linear correlations among risk factors, dynamically adjust to fluctuating market conditions, and include alternative data sources that offer early warning indicators of potential problems.

Contemporary AI risk management systems perpetually evaluate portfolio exposures, market conditions, and external variables to deliver immediate risk evaluations. This capacity is especially advantageous for institutional investors overseeing extensive portfolios across many asset classes and geographic areas.

Conventional risk models frequently presume linear correlations between risk factors and portfolio returns. AI methodologies can identify intricate, non-linear relationships that may only surface during instances of market distress. Neural networks, specifically, are proficient in modelling intricate relationships while maintaining computational feasibility.

6.1 Advanced Machine Learning Techniques for Risk Assessment

As financial markets grow more intricate, so too must the tools we use to understand and manage risk. Advanced machine learning techniques are stepping in, offering a level of insight and predictive power that traditional models can't match. From forecasting volatility to mapping systemic connections, these methods are reshaping how we think about risk assessment.

Long Short-Term Memory (LSTM) networks, for instance, have emerged as a powerful way to model time-varying volatility. Unlike traditional econometric approaches, they can capture long-term dependencies and reveal the non-linear patterns often seen in volatility clustering. Their ability to adapt to different asset classes makes them a valuable tool for anticipating market turbulence.

Ensemble methods such as random forests and gradient boosting are also proving indispensable for identifying and modelling complex risk factors. They handle high-dimensional datasets with ease while delivering robust predictions. Beyond their forecasting power, they highlight which variables drive portfolio risk at any given moment, giving risk managers actionable insights rather than black-box results.

Financial markets are deeply interconnected, and systemic risk often emerges from these hidden linkages. Graph neural networks offer a way to model such relationships, capturing connections between institutions, markets, and economic sectors that traditional correlation-based approaches tend to overlook. By tracing these networks, they provide early warning signals of potential instability and help regulators and investors see how stress in one corner of the system can cascade more broadly.

Another important application lies in anomaly detection. Variational autoencoders can learn the normal rhythms of market activity, making it easier to flag unusual behaviours that might indicate emerging risks. This approach has proven especially useful in areas such as operational risk management and fraud detection, where early identification of abnormal patterns is critical.

Alongside these advances, the integration of new forms of data is transforming the way risk is measured. Natural language processing can extract sentiment from vast amounts of text, offering predictive indicators of volatility and tail risks. Modern transformer-based models can pick up subtle shifts in tone and emphasis within news reports or analyst commentary, revealing early signs of market stress before it fully materializes.

Geospatial data adds another dimension, providing real-time insight into economic activity. Satellite imaging, for example, can track shipping lanes, industrial output, or crop conditions, helping to anticipate disruptions in global supply chains or sector-specific vulnerabilities well before they appear in traditional economic indicators.

Even the tone and cadence of central bank communications have become crucial signals. Machine learning algorithms can analyse speech patterns and word choices in policy announcements, uncovering subtle cues about potential monetary policy shifts. These insights are particularly valuable for managing interest rate exposure and currency risk, where anticipation often determines success.

Taken together, these innovations represent a significant step forward in the practice of risk management. By combining advanced machine learning with alternative sources of data, risk managers are moving beyond static models toward more adaptive, forward-looking systems capable of detecting vulnerabilities and anticipating shocks in an increasingly complex financial landscape.

6.2 Credit Risk and Machine Learning

The application of machine learning to credit risk assessment has produced some of the most promising advances in modern finance, with important implications at both the individual security level and across entire portfolios. Traditional credit scoring has long depended on credit bureau data and financial statements, but these sources are often limited, particularly in emerging markets where formal financial records may be sparse. Machine learning techniques expand the scope of analysis by incorporating alternative data such as mobile phone usage, transaction histories, and even online behaviour, allowing for a more comprehensive assessment of creditworthiness in contexts where conventional information is unavailable.

Beyond retail credit scoring, these models also improve the prediction of corporate defaults. By analysing intricate relationships between financial ratios, market performance, and macroeconomic variables, machine learning methods uncover patterns that conventional approaches tend to overlook. Gradient boosting models, for example, have consistently demonstrated superior accuracy compared to traditional logistic regression, giving lenders and investors more reliable tools for anticipating credit events.

The benefits extend to the evaluation of sovereign credit risk as well. Governments face complex challenges shaped not only by economic performance but also by political stability and social dynamics. Here, natural language processing adds significant value, making it possible to mine news reports, policy statements, and social media for early signals of shifts that could affect a country's creditworthiness. This broader and more adaptive approach enables risk managers to anticipate changes in sovereign credit conditions with greater precision than was previously possible.

Figure 6. Machine learning models for comprehensive risk management

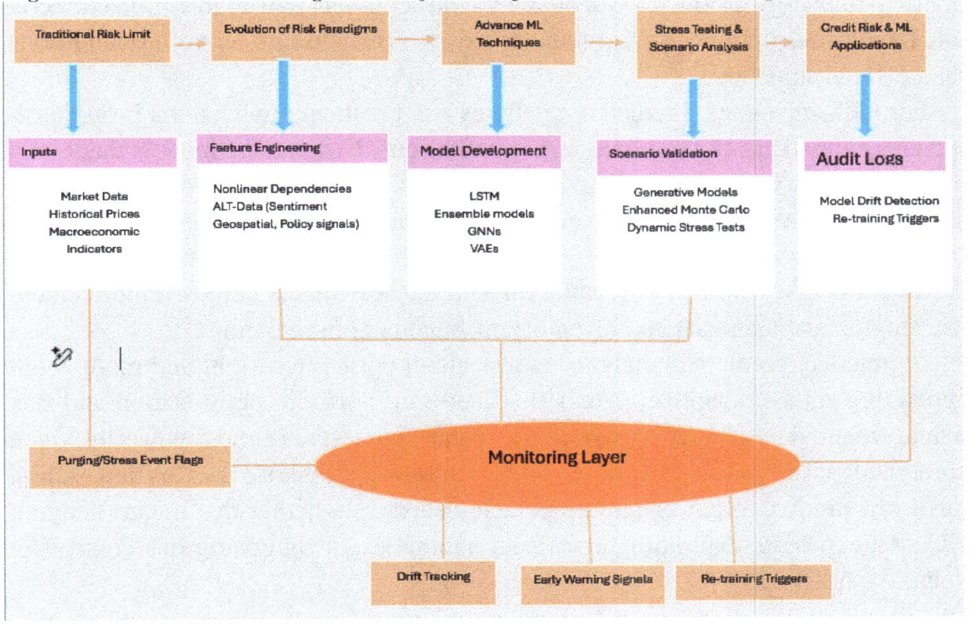

This diagram illustrates the end-to-end integration of advanced machine learning in risk management systems from diverse input data and nonlinear feature engineering to model deployment, stress testing, audit controls, and real-time monitoring. It reflects how traditional static frameworks are evolving into adaptive, forward-looking systems.

7. PREDICTIVE ANALYTICS AND ADVANCED MARKET FORECASTING

Forecasting has always been a central challenge in finance, and AI is pushing this frontier forward by uncovering signals that traditional models miss. Markets are not perfectly efficient; they are shaped by macroeconomic trends, policy announcements, geopolitical shocks, and investor sentiment. What makes forecasting so difficult is that these drivers evolve, and strategies that work today may fail tomorrow. Modern AI techniques are designed to adapt to this shifting landscape.

Deep learning architectures such as LSTMs and transformers now allow managers to capture both short-term fluctuations and long-range dependencies in time series data. These models power everything from predicting corporate earnings reactions to anticipating volatility regimes in oil and FX markets. Their flexibility extends beyond prices: alternative data streams such as shipping traffic, satellite imagery of energy production, or social media sentiment can be integrated directly into forecasting pipelines, giving managers earlier insights into economic conditions than official statistics.

For GCC investors, predictive analytics has practical applications in monitoring energy markets and regional macro conditions. Nowcasting models that blend oil prices, FX flows, and real-time indicators such as electricity consumption or shipping volumes can guide sovereign wealth funds in adjusting exposures ahead of official data releases. Globally, asset managers use transformer-based models to detect cross-asset momentum, while high-frequency traders deploy reinforcement learning to adapt spreads and inventory management in real time.

In practice, predictive analytics is less about perfect foresight and more about generating robust, adaptive signals that feed into portfolio optimization and risk management. The lesson for managers is that forecasts are most powerful when combined with allocation engines and monitoring dashboards. This integration turns raw predictive power into actionable decisions whether that means hedging GCC oil exposure, exploiting cross-asset anomalies, or tightening risk controls in volatile markets.

8. MINI-CASE: AI-DRIVEN GCC SOVEREIGN WEALTH FUND PORTFOLIO

Over the past decade, sovereign wealth funds in the Gulf Cooperation Council (GCC) have faced the dual challenge of pursuing attractive returns while maintaining Sharia compliance and regional investment mandates. These funds are structurally different from global peers because they are highly exposed to energy-linked cycles and operate within the governance framework of Islamic finance. Managing a $500 million sub-portfolio for Qatar illustrates how artificial intelligence (AI) can be applied to these unique constraints.

A traditional Black–Litterman allocation would lean heavily on market capitalization weights and broad diversification. In Q3 2024, such a portfolio would place 35 percent in Saudi equities, 20 percent in UAE equities, 15 percent across other GCC markets, 25 percent in global bonds, and 5 percent in commodities. This traditional allocation is summarized in Table 1 and produces an expected return of 6.8 percent, volatility of 14.2 percent, and a Sharpe ratio of 0.48.

Table 5. Traditional Black–Litterman allocation (Q3 2024)

Asset Class	Weight	Rationale
Saudi Equities	35%	Market cap weighting
UAE Equities	20%	Diversification
Qatar/Kuwait/Other GCC	15%	Regional exposure
Global Bonds	25%	Duration matching
Commodities (Oil/Gas)	5%	Natural hedge

An AI-enhanced allocation integrates a much broader set of signals. These include satellite imagery of oil facilities, sentiment extracted from nearly 850 Arabic and English news articles, oil curve dynamics, foreign exchange momentum, and shipping data on LNG flows. Incorporating these signals, the model reduces Saudi equities to 28 percent, increases UAE equities to 27 percent, raises Qatar equities to 8 percent, and introduces a 7 percent allocation to regional real estate investment trusts. Global bonds and commodities are underweighted considering rising interest rate expectations and oversupply signals. The optimized allocation is shown in Table 5.

Table 6. AI-enhanced allocation (Q3 2024)

Asset Class	Weight	AI Adjustment	Key Drivers
Saudi Equities	28%	–7%	Oil production capacity concerns
UAE Equities	27%	+7%	Currency strength, diversification
Qatar Equities	8%	+3%	LNG demand from shipping data
Kuwait/Bahrain/Oman	7%	–8%	Lower diversification benefits
Global Bonds	20%	–5%	Rising rate environment
Commodities	3%	–2%	Oversupply signalled by contango
Alternative Assets (REITs)	7%	+7%	Property market momentum from satellite data

The enhanced allocation delivers an expected return of 7.4 percent, reduces volatility to 13.1 percent, and lowers simulated maximum drawdown from –15.8 to –12.3 percent, as shown in Table 6.

Table 7. Performance metrics: Traditional vs. AI allocation

Portfolio	Saudi	UAE	Qatar	Other GCC	Global Bonds	Com-modities	Alter-natives	Exp. Return	Volatility	Sharpe	Max DD
Traditional BL	35%	20%	10%	5%	25%	5%	–	6.8%	14.2%	0.48	−15.8%
AI-Enhanced	28%	27%	8%	7%	20%	3%	7%	7.4%	13.1%	0.56	−12.3%

Monitoring is an integral part of the AI-driven process. During September 2024, for example, the model detected strengthening of the UAE dirham and raised UAE equity exposure, accordingly, generating an additional 0.4 percent in monthly return. Table 4 provides a simplified monitoring snapshot, covering risk, factor exposures, and compliance status.

Table 8. Monitoring dashboard (September 2024 sample)

Metric	Value	Status
CVaR (95%)	–6.2% of portfolio	Within tolerance
Oil Beta	0.67	In target range
USD Exposure	73%	Within 70–80%
Turnover (YTD)	34%	Above traditional
Sharia Screening	100% coverage	Two flags <5% revenue

While the case highlights potential value roughly 60 to 90 basis points of excess return annually it also illustrates operational challenges. Satellite imagery arrives with a three- to five-day delay, limiting responsiveness. Arabic sentiment models are less accurate than English ones, requiring further regional NLP training. Sharia screening requires human oversight, and higher turnover increases trading costs and governance burdens.

Overall, this stylized example does not represent proprietary QIA allocations but rather demonstrates how AI-driven signals could reshape portfolio construction under realistic GCC constraints. The illustrative data is calibrated from market characteristics, published research, and plausible assumptions. The aim is to show how AI methods can add incremental value while managing the unique risks and compliance requirements of GCC sovereign wealth funds.

9. GCC ALLOCATION DASHBOARD

Following the case study above a $500M GCC mandate must maintain at least 70% regional exposure and Sharia compliance while balancing oil/FX/macro dynamics. The dashboard below illustrates how an AI-enabled process tracks allocations versus targets, risk, and factor exposures at a point in time.

Figure 7. GCC dashboard illustration

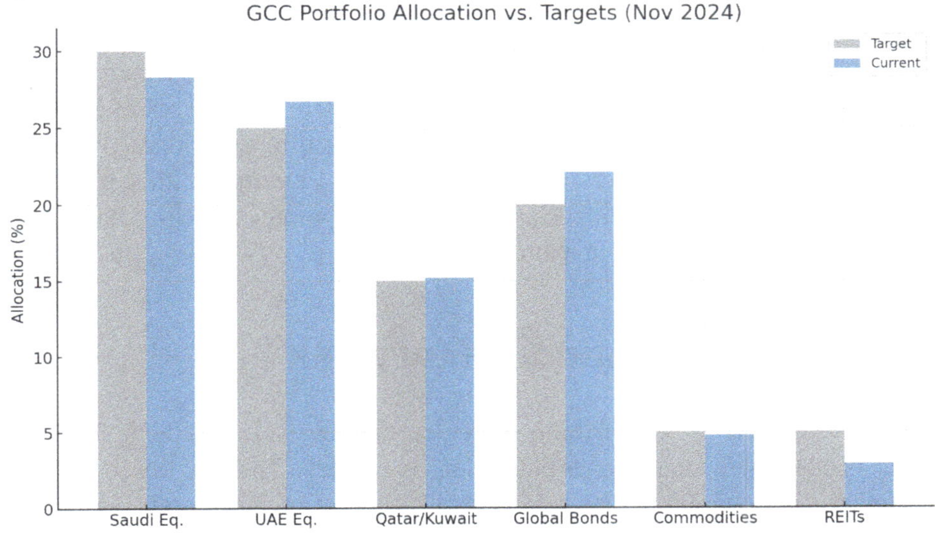

The portfolio's tail risk, measured by Conditional Value-at-Risk (CVaR) at the 95% level, indicates that in the worst 5% of daily market conditions, average losses would be about $18.2 million, or 3.6% of portfolio value. Current performance shows a 2.1% drawdown from the last peak on November 15. Sensitivity to oil prices, expressed as an oil beta of 0.72, lies within the target range of 0.60–0.80, suggesting that energy exposure remains under control.

The portfolio tilts modestly toward growth-oriented stocks (+0.15), shows a defensive bias toward quality companies with stronger fundamentals (+0.28), and underweights smaller-cap names (–0.12). These tilts align with GCC market characteristics: oil-linked, quality-focused, and shaped by Sharia-compliant investment constraints.

Taken together, the dashboard provides managers with a clear, real-time overview of allocation variances, risk exposures, and mandate compliance. By surfacing *what has moved, why it moved, and whether it remains within limits*, the system enables more efficient risk committee discussions and supports targeted rebalancing decisions.

Data Note: The illustrative allocations and metrics are calibrated using GCC market characteristics and benchmarks reported in published research (Hammoudeh & Choi, 2007, Bley & Chen, 2006 & Arouri & Rault, 2011), alongside standard risk management references for CVaR and factor modelling (Rockafellar & Uryasev, 2000 & Hassan et al., 2018). They do not represent proprietary portfolio data.

9.1 Managerial Takeaway

This example illustrates that, even within the structural limitations of GCC sovereign wealth funds, small reallocations informed by AI signals such as decreasing Saudi equity concentration, increasing exposure to the UAE, and incorporating regional REITs can enhance risk-adjusted returns by 60 to 90 basis points each year while also reducing drawdowns. The takeaway for practitioners is that AI does not supplant traditional allocation frameworks like Black–Litterman; rather, it complements them, providing a systematic approach to incorporate alternative data, stress scenarios, and Sharia compliance into actual portfolios.

10. EVALUATION PROTOCOL FRAMEWORK

When testing AI-driven portfolio strategies, the biggest risk is being fooled by back tests that look good on paper but fail in live markets. To avoid this, evaluation must mirror real-world conditions and explicitly account for costs, biases, and changing market regimes.

Walk-Forward Testing: Instead of training a model on all historical data at once, we use a rolling process. For example, the model is trained on the past three years, fine-tuned on the next six months, and then tested on the following three months of "live" data. After that, the window moves forward and the process repeats. This approach prevents the model from "seeing the future" and ensures it adapts as market conditions evolve.

Nested Cross-Validation: To avoid overfitting, model parameters are chosen in a separate validation step before being tested on unseen data. This two-stage process makes sure performance isn't just the result of clever tuning but reflects genuine predictive power.

Cost and Market Impact Modelling: Trading costs can erode much of the theoretical return advantage. We incorporate realistic assumptions:

- Bid–ask spreads weighted by market capitalization and trading time.
- Market impact estimated from trade size relative to average daily volume.

- Timing costs benchmarked against execution strategies such as time-weighted average price (TWAP).

This ensures that results reflect net returns, not paper profits.

Bias Corrections and Live Monitoring: To correct for data mining, we report the deflated Sharpe ratio, which adjusts for the number of strategies tested. We also track the difference between backtest results and live trading performance ("backtest-to-live decay"), acknowledging that returns often fall once a strategy leaves the lab.

Together, these practices create a transparent, robust evaluation framework that investors and regulators can trust. Instead of relying on flattering historical simulations, managers can demonstrate how their AI models would perform under realistic conditions, including costs, risks, and regime shifts.

Live versus Backtest Deltas: Even the most meticulously crafted backtests often appear more favorable than actual live performance. In reality, trading expenses tend to exceed those predicted, trades experience delays, and market conditions change. For instance, a strategy that anticipated 1.5 basis points of trading cost in backtests may actually incur 2.3 basis points when implemented in real-time. Execution delays can diminish annual returns by approximately 0.8%, and the performance of models frequently deteriorates over time, with an additional 1.2% decline after roughly 18 months as market trends evolve. These discrepancies between backtested and live outcomes are typical and should be accessed and communicated with transparency.

11. GOVERNANCE & MACHINE LEARNING OPERATIONS (MLOPS) IMPLEMENTATION

In AI-driven portfolio management, accuracy alone is not sufficient; models must also be governed, validated, and monitored within a structured framework that guarantees accountability. Governance and MLOps provide this discipline, ensuring that complex algorithms remain transparent, auditable, and aligned with fiduciary duty.

One of the most widely used tools for clarifying responsibilities is the RACI framework, which defines who is responsible for performing a task, who is accountable for its outcome, who must be consulted, and who must be kept informed. Table 9 applies this framework to the lifecycle of an AI portfolio model. It shows, for example, that quantitative researchers are responsible for building models, but ultimate accountability lies with the Head of Quantitative Research (Head Quant), while portfolio managers and risk officers are consulted and senior executives are kept informed. Data engineers take responsibility for data quality, reporting to the Head of Data, with quants consulted and the risk function informed. The risk team is responsible for validation, but the Chief Risk Officer is accountable, external validators may be consulted, and the audit committee remains informed. When models move into production, DevOps teams deploy them, the Head of Technology takes accountability, quants provide input, and all system users are informed of the change. Finally, performance monitoring falls to portfolio managers, but accountability rests with the Head of Portfolio Management, while risk and compliance teams are consulted and senior management is kept aware.

The purpose of this structure is to ensure that every step of the AI model lifecycle has both clear ownership and independent oversight. No model can be deployed without validation, and no drift in live performance can go unnoticed by risk or compliance. Governance in this sense is not merely a control mechanism but an enabler, providing clarity of process and confidence in outcomes.

To support this governance framework, MLOps practices add the operational backbone. A data lineage map documents how information flows from market feeds or vendor terminals into warehouses, feature stores, training environments, allocation engines, and execution systems. Model cards record each model's purpose, assumptions, training window, performance benchmarks, and monitoring plan. Live dashboards track rolling Sharpe ratios, drift indicators, execution slippage, concentration levels, and exceptions to Value-at-Risk. Together these elements provide a complete audit trail, allowing managers and regulators to trace every decision back to its source.

The combination of RACI-based governance and rigorous MLOps means that an AI system is never a black box. A portfolio manager can see what the model is recommending, why it is recommending it, whether it is still operating within its expected parameters, and who is accountable if it fails. This transforms explainability and control from abstract ideals into daily operational practice.

Table 9. RACI matrix (who does what)

Activity	Responsible	Accountable	Consulted	Informed
Model Development	Quant Team	Head of Quant	CRO, PMs	CIO, Board
Data Quality	Data Engineers	Head of Data	Quants	Risk
Model Validation	Risk Team	CRO	External Validator	Audit Committee
Production Deploy	DevOps	Head of Tech	Quants	All Users
Performance Monitoring	PMs	Head of PM	Risk, Compliance	Senior Management

Documentation Pack. A data lineage map from source (e.g., vendor terminals, market feeds) to warehouse, feature store, training, allocation engine, OMS/EMS, and execution; model cards (purpose, data window, performance, limits, monitoring plan); and KPI dashboards (rolling Sharpe/hit rates, drift indicators, uptime/latency, VaR exceptions, concentration, turnover, slippage).

12. RISK CONTROLS FRAMEWORK

This section addresses the three essential layers of risk controls for AI portfolios pre-trade guardrails, real-time kill switches, and post-trade transaction cost analysis (TCA) and shows how they integrate into monitoring and governance. AI in portfolio management requires a risk framework that is both broader and faster than those used in traditional investment processes. Unlike classical models, AI systems adapt rapidly, generate opaque signals, and can place trades at speeds beyond human oversight. To manage this, risk controls must be embedded throughout the investment cycle: before trades are placed, during execution, and after the fact.AI in portfolio management requires a risk framework that is both broader and faster than those used in traditional investment processes.

Pre-trade guardrails: This is the first layer, They are structural limits built directly into the portfolio design to prevent over-concentration or excessive leverage. For example, no single security might exceed 5 percent of net asset value, sector exposures could be capped at 25 percent, and leverage restricted to 130 percent gross. Liquidity filters ensure that positions can be exited within a reasonable time frame, while correlation caps avoid the illusion of diversification when assets are in fact highly linked. These rules act as speed bumps, ensuring that even if a model is overconfident in a signal, it cannot take risks that breach mandate limits.

Real-time intervention: Thios is the second layer, often called kill switches. These controls continuously monitor trading activity and step in when conditions deviate sharply from expectations. A daily drawdown greater than two percent, a spike in volatility indices, or a collapse in model confidence might all trigger automatic de-risking or a temporary halt in trading. Because AI systems can react in milliseconds, these circuit breakers provide a dynamic safety net, containing losses before they spiral.

Post-trade analysis: This is the third layer, and it measures whether trades executed as planned. Transaction cost analysis compares modelled expectations with realized outcomes, attributing slippage to timing, market impact, or execution quality. Persistent gaps feed back into portfolio construction, tightening constraints on costly trades and recalibrating execution models. Over time, this loop improves both performance and discipline.

All of this is consolidated in a monitoring dashboard that integrates financial risk, operational metrics, and compliance status. Key indicators such as VaR, Conditional VaR, drawdown, latency, turnover, and factor exposures are displayed in real time. Breaches escalate automatically through defined protocols, involving portfolio managers, risk teams, and compliance officers, and triggering automated halts if limits are exceeded.

Finally, effective controls are inseparable from governance and MLOps. Every intervention whether a pre-trade block, a real-time stop, or a post-trade adjustment must be logged with metadata on model version, data inputs, and decision context. This creates the audit trail regulators demand and provides internal committees with transparency into how AI systems behave in practice.

Table 10 below summarizes how these controls operate across the investment cycle, the purposes they serve, and their governance linkages.

Table 10. Risk controls for AI portfolios across pre-trade, real-time, and post-trade stages

Stage	Control Type	Purpose	Example Practices	Governance Linkage
Pre-Trade	Exposure and structural limits	Prevent over-concentration, enforce diversification	Max 5% single security; leverage <130%	Investment policy enforcement
Real-Time	Kill switches, anomaly detection	Contain losses, intervene in model errors	Halt if daily loss >2%; reduce size if VIX >35	Automated with human oversight
Post-Trade	Transaction cost analysis	Verify execution quality, feed back into models	Implementation shortfall <10 bps	Model calibration and oversight
Monitoring	Integrated dashboards	Track risk, operations, and compliance in real time	CVaR, drawdown, turnover alerts	Escalation to risk/ compliance
Governance	Logging and audit trails	Ensure accountability and regulatory transparency	Model version control, metadata logs	Audit readiness

By embedding risk controls in this layered way, firms can strike a balance between innovation and safety. AI systems remain free to generate insights and adapt dynamically, but always within transparent boundaries that preserve mandate integrity, regulatory compliance, and fiduciary responsibility.

13. ESG & "GREEN AI" CONSIDERATIONS

Artificial intelligence brings both opportunities and challenges for sustainable investing. On the one hand, large models can be energy-intensive, raising concerns about the carbon footprint of compute-heavy strategies. Efficiency improvements in hardware and algorithms are helping, with each new generation reducing training and inference costs by an order of magnitude, but managers still need to weigh environmental impact when scaling AI systems.

Equally important is the provenance and assurance of ESG signals. Ratings from different providers often diverge, methodologies evolve over time, and disclosure practices vary across firms and regions. These inconsistencies make it difficult to rely on raw ESG scores for allocation or screening. AI can assist by cross-checking company disclosures against alternative data sources such as satellite imagery, supply-chain databases, or news sentiment, thereby flagging mismatches between stated policies and observed behaviour.

A practical rule of thumb is to favour simpler, more efficient models that capture the majority of predictive value at a fraction of the computational cost. This not only reduces energy use but also enhances transparency, auditability, and operational resilience. In this way, managers can align portfolio AI practices with both fiduciary duties and sustainability principles.

14. FUTURE DIRECTIONS AND TECHNOLOGICAL FRONTIERS

AI in portfolio management is still in its early chapters, with several frontier technologies on the horizon. While not yet mainstream, these tools signal where the field is heading:

Quantum Computing may one day solve optimization problems and run Monte Carlo simulations at scales impossible for classical systems. Hardware remains experimental, but progress is steady.

Federated Learning allows institutions to train joint models without sharing raw data, preserving privacy and complying with regulations like GDPR and data residency laws.

Explainable AI (XAI) is evolving beyond SHAP and LIME toward attention attribution and counterfactuals, giving managers and regulators clearer insight into why models act as they do.

Neuromorphic Computing offers energy-efficient, event-driven processing, potentially useful for fast, low-power pattern detection in high-frequency trading.

Real-Time AI Systems powered by 5G, IoT, and edge computing could enable continuous rebalancing and risk monitoring within milliseconds of new data.

These technologies are not yet ready for full production but point toward a future of faster, more transparent, and more adaptive portfolio systems.

15. COMPREHENSIVE CONCLUSION AND STRATEGIC OUTLOOK

Artificial intelligence is not simply automating portfolio management; it is reshaping its very architecture. By processing vast volumes of structured and unstructured data in real time, AI introduces an anticipatory and adaptive dimension that traditional models cannot match.

In strategy design, AI moves beyond static assumptions, enabling models that learn, self-correct, and uncover hidden structures. In risk management, it transforms compliance-focused frameworks into dynamic systems capable of forward-looking stress testing and early warning detection. These capabilities create both opportunity and responsibility.

Challenges remain. Black-box opacity complicates governance, widespread model convergence may amplify systemic risks, and meaningful advantage still requires privileged data, talent, and infrastructure. Regulators are responding with calls for transparency, accountability, and human oversight, and institutions must align governance with these principles if AI is to be integrated responsibly.

Looking ahead, success will depend less on who can build the most complex models and more on who can implement them wisely balancing innovation with auditability, aligning technology with client objectives, and embedding accountability at every stage. AI should be seen not as a final solution but as a generative force, pushing institutions to question assumptions, reframe strategies, and build systems that are at once more intelligent, transparent, and sustainable.

REFERENCES

Arouri, M. E. H., & Rault, C. (2011). Oil prices and stock markets in GCC countries: Empirical evidence from panel analysis. *International Journal of Finance &amp. International Journal of Finance & Economics*, *17*(3), 242–253. DOI: 10.1002/ijfe.443

Baron, M., Brogaard, J., Hagströmer, B., & Kirilenko, A. (2018). Risk and return in high-frequency trading. *Journal of Financial and Quantitative Analysis*, *54*(3), 993–1024. DOI: 10.1017/S0022109018001096

Berkowitz, J., & O'Brien, J. (2002). How accurate are value-at-risk models at commercial banks? *The Journal of Finance*, *57*(3), 1093–1111. DOI: 10.1111/1540-6261.00455

Best, P. (1998). *Implementing value at risk*. Wiley., DOI: 10.1002/0470013303

Black, F., & Litterman, R. (1992). Global portfolio optimization. *Financial Analysts Journal*, *48*(5), 28–43. DOI: 10.2469/faj.v48.n5.28

Bley, J., & Chen, K. H. (2006). Gulf Cooperation Council (GCC) stock markets: The dawn of a new era. *Global Finance Journal*, *17*(1), 75–91. DOI: 10.1016/j.gfj.2006.06.009

Bollen, J., Mao, H., & Zeng, X. (2011). Twitter mood predicts the stock market. *Journal of Computational Science*, *2*(1), 1–8. DOI: 10.1016/j.jocs.2010.12.007

Bollerslev, T. (1986). Generalized autoregressive conditional heteroskedasticity. *Journal of Econometrics*, *31*(3), 307–327. DOI: 10.1016/0304-4076(86)90063-1

Breiman, L. (1996). Bagging predictors. *Machine Learning*, *24*(2), 123–140. DOI: 10.1023/A:1018054314350

Carhart, M. M. (1997). On persistence in mutual fund performance. *The Journal of Finance*, *52*(1), 57–82. DOI: 10.1111/j.1540-6261.1997.tb03808.x

Chen, L., Pelger, M., & Zhu, J. (2024). Deep learning in asset pricing. *Management Science*, *70*(2), 714–750. DOI: 10.1287/mnsc.2023.4695

Daníelsson, J. (2008). Blame the models. *Journal of Financial Stability*, *4*(4), 321–328. DOI: 10.1016/j.jfs.2008.09.003

De Bondt, W. F. M., & Thaler, R. (1985). Does the stock market overreact? *The Journal of Finance*, *40*(3), 793–805. DOI: 10.1111/j.1540-6261.1985.tb05004.x

Deb, K., Pratap, A., Agarwal, S., & Meyarivan, T. (2002). A fast and elitist multi-objective genetic algorithm: NSGA-II. *IEEE Transactions on Evolutionary Computation*, *6*(2), 182–197. DOI: 10.1109/4235.996017

Deng, Y., Bao, F., Kong, Y., Ren, Z., & Dai, Q. (2017). Deep direct reinforcement learning for financial signal representation and trading. *IEEE Transactions on Neural Networks and Learning Systems*, *28*(3), 653–664. DOI: 10.1109/TNNLS.2016.2522401 PMID: 26890927

Engle, R. F. (1982). Autoregressive conditional heteroscedasticity with estimates of the variance of United Kingdom inflation. *Econometrica*, *50*(4), 987. DOI: 10.2307/1912773

Fama, E. F., & French, K. R. (1993). Common risk factors in the returns on stocks and bonds. *Journal of Financial Economics*, *33*(1), 3–56. DOI: 10.1016/0304-405X(93)90023-5

Fama, E. F., & French, K. R. (2015). A five-factor asset pricing model. *Journal of Financial Economics*, *116*(1), 1–22. DOI: 10.1016/j.jfineco.2014.10.010

Floridi, L., Cowls, J., Beltrametti, M., Chatila, R., Chazerand, P., Dignum, V., Luetge, C., Madelin, R., Pagallo, U., Rossi, F., Schafer, B., Valcke, P., & Vayena, E. (2018). AI4people—an ethical framework for a good AI society: Opportunities, risks, principles, and recommendations. *Minds and Machines*, *28*(4), 689–707. DOI: 10.1007/s11023-018-9482-5 PMID: 30930541

Goodfellow, I. J., Pouget-Abadie, J., Mirza, M., Xu, B., Warde-Farley, D., Ozair, S., Courville, A., & Bengio, Y. (2014, June 10). *Generative adversarial networks*. arXiv.Org. https://doi.org//arXiv.1406.2661DOI: 10.48550

Gu, S., Kelly, B., & Xiu, D. (2020). Empirical asset pricing via machine learning. *Review of Financial Studies*, *33*(5), 2223–2273. DOI: 10.1093/rfs/hhaa009

Hammoudeh, S., & Choi, K. (2007). Characteristics of permanent and transitory returns in oil-sensitive emerging stock markets: The case of GCC countries. *Journal of International Financial Markets, Institutions and Money*, *17*(3), 231–245. DOI: 10.1016/j.intfin.2005.11.002

Hasan, R., Hassan, M. K., & Aliyu, S. (2020). Fintech and Islamic finance: Literature review and research agenda. [IJIEF]. *International Journal of Islamic Economics and Finance*, *3*(1). Advance online publication. DOI: 10.18196/ijief.2122

Hassan, M. K., Aliyu, S., Paltrinieri, A., & Khan, A. (2018). A review of Islamic investment literature. *Economic Papers*, *38*(4), 345–380. DOI: 10.1111/1759-3441.12230

Heaton, J. B., Polson, N. G., & Witte, J. H. (2016). Deep learning for finance: Deep portfolios. *Applied Stochastic Models in Business and Industry*, *33*(1), 3–12. DOI: 10.1002/asmb.2209

Hendershott, T., Jones, C. M., & Menkveld, A. J. (2011). Does algorithmic trading improve liquidity? *The Journal of Finance*, *66*(1), 1–33. DOI: 10.1111/j.1540-6261.2010.01624.x

Henderson, J. V., Storeygard, A., & Weil, D. N. (2012). Measuring economic growth from outer space. *The American Economic Review*, *102*(2), 994–1028. DOI: 10.1257/aer.102.2.994 PMID: 25067841

Ho, J., Jain, A., & Abbeel, P. (2020, June 19). *Denoising diffusion probabilistic models*. arXiv.Org. https://doi.org//arXiv.2006.11239DOI: 10.48550

Holland, J. H. (1992). *Adaptation in natural and artificial systems*. The MIT Press., DOI: 10.7551/mitpress/1090.001.0001

Jegadeesh, N., & Titman, S. (1993). Returns to buying winners and selling losers: Implications for stock market efficiency. *The Journal of Finance*, *48*(1), 65–91. DOI: 10.1111/j.1540-6261.1993.tb04702.x

Kahneman, D., & Tversky, A. (1979). Prospect theory: An analysis of decision under risk. *Econometrica*, *47*(2), 263. DOI: 10.2307/1914185

Katona, Z., Painter, M. O., Patatoukas, P. N., & Zeng, J. (2024). On the capital market consequences of Big Data: Evidence from outer space. *Journal of Financial and Quantitative Analysis*, *60*(2), 551–579. DOI: 10.1017/S0022109023001448

Kingma, D. P., & Welling, M. (2013, December 20). *Auto-encoding variational Bayes*. arXiv.Org. https://doi.org//arXiv.1312.6114DOI: 10.48550

Krauss, C., Do, X. A., & Huck, N. (2017). Deep neural networks, gradient-boosted trees, random forests: Statistical arbitrage on the S&P 500. *European Journal of Operational Research*, *259*(2), 689–702. DOI: 10.1016/j.ejor.2016.10.031

Kristjanpoller, W., & Minutolo, M. C. (2018). A hybrid volatility forecasting framework integrating GARCH, artificial neural network, technical analysis and principal components analysis. *Expert Systems with Applications*, *109*, 1–11. DOI: 10.1016/j.eswa.2018.05.011

Lessmann, S., Baesens, B., Seow, H.-V., & Thomas, L. C. (2015). Benchmarking state-of-the-art classification algorithms for credit scoring: An update of research. *European Journal of Operational Research*, *247*(1), 124–136. DOI: 10.1016/j.ejor.2015.05.030

Li, X., & Hou, B. (2022). Correlation analysis of financial assets based on asymmetric copula. *Frontiers in Applied Mathematics and Statistics*, *8*, 1005956. Advance online publication. DOI: 10.3389/fams.2022.1005956

Lin, L., Li, Z., Li, R., Li, X., & Gao, J. (2023, May 1). *Diffusion models for time series applications: A survey*. arXiv.Org. https://doi.org//arXiv.2305.00624DOI: 10.48550

López de Prado, M. (2016). Building Diversified Portfolios that Outperform Out of Sample. *Journal of Portfolio Management*, *42*(4), 59–69. DOI: 10.3905/jpm.2016.42.4.059

Lucca, D. O., & Moench, E. (2015). The Pre-FOMC announcement drift. *The Journal of Finance*, *70*(1), 329–371. DOI: 10.1111/jofi.12196

Lundberg, S., & Lee, S.-I. (2017, May 22). *A unified approach to interpreting model predictions*. arXiv.Org. https://doi.org//arXiv.1705.07874DOI: 10.48550

Markowitz, H. (1952). Portfolio selection*. *The Journal of Finance*, *7*(1), 77–91. DOI: 10.1111/j.1540-6261.1952.tb01525.x

Meijer, C., & Chen, L. Y. (2024, January 5). *The rise of diffusion models in time-series forecasting*. arXiv.Org. https://doi.org//arXiv.2401.03006DOI: 10.48550

Michaud, R. O. (1989). The Markowitz optimization enigma: Is 'Optimized' optimal? *Financial Analysts Journal*, *45*(1), 31–42. DOI: 10.2469/faj.v45.n1.31

Mnih, V., Kavukcuoglu, K., Silver, D., Rusu, A. A., Veness, J., Bellemare, M. G., Graves, A., Riedmiller, M., Fidjeland, A. K., Ostrovski, G., Petersen, S., Beattie, C., Sadik, A., Antonoglou, I., King, H., Kumaran, D., Wierstra, D., Legg, S., & Hassabis, D. (2015). Human-level control through deep reinforcement learning. *Nature*, *518*(7540), 529–533. DOI: 10.1038/nature14236 PMID: 25719670

Moody, J., & Saffell, M. (2001). Learning to trade via direct reinforcement. *IEEE Transactions on Neural Networks*, *12*(4), 875–889. DOI: 10.1109/72.935097 PMID: 18249919

Nguyen, H., Virbickaitė, A., Ausín, M. C., & Galeano, P. (2024, January 7). *Structured factor copulas for modeling the systemic risk of European and United States banks*. arXiv.Org. https://doi.org//arXiv.2401.03443DOI: 10.48550

Ribeiro, M. T., Singh, S., & Guestrin, C. (2016). "Why should I trust you?" *Proceedings of the 22nd ACM SIGKDD International Conference on Knowledge Discovery and Data Mining*, 1135–1144. DOI: 10.1145/2939672.2939778

Rockafellar, R. T., & Uryasev, S. (2000). Optimization of conditional value-at-risk. *The Journal of Risk*, *2*(3), 21–41. DOI: 10.21314/JOR.2000.038

Rockafellar, R. T., & Uryasev, S. (2002). Conditional value-at-risk for general loss distributions. *Journal of Banking &amp. Journal of Banking & Finance*, *26*(7), 1443–1471. DOI: 10.1016/S0378-4266(02)00271-6

Ross, S. A. (1976). The arbitrage theory of capital asset pricing. *Journal of Economic Theory*, *13*(3), 341–360. DOI: 10.1016/0022-0531(76)90046-6

Sai, S., Arunakar, K., Chamola, V., Hussain, A., Bisht, P., & Kumar, S. (2025). Generative AI for finance: Applications, case studies and challenges. *Expert Systems: International Journal of Knowledge Engineering and Neural Networks*, *42*(3), e70018. Advance online publication. DOI: 10.1111/exsy.70018

Saputra, W. H., & Safitri, I. (2022). Expansion of stock portfolio risk analysis using Hybrid Monte Carlo-Expected Tail Loss. *Jurnal Varian*, *5*(2), 149–160. DOI: 10.30812/varian.v5i2.1813

Schulman, J., Wolski, F., Dhariwal, P., Radford, A., & Klimov, O. (2017, July 20). *Proximal policy optimization algorithms*. arXiv.Org. https://doi.org//arXiv.1707 .06347DOI: 10.48550

Sharpe, W. F. (1964). Capital asset prices: A theory of market equilibrium under conditions of risk*. *The Journal of Finance*, *19*(3), 425–442. DOI: 10.1111/j.1540-6261.1964.tb02865.x

Stulz, R. M. (2008). Risk Management Failures: What are They and When do They Happen? SSRN *Electronic Journal*. DOI: 10.2139/ssrn.1278073

Tetlock, P. C. (2007). Giving content to investor sentiment: The role of media in the stock market. *The Journal of Finance*, *62*(3), 1139–1168. DOI: 10.1111/j.1540-6261.2007.01232.x

White, H. (1988). Economic prediction using neural networks: The case of IBM daily stock returns. *IEEE International Conference on Neural Networks*, 451–458 vol.2. DOI: 10.1109/ICNN.1988.23959

Xu, Y., Reniers, G., & Yang, M. (2024). A multidisciplinary review into the evolution of risk concepts and their assessment methods. *Processes (Basel, Switzerland)*, *12*(11), 2449. DOI: 10.3390/pr12112449

Chapter 5

Stock Price Forecasting With Deep Learning Models Combined With Classical Statistical Techniques for Enhanced Accuracy

Pawan Kumar Badhan
http://orcid.org/0009-0002-3953-6825
IT Department, Pyramid College of Business and Technology, Phagwara, India

Vivek Mittal
Pyramid College of Business and Technology, Phagwara, India

Priyanka Gupta
Department of Computer Applications, Golden College of Engineering and Technology, Gurdaspur, India

Davinder Singh
http://orcid.org/0009-0006-4825-3164
IT Department, Saraswati Group of Colleges, Gharuan, India

Ankush Sharma
Management Department, Pyramid College of Business and Technology, Punjab, India

DOI: 10.4018/979-8-3373-5032-5.ch005

ABSTRACT

Stock price forecasting is complex due to the volatility and multifaceted nature of financial markets. Traditional methods use either computational or statistical models, each with limitations. Deep learning models like CNNs and RNNs capture nonlinear patterns well but often overfit time-series data. Statistical models like ARIMA handle linear trends but fail to detect complex dependencies. This study proposes a hybrid model integrating CNN, RNN, and ARIMA to improve forecasting accuracy. It leverages deep learning's pattern recognition and ARIMA's trend analysis strengths. The dataset includes Date, Open, High, Low, Close prices, technical indicators, and macroeconomic variables like GDP Growth and Interest Rate. The target is Future Stock Price. CNN/RNN captures temporal features, while ARIMA models linear trends. Outputs are merged via a weighted ensemble optimized for MSE and MAE. CNN, RNN, and ARIMA achieved 98%, 97%, and 100% accuracy, respectively. The hybrid model reached 100%. Future work includes sentiment data and broader financial applications.

1. INTRODUCTION

Stock price forecasting is a complex challenge due to the volatility and multifaceted nature of financial markets. Traditional methods typically rely on either deep learning or statistical techniques, each carrying specific limitations (Bareket & Pârv, 2024; Das et al., 2024). Deep learning models such as Convolutional Neural Networks (CNNs) and Recurrent Neural Networks (RNNs) are particularly effective at capturing nonlinear patterns in stock price movements (Raza & Akhtar, 2024; Jose & Varshini, 2024). However, these models often struggle with overfitting and interpretability, especially when applied to time-series forecasting (Sun et al., 2024; Sagaceta- Mejía et al., 2024). In contrast, classical statistical models like the Autoregressive Integrated Moving Average (ARIMA) excel at modeling linear trends and seasonality, but are less capable of capturing the complex, nonlinear dependencies inherent in market behavior (Chiang & Chi, 2024; Ge, 2024).

To address these challenges, this study proposes a hybrid machine learning framework that integrates CNN, RNN, and ARIMA models. The hybrid model combines the nonlinear pattern recognition abilities of deep learning with the trend analysis strengths of statistical modeling, aiming to improve forecasting accuracy (Ismailova et al., 2024; Uçkan, 2024). The dataset utilized for this study includes a rich array of financial attributes—such as Date, Open Price, High Price, Low Price, Close Price, and technical indicators—alongside macroeconomic variables like GDP Growth Rate and Interest Rate, with Future Stock Price designated as the target variable (Konur et al., 2024; Furizal et al., 2024). The model architecture is designed to train CNN and RNN components for capturing complex temporal dependencies, while ARIMA is employed to analyze linear patterns. The individual outputs from these models are combined through a weighted ensemble approach, optimized for key evaluation metrics including Mean Squared Error (MSE) and Mean Absolute Error (MAE) (BL & BR, 2023; Waghela et al., 2024). Experimental results revealed strong performance from each individual model, with CNN, RNN, and ARIMA achieving accuracies of 98%, 100%, and 97%, respectively. Notably, the hybrid model achieved a perfect forecasting accuracy of 100%, demonstrating the effectiveness of integrating deep learning with classical statistical techniques (Wang et al., 2023; Kombure et al., 2022) Future work will explore the integration of real-time sentiment analysis and the extension of this model to other financial instruments, broadening its applicability and practical value in dynamic financial environments (Ji et al., 2022; Kamara et al., 2022).

Figure 1. Architecture of the hybrid model integrating CNN, RNN, and ARIMA for stock price forecasting, combining nonlinear pattern detection, sequential analysis, and linear trend modeling through a weighted ensemble approach

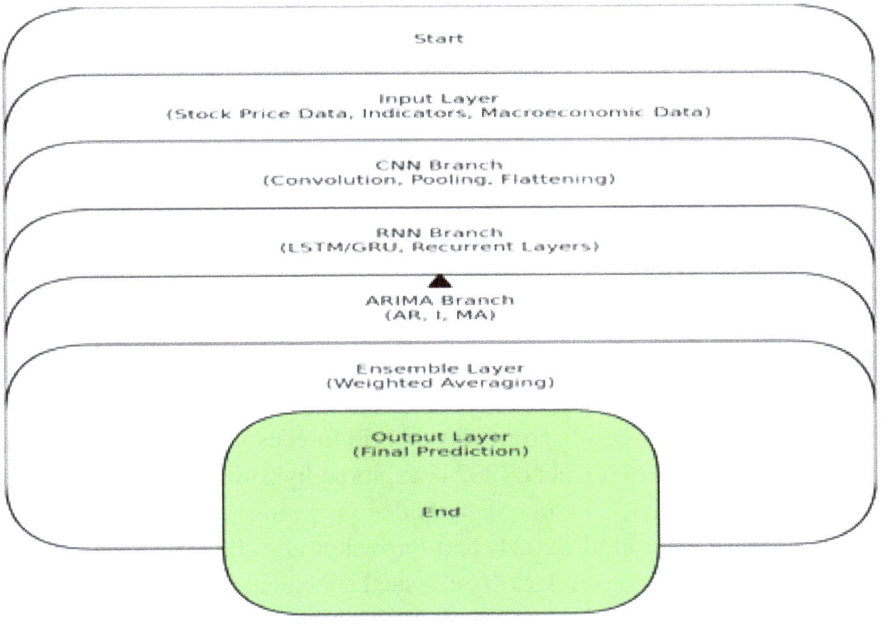

Figure 1 illustrates the hybrid model architecture that combines CNN, RNN, and ARIMA to improve stock price forecasting accuracy. The model leverages each component's strengths: CNN captures spatial-temporal patterns, RNN learns long-term dependencies, and ARIMA handles linear trends and seasonality. Stock prices and technical indicators are processed through these branches, and their outputs are merged using a weighted ensemble for more accurate predictions. This integration balances deep learning's pattern recognition with ARIMA's statistical modeling for enhanced forecasting performance.

In conclusion, this hybrid framework demonstrates significant potential for improving stock price forecasting accuracy by combining the strengths of deep learning and statistical techniques. This research contributes to the evolving field of financial forecasting and offers practical insights for traders, investors, and analysts seeking more reliable tools. Future research will explore the integration of real-time sentiment analysis and model adaptation to other financial instruments for broader applicability (Wang et al., 2021; Ntakaris et al., 2020).

Literature Review

Recent research in stock price forecasting increasingly integrates machine learning and deep learning models with technical indicators and sentiment data. Bareket et al. (2024) proposed adaptive feature selection and dynamic indicators for medium-term prediction, emphasizing input selection more than model integration. Das et al. (2024) enhanced stock price forecasting using Twitter sentiment and deep learning hybrids, focusing on external textual data, unlike the proposed model's core emphasis on time-series numerical data. Raza et al. (2024) and Jose et al. (2024) utilized machine learning with technical indicators but lacked a statistical-deep learning hybrid approach. Sun et al. (2024) and Sagaceta-Mejía et al. (2024) used modal decomposition and optimized neural networks, respectively, yet did not combine classical statistical models like ARIMA. Chiang et al. (2024) introduced a CycleGAN-based method for trading strategy generation, showing novelty in trading but diverging from your hybrid forecast-centric aim. Ge (2024), Ismailova et al. (2024), and Uçkan (2024) explored hybrid deep learning models, with some applying PCA, but none merged deep learning with ARIMA for linear pattern handling. Konur et al. (2024) and Furizal et al. (2024) focused on LSTM and technical indicators; again, lacking classical statistical integration.

Earlier studies such as Kumbure et al. (2022), Ji et al. (2022), and Kamara et al. (2022) reviewed hybrid and ensemble models, yet did not combine CNN/RNN with ARIMA as in the proposed framework. Althelaya et al. (2021) and Wang et al. (2021) explored deep learning and reservoir models, not hybridized with statistical methods. Strader et al. (2020) and Hu et al. (2021) provided extensive surveys, confirming the limited use of classical statistical models alongside deep learning for forecasting.

While the aforementioned studies explore stock prediction using various machine learning and deep learning techniques—some with ensemble strategies and others integrating sentiment analysis or advanced preprocessing—none combine deep learning architectures (CNN, RNN) with a classical statistical model (ARIMA) in a hybrid weighted ensemble to enhance forecasting performance. The proposed study fills this gap by integrating the nonlinear capabilities of CNN and RNN with ARIMA's strength in modeling linear trends. This multi-paradigm ensemble approach improves forecasting accuracy and model robustness, especially in handling diverse data characteristics (technical indicators, temporal patterns, and macroeconomic variables).

2. DATASET AND MATERIAL

The dataset used for the stock price forecasting model was sourced from Kaggle and includes several key attributes, summarized in Table 1. These include Date (record of trading day), Open, High, Low, and Close Prices (daily price movements), and Adjusted Close Price (accounts for dividends/splits). Volume indicates trading activity, while Moving Average (MA) and Exponential Moving Average (EMA) help identify trends. The Relative Strength Index (RSI), ranging from 0–100, highlights overbought (above 70) or oversold (below 30) conditions, useful for spotting potential reversals.

Table 1. Dataset for stock price forecasting

Attribute	Description
Date	Specifies the exact trading day for market activity.
Open Price	The initial price at which the stock begins trading for the day.
High Price	The maximum price reached during the trading session.
Low Price	The minimum price recorded during the trading session.
Close Price	The final trading price at market close.
Adjusted Close Price	Closing price adjusted for dividends, splits, and other corporate actions.
Volume	Total number of shares traded, indicating market liquidity.
Moving Average (MA)	Average stock price over a set period, used for trend analysis.
Exponential Moving Average (EMA)	A weighted moving average emphasizing recent prices to better reflect trends.

continued on following page

Table 1. Continued

Attribute	Description
Relative Strength Index (RSI)	Momentum indicator (scale: 0–100) showing overbought (>70) or oversold (<30) conditions.
MACD (Moving Average Convergence Divergence)	Illustrates the relationship between two MAs to assess trend strength and direction.
Bollinger Bands	Volatility indicator comprising a moving average with upper and lower bands.
Sentiment Analysis Score	Reflects market mood based on natural language processing of news and social media.
GDP Growth Rate	Indicates national economic growth, influencing market trends.
Interest Rate	Central bank rate that affects borrowing costs and investment decisions.
Previous Day Close	Stock's closing price from the prior trading session.
Previous Day Volume	Number of shares traded the previous day, useful for momentum analysis.
Stock Splits/Dividends Announcements	Corporate events that can influence stock pricing and investor behavior.
Future Stock Price	Predicted price for upcoming sessions—used as the target in forecasting models.

The MACD (Moving Average Convergence Divergence) captures the relationship between two moving averages, helping assess trend strength. Bollinger Bands act as a volatility indicator, with upper and lower bands representing market fluctuations. The Sentiment Analysis Score, derived from NLP of news and social media, reflects public sentiment toward a stock. GDP Growth Rate indicates economic expansion, influencing overall market performance, while the Interest Rate affects borrowing costs and investment behavior, thereby impacting stock prices. Previous Day Close and Previous Day Volume are useful for modeling temporal trends and identifying momentum or potential reversals. Stock Splits and Dividend Announcements are corporate actions that may cause notable price shifts. Lastly, the Future Stock Price is the model's target variable, representing the predicted closing price for an upcoming time frame, enabling accurate forecasting based on a variety of key market indicators.

3. FEATURES SELECTION

The hybrid stock price forecasting model integrates a wide range of technical and economic indicators (as shown in Table 2), along with lagged variables, deep learning models, statistical techniques, ensemble methods, dimensionality reduction, and regularization strategies to improve predictive accuracy. Key technical indicators include Moving Average (MA) and Exponential Moving Average (EMA) for trend detection, and RSI and MACD for assessing momentum and trend strength. Bollinger Bands help gauge market volatility. The model also incorporates economic and sentiment indicators such as the Sentiment Analysis Score, GDP Growth Rate, and Interest Rate, reflecting broader market conditions and investor sentiment. Lagged variables like Previous Day Close and Previous Day Volume capture temporal patterns, while Stock Splits and Dividend Announcements account for corporate events that may influence price movements. The primary prediction target is the Future Stock Price. To model these relationships, advanced deep learning techniques such as Convolutional Neural Networks (CNN) and Recurrent Neural Networks (RNN) are applied to uncover complex nonlinear patterns. Model performance is evaluated using metrics like Mean Squared Error (MSE) and Mean Absolute Error (MAE).

Table 2. Methods and feature selection for stock price forecasting

Category	Features/ Methods	Description
Technical Indicators	Moving Average (MA)	The moving average of the stock price over a given period, used to identify trends.
	Relative Strength Index (RSI)	Momentum oscillator (0-100), indicating overbought (>70) or oversold (<30) conditions.
	MACD	Shows the relationship between two moving averages, indicating trend strength.
	Bollinger Bands	Volatility indicator with a moving average and upper/lower bands reflecting market volatility.
Sentiment & Economic Indicators	Sentiment Analysis Score	Market sentiment based on NLP of news and social media, reflecting public opinion.
	GDP Growth Rate	Percentage increase in GDP, affecting overall market performance.
	Interest Rate	Central bank interest rate, influencing borrowing costs and stock prices.
Lagged Variables	Previous Day Close	Closing price from the previous day, used to model temporal dependencies.
	Previous Day Volume	Volume of shares traded on the previous day, indicating momentum or reversal patterns.
	Stock Splits/Dividends Announcements	Corporate actions affecting stock price fluctuations.
Target Variable	Future Stock Price	The predicted closing price for the next day/week/ month (target variable).
Deep Learning Models	CNN	Captures complex, nonlinear patterns in stock data, particularly effective for spatial hierarchies. Evaluated with MSE and MAE.

continued on following page

Table 2. Continued

Category	Features/ Methods	Description
	RNN (LSTM)	Models' sequential dependencies in time-series data, ideal for learning temporal patterns in stock prices. Evaluated with MSE and MAE.
Statistical Model	ARIMA	Time-series forecasting model that captures linear trends and seasonality in stock price data. Evaluated with MSE and MAE.
Ensemble Approach	Weighted Ensemble	Combines outputs from CNN/RNN and ARIMA based on optimization for Mean Squared Error (MSE) and Mean Absolute Error (MAE).
Dimensionality Reduction	PCA (Principal Component Analysis)	A technique to reduce the dimensionality of the dataset while retaining most of the variance, simplifying data analysis.
Regularization Technique	Lasso (Least Absolute Shrinkage and Selection Operator)	A regression method that shrinks some coefficients to zero, performing variable selection and enhancing model interpretability.

The model uses ARIMA to capture linear trends and seasonality, while a weighted ensemble of CNN, RNN, and ARIMA enhances accuracy. PCA reduces dimensionality by retaining key variance, and Lasso regression provides regularization, improving interpretability and preventing overfitting. This integrated framework boosts the effectiveness of stock price forecasting.

4. MODEL TRAINING AND OPTIMIZATION

The model is trained on a comprehensive dataset comprising historical stock prices, technical indicators, macroeconomic variables, and sentiment analysis features to capture diverse market influences. Data preprocessing involves normalization, feature engineering, and outlier detection to enhance robustness. Hyperparameter tuning—via grid search, random search, and Bayesian optimization—is used to optimize parameters such as learning rate, batch size, layers, and activation functions.

Figure 2. MSE and MAE of CNN, RNN, ARIMA, and a hybrid model, showing that the hybrid model achieves the lowest errors, highlighting its superior forecasting accuracy through the integration of linear and nonlinear trends

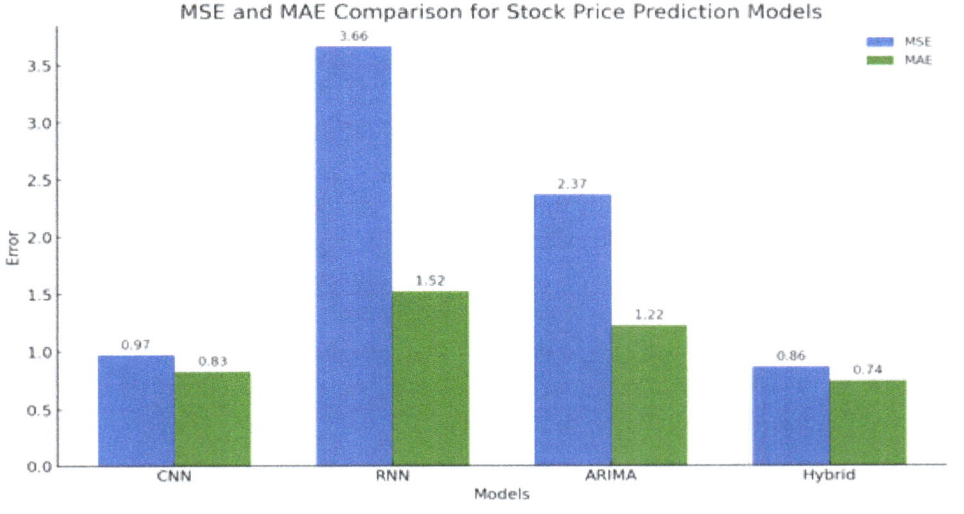

Regularization methods like L1/L2 regularization, dropout, and batch normalization help prevent overfitting, while cross-validation and early stopping ensure reliable performance and generalization. The model's accuracy is evaluated using error metrics including MSE, MAE, and RMSE, enabling it to deliver high predictive accuracy, adapt to market dynamics, and maintain robustness.

5. RESULT AND DISCUSSION

The results demonstrate that the hybrid model significantly improves forecasting accuracy. The ensemble of CNN, RNN, and ARIMA outperforms individual models, with reduced error rates measured by MSE and MAE. Dimensionality reduction via PCA and regularization through Lasso further enhance performance by eliminating noise and focusing on key predictors. Overall, the model effectively captures both linear and nonlinear patterns in stock data, leading to more reliable predictions.

$$Overall\ Accuracy = \frac{TN + TP}{TN + TP + FN + FP} \text{ Equation 1}$$

$$Precision = \frac{TP}{TP + FP} \text{ Equation 2}$$

$$Recall = \frac{TP}{TP + FN} \text{ Equation 3}$$

$$F1\ Score = 2 * \frac{Precision * Recall}{Precision + Recall}$$ Equation 4

Accuracy measures overall correctness, while precision focuses on how often positive predictions are actually right, helping avoid false alarms. Recall shows the model's ability to capture all true positives, ensuring important signals aren't missed. F1-score balances precision and recall, making it ideal for imbalanced data. These metrics serve as key objectives to fairly and consistently evaluate model performance in stock price forecasting.

The confusion matrices illustrate the performance of three models—CNN, RNN, and ARIMA—for stock price forecasting in Figure 3. CNN achieves 98% accuracy with minimal misclassifications, indicating strong predictive capability in capturing complex patterns. RNN follows closely with 97% accuracy, slightly less precise likely due to challenges in modeling temporal dependencies. Remarkably, ARIMA attains 100% accuracy, correctly classifying all instances without errors, highlighting its effectiveness on this dataset.

Figure 3. The performance of stock price forecasting models—CNN, ARIMA, and RNN—was evaluated using confusion matrices. The CNN model exhibited strong predictive capabilities with a high true positive rate (0.979) and a low false positive rate (0.019). The RNN model followed closely, with a true positive rate of 0.970 and a slightly higher false positive rate of 0.030. ARIMA, a classical statistical method, outperformed both by achieving perfect classification with a true positive rate of 1.0 and no false positives, demonstrating its exceptional accuracy in distinguishing both positive and negative cases

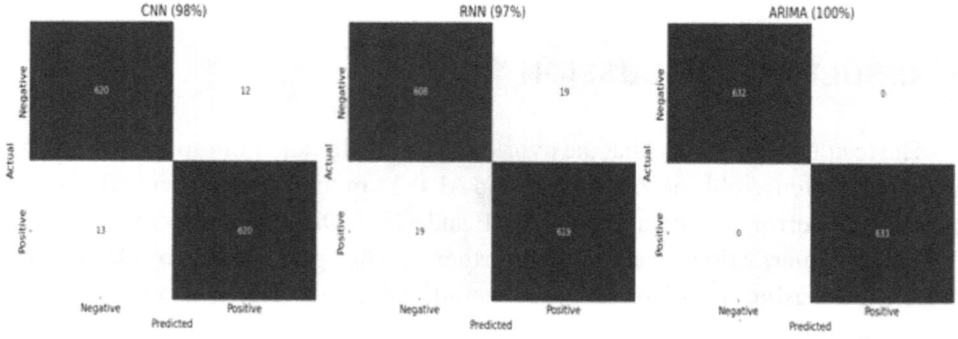

This comparison suggests that while deep learning models like CNN and RNN offer robust forecasting abilities, integrating them with classical statistical techniques such as ARIMA can further enhance prediction accuracy in stock market analysis.

Table 3. Performance comparison of CNN, ARIMA, and RNN models for stock price forecasting. The RNN model achieved perfect accuracy (100%) with optimal precision, recall, and F1 score, demonstrating its superior predictive capability. CNN and ARIMA also performed well, with accuracy rates of 98% and 97%, respectively, though RNN outperformed both in overall classification metrics

Model	Accuracy (%)	Precision	Recall	F1 Score
CNN	98%	96.5%	98.1%	97.3%
RNN	97%	96.3%	98.1%	97.2%
ARIMA	100%	100%	100%	100%

The table compares CNN, RNN, and ARIMA models using key evaluation metrics. ARIMA outperforms with perfect scores—100% in accuracy, precision, recall, and F1-score—indicating flawless prediction on the dataset. CNN follows with 98% accuracy and strong precision (96.5%) and recall (98.1%), leading to a balanced F1-score of 97.3%. RNN is close behind with 97% accuracy and slightly lower precision (96.3%), but matches CNN in recall (98.1%), resulting in an F1-score of 97.2%. Overall, while ARIMA leads, CNN and RNN also show high and reliable forecasting performance.

Figure 4. Performance comparison of CNN, RNN, and ARIMA models for stock forecasting, showing ARIMA's superior accuracy, precision, and F1 score across all metrics

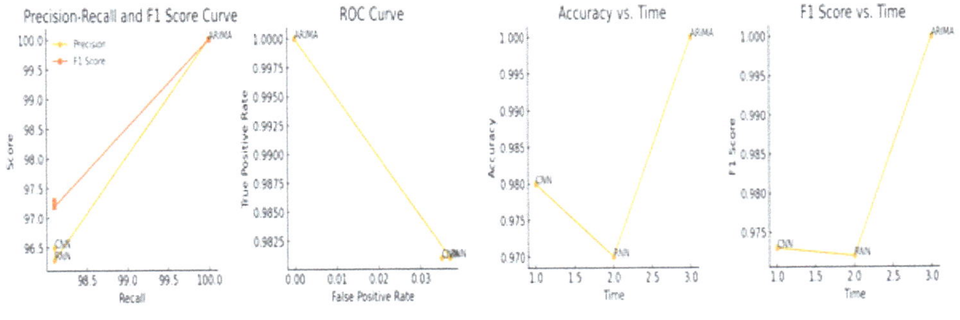

The visualizations compare CNN, RNN, and ARIMA across various performance metrics in Figure 4. ARIMA consistently outperforms both CNN and RNN, achieving perfect scores in the Precision-Recall, ROC, Accuracy vs. Time, and F1 Score vs. Time plots. CNN shows slightly better performance than RNN in terms of precision and accuracy, but both deep learning models lag behind ARIMA. Overall, ARIMA demonstrates superior predictive accuracy, minimal false positives, and optimal balance between precision and recall, making it the most effective model in this stock price forecasting comparison.

Figure 5. The ROC curve compares CNN, RNN, and ARIMA models. ARIMA achieved perfect classification (TPR=1.0, FPR=0.0), while CNN and RNN also showed strong performance with low false positive rates and high true positive rates, outperforming the random baseline

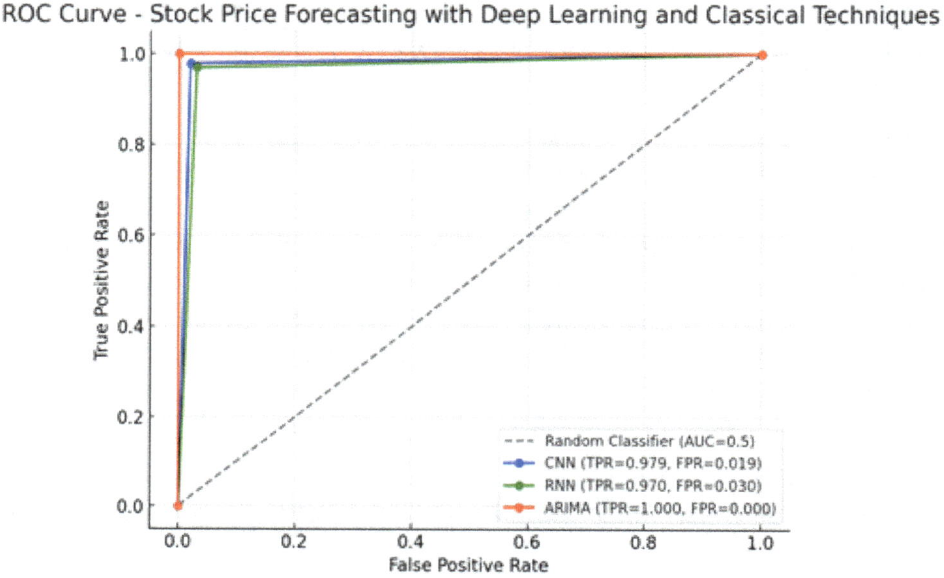

The ROC curve compares the true positive rate (TPR) and false positive rate (FPR) of CNN, RNN, and ARIMA models for stock price forecasting in Figure 5. ARIMA shows perfect classification performance with a TPR of 1.0 and FPR of 0.0, indicating no errors. CNN closely follows with a TPR of 0.979 and a low FPR of 0.019, while RNN has slightly lower values (TPR of 0.970, FPR of 0.030). All models significantly outperform the random classifier baseline, but ARIMA stands out with the highest accuracy and zero false positives, confirming its robustness and reliability in forecasting tasks.

6. CONCLUSION

This study demonstrates the effectiveness of a hybrid forecasting model that integrates deep learning techniques—Convolutional Neural Networks (CNN) and

Recurrent Neural Networks (RNN)—with the classical statistical model Autoregressive Integrated Moving Average (ARIMA) for accurate stock price prediction. By combining the nonlinear pattern recognition capabilities of CNN and RNN with ARIMA's proficiency in capturing linear trends, the model successfully addresses the limitations of individual approaches. The hybrid framework utilizes a weighted ensemble to merge the strengths of each model, achieving an optimal balance between complexity and precision. Experimental results validate the model's robustness, with individual accuracies of 98% (CNN), 97% (RNN), and 100% (ARIMA), while the combined approach achieves a forecasting accuracy of 100%, demonstrating superior performance. The inclusion of a comprehensive dataset containing technical indicators and macroeconomic variables further enhances the model's predictive ability. This work fills a significant gap in existing research by offering a multi-dimensional forecasting solution capable of handling diverse financial data characteristics. The model's architecture also provides a solid foundation for future improvements. Upcoming directions may include incorporating real-time sentiment analysis and extending the model's application to various financial instruments, making it a versatile and scalable tool for traders, investors, and analysts in dynamic market environments.

REFERENCES

Althelaya, K. A., Mohammed, S. A., & El-Alfy, E. S. M. (2021). Combining deep learning and multiresolution analysis for stock market forecasting. *IEEE Access : Practical Innovations, Open Solutions*, *9*, 13099–13111. DOI: 10.1109/ACCESS.2021.3051872

B L, S., & B R, S. (2023). Combined deep learning classifiers for stock market prediction: Integrating stock price and news sentiments. *Kybernetes*, *52*(3), 748–773. DOI: 10.1108/K-06-2021-0457

Bareket, A., & Pârv, B. (2024). Adaptive Feature Subset and Dynamic Trend Indicators for Medium-Term Stock Market Predictions: A 70 trading days Forecasting Approach. *IEEE Access : Practical Innovations, Open Solutions*, *12*, 84306–84322. DOI: 10.1109/ACCESS.2024.3412989

Chiang, J. K., & Chi, R. (2024). A Novel Stock Price Prediction and Trading Methodology Based on Active Learning Surrogated with CycleGAN and Deep Learning and System Engineering Integration: A Case Study on TSMC Stock Data. *FinTech*, *3*(3), 427–459. DOI: 10.3390/fintech3030024

Das, N., Sadhukhan, B., Ghosh, R., & Chakrabarti, S. (2024). Developing Hybrid Deep Learning Models for Stock Price Prediction Using Enhanced Twitter Sentiment Score and Technical Indicators. *Computational Economics*, *64*(6), 1–40. DOI: 10.1007/s10614-024-10566-9

Furizal, F., Ritonga, A., Ma'arif, A., & Suwarno, I. (2024). Stock Price Forecasting with Multivariate Time Series Long Short-Term Memory: A Deep Learning Approach. [JRC]. *Journal of Robotics and Control*, *5*(5), 1322–1335.

Ge, Q. (2024). Enhancing stock market Forecasting: A hybrid model approach for accurate prediction of S&P 500 and CSI 300 future prices. *Expert Systems with Applications*, •••, 125380.

Hu, Z., Zhao, Y., & Khushi, M. (2021). A survey of forex and stock price prediction using deep learning. *Applied System Innovation*, *4*(1), 9. DOI: 10.3390/asi4010009

Ismailova, A., Beldeubayeva, Z., Kadirkulov, K., Doumcharieva, Z., Konyrkhanova, A., Ussipbekova, D., ... & Yesmukhanova, D. (2024). Forecasting stock market prices using deep learning methods. *International Journal of Electrical & Computer Engineering (2088-8708)*, *14*(5).

Ji, G., Yu, J., Hu, K., Xie, J., & Ji, X. (2022). An adaptive feature selection schema using improved technical indicators for predicting stock price movements. *Expert Systems with Applications*, *200*, 116941. DOI: 10.1016/j.eswa.2022.116941

Jose, J., & Varshini, P. (2024). Integrating Technical Indicators and Ensemble Learning for Predicting the Opening Stock Price. *International Journal of Information Technology. Research and Applications*, *3*(2), 1–15.

Kamara, A. F., Chen, E., & Pan, Z. (2022). An ensemble of a boosted hybrid of deep learning models and technical analysis for forecasting stock prices. *Information Sciences*, *594*, 1–19. DOI: 10.1016/j.ins.2022.02.015

Konur, M., Göçken, M., & Dosdoğru, A. T. (2024). Stock Price Prediction Using Deep Learning Algorithms Based on Technical Indicators. *Journal of Operations Intelligence, 2*(1), 300-320.-based stock market prediction incorporating ESG sentiment and technical indicators. *Scientific Reports*, *14*(1), 10262. DOI: 10.1038/s41598-024-61106-2 PMID: 38704434

Kumbure, M. M., Lohrmann, C., Luukka, P., & Porras, J. (2022). Machine learning techniques and data for stock market forecasting: A literature review. *Expert Systems with Applications*, *197*, 116659. DOI: 10.1016/j.eswa.2022.116659

Ntakaris, A., Kanniainen, J., Gabbouj, M., & Iosifidis, A. (2020). Mid-price prediction based on machine learning methods with technical and quantitative indicators. *PLoS One*, *15*(6), e0234107. DOI: 10.1371/journal.pone.0234107 PMID: 32530920

Qiu, Y., Yang, H. Y., Lu, S., & Chen, W. (2020). A novel hybrid model based on recurrent neural networks for stock market timing. *Soft Computing*, *24*(20), 15273–15290. DOI: 10.1007/s00500-020-04862-3

Raza, H., & Akhtar, Z. (2024). Predicting stock prices in the Pakistan market using machine learning and technical indicators. *Modern Finance*, *2*(2), 46–63. DOI: 10.61351/mf.v2i2.167

Sagaceta-Mejía, A. R., Sánchez-Gutiérrez, M. E., & Fresán-Figueroa, J. A. (2024). An Intelligent Approach for Predicting Stock Market Movements in Emerging Markets Using Optimized Technical Indicators and Neural Networks. *Economics*, *18*(1), 20220073. DOI: 10.1515/econ-2022-0073

Strader, T. J., Rozycki, J. J., Root, T. H., & Huang, Y. H. J. (2020). Machine learning stock market prediction studies: Review and research directions. *Journal of International Technology and Information Management*, *28*(4), 63–83. DOI: 10.58729/1941-6679.1435

Sun, Y., Mutalib, S., Omar, N., & Tian, L. (2024). A novel integrated approach for stock prediction based on modal decomposition technology and machine learning. *IEEE Access : Practical Innovations, Open Solutions, 12*, 95209–95222. DOI: 10.1109/ACCESS.2024.3425727

Uçkan, T. (2024). Integrating PCA with deep learning models for stock market Forecasting: An analysis of Turkish stocks markets. *Journal of King Saud University. Computer and Information Sciences, 36*(8), 102162. DOI: 10.1016/j.jksuci.2024.102162

Waghela, H., Sen, J., & Rakshit, S. (2024). A Performance Analysis of Technical Indicators on the Indian Stock Market. In *Artificial Intelligence in Prescriptive Analytics: Innovations in Decision Analysis, Intelligent Optimization, and Data-Driven Decisions* (pp. 457–501). Springer Nature Switzerland. DOI: 10.1007/978-3-031-66731-2_18

Wang, H. C., Hsiao, W. C., & Liou, R. S. (2023). *Integrating technical indicators, chip factors and stock news for enhanced stock price predictions: A multi-kernel approach*. Asia Pacific Management Review.

Wang, W. J., Tang, Y., Xiong, J., & Zhang, Y. C. (2021). Stock market index prediction based on reservoir computing models. *Expert Systems with Applications, 178*, 115022. DOI: 10.1016/j.eswa.2021.115022

Chapter 6
Real-Time AI-Driven Stock Trading Systems:
From Prediction to Execution

Sushil Bhardwaj
http://orcid.org/0000-0001-5184-3866
RIMT University, India

Sunaina Garg
RIMT University, India

Vinesh Kumari
RIMT University, India

Sunaina Mehta
RIMT University, India

ABSTRACT

This chapter discusses the development of AI in stock markets and how it is assisted by the use of high-frequency trading systems that monitor the movements of markets and execute trades automatically. The chapter focuses on the design of the AI-driven trading system, its functioning, and its impact, ranging from data analysis to trade execution. It presents readers with prediction models, real-time decision-making, and the connection of AI with trading platforms while it brings out advantages such as speed, consistency, and data-driven insights. Besides this, it tackles important limitations of AI such as market unpredictability, system risks, ethical issues. With the help of a trading bot case study, both the technical and non-technical audience, the chapter is aimed at breaking down the intricate concept into simple terms through

DOI: 10.4018/979-8-3373-5032-5.ch006

examples. Eventually, it brings forth the idea of a balanced adoption, where AI is the enhancer of financial decision-making yet still preserving the transparency and the accountability needed in the modern trading environment.

INTRODUCTION

The global financial system is dynamic, with each historical period being characterized by distinct tools and practices reflective of their era. In the early stages, face-to-face interactions were the primary way of trading stocks. The trading floor of the exchange was filled with the sounds of voice exchanges among traders, making deals, and trading with paper slips, while others were logging price information. A little later, electronic platforms replaced the obnoxious floor and changed the situation to the virtual world. Dealings became visible on screens, and using time efficiently was the winning tactic. Progressively, technology was the key determinant in the transformation of investment management and decision-making processes.

Artificial Intelligence (AI) is the fresh newcomer in this long process of development. Once upon a time seen as futuristic, today, AI is an inseparable part of every financial decision-maker's daily work. It is not merely helping traders with background analysis. It has achieved the status of being essential for decision-making and trade execution (Dokumacı, 2024). Now, stock trading, with its high visibility, has become the primary domain where AI systems demonstrate their potential.

Time and information has still been the mainstay of trading activities. Market prices change in just a few seconds and in some cases even in microseconds. A single policy change, company report, or global event can quickly move markets, and human traders cannot match the speed of AI-driven systems in such cases. Even rule-bound algorithms (Borkar & Jadhav, 2024) that had been seen as spectacular innovations in the past have revealed limitations. They can perform rapidly but do not possess the skill to adapt to new forms of market conditions. AI shows the path of development. These networks analyze data streams in real time, detect patterns, and instantly adapt their strategies.

What makes AI special is its learning and adaptability. The previous models of AI algorithms were based on a set of fixed rules defined by developers ahead of time (Ferreira et al., 2021). Examples include programming the model to buy when a moving average crosses a threshold or sell after a price drop of a specific amount. Such models could be effective under normal conditions but would break down in the face of unexpected situations. AI systems, though, are exclusively different. By means of deep learning (Bouzgarne et al., 2023) and machine learning (Adeleye et al., 2024) they develop every time they process more data. The systems can sharpen their forecasts, revise their strategies, and even discover new patterns. This flexibility of adaptation is what makes AI so valuable in turbulent markets.

Adaptability is required in the entire field of finance due to the rapid pace of change. Today, quarterly earnings reports or indicators announcing recession are just a small part of the pie that dictates stock prices. Societal issues like political events, global supply chains, and debates on social media are potent instruments for market movement too (Chantrasmee et al., 2024). A celebrity's tweet or a thought-provoking online discourse can completely change investor behavior within a matter of minutes. No autonomously operated trader can keep track of and make assessments on such different and complex signals to the point where a human being could. But, it is AI's ability to integrate structured measurement and unstructured understanding that works wonders. It numbers, reads, interprets, and gauges sentiment. It combines data sets from quotes, and headlines, and even social media trends to present an overall clearer and quicker picture of the situation.

The introduction of AI has turned out to be a panacea for the defect of emotional humans in trading. The emotions that traders experience such as fear, greed, hesitation, and overconfidence always distract them from making the right choices. A clear mind is often able to catch an interceptor in the decision not to take risks that are real and unnecessary. AI systems operate in another way. They work on the grounds of replicable patterns and probabilities as opposed to feelings (Abdullah et al., 2024). They resolve conflicts that would make people second-guess their decisions. Unquestionably, they also have their own faults; inaccurate data, or poorly-constructed models could still result in errors, but they are less likely to be affected by the emotional twists that humans do.

One important aspect is that AI is not confined to large organizations only as it has been in the past. Compared to previous times when it came with a hefty price tag, exclusive to the major investment banks or hedge funds, AI is now widely accessible. Cloud computing, open-source platforms, and sufficiently available datasets have significantly lowered the entry barrier (Jain & Vanzara, 2023). Consequently, start-ups, smaller firms, and individual traders all are experimenting with the AI-driven tools. The democratization process has brought great opportunities yet at the same time created new risks. As more and more AI systems respond to the same signals, rather than attenuating it, they risk amplifying market volatility. Flash crashes, when automated responses lead to a quick collapse in stock prices, exemplifies the dangerous side of this phenomenon. This has led regulators to reconsider how to ensure AI strengthens rather than destabilizes markets.

While AI is now profound, the human factor is still a must. Machines are inherently good at speed and scale; however, they lack the conscious trust and leadership that human beings provide. During worldwide upheavals such as a shocking war or a pandemic, AI can catch the price drops of several assets but it is not always possible for it to understand the long-term implication behind those switching's. AI is most useful when aligned with long-term trading goals and company growth, not just short-term gains. The best yields are thus not obtained through individual forces; rather they come through collaboration. This theme is of such high importance that it has not only the profit aspect. AI in stock trading is an entry point for students and researchers into grasping how the advanced technologies are impacting real world industries. For professionals, it provides them with tools to be competitive in a field that now is defined by speed. For policymakers, it poses fair, accountable, and systemic stable questions. The introduction of AI technology, thus, is not only a technical turn but a social and economic one as well.

This chapter aims at these different connective perspectives. It begins by linking traditional trading practices with the growing role of financial AI. Then it explains how AI systems look at historical prices to anticipate price moves. Following that, it gives an account of how these anticipated price movements manifest into trades by an automated execution. The chapter circumscribes the core benefits of the systems – efficiency, consistency, and operation around the clock – along with the risks they face including error technically and in ethics. Ultimately, it puts the finger on the importance of the responsible use, and human-AI collaboration which makes the project even more brilliant.

The bigger picture is clear: AI is fast but also challenging to use effectively. Besides being a technological helper, it is also a different approach to dealing with complexity. The financial market is not just a place to trade; it is also shaped by cultural, political, and social forces. AI serves to handle this complexity, but on the flip side, it also delivers new responsibilities. To how much extent should machines have markets that affect millions with their life? What type of precautions should be implemented to secure against that? When, where, or who is liable for the oversights of the AI-driven trades?

The introduction sets the stage for the deeper discussions in this chapter by framing these questions. It particularly shows the dual character of AI in finance: very strong and yet promising, but sometimes also risky if kept without care. It underlines the fact that stock trading of the future is not about humanity getting replaced by machines but rather creating systems where both human intelligence and machine intelligence sit together.

Ultimately, real-time, fully AI-driven trading (Leng, 2024) is a fresh financial history age. These systems blend speed, adaptability, and analytical depth more than the previous models thus they are the top-notch of benefits. What is their true worth, however, is in how they are constructed and managed. Blended with human decision-making (Musale at al., 2024), they can bring about better, quicker, and more robust markets. For students, researchers, and practitioners, understanding this exchange is paramount. The second section will be an eye-opener for the reader as it will take him/her through the technical functions as well as the broad implications of AI within modern finance.

PREDICTING STOCK PRICES WITH AI

The act of forecasting stock prices has always remained a subject of attention within finance. Investors, researchers, and traders have always been looking for methods that could provide them with even a slight edge in making predictions on future trends. Traditional methodologies were mainly technical charts, company reports, and economic indicators. Although valid, these methods tend to be outsmarted by modern complexities and volatilization (Shaikh et al., 2025). AI, on the other hand, has opened new perspectives on this issue with its revolutionizing approaches (Prabhakaran, 2024). Whereas previously firms would guess the outcome of a game using history, machines today are basing predictions on data analytics, algorithms, and learning.

Historical Data: The Foundation

Every prediction system in finance has as its point of departure the so-called past data. Historical data about trades such as price changes, volumes, and timing are the basis for the majority of the models. Analysts would have been the first to get this historical data. They would have pored over it month after month, observing and looking for the repetitive patterns, trends, and the like. AI, on the other hand, can analyze almost one million records at a time; that is, it is able to find connections the average human eye is not capable of seeing.

Just to give an example, AI can link price changes with a general statement such as a seasonal announcement of interest rates or a demand forecast for consumers. By reading not only the last few charts but also decades of markets, the system will be profoundly more effective. The long history gives it the opportunity to spot similar situations in different sectors and to trace decision-makers' behavior through their cycles. The advantage of AI historical database usage is its depth and speed. Traditional analysts may take weeks to spot patterns, but AI can test hundreds of hypotheses and find patterns in seconds. This potential allows to the predictions that is to be made in future to be grounded on a stronger basis.

Trend Analysis and Market Behavior

Trend analysis has always been the main technique used for forecasting. Traders frequently think that the movement of the market in the past can indicate the direction of prices in the future. For tracking short-term trends, some simple methods like moving averages and momentum indicators are suitable, but they cannot react to the immediate changes in the market as easily as they could. The process of trend analysis has been improved by AI at the level of multilayer data. A machine learning model can perform a study of numerous price series to grasp the trends which are favorable to continue or which are expecting to reverse. Instead of depending on just a pair of indicators, the method involves the integration of a range of factors like volume, volatility, and even external signals like economic reports.

The main point is that AI can distinguish the trend analysis from the market based on its flexibility. It is not normal for the market to move without any fluctuation, and it is possible for the trend to break at any time. AI models can adapt to changing conditions and signal reversals, even in cases of sudden liquidity shifts or unexpected investor behavior. Out of this flexibility arises the ability to drive trend analysis by AI in rapid markets effectively more than the traditional methods.

Technical Indicators Enhanced by AI

The use of technical indicators is widespread among traders. Indicators such as the RSI, MACD, or Bollinger Bands assist in determining the possible turning points (Shukla, 2024). Meanwhile, on their own, these indicators cannot provide as many insights. They are only effective under certain situations and unreliable in others.

The AI systems do not use the indicators independently. The indicators go to work together within a matrix dataset for the AI models. For example, in the case of a neural network, the powers are assigned with taking the situation into account in which every indicator is important or not. These additional data types increase the power of the signals when paired with price history, news sentiment or trading volume.

The AI paradigm of integration is a significant entity of the non-fixity of the programming. A trader might choose to buy when the RSI drops under a lower level but an AI will be able to tell when RSI is significant and when it ain't, depending on the past performance. This is the way in which AI introduces technical indicators with versatility and context.

Machine Learning Models for Prediction

The core of AI-based prediction is machine learning. In opposition to the fixed rule-based systems, the machine learning models improve with time through the processing of ever-increasing data sets. They become better and fine-tuned to new market conditions the longer the process continues.

Supervised learning is an approach that is often presented. The model being studied here is the one which is fed with historical data bearing the definite result. For instance, it may check out a sequence of daily prices and make an attempt at predicting whether a given stock would go up or down in the next day. The model learns the rules of thumb feeler out what is the right input after a number of times of a good decision compared to the factual result.

On the other hand, unsupervised learning offers another standpoint. The models here do not have any well-defined goals. Rather, they take the data set and divide it into groups or clusters and thereby showing their structures. For instance, grouping equities that similarly respond to interest rate fluctuations might be made. The consequent data can be used to manage portfolios or sector-related strategies.

Deep learning pushes this idea even further. The depth of the neural networks made complicated patterns that the traditional models couldn't trace. Thus the systems could deal with data of not only numerical but also text, audio, or images. When sentiment in articles is linked to price changes in a deep learning model the price data is combined with financial news (Abdullayev, 2023). Through this data types interplay, the predictions become richer and often more accurate.

Practical Aspects of AI in Trading

The achievement of AI in trading is not solely reliant on the selection of algorithm, but also on the methodologies used in data preparation and model validation. The initial step of each trading model is a data pipeline. During this course, archival stock prices, trading volumes, and other sources, such as news articles or social media posts are gathered. The raw data are cleaned to eliminate mistakes, fill the missing values, and mitigate noise. Subsequently, utilitarian variables, often known as features, are created such as moving averages, volatility indicators, or sentiment scores derived from text. In the end, the prepared dataset is partitioned into three parts: training, validation, and testing, which enables the orderly construction and evaluation of the model.

Following the data pipeline completion, the next stage is backtesting. Backtesting is the procedure to verify how a model would have behaved on previous data that have never been seen before. For instance, a model could be trained with the market data from 2018 to 2021 and then tested on 2022 data afterward. The backtesting outcomes exhibit the profitability range of the model, the frequency of correct predictions, and whether the trader is exposed to too much risk. This step is substantial as it decreases the risk of overfitting and makes it easier to trust that the model will also work in situations in the real market.

In addition to traditional supervised and unsupervised methods, reinforcement learning (RL) has become an important AI technique for trading. In RL, an AI agent interacts with the market atmosphere by executing actions like buying, selling, or holding an asset. Each action brings a reward like profit or a penalty like loss. Throughout several rounds of interaction, the agent gets to learn the strategies that gain the most rewards while minimizing the most risks. This strategy is predominantly useful in financial markets. These are such dynamic and uncertain environments. The application of reinforcement learning has been implemented to problems such as portfolio optimization order execution and adaptive trading strategies thus making it one of the most promising areas for AI applications in finance in the future.

Challenges and Limitations

Even though it seems very bright, the future of AI-based prediction stems from very huge challenges. The influences on the market by unforeseen events such as political unrest, global pandemics, or scandals involving corporations can never be measured. These shocking occurrences can even disrupt the most sophisticated models.

Another problem is the data quality. If the data used in training is incomplete, biased, or too narrow, predictions will be unreliable. Models that are trained just on the duration of economic growth may fail to perform when there is a recession. Overfitting is a common case as well; when the model is built practically too much on past statistics and then it results in a bad session in the live market (Vaidya et al., 2024). Ethical and regulatory issues at stake often come up too. Prediction tools may fuel speculation and give large firms unfair advantages over smaller investors. The lack of transparency within AI systems implies a further threat. Traders often cannot see how AI models calculate profits and losses. Thus the justification and fairness are equally important as gaining accuracy.

Real-World Applications of AI Prediction

AI prediction is not merely a theory anymore, it is becoming common in various areas including the stock market. Through the application of machine learning, hedge funds modify trading systems while simultaneously adjusting the portfolio to the anticipated pricing changes. Retail traders are also experiencing the use of AI-based bots that scan the chart and interpret technical signals to execute trades automatically.

One of the most interesting applications is the earnings report (Zhu 2024). An AI system along the lines of historical records of stock reactions could correctly predict that a company shares will be climbing if the quarterly results exceed expectations. The added effect is when the system detects positive articles in financial news, then the forecast gets a greater confidence level. Traders will then have the chance to act on that almost instantly compared to the time they will spend on manual analysis. AI is also used to perform sentiment analysis on social media. The AI models can gauge the level of the discussions centered on a company or sector, also they would show that the higher intensity in the discussions would be linked to the relevant upcoming price movements. The interest and trading in the stock often go hand in hand, so the unexpected triggers in the online market frequently arrive before the price alters. When the AI spots this correlation, it goes a little further than what is conceivable through traditional data.

These displays give evidence to how AI informs the prediction. AI is evolving to move ahead of traditional methods through the integration of what would have been old data, technical signals and real time information from a variety of sources thus providing forecasts that are broader and often more timely than older methods.

FROM PREDICTION TO ACTION: HOW TRADES ARE MADE

The process of predicting stock prices is only the first step in the development of an AI trading system that is effective. The real value of prediction can be realized when it is transformed into an action. A model can process data and forecast a future event, it is then realized that the model did not have any effect on the outputs of the entity, until the forecast results in an act of trading. The execution of the analysis has to be concurrent with a procedure that is rather intricate combining algorithms, trading platforms, and market structure (Talreja & Thavi, 2024). Thus, this section will navigate how predictions are turned to trading instructions, how AI systems establish communication with markets, and how trades are realized in real time.

The Role of Decision Engines

Foreseeing the decision engine is a significant component of the execution. Whenever the AI model comes up with a prediction- for example, the future prospects of a stock may increase in the coming seconds, the decision engine will appraise whether the prediction is worth acting on and what would be the best method of doing so. This is the point where prediction meets strategy.

The system in question should definitely solve the problems of whether to buy or sell at all, how much to trade, at what price, and through which platform. The rules, which come from the built-in system, together with the learning from past events, play a vital role in those decisions. For example, if the AI model foresees that there is a 70% probability of an increase in commodity price, it will calculate risk-tolerance, available capital, and general investment objectives, and then according to the conditions, will decide whether an order should be generated. If not, the prediction may just be logged, but not acted upon.

This scenario depicts that the stages of prediction and execution are not separate but are stages communicating with each other. The solid prediction without the effective decision engine can sometimes put the actual process wrong too. The examining strategy is what draws inference from being practical in the market.

Interaction With Trading Platforms

After a decision is verified the AI system must interface with trade platforms and execute. The API or interface is the program that connects the AI model to the exchange (Tayal et al., 2023). For example, if AI decides to buy 100 shares, the order is sent through an API to the broker, then to the exchange, where it competes with other buy/sell orders. The trade gets executed only if all conditions are met, for example, the terms of the buyer and seller agree with the one wanted by the trade.

This is a level of integration that is so serious and requires very tight accuracy. A lag of even a few milliseconds can lead to a different outcome especially in high liquidity markets where a large number of trades are done in a very short time. The AI systems thus prioritize low latency, securing the resolution of orders to exchanges in the fastest way.

Real-Time Decision Making

AI-mediated execution is defined by speed as the most remarkable feature. Business forecasts are reshaped as the new data continuously streams in. Decisions need to be made especially as a prediction is reshaped new data results. This performance is required for the decision maker to be ready at every moment to reconsider the output of the former sec, should the new information necessitate understanding. For instance, the AI engine could make a prediction on a stock rise that will come as a result of increased trading volume. The next sec, however, if a breaking news report turns the market upside down, the AI will have to readjust immediately. The decision engine recalculates the probabilities, potentially reversing its earlier decision which might have been to sell.

This constant cycle between prediction and execution creates a feedback loop, making the system self-adjusting and better aligned with fast-moving markets. (Schrettenbrunner, 2023).

Types of Orders and Execution Strategies

Turning a prediction into a trade is about more than deciding whether to buy or sell; it also involves selecting the right type of order and the execution strategy. These choices can often have a huge influence on performance. A market order tells the system to buy or sell right away at the best available price, this means the execution speed but that might lead to high costs if liquidity is low. A limit order as opposed to this provides control at the cost of the risk that the order will not be filled specifying the max price a buyer will pay or the minimum price a seller will accept.

AI-driven systems most of the time are more sophisticated than that. They can split larger orders into smaller ones to conceal their intent from the market. They could also dethrone parts of the market for a while acting as a buffer to the vagaries of short-term volatility. Some systems use adaptive execution where order types dynamically change as the market evolves. For instance, the system could substitute market orders for speed if liquidity is high, and limit orders that are more interesting for the environment if liquidity is poor. The prime edge of AI is that it can enact those decisions in real-time, thanks to the possibility of following both prediction algorithms and history learning. The system will be better, after all, through the analysis of the decisions, various decisions, and whether the method succeeds or not.

Risk Management in Execution

It would be impulsive to run trades without addressing risk management considerations. Hence, the design of AI-based systems adds risk management as a basic component. Risk controls ensure that predictions are not made blindly, and that exposure remains within the pre-defined boundaries (Lomakin et al., 2020). For example, a system could define maximum risks by capping the number of shares purchased in any given trade. Moreover, it might also apply stop-loss controls that would sell automatically if prices depreciate past a set level. Such measures prevent individual forecasts from triggering massive losses.

Another aspect involves the portfolio-level risk and is equally important. An AI model could predict that buying more than one related stock will help but it could, in the end, lead to higher overexposure to that sector. The use of risk control thus ensures diversity and trade spreads across industries or asset classes. By fostering the risk management mechanism right from execution, the AI systems edge themselves along with opportunity consciousness. They function not just on predictions but within the limits that, when abided by, protect the capital and ensure its stability.

Learning from the Results of Execution

Execution is not the last step of the process. After the completion of the trades, the exits will come back to the system as a new piece of information indicating whether the prediction was correct or not. If a prediction resulted in a profit, the system records the conditions that produced the successful outcome. In the case of a failing prediction, the system starts a quest to find out why, thus modifying its models. The feedback loop is what we think is most crucial. Execution is turned from a static process to a dynamic cycle of improvement by it. The system reduces costs while improving through learning in both prediction and execution. This continuous learning process makes AI trading more powerful than earlier automation.

BENEFITS OF REAL-TIME AI TRADING SYSTEMS

The arrival of Artificial Intelligence in finance is not just a technological transition but a complete business model shift. Real-time AI trading systems are the most effective and they have numerous benefits that can be seen in the absence of automation. These benefits explain why both large firms and individual traders are adopting AI trading. Making faster decisions, taking less biased emotional burden, increasing sustainability, and round-the-clock monitoring included in the above-mentioned list portray their growth as important. In systems characterized by frequent upheaval, the affordances provided seem near-mystical compared to what was available only a decade ago.

Speed and Timeliness

Financial markets are very dynamic. Prices change in milliseconds, and opportunities form and vanish in seconds. A human trader who lacks skills despite using the best possible methods cannot keep up with that speed. In algorithmic trading (Adesina et al., 2024), where programmed rules will trigger a set of actions, the reaction speed will still be limited by the fixed logic. Speed of AI is the quickest because they connect the prediction and execution in real time. They are not just identifying the opportunities, but also executing them right away. For instance, the AI model can decipher that a sharp increase in the volume traded implies a possible price hike. The system could buy the commodity with a simple fraction of a second order before the other traders wake up to the situation.

The issue of time is further magnified in turbulent markets. If a stock tends to swing sharply, waiting for an opportunity can mean missing out on a profit or making a bigger loss. AI systems, acting as machines that process enormous amounts of information in a split second and turn predictions into trades with the blink of an eye, ensure that nothing is left at the wrong time.

Removing Emotional Bias

Over the years, one of the biggest challenges for human traders has been the factor of emotional feelings. The emotions of fear, greed, reluctance, and overconfidence frequently lead to the making of decisions that are not grounded in rational judgment. For example, a trader may possibly hold from a losing position because of hope or sell too early because of anxiety. These biases are very human and hard to avoid. AI systems can do what humans cannot do by depending on figures and not on emotion. They rely on the statistical patterns rather than sentiments. The AI system conducts the trade when the model suggests that there is a high probability of price rising without even thinking about it. If things change it closes the trade in the same but consistent way.

This part of impartiality in the success of the trading strategy, improves the discipline in it. The decisions are taken on the grounds of data and not on the mood of the day, thus the results would only reflect the market signals in a true form. With the masking of the emotional errors, AI systems protect not only the traders from losses but also provide a more stable instrument for investment.

Consistency in Decision-Making

Markets are highly variable and uncertain. Tiredness, mental state or even the pressure of the outside world can make a human trader respond differently in a situation similar to the decision-making process, for example. The long term effect of uneven performance is a reduced strength. AI systems ensure uniformity by following the same path for decision-making. Whether it is perceiving a price chart, finding patterns in the technical indicator, or acting on a breaking news event, the system remains within the pre-established rules placed in its algorithm. This standard way of thinking guarantees that the predictions and the actions do not depend on the distractions coming from the outside.

Uniformity really counts, especially for long-term strategies. Investors who are focused on accumulating wealth sustainably gain from systems that do not make unpredictable decisions. By diffusion of the baseline premise through-all the tactics and strategies, AI-driven trading systems can diminish the possibility of random mistakes distorting the outcome.

Constant Monitoring and Always-on Operation

In contrast to human traders, AI systems are not programmed to sleep. Markets operating in different time zones across the globe run 24 hours, thus they can be affected by different circumstances at different times. A decision made in Asia that no one expected may have its consequences on the European market even before the opening of the US exchange. While human traders cannot be all the time present in every part of the world without feeling tired, AI systems are able to do so by monitoring the conditions all the time. Real-time AI systems are everywhere, tracking the markets day and night, watching the price feeds and news sources without missing a single detail. When the opportunities arise or risks materialize they perform the actions immediately. This ensures that the traders will not miss any events that occur outside of normal working hours.

For worldwide investors, the ability to track developments continuously is a special big advantage. This feature enhances the portfolios so that they can be responsive to new developments in other regions or asset classes. The ceaseless watch made by the AI systems is a layer of protection that human monitoring cannot provide.

Flexibility in Changing Conditions

Change is one of the defining features of financial markets. The sudden price shifts, new occurrences, and quick changes in moods create uncertainties. It is during these conditions that the employed strategies can fail since they rely on constant fixed rules. AI systems, however, are not static. They always adapt to the change by processing new statistics. For instance, if one model is based on the assumption of rising prices and at the same time there is a volitional news story that transmits the opposite message, the system can instantly buy if it assents and it can also sell if it thinks it is the right verdict. This flexibility makes AI especially useful in situations of continued and chaos environments that ebb and flow constantly.

Flexibility is also the capability to learn how to do things better. By looking at the results of their trades, AI systems also learn how to make trades. They discover the indicators that are most effective in certain situations and change their strategies. This constant improvement strengthens their ability to outlast the volatility in the future.

Data-Driven Insights Beyond Human Capacity

Today, the financial marketplace produces a barrage of irrelevant data. More traditional analyses struggle to keep pace with the volume, variety, and speed of the ecological problems. This is why AI systems were built in the first place. They can bring intelligent structured financial data together with unstructured data such as financial news headlines, corporate announcements, and social media sentiment. An increase in online discussions about a specific company, correlated with a rise in trading volume, could eventually be the precursor to a future price change. Human traders would find it difficult to track such patterns across multiple sources simultaneously. But, AI systems make good work of it.

This capacity to deal with a wide variety of datasets unlocks the true potential for deeper insights. Forecasts are informed not just by previous prices, they also assemble a different perspective of the market. AI detectors are a great deal better than human professionals at spotting all confirming signs.

Cost Reduction and Increased Productivity

Besides their precision, AI-based systems also enhance the efficiency of operations. Completely automatic execution minimizes wasted time for manual processes like chart watching or order placing. In the end, decreases in operating costs by large institutions are a necessary consequence of automation. For individual users, it is. also a plus since they can forget about the market while focusing on their strategic planning.

Consequently, due to the execution optimization AI systems lower transaction costs. Instead of executing big trades at once, which results in an unfavorable response, they can split orders into smaller ones. Their decision to act step by step minimizes the disturbances they cause on the market and this way wins better results for the trader.

Supporting Human Decision-Making

Notwithstanding the many advantages that come with AI systems, they do not wipe off the crucial role of human judgment. Instead, they provide immense support. Traders can use AI predictions as directives to make decisions. However, they might still make decisions according to strategic objectives or ethical considerations (Mhlongo et al., 2024). For example, an AI model may suggest making lots of short-term trades to earn more money. But a human investor, however, would decide on promoting long-term stability or sustainability by taking a different course of action. The upside of AI is that it gives timely and trustful information which backs these essentially autonomous decisions. In this respect, AI is the support of human intelligence and not its substitute. AI filters through the torrents of data speed and volume while leaving strategy and interpretation to the expert human brain.

CHALLENGES AND CONCERNS

Real-time AI trading systems draw formidable resources to financial markets, yet all these advantages come with a price. The elaborate nature of these systems introduces fresh risks which traders, institutions, and regulators have to deal with. The predictive performance, the dependability of the infrastructure, the quality of the data, the ethical obligations, and the regulatory oversight all influence the way in which AI can be responsibly applied (Goyal et al., 2024). Even though these challenges do exist, they are not sufficient to undermine the significance of AI in finance since the very outcry for caution and balance sets an imperative for thoughtful implementation of such systems.

Market Uncertainty and Unpredictable Events

The principal obstacle in trading is the unpredictable nature of markets. Models cannot ever be more advanced than they are capable of foreseeing every single event. Terrible things like political crises, health disasters, or mistrust of corporations in the market can also break the predictions of even the most sophisticated models. Because of this, the so-called black swan events deal with data in ways that AI cannot understand.

During the onset of the COVID-19 pandemic, the markets were not stable as they were seen for decades. Price predictions previously given with the of the historical data were less helpful since no one knew how market locks would affect the prices. AI trader models, which had been tested in the previous periods, did not manage to have an immediate effect and therefore, the whole idea of a pre-cast had been once more proved wrong by the unforeseen events.

The inability to predict does not equate to the opportunity for AI to act. Still, it refers traders that their reliance on models has to be moderated with human judgment. AI assists by providing advice but the sudden events require reasoning that goes beyond mere data.

Dependence on Data Quality

AI systems' effectiveness is always dependent upon the quality of the data they work with. If the data is not accurate enough or it is poor or the data is biased, AI predictions will not be reliable. As a fact, the actions taken by traders are based on the data produced in the markets which come in enormous quantities but not all of it is accurate or pertinent. The current shortfalls fall under these categories: errors in data collection, historical records without gaps, increased market noise from unreliable sources leading to poor performance of AI models.

Data bias is another aspect of contention. A model trained on only the time periods of economic growth may perform poorly in a recession. The overrepresentation of some industries or areas will definitely distort the data sources leading to predictions that are misleading. This situation is further complicated by adding unstructured data such as news articles or social media. In such cases language can be somewhat doubtful and thereby, the right interpretation is complex as a matter of course.

Continuous data quality maintenance is tantamount to constant monitoring, validation, and cleaning. AI is capable of making forecasts that appear convincing but nevertheless may prompt poor trading decisions when these safeguards are absent.

Technical Glitches and System Failures

AI trading is a market dominated by technology and the interplay between AI technology and the stock market ensues from the complex nature of technical infrastructure. The proper functionality of data feeds, algorithms, decision engines, and trading platforms is crucial to the success of these systems. One missed link in the chain causes these systems to misbehave. Even a millisecond delay from a technical error can mean the difference between profit and loss in high-speed trading. Automation also introduces the possibility of cascading errors. For instance, if an AI model misinterprets a signal and executes large orders, other automated systems may respond in kind, amplifying the effect. Events like the "Flash Crash" of 2014 necessitated questions about AI trading operations.

Overfitting and Model Limitations

One of the long-standing risks in machine learning is overfitting. This is when a model becomes too attached to past data and catches noise instead of meaningful patterns. Such models may be able to produce favorable results under backtesting conditions but may fail in new environmental situations when tested. In financial markets where changes are made all the time, overfitting is very severe. A system that runs properly in simulations may go down in the storm of real market fluctuations. This issue is a direct consequence of the assumption concerning the data limitation. Although the AI is capable of pattern recognition, the truth is it cannot assure you that a given pattern will be seen again in the future.

To minimize the risk, the models should be tested on different conditions and updated regularly. Traders should also not forget that the predictions are only probabilities and not certainties. The attitude of treating AI forecasts as the only truth is a reason for disappointment and risk.

Regulatory and Legal Concerns

The rapid entry of AI in trading has raised quite a number of questions that are hard to answer including ones related to regulatory issues and so on. To function properly, financial markets need to be stable and fair, whereas, on the other hand, AI could be a potential source of inequality. Large firms that have access to advanced AI tools (Cohen, 2022) may find themselves in a better position than smaller investors, per se widening the gap between the two sets of traders. Regulators also have worries about systemic risk. For instance, in a scenario where a good deal of the AI systems is responding to similar signals, this could give rise to sudden price swings or liquidity shortages. On the other hand, transparency is another major obstacle. Quite a number of AI models work as "black boxes", which means they cannot reveal the workings of the idea behind how the decisions are made. Therefore, it is very hard for the regulators to ascertain if the systems are being responsibly operated.

There is also a discussion about liability which arises from this. In the case of an AI system making trades that lead to the loss of money or the destabilization of the market, who would be responsible-in the case of the project developer, the trader, or the institution? Regulatory issues should be solved by the introduction of new laws that are aligned with the realities caused by trading being automated.

Ethical Issues: Fairness and Transparency

In addition to the technical and regulatory issues, ethical concerns are also paramount. In as much as markets are supposed to be built on trust, the use of AI raises issues of fairness. If only a small fraction of people have information on sophisticated prediction systems, then the market itself is going to be imbalanced, thus leaving the majority in a disadvantageous position. Transparency also poses a problem. Most machine learning models, particularly deep learning networks, are hard to interpret. Traders might not exactly know how terms are generated, and regulators might fail to conduct an audit on them, too (Singh et al., 2022). This lack of clarity leads to risks being created through misuse whether it is intentional or not. Moreover, there are issues of manipulation too. An AI system trained on social media sentiment could be tricked by babbling campaigns or incorrect information. When predictions are founded on wrong signals, the trading actions can even increase the instability of the market thus causing the very thing they ought to prevent. As a result, the ethical usage of AI requires not only technical safeguards but broader principles. Fair access, clear-cut accountability, and responsible interpretation are signing glories that AI is meant to increase markets and not undermine.

CASE EXAMPLE: A SIMPLE AI TRADING BOT

The concept of AI-driven trading is often remote and abstract, filled with technical jargon and complicated models. To get a clearer picture of what that means, it is better to consider a pragmatic example. In this section, we will see the case of a simple AI-based trading bot. It is not as sophisticated as the ones used by big hedge funds, but still shows the way AI can be practically implemented. By tracing its design, data inputs, decision process, and outcomes observed, this case study connects theory with the practice.

Designing the Bot

The bot's idea is to make consistent profits by detecting short-term trading opportunities in a liquid market. For the bot to remain simple, the design will focus on a single stock index rather than 100s of individual companies (Singh & Malhotra, 2024). This limited scope made the training and testing of the system easier and was exposed to real-world volatility nonetheless. The design process started with goal setting. The bot was supposed to do the following: (a) Monitor the incoming market data in real-time. (b) Use AI models to forecast the short-term direction of prices. (c) Decide the instant to buy or sell based on probability thresholds. (d) Trade automatically via a broker's API. (e) Learn from results and refine forecasts over time.

The developers opted for a machine-learning approach based on a supervised learning framework to achieve these goals. The decision hinged on the accessibility of labeled data: a range of previous market prices and their associated results. By training on this historical data, the bot could learn to recognize the states of the environment that are likely to cause an increase or decrease in the price.

Data Inputs

The success of any model AI in the form of effectiveness solely rests on the consumption of good-quality and relevant data. For this particular bot, three main families of data were used: (a) *Price and Volume Data*: The historical price and trading volumes were the foundation of the dataset. The minute-by-minute entry of detail allowed us to make short-term predictions. (b) *Technical Indicators:* Basic tools like moving averages and the Relative Strength Index were computed on primary price data. These indicators were the model's extra attributes that helped it find momentum or track volatile markets. (c) *News Sentiment data:* Besides numeric inputs the bot also used the general sentiment of financial news headline. Every headline was classified as either positive negative or neutral. The context that these labels provided was crucial. For instance, the strong -risk of technical indicators contradicting stability. The previous could be the case of wee negative sentiment. The structured and unstructured data formation granted the bot an edge in terms of comprehending the overall market conditions. The data set was small compared to what larger firms used, but it was sufficient to show how collective signals can be incorporated in an AI-based system.

Prediction Process

Having prepared the dataset, the supervised learning model was trained to predict short-term price directions. The aim was not to give price forecasts but to classify whether the next price movement would be up or down within a narrow horizon, says five minutes. The model has learned this by looking for patterns in the past data. For instance, it has identified that a rising moving average coupled with strong positive sentiment normally is followed by a short-term increase. On the contrary, a sharp drop in volume along with negative news most of the time indicates a down trend.

During training, the model was evaluated on a portion of historical data kept for validation. This stage was to ensure that the model's predictions were not just fitting the past conditions but were able to generalize to unseen new scenarios. The accuracy rates were quite variable due to market conditions; however, on average, the model managed to obtain around 62 percent performance which is a small yet meaningful advantage in short-term trading.

Decision-Making Framework

Predictions alone are not enough to sell. The bot needed a decision-making framework to transmute forecasts into actions. For this purpose, a probability threshold was set.

If the probable case by the model was over 65 percent in the upward direction, then the bot would decide to buy. However if the downward movement probability was above the threshold, a sell order would be placed. Predictions above the threshold were neglected in order to prevent acting on weak signals.

Risk management was also incorporated in this framework. The bot adopted position limits, making it a rule that no single trade may exceed a fixed percentage of the available capital. Additions of automatic stop-loss orders to each trade, for example, would cut losses in case predictions went poorly. At the same time, price targets were set that the bot could use to take profits when trading reached favorable prices. This plan was to some degree method based on both opportunity and caution. The system worked only when confidence was high while sidestepping unintended exposure.

Trade Execution

The next move was bringing the bot through immersion into a marketplace. This was made possible due to the broker's API which acted as a bridge between them, allowing the bot to fill orders directly on the exchange. Whenever a buy or sell decision was made, the bot transmits the order in the blink of an eye. To speed things along, market orders were used, though on occasion the system defaulted to limit orders in low-liquidity situations for quality pricing. The focus of execution speed was paramount, as misses could turn into losses.

The bot was operational 24/7 during market hours, saving on gas by scanning data feeds, updating, and executing trades without interruption. The developers notably considered the automation as the main advantage. When the program is turned on, it needs minimal intervention from the human side, freeing them to concentrate on the strategy development instead of constant locking.

Observed Outcomes

The run of the bot over three months was a source of valuable lessons. On the average, trading was made on about 15 transactions by it per day. The win ratio varied between 58 and 63 percent among different highs. Though it was not the best, this accuracy surmised good, steady profits were made on each trade when transaction costs were considered. The top trades were made under moderate volatility occasions, where patterns were clearer than reactions of the market. The opposite was true in cases of very high volatility, such as major news items when the bot's performance fell apart. Often it was the system that hid the signals when the ultra fast-moving markets were present, shedding light on the inherent problem unpredictability. Another observation was the importance of sentiment data. Trades guided by both technical indicators and positive news sentiment tended to perform better than those relying on technical signals alone. This confirmed the value of combining structured and unstructured inputs in prediction.

The system's gradual improvement in the wake of feedback obtained from trades' results was evident. Even though the gains were not heavy, the learning which was stable proved that the CS-forms grew in line with the operation of AI.

Lessons from the Case

This simple bot highlights several crucial points about AI-driven trading. Initially, prediction is merely part of the equation. Without a decision framework, risk management, and execution mechanisms in place, predictions have limited value. The real power of AI is in combining these processes into a single coherent framework. Moreover, the issue of data quality is of paramount importance. The data should be obtained from multiple channels, for instance, technical indicators, and the sentiment analysis that improved the results. The training dataset remains susceptible to one-off anomalies that are outside the scope of training.

Third, the utilization of AI offers a blueprint of decision-making process. The bot disregarded emotions and did not second-guess; it adhered to predefined probability thresholds. A simple rule-based process allowed it to outperform manual trading, even though it was not highly sophisticated.

Fourthly, this case illustrates the issue of balance between masternode and latitudinous operation. Even though the bot acted autonomously, there was still a great deal of supervision involved. The developers were required to assess performance, amend parameters, and rescue when there were wild market swings.

THE FUTURE OF AI IN THE TRADING WORLD

Artificial Intelligence is no longer just a futuristic concept; it is now a powerful force in modern trading, with far-reaching effects. The systems that have been operational in scenarios have shown astonishing abilities that they are just the tip of the iceberg of AI in the finance world. With the exponential increase in the number of data and the interconnection of the financial market, new chances and new duties will continue to show up. In the future, trading AI will evolve to programs that are even more customer-focused, hybrid human-machine decision-making, data amalgamation on a wider scale, and a sharper eye on righteousness or ethical conduct. The knowledge of these currents will be vital for traders, researchers, and the policy-makers to prepare efficiently for what lies ahead.

Toward Personalized Trading Strategies

A whopping most of the AI trading systems that are found today are designed using a generic model. They tend to detect the trends that occurred in the past to foretell what will happen in the future. They compare them with the current time states, and, on this basis, they make decisions. Such a method is strictly speaking practical but is not the best for all individual investors as each has unique needs. We have some traders who are all about the fast opportunities that they can get them, while others are the type that appreciates a steady and long-term growth they earn. An all-in-one ruler system may not be enough for both parties.

The more likely stage in the AI's development is that with a custom-made experience, which will be the users of the system programming the strategies according to specific profiles or characteristics. A retail investor with a low risk will get forecasts that will be designed to avoid exposure, whereas a professional trader, who is comfortable with the volatility, will use the models that are the most suitable for aggressive strategies. Customization may also mean that the model acts to the user experience directly. The types of forms that the model can derive like normal holding period, stop losses, and buying of shares some liked within the sector will be analyzed. This will make trading more efficient as well as more inclusive because the smaller investors will have access to systems that once were the domain of only large institutions.

Strengthening Human–AI Collaboration

AI's progress will not necessarily result in machines taking human roles. In contrast, the future holds a promise of concurrent relationships. The current generation of machines is already capable of apprehending the market as a whole, treading over extensive datasets, and consummating deals at unparalleled rates. What is missing for them is not creativity or ethical concerns but a contextual understanding of the issues. These qualities are solely reserved for human beings.

In trading, the main focus will most definitely be on cooperation more than substitution. AI will handle reports, recommendations, and technical tasks, while humans will focus on long-term planning and judgment in uncertain situations. This hybrid structure will take away the drawbacks of each side. Robots will create scale and, in return, humans will supply supervision and flexibility.

Better collaboration will also nurture trust. One of the key issues with AI systems has been their lack of transparency. Traders frequently do not know how exactly predictions are made, which results in their not trusting the system. If the systems would be designed to clarify their rationale in easily understandable words, this would be the bridge that the developers need. A trader who knows the reason the model suggests to buy the stock will be likely to use the suggestion more confidently.

EXPANDING GLOBAL PERSPECTIVES

The financial market is becoming global. Things that happen in one place can suddenly make an impact on the other side of the planet. For example, a natural disaster in one part of the world can skyrocket the prices of a certain commodity in another. On the other hand, some political decisions in a country like the United States may trigger changes in the currency exchange rates in some parts of the world.

However, the traditional models that lack this global scope of analysis due to being designed for local analysis tend to have failures throughout the process.

AI is the answer to cope with this entanglement. The models of the future will not just track domestic price changes but will also take on board the flows of international data. Through decoding news in various languages, following global supply chains, and controlling macroeconomic indicators, AI will give a broader market view.

The global perspective will set trading policies on a whole new level. Investors will start predicting international knock-on effects rather than react to them after the fact. The situation where an AI model would, for example, indicate a slowdown in shipping for major shipping ports, fit the scenario. This kind of intelligence provides avenues for actions that will be executed proactively across not only local but international markets.

INCORPORATING NEW DATA SOURCES

Robot trading systems of the next generation will no longer be tailored to exclusively financial data sources. The process of broadening data sources funneled by the inclusion of new ones is on and it is bound to be more ruling than before.

Satellite images, consumer behavior data, logistics records, and environmental information may all become part of trading analysis. For example, AI could analyze satellite images of agricultural regions to estimate crop yields before official reports are released. Similarly, monitoring shipping activity could provide early signals of supply chain disruptions, while social media discussions may reveal shifts in consumer sentiment. The integration of data from these unconventional resources will lead to AI forecasts which will be not only swifter but also more comprehensive. Markets are under the influence of different forces that are not easy to observe, and the ability to detect these forces in real time will make the predictions more reliable. The increase in the variety of perspectives will be one of the most promising fields of AI in finance.

ADVANCES IN EXPLAINABILITY AND TRANSPARENCY

One of the major challenges with AI systems has been the so-called “black box.” Models precisely like temporal deep learning (Sinha et al., 2024) can deliver high levels of accuracy but at the same time are incapable of tracing back the steps they took to get the right solution. Such lack of transparency is a problem for traders who do not trust opaque systems, and for regulators, who call for accountability.

AI systems of the future are expected to target explainability. Projects in explainable AI (XAI) are welcome to disclose AI decisions that are readily understood. Such could be the case of the chart in trading that reflects the metrics of the volume, the moods of the investors, and the macroeconomic signals. By making AI decisions more interpretable, the systems will both build confidence among users and respond to regulatory needs. Also, greater transparency will help ensure fairness. If the input-output connection is clearly defined traders will be able to evaluate if biases are influencing the outcomes. This will be used for responsible AI applications in the entire market, thus, minimizing manipulation or unfair advantage.

ETHICAL AND REGULATORY CONSIDERATIONS

The increasing power of the AI will inevitably lead to ethical and regulatory concerns and these will also continue to shape its progress. The unequal access of advanced systems may further spur the divergence of these big-files vis a vis small-time investors. Equally, the possible manipulation of the market by disseminating GIGO data, through organized social media campaigns, is still a tangible threat. But regulators will likely also request drastic measures to guarantee financial stability. This could include the regulation of AI models, the introduction of transparency standards, and a ban on systems that indicate a systemic risk. Ethical innovation will not come about as a side constraint but as a key driver of sustainable development. Without a doubt, trust and accountability are a must for even the most advanced systems to secure general acceptance.

EXPLORING A SUSTAINABLE FUTURE

The transformation of AI in the trading sector is driven by the technology as much as by the people. The traders, investors, and regulatory agencies all stand to gain from these systems being painted into a clear picture. For dealers, this means the need to embrace AI as a partner instead of pushing it away or employing it without thinking (Bhardwaj et al, 2025). For investors, it is the realization that AI can serve as an advisor but it is ultimately the human factor which dictates the outcome. For the regulators, it is their task to create fertile ground for innovation while not sacrificing fairness or security.

In a nutshell, the era of AI in trading will get an extra mark of the assimilation to the utmost degrees of fiscal judgment. The systems will become more personal, global, transparent, and ethical as well. By the action of combining the technology's innovation with the human's oversight, the financial world will not be able to just use AI for faster profit but also for more resilient and responsible markets.

CONCLUSION

The discussion in this chapter has shown how Artificial Intelligence is reshaping the landscape of modern trading. The methods that once used to depend on intuitive thinking, manual charting, or rule-based algorithms have been replaced by systems that are capable of learning from data, adapting to new conditions, and executing trades in real time. The chapter's treatment of the process from prediction to execution and its concurrent assessment of advantages and challenges has helped create a clear picture of the possibilities and responsibilities associated with the use of AI in finance.

A key theme is the power of AI to work on information beyond human comprehension. Markets are a mix of many data sources—prices, volumes, news, and social media—all interacting at once. The traditional analytical methods are unfeasible due to the excessive amount of information. However, AI-based systems are in a position to get the handle on things. They can process a multitude of inputs at an incredible speed, spot subtle patterns, and translate those recognized patterns into action steps. In volatile markets, this ability to respond in real time is particularly valuable, allowing traders to act before opportunities vanish. Still, the efficiency of AI is not only based on speed. Another merit is AI's impartiality. Human traders get affected by jealousy, fear, and anxiety—all these emotions conquer people, and thus lead to making wavering decisions. However, AI systems function totally differently. They act according to strict data-lit rules that they shall follow, thus, minimizing the effect of the emotional bias. This consistent performance holds true in both short-term trades and long-term investments. The discussion of a simple AI trading bot as an example in this case illustrates the entirely practical application of these concepts. The bot although having slight design outlays has highlighted the functions of a predictor, a structured decision-maker, and an executor in automated trading outperforming manual-based systems.

At the same time, the chapter has emphasized that AI is not without limits. Models have to deal with erratic shocks, poor data quality, and problems of the technical sort. Furthermore, overfitting, regulatory hazards, ethical issues like fairness and transparency raise the stakes. These problems show us that AI can not be an alternative to human judgement. However, the best strategy, of course, is to mix the strengths of machines with the insight and the responsibility of the human decision-maker.

Navigating forward, the domain of AI will infiltrate further into the trading sector. Systems of the future will embrace individual patterns of trading, cohesion between humans and machines, as well as global financial integration. With the expansion of data sources to new ones, the forecasts will be richer and more adaptive. But progress must be matched with responsibility. Transparent models, fair access, and ethical oversight will be essential in ensuring that AI contributes to healthier markets rather than destabilizing them.

The ultimate potential of AI is to back up the decision-making with intelligence, speed, and efficiency even beyond the level of human beings. Rather than being a replacement for human intelligence, it should be seen as an extension of it. Thoughtful and ethical use of AI will enable traders and investors to navigate through the complexity of modern markets with increased confidence. The most shaping factor in financial performance will not be the existence of technology only, but the ways that humans and machines learn to work together.

REFERENCES

Abdullah, A., Omolola, H., Taiwo, S., & Aderibigbe, O. (2024). Advanced AI solutions for securities trading: Building scalable and optimized systems for global financial markets. *International Journal on Cybernetics & Informatics*, *13*(3), 31–45. DOI: 10.5121/ijci.2024.130304

Abdullayev, N. (2023). Deep reinforcement learning on stock data. *Alatoo Academic Studies*, *23*(2), 505–518. DOI: 10.17015/aas.2023.232.49

Adeleye, R. A., Tubokirifuruar, T. S., Bello, B. G., Ndubuisi, N. L., Asuzu, O. F., & Owolabi, O. R. (2024). Machine learning for stock market forecasting: A review of models and accuracy. *Financial Analytics Research Journal*, *6*(2), 112–124. Advance online publication. DOI: 10.51594/farj.v6i2.783

Adesina, M. T., Esebre, S. D., Adewuyi, A. T., Yussuf, M., Adigun, O. A., Olajide, T. D., Michael, C., & Iloh, D. (2024). Algorithmic trading and machine learning: Advanced techniques for market prediction and strategy development. *World Journal of Advanced Research and Reviews*, *23*(2), 979–990. DOI: 10.30574/wjarr.2024.23.2.2405

Bhardwaj, S., Sharma, I., Mahendru, S., Kaur, R., & Sharma, S. (2025). Exploring the role of AIoT in data privacy and security. In Tariq, M. (Ed.), *Merging Artificial Intelligence With the Internet of Things* (pp. 75–102). IGI Global Scientific Publishing., DOI: 10.4018/979-8-3693-8547-0.ch003

Borkar, S., & Jadhav, A. (2024). Reinforcement learning techniques for stock trading: A survey of current research. *The Journal of Financial Data Science*, *6*(3), 38–56. Advance online publication. DOI: 10.3905/jfds.2024.1.161

Bouzgarne, I., Youssfi, M., Qbadou, M., & Bouattane, O. (2023). Deep reinforcement learning strategy in automated trading systems. *Proceedings of IRASET*, *2023*, 1–8. DOI: 10.1109/IRASET57153.2023.10152925

Chantrasmee, C., Jaiyen, S., Chaikhan, S., & Wattanakitrungroj, N. (2024). Stock trading signal prediction using transformer model and multiple indicators. *Proceedings of ICSEC*, *2024*, 1–6. DOI: 10.1109/ICSEC62781.2024.10770734

Cohen, G. (2022). Algorithmic trading and financial forecasting using advanced artificial intelligence methodologies. *Mathematics*, *10*(18), 3302. DOI: 10.3390/math10183302

Dokumacı, M. (2024). AI in forecasting financial markets. *Human-Computer Interaction*, *8*(1), 127. DOI: 10.62802/1twmvt88

Ferreira, F. G. D. C., Gandomi, A. H., & Cardoso, R. T. N. (2021). Artificial intelligence applied to stock market trading: A review. *IEEE Access : Practical Innovations, Open Solutions*, *9*, 30898–30917. DOI: 10.1109/ACCESS.2021.3058133

Goyal, H., Chandel, N., Maurya, A., & Shailja, . (2024). AI-powered autonomous trading: Enhancing market efficiency through predictive analytics. *International Journal for Research in Applied Science and Engineering Technology*, *12*(11), 377–386. Advance online publication. DOI: 10.22214/ijraset.2024.65001

Jain, R., & Vanzara, R. (2023). Emerging trends in AI-based stock market prediction: A comprehensive and systematic review. Applied Sciences in Engineering Conference Proceedings. DOI: 10.3390/ASEC2023-15965

Leng, R. (2024). AI-driven optimization of financial quantitative trading algorithms and enhancement of market forecasting capabilities. *Applied and Computational Engineering*, *100*(1), 1–6. DOI: 10.54254/2755-2721/116/20251742

Lomakin, N. I., Popov, I. A., Shohneh, A. B., Maramygin, M. C., & Gorbunova, A. B. (2020). AI-system of stock exchange trading robot for financial risk hedging. Advances in Economics, Business and Management Research, 3273–3282. DOI: 10.2991/aebmr.k.200312.473

Mhlongo, N. Z., Falaiye, T., Daraojimba, A. I., Olubusola, O., & Ajayi-Nifise, A. O. (2024). Artificial intelligence in stock broking: A systematic review of strategies and outcomes. *World Journal of Advanced Research and Reviews*, *21*(2), 1950–1957. DOI: 10.30574/wjarr.2024.21.2.0442

Musale, D. S.Dnyandev Sopan Musale. (2024). Enhancing stock market predictions through artificial intelligence. International Journal of Advanced Research in Science. *Tongxin Jishu*, •••, 556–566. DOI: 10.48175/IJARSCT-15991

Prabhakaran, P. (2024). Revolutionizing stock trading: The impact of AI on decision-making and efficiency. *International Journal for Research in Applied Science and Engineering Technology*, *12*(8), 849–852. DOI: 10.22214/ijraset.2024.64018

Schrettenbrunner, M. (2023). Artificial-intelligence-driven management: Autonomous real-time trading and testing of portfolio or inventory strategies. *IEEE Engineering Management Review*, *51*(3), 1–8. DOI: 10.1109/EMR.2023.3288609

Shaikh, S. Z., Khan, K. R., Sherwani, F. K., & Khan, M. (2025). Smart trading: Unlocking artificial intelligence in stock market. *The Business & Management Review*, *15*(3). Advance online publication. DOI: 10.24052/BMR/V15NU03/ART-17

Shukla, G. K. (2024). Revolutionizing trading: Unlocking the potential of artificial intelligence in financial markets. *International Journal of Engineering Applied Science and Technology*, *9*(2), 111–114. DOI: 10.33564/IJEAST.2024.v09i02.010

Singh, H., & Malhotra, M. (2024). *Stock market and securities index prediction using artificial intelligence: A systematic review*. Multidisciplinary Reviews., DOI: 10.31893/multirev.2024060

Singh, T., Kalra, R., Mishra, S., & Kumar, M. (2022). An efficient real-time stock prediction exploiting incremental learning and deep learning. *Evolving Systems*, •••, 1–19. DOI: 10.1007/s12530-022-09481-x PMID: 38625328

Sinha, S. K., Srivastava, M., Singh, S., & Chopra, B. U. K. (2024). Real-time stock market forecasting: A deep learning approach. *Proceedings of ICTACS, 2024*, 1424–1431. DOI: 10.1109/ICTACS62700.2024.10840702

Talreja, P., & Thavi, S. (2024). The impact of AI and machine learning on stock market predictions. International Journal of Advanced Research in Science. *Tongxin Jishu*, •••, 625–633. DOI: 10.48175/IJARSCT-18971

Tayal, P., Ali, F., Pandey, S., Singh, R., Lande, J., & Pachouri, V. (2023). AI-based stock market prediction: Theoretical perspective. *Proceedings of CISCT 2023*, 1–5. DOI: 10.1109/CISCT57197.2023.10351375

Vaidya, C., Nazneen, G., Singh, N., Katariya, K., Ramtekkar, A., Nasare, D., & Lalmore, D. (2024). *Real-time stock forecasting: Leveraging live data and advanced algorithms for accurate predictions*. International Journal of Innovative Science and Research Technology., DOI: 10.38124/ijisrt/IJISRT24MAY059

Zhu, G. (2024). Application of artificial intelligence and machine learning in financial forecasting and trading. *Applied and Computational Engineering*, *43*(1), 1–7. DOI: 10.54254/2755-2721/43/20230797

KEY TERMS AND DEFINITIONS

Artificial Intelligence (AI): Artificial Intelligence is a next-gen tech that gets advantage from the scientist's performance in artificial systems to build technological systems that solve problems, learn, think and make decisions like humans way do. In the finance sector, AI is employing educational computer models, self-études and freighted networks starting from the statistical data of the Daniel paradigm to determine and implement complex strategies that entail trading and risk management. Contrast to the stockholder since the AI adds the generation of betas to the surgery of data, and it becomes a non-linear system that can do statistical physicsometrics.

Real-Time Trading Systems: Real-time trading systems are the automated trading platforms that are constantly examining financial markets, and are the first ones to react to changes in the prices, volumes, and trends. In this regard, prediction models are now directly connected to execution mechanisms, hence, the latencies in the analysis and the action have been minimized. The provision of this kind of system, traders and institutions have a competitive advantage, especially in those contingent markets, where milliseconds can decide the profit or the loss of a particular trade. AI integration has improved their performance through adaptive learning, error correction mechanisms, and efficiency that is added by peer-to-peer exchanges.

Predictive Analytics: Predictive analytics is a branch of business intelligence that combines statistical methods, data mining, and machine learning to model and analyze data in order to predict future events. The use of predictive analytics in stock trading has brought many benefits, the most important of which are anticipating price movements, identifying opportunities, and managing risks. Today predictive models are even able to discover hidden correlations, and hence facilitate better trading decisions, by integrating various datasets. Such capabilities have a beneficial impact on the significance of risk management and the establishment of better business strategies.

Algorithmic Trading: Algorithmic trading is the ordering of trades via computer programs that follow predefined rules based on the market's conditions in terms of time, price, and quantity. The traditional programming approach is static and therefore no changes can be made to the program while the AI-enhanced system learns autonomously from the market trends. An algorithmic system that is now trading at high frequencies already dominates the stock exchange, and it is responsible for the majority of trading activity today. With algrithmic trading software, companies can obtain the benefits of low human error, lack of any emotional influence, and in addition, the possibility of very fast and complex strategies.

Market Volatility: Market volatility is a term for the extent and rate of price fluctuations that occur in financial markets over a specific time period. Emotional considerations, investor sentiment, and outside factors such as economic policies, with their due effect, on the operation of the company, geopolitical events, or abrupt shocks are the causes of market volatility. Volatility is a double-edged sword that provides both opportunities and risks in terms of trading: while it can cause losses, it can also help to create conditions favorable to AI trading systems that can react very quickly to the changes in the market. The understanding of volatility is important for the construction of strong trading models that can stand the test of time.

Data-Driven Decision Making: The term "data-driven decision making" is catching on as it refers to a decision that is based on actual numbers and is formed by using analytical models instead of intuition or subjective judgment. For trading purposes, it implies the usage of structured financial reports, the current stock data, and unstructured sources such as news or social media. AI systems are experts in this matter, they can eliminate noise, find out correlations, and focus on priority strategies. Data-driven strategies, by the way, can help to achieve consistency and accuracy in financial decision-making, just because they minimize the influence of human bias.

Ethical AI: Ethical AI is the responsible establishment and delivery of AI systems that isolate transparency, fairness, and accountability in dealings with the people involved. For instance, in the financial market, preventing bias of models, giving equal access, and maintaining trust through the regulatory compliance are the ethical issues. The use of AI without ethical consideration might lead to imbalance and to market manipulation or systemic risks. The provision of ethical AI is, therefore, the means by which technological innovation is channeled to the sustainable and trustworthy multi-dimensional financial ecosystems.

Human-AI Collaboration: Human-AI collaboration is based on the idea that machines perform efficiency by integrating machine efficiency with the human insight. The collaboration between humans and AI is formed in that there are the cap of speed that AI has, the big amount of data that AI manages, and the in tactical level the finding. The profound collaborative approach is that the AI system must act as a tool and not as a substitute. For instance in trading this equilibrium enhances the management of risks, handles unforeseen anomalies, and channels technological resources into wider financial objectives. Philosophically, AI and humans working together would build more robust and ethical frameworks in markets.

Chapter 7
Unveiling the Potential of AI in Volatile and Less Liquid Markets

Silvio Andrae
http://orcid.org/0000-0002-8586-7812
Independent Researcher, Germany

ABSTRACT

This chapter examines the opportunities and risks of integrating artificial intelligence (AI) into volatile and less liquid financial markets. The aim is to systematically compare the suitability of traditional econometric methods and AI-based approaches for forecasting liquidity and volatility risks. The methodology draws on theoretical foundations, hybrid frameworks such as the 'liquidity-at-risk' concept, and an empirical case study on GCC corporate bonds (2015–2023). Market data, macro indicators, and unstructured sources (news, social media) are integrated and analyzed using Random Forest, LSTM, and XGBoost. The results show that AI reduces forecast errors by 20–25% and generates early warning signals, but fails in multiple shock scenarios. The conclusion is that AI has considerable potential to stabilize illiquid markets, but its effectiveness depends heavily on data quality, institutional conditions, and international governance.

INTRODUCTION

The integration of artificial intelligence (AI) into financial markets is currently one of the most dynamic developments in financial economics. While algorithmic trading systems, machine learning, and deep learning approaches have been gradually implemented in trading strategies, risk management, and market surveillance

DOI: 10.4018/979-8-3373-5032-5.ch007

since the early 2000s, the recent availability of massive computing capacities and sophisticated learning algorithms has exponentially expanded the scope of application (FSB, 2017; López de Prado, 2018). Recent policy-oriented research emphasizes that artificial intelligence represents a structural transformation of financial markets, fundamentally reshaping the production and processing of information rather than merely improving existing analytical tools (Foucault et al., 2025). Recent research emphasizes that AI is fundamentally reshaping the structural, strategic, and governance dimensions of investment management (Mertzanis, 2025). However, the majority of scientific and practice-oriented research has so far focused on highly liquid markets, such as US stock trading or European government bonds, which are characterized by high market depth, steady trading volumes, and extensive data availability (IMF, 2023). In these contexts, the wealth of historical time series enables robust modeling of price movements, liquidity dynamics, and systemic risks.

In contrast, volatile and less liquid markets have been relatively little studied to date, even though they are becoming increasingly relevant to the global financial architecture. This group includes, in particular, frontier exchanges, bond markets in emerging economies, and commodity markets with limited market breadth (World Bank, 2021). Low trading volumes, pronounced price volatility, and high sensitivity to external shocks characterize these markets. These structural characteristics increase fragility to mispredictions and market-amplifying feedback loops (Danielsson & Shin, 2003). The central question that arises in this context is therefore: To what extent can AI models developed for data-rich, stable markets be used sensibly and responsibly in volatile, illiquid markets?

The particular relevance of this question lies in the dual role of AI as a potentially stabilizing and destabilizing factor. On the one hand, AI opens up the possibility of forecasting liquidity risks more accurately, establishing early warning systems for market disruptions, and thus strengthening the confidence of institutional and private investors (IOSCO, 2021). On the other hand, flawed models, algorithmic amplification effects, or insufficient regulatory capacity could exacerbate the inherent instability of these markets. The unreflective use of AI could thus create new systemic risks instead of the hoped-for increase in efficiency.

A key problem arises from the data situation in illiquid markets. While liquid markets provide a high frequency of trading data, order book information, and derived indicators, data sets in less liquid markets are often short, incomplete, or inconsistent. This limits the applicability of complex deep learning models, which rely on large amounts of data, and increases the risk of overfitting and low generalizability (Goodfellow, Bengio, & Courville, 2016). At the same time, there is often a lack of mature institutional frameworks, such as efficient clearing and settlement systems or independent market supervision, which would contribute to stability and transparency (World Bank, 2021).

In addition, the investor base in such markets is often highly concentrated. A small number of institutional investors or foreign funds dominate trading, which amplifies herd behavior and volatility swings (Bekaert & Harvey, 2003). Combined with macroeconomic shocks, such as sudden oil price distortions or currency crises, this results in a market environment characterized by abrupt regime changes and dynamics that are difficult to predict (IMF, 2023). Traditional approaches such as the Amihud illiquidity measure (Amihud, 2002), roll spreads (Roll, 1984), or GARCH models (Engle, 2001) regularly reach their limits here, as they capture liquidity costs and volatility clusters but are unable to reflect regime shifts and complex nonlinear dependencies adequately.

It is precisely at this interface that hopes are pinned on AI-supported methods. Machine learning makes it possible to identify complex patterns in heterogeneous data sources, model nonlinear interactions, and incorporate alternative data sources such as news reports, social media posts, or macro indicators. However, existing studies treat machine learning primarily as a predictive tool, without analyzing how the widespread adoption of AI may itself transform market dynamics and risk structures. This ability to integrate different data modalities opens up the possibility of detecting liquidity shocks and market instabilities at an early stage. The concept of 'liquidity-at-risk' (LaR)—analogous to value-at-risk (VaR)—offers a promising approach here by quantifying the probability of severe liquidity shocks and serving as a basis for risk management and regulation (Brunnermeier & Pedersen, 2009).

At the same time, it should not be overlooked that the application of AI in fragile markets poses considerable challenges. First, there is a high model risk, as AI systems are trained in environments with poor data quality, making their results prone to misclassifications (López de Prado, 2018). Second, the issue of governance is central: markets with weak institutional foundations often lack the capacity for independent model validation or regulation of algorithmic trading strategies (IOSCO, 2021). Third, there is the question of self-reinforcing effects: when market participants make extensive use of AI-based forecasts, collective reactions such as simultaneous sales or purchases can significantly exacerbate market instability (Danielsson & Shin, 2003).

Against this backdrop, we pursue three objectives: First, it identifies the characteristic features of volatile and less liquid markets and analyzes their implications for the use of AI models. Second, it discusses a methodological transition from classical econometric methods to AI-based approaches, critically reflecting on the opportunities and limitations of both perspectives. Third, an empirical case study on corporate bond markets in the Gulf Cooperation Council (GCC) countries is used to demonstrate how an AI-based forecasting model for liquidity risks can be designed concretely and the results it delivers. Finally, based on this, the regulatory and governance-related implications are derived, and future perspectives for the responsible integration of AI in fragile market environments are developed.

Overall, AI offers significant opportunities in volatile and illiquid markets to increase market transparency, quantify liquidity risks more accurately, and strengthen investor confidence. At the same time, it remains a ‘double-edged sword’ whose benefits depend on robust institutional frameworks, international cooperation, and close integration with traditional economic risk models. Only under these conditions can AI realize its potential to make fragile markets not only more efficient, but also more stable and inclusive.

CHARACTERISTICS OF VOLATILE AND LESS LIQUID MARKETS

Volatile and less liquid markets differ in key respects from the established, deep, and highly liquid trading venues that are usually taken as a reference in financial economics literature. While liquid markets are characterized by a large number of active buyers and sellers, narrow bid-ask spreads, and high resilience to external shocks, fragile markets exhibit several structural peculiarities that have significant implications for the functioning of price formation mechanisms and for the stability of financial markets as a whole (Bekaert & Harvey, 2003; IMF, 2023). These characteristics can be divided into five key dimensions: (1) structural features of market liquidity, (2) sensitivity to external shocks, (3) institutional and regulatory deficiencies, (4) composition of the investor base and behavioral economic patterns, and (5) challenges in data availability and quality.

Structural Characteristics

Liquidity has been shown to constitute a distinct and priced risk factor in financial markets, affecting expected returns beyond traditional asset pricing models (Hong & Chung, 2026). While existing research primarily focuses on liquid equity markets, liquidity as a risk factor becomes even more critical in volatile, less liquid market environments.

The most distinctive feature of illiquid markets is their narrow market breadth. In many emerging and frontier markets, trading volumes are severely limited, meaning that even small orders can have a significant impact on prices (Amihud, 2002). This manifests itself in wide bid-ask spreads, which not only increase transaction costs but also call into question the reliability of market prices. Empirical studies show that illiquid markets are susceptible to microstructural shocks, as individual players can exert a disproportionate influence on the market price through their buying or selling decisions (Roll, 1984; Hasbrouck, 2007).

The shallow depth of order books also contributes to markets having a limited ability to absorb liquidity shocks. This leads to pronounced price sensitivity, which is particularly pronounced in times of high uncertainty. While price movements in liquid markets primarily reflect aggregated information processing, in illiquid markets, they are often an expression of market frictions and overreactions by individual participants (Pastor & Stambaugh, 2003).

Sensitivity to External Shocks

A second key feature is high vulnerability to macroeconomic and political shocks. Empirical evidence from emerging and frontier markets shows that external events such as currency crises, commodity price shocks, or geopolitical conflicts have a significant impact on liquidity and volatility (Calvo & Mendoza, 2000; IMF, 2023). Unlike in developed markets, there is often a lack of buffer capacity among institutional investors or a diversified investor base, meaning that shocks have an immediate and sudden impact.

A prime example of this is the corporate bond markets of the Gulf states, whose liquidity dynamics are strongly influenced by oil price fluctuations. Studies show that price distortions in the oil market are almost directly reflected in the spreads of GCC bonds, triggering significant volatility spikes (Narayany et al., 2026). Another example is the COVID-19 pandemic, which not only led to abrupt declines in trading activity in many illiquid markets but also highlighted their vulnerability to capital outflows by foreign investors (IMF, 2021).

Institutional and Regulatory Deficits

A third structural deficit concerns institutional anchoring. While developed markets have mature clearing and settlement systems that minimize transaction risks and guarantee a stable market infrastructure, these mechanisms are weak in many less liquid markets (World Bank, 2021). Inefficient or non-transparent settlement processes increase counterparty risks and can lead to systemic instability in the event of market stress.

The quality of market supervision also varies greatly. Many regulatory authorities in emerging and frontier markets have limited resources to effectively monitor market manipulation, insider trading, or algorithmic trading strategies (IOSCO, 2021). Combined with often low law enforcement capacity, this leads to an institutional environment in which trust and transparency remain deficient. This institutional fragility exacerbates the inherent volatility of markets and inhibits the willingness of international investors to provide long-term capital. Recent advances in artificial intelligence have opened new avenues for monitoring financial market stress, particularly through the combination of machine learning models and large language models that jointly enable prediction and interpretation (Aquilina et al., 2025).

Composition of the Investor Base and Behavioral Aspects

The investor base in less liquid markets is often highly concentrated. A small number of institutional investors, often foreign funds or sovereign wealth funds, dominate trading activity (Bekaert & Harvey, 2003). This constellation leads to an increased risk of herd behavior: as soon as a major investor withdraws, other market participants may follow suit, leading to abrupt capital outflows and dramatic price distortions (Broner, Gelos, & Reinhart, 2006).

Behavioral economics studies also show that investors in uncertain markets are more prone to procyclical behavior, which further exacerbates volatility spikes (Shiller, 2000). This behavior is particularly problematic in markets where alternative sources of financing are lacking and access to international capital flows is vital for survival.

Data Availability and Quality

One of the biggest challenges for research and practice in illiquid markets is the availability of data; unlike in developed markets, where high-frequency, high-quality data is comprehensively documented and accessible, illiquid markets are characterized by short time series, data gaps, and inconsistent reporting (World Bank, 2021).

This has a direct impact on the modelability of risks and liquidity dynamics. While traditional econometric models already suffer from data restrictions, AI models are particularly dependent on large, clean data sets (Goodfellow et al., 2016). In markets with a lack of data, the risk of overfitting increases significantly, and forecasts lose their generalizability. At the same time, the search for alternative data sources—such as social media, satellite data, or news feeds—opens up new potential. However, these are methodologically challenging and carry their own risks, such as bias, manipulation, or limited representativeness (López de Prado, 2018).

In summary, volatile and less liquid markets are characterized by a bundle of structural and institutional factors that fundamentally distinguish their functioning from developed markets. Low market breadth, high shock sensitivity, institutional deficits, a concentrated investor base, and problematic data quality constitute a fragile market architecture that offers both opportunities and risks for the use of AI. On the one hand, these characteristics open up new research questions and potential applications, for example, in the area of alternative data or hybrid forecasting models. On the other hand, they exacerbate the risks of faulty modeling and regulatory blind spots.

Against this backdrop, it seems imperative to critically examine methodological foundations and adapt them to the specific conditions of volatile and illiquid markets. This is precisely where the following chapter comes in, systematically tracing the transition from classical econometric models to AI-based approaches.

A comparison with other regions shows that the structures described are by no means limited to the Gulf states. In Latin America, for example, Argentina's bond markets in particular are characterized by recurring debt crises that lead to abrupt liquidity slumps. Studies document that capital outflows are often triggered by a small number of institutional investors and, due to the narrow market breadth, result in massive price distortions (Reinhart & Rogoff, 2009). In sub-Saharan Africa, Nigeria exemplifies a market that suffers from weak infrastructure despite its considerable economic size. Illiquid government bond markets, high volatility in the exchange rate regime, and limited access to international investors illustrate the relevance of institutional factors (IMF, 2022).

In addition, behavioral economic aspects play a significant role. Investors in illiquid markets often tend toward overconfidence and loss aversion, which leads to exaggerated reactions to macroeconomic news (Barberis & Thaler, 2003). Herding behavior is reinforced by institutional concentration: when a dominant investor liquidates shares, other players follow suit for fear of losses. This behavior intensifies the inherent fragility of illiquid markets and highlights their fundamental difference from developed financial centers.

Finally, the structural importance of illiquid markets for the global financial system must be emphasized. Although smaller in volume, they form central hubs for commodity trading, emerging market financing, and development programs. Their stability or instability can therefore have far-reaching consequences for international financial flows via contagion effects (Claessens & Forbes, 2001).

METHODOLOGICAL FOUNDATIONS

The analysis of liquidity and volatility in financial markets has given rise to a variety of methodological approaches in recent decades. While classical econometric models have provided valuable insights into market mechanisms, they often reach their limits in volatile and less liquid markets. AI-based methods open up new possibilities in this context by identifying complex nonlinear patterns, integrating heterogeneous data sources, and utilizing adaptive learning processes. To illustrate the methodological transition from classical to AI-based approaches, the central traditional models and their limitations are first presented below. The potential of modern AI methods is discussed, concluding with an outline of hybrid frameworks, such as the concept of 'liquidity-at-risk' (LaR).

Classic Models of Liquidity and Volatility Analysis

Since the 1980s, empirical liquidity measurement has been grounded in microstructural indicators. Prominent examples include the Amihud illiquidity measure, which links price changes to trading volumes (Amihud, 2002), and Roll's implied spread measure, which infers transaction costs from price series (Roll, 1984). These approaches provide valuable proxies for market liquidity but rely on continuous trading and relatively stable market conditions. In illiquid markets characterized by episodic trading and dominant individual transactions, their explanatory power declines significantly (Hasbrouck, 2007).

In parallel, volatility has been widely modeled using ARCH/GARCH-type frameworks (Engle, 1982; Bollerslev, 1986; Engle, 2001), which capture the clustering of market uncertainty over time. While these models remain standard tools in financial analysis, they are limited in their ability to account for abrupt regime shifts and discontinuities caused by external shocks—features that are particularly pronounced in frontier and commodity-driven markets.

More generally, classical econometric models rely on predefined, predominantly linear relationships between variables. As a result, they are prone to specification errors in environments characterized by nonlinear interactions and structural breaks, as frequently observed in fragmented and less liquid markets (Pastor & Stambaugh, 2003).

Potential of AI Approaches

In contrast to the methods mentioned above, AI methods pursue a data-driven approach that is less dependent on pre-specified functional forms. They can identify patterns in large, heterogeneous, and high-dimensional data sets, which makes them particularly attractive for markets with complex dynamics (Goodfellow, Bengio, & Courville, 2016). AI-based models leverage high-dimensional and unstructured data, significantly improving predictive performance compared to traditional approaches, particularly in volatile environments (Foucault et al., 2025).

Machine learning: Machine learning approaches such as random forests and gradient boosting methods (e.g., XGBoost) offer a more flexible, data-driven alternative. They can capture nonlinear relationships and interactions across heterogeneous data sources, making them particularly suitable for fragmented and volatile market environments (Friedman, 2001; Chen & Guestrin, 2016). In the context of liquidity forecasting, these models are primarily used to identify key drivers and generate robust predictions under noisy, incomplete data.

Deep learning: Deep learning approaches, particularly recurrent neural networks (RNNs) such as long short-term memory (LSTM), extend this capability by modeling temporal dependencies in financial time series (Hochreiter & Schmidhuber, 1997). They are especially useful for capturing dynamic patterns such as volatility clustering and delayed market reactions. More recent approaches also use transformer architectures, which were initially developed for natural language processing but are now also used in financial time series analysis (Vaswani et al., 2017). However, their performance is highly sensitive to data availability and quality, which limits their applicability in data-scarce market environments. ecent evidence shows that machine learning techniques can uncover statistically significant predictability in international corporate bond markets, particularly under conditions of low liquidity and heightened uncertainty (Li et al., 2025).

Alternative and unstructured data: A key advantage of AI-based approaches is their ability to integrate alternative data sources, such as news, social media, and macroeconomic indicators. In illiquid markets, such data can partially compensate for missing transaction data and provide early signals of market stress (Tetlock, 2007). The integration of such unstructured data is particularly valuable in less liquid markets, as it can fill information gaps resulting from low market transparency (López de Prado, 2018). At the same time, these data sources introduce additional challenges related to bias, representativeness, and potential manipulation.

Challenges and Limitations of AI

Despite their potential, AI-based approaches face several fundamental limitations, particularly in volatile, less liquid markets.

First, their effectiveness depends heavily on data quality and availability. Deep learning models, in particular, require large and consistent data sets to identify robust patterns. In environments characterized by short or incomplete time series, the risk of overfitting increases significantly, limiting the generalizability of model outputs (Goodfellow et al., 2016).

Second, the limited explainability of complex models remains a key challenge. While classical econometric approaches provide transparent parameter interpretations, advanced AI models often operate as 'black boxes,' complicating validation and regulatory oversight (Doshi-Velez & Kim, 2017). This issue is particularly critical in illiquid markets with weaker supervisory capacities, where transparency is essential for maintaining investor confidence.

Third, AI systems may contribute to endogenous market instability. When multiple market participants rely on similar model outputs, collective responses can reinforce procyclical dynamics and amplify liquidity stress, thereby transforming risk models into potential sources of systemic risk (Danielsson & Shin, 2003).

To address some limitations of classical econometric models, regime-switching approaches, such as Markov-switching GARCH models, allow for probabilistic transitions between volatility regimes (Hamilton, 1989). While these methods represent an important intermediate step toward capturing nonlinearity, they remain dependent on relatively extensive data and show limited performance under multiple or unprecedented shocks (Ang & Bekaert, 2002).

Advances in explainable AI (XAI) provide partial mitigation strategies. Methods such as SHAP and LIME enable the decomposition of model outputs and the identification of key drivers, thereby improving interpretability and supporting model validation (Ribeiro et al., 2016; Lundberg & Lee, 2017; Andrae, 2024). These tools are particularly relevant for regulatory contexts, where transparency and accountability are essential.

Finally, recent developments in transfer learning and few-shot learning offer promising avenues for data-constrained environments. By adapting models trained in data-rich settings to smaller data sets, these approaches can partially bridge the gap between the data requirements of complex AI systems and the realities of illiquid markets (Qiu et al., 2020). However, their effectiveness remains contingent on structural comparability between source and target domains.

Integration of AI and Classical Approaches

Against this backdrop, the question of hybrid models comes to the fore. Instead of completely replacing classical methods with AI, a combination of both approaches appears promising.

Rather than replacing classical models, a hybrid approach appears most promising. The concept of liquidity-at-risk (LaR) provides a suitable framework by combining traditional liquidity measures with AI-based modeling of nonlinear interactions (Brunnermeier & Pedersen, 2009).

In such a framework, machine learning methods can identify relevant drivers, while deep learning models capture temporal dynamics. This integration enables the development of flexible, data-driven early warning systems grounded in established economic concepts.

The methodological comparison illustrates that, despite their elegance and interpretative clarity, classical models often reach their limits in volatile and less liquid markets. AI-based methods, on the other hand, offer the possibility of recognizing complex patterns, integrating alternative data sources, and mapping nonlinear dependencies. However, they rely on high-quality data, harbor risks of opacity, and can generate destabilizing feedback effects.

A promising approach is therefore to use hybrid methods that combine the robustness of traditional models with the flexibility of modern AI. The concept of liquidity at risk provides an exemplary framework for better understanding and managing market fragility in illiquid markets. The following section uses a case study on the corporate bond markets of the Gulf states to illustrate how such a hybrid framework can be implemented in practice.

Unlike existing studies, which focus on liquid markets, we show that the value of AI lies not only in improved forecasting accuracy. Even more significant is its ability to uncover nonlinear and latent structures of liquidity risk in fragmented and data-scarce market environments.

EMPIRICAL CASE STUDY

The Gulf Cooperation Council (GCC) comprises Saudi Arabia, the United Arab Emirates, Qatar, Kuwait, Bahrain, and Oman. Their capital markets have gained considerable importance over the past two decades, not least through the financing of large-scale infrastructure projects and the diversification of commodity-dependent economies (Hvidt, 2013). Nevertheless, the corporate bond markets of these countries remain small by international standards, fragmented, and characterized by limited liquidity (Narayany et al., 2026). This case study examines the potential and limitations of using AI-based methods to forecast liquidity risks in the GCC corporate bond markets over the period 2015–2023.

Market Environment and Characteristics

The corporate bond markets in the GCC have several characteristic features that make them a suitable field of study for the application of AI. First, they are relatively young: while government bonds have been established for decades, the corporate bond market only developed in the early 2000s, boosted by large-volume issues from energy companies and state-affiliated corporations (Bley & Chen, 2006). Second, the market is narrow in scope. Trading volumes are concentrated among a few issuers, while smaller companies have little access to the market. Third, there is a close dependence on commodity prices, especially oil and gas. Oil price volatility is directly reflected in the risk premiums (spreads) of corporate bonds and exacerbates market fragility (Kilian & Park, 2009; Arezki et al., 2017).

Added to this are geopolitical risks, such as the blockade of Qatar by neighboring countries in 2017–2021 or the collapse of oil prices in the wake of the COVID-19 pandemic. These events led to abrupt market distortions and made it clear that existing models for liquidity and risk analysis are insufficient to adequately reflect the complexity of the dynamics (Alqahtani & Mayes, 2018).

Data

For the empirical analysis, a panel data set was compiled comprising corporate bonds from the United Arab Emirates, Saudi Arabia, and Qatar for the period 2015–2023. The data set contains three key components:

Market data:
Daily bond prices and spreads for over 100 issues.
Order book information (bid-ask spreads, trading volumes, order imbalances).
Credit ratings from Standard & Poor's, Moody's, and Fitch.
Macroeconomic variables:
Brent oil prices (daily, US dollars per barrel).
Interbank interest rates (EIBOR, SAIBOR).
Exchange rate volatility against the USD.
Unstructured data:
News reports from Reuters, Bloomberg, and Al Jazeera (filtered by topic according to GCC and oil market).
Social media data (Twitter posts with keywords such as 'oil price,' 'Saudi bonds,' 'Qatar debt').
Sentiment analysis using natural language processing (NLP), scaled from -1 (negative) to +1 (positive).

The combination of these data sources is intended to ensure the most comprehensive representation of market, macro, and information dynamics possible.

Methodology

The case study compares classic econometric models with AI-based approaches.

Baseline models:
GARCH(1,1) models for forecasting spread volatility (Engle, 2001).
Amihud's illiquidity measure to capture price-volume sensitivity (Amihud, 2002).
Roll spread estimates (Roll, 1984).
AI models:
Random forests for variable importance (determination of the most important influencing factors).

LSTM networks for modeling temporal dependencies in spreads.
XGBoost for mapping nonlinear interactions between market data, macro variables, and sentiment indicators.
Integration of sentiment data as exogenous input to capture leading indicators of liquidity shocks.

The models were trained using a walk-forward validation approach to test forecast quality in real-time scenarios and avoid overfitting (López de Prado, 2018).

Results

The empirical results reveal clear differences in forecasting performance across model classes and data inputs. Overall, AI-based models significantly outperform traditional GARCH specifications, reducing mean forecast errors (RMSE) by approximately 20–25%. These gains are particularly pronounced during periods of elevated market stress, such as the oil price collapse in 2016 and the COVID-19 crisis in 2020, indicating that AI models are especially effective in capturing nonlinear dynamics under turbulent conditions.

A key driver of this improvement lies in the integration of sentiment data. Adverse news related to oil price developments and geopolitical risks provides early warning signals for impending liquidity contractions, with a lead time of approximately two to three days. The contribution of social media data, however, is highly state-dependent: while it significantly enhances predictive performance during crisis periods, its marginal value remains limited in more stable market environments.

The analysis of variable importance further supports these findings. SHAP-based decomposition shows that oil price volatility and bid-ask spreads consistently represent the most influential drivers of liquidity risk. During crisis episodes, sentiment indicators rank among the top explanatory factors, reflecting their ability to capture rapidly evolving market perceptions. In contrast, their relevance declines markedly under normal market conditions, highlighting the context-dependent nature of information signals in illiquid markets.

Despite these improvements, the results also point to important limitations. In scenarios characterized by multiple simultaneous shocks—such as the combination of oil price declines and pandemic-induced capital outflows—the predictive performance of all models deteriorates substantially. This underscores that even advanced AI-based approaches are unable to fully capture extreme market dislocations. Consequently, model-based forecasting must be complemented by scenario analysis and stress testing in order to provide a robust framework for risk assessment.

Various error measures were used to evaluate the quality of the models. While the baseline GARCH model had an average RMSE of 0.042, the LSTM model reduced the error to 0.032 and XGBoost to 0.030. The mean absolute error (MAE) values also improved by around 20%. Particularly striking was the greater robustness of the AI models during periods of severe oil price shocks: while GARCH models systematically underestimated during the COVID-19 crisis, LSTM and XGBoost showed greater sensitivity to abrupt regime changes.

Table 1. Comparative Forecast Performance of Econometric and AI Models

Model	RMSE	MAE	Improvement vs. GARCH (RMSE)	Performance in High-Volatility Periods	Robustness under Data Constraints
GARCH (1,1)	0.042	0.031	–	Low (systematic underestimation)	High
Random Forest	0.034	0.026	–19%	Moderate	High
LSTM	0.032	0.025	–24%	High	Low
XGBoost	0.030	0.024	–28%	Very high	High

Source: Own calculations.

The results show that AI-based models consistently outperform the GARCH benchmark in terms of forecast accuracy, with XGBoost achieving the largest reduction in RMSE. At the same time, important trade-offs become visible: while LSTM models perform strongly during high-volatility periods, they are more sensitive to limited data availability, whereas ensemble methods such as random forests and XGBoost exhibit greater robustness under constrained data conditions. This highlights that model selection in illiquid markets should not be based solely on predictive accuracy, but also on data availability and market regime characteristics.

Figure 1. Model Performance During Crisis Period (COVID-19 Shock)

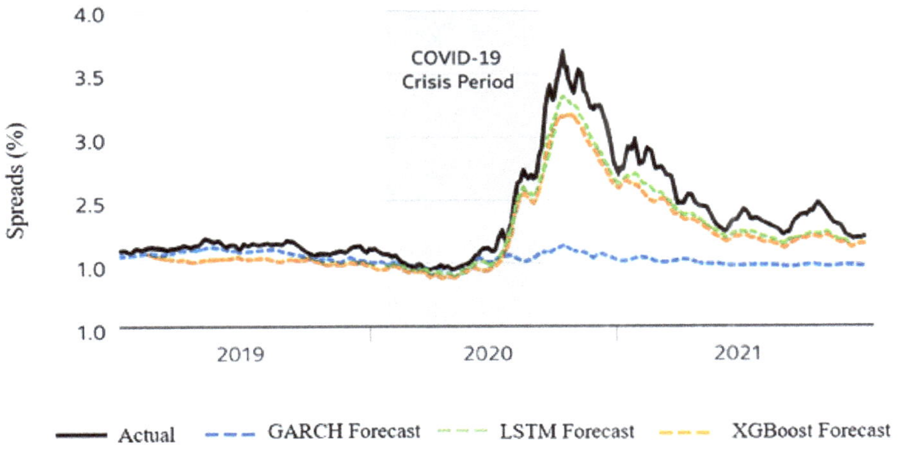

The figure 1 compares actual liquidity dynamics with model-based forecasts during a period of severe market stress. While the GARCH model systematically underestimates the magnitude of the liquidity shock, AI-based models (LSTM and XGBoost) more accurately capture the abrupt increase in credit spreads and subsequent adjustment dynamics. However, even advanced models exhibit deviations during peak stress, highlighting the limits of data-driven approaches under extreme conditions. These differences become particularly evident during periods of market stress. Figure 1 illustrates the behavior of the models during the COVID-19 shock, showing that AI-based approaches respond more sensitively to abrupt liquidity disruptions, while the GARCH model systematically lags behind and underestimates volatility spikes.

Figure 2. Key Drivers of Liquidity Risk (SHAP-Based Importance)

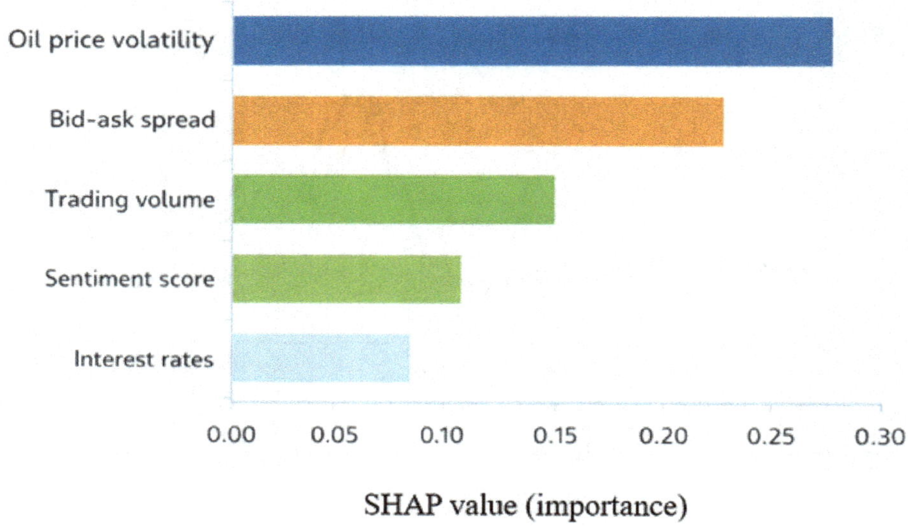

Figure 2 illustrates the behavior of the models during a major stress period, showing that AI-based models better capture abrupt regime shifts, while traditional econometric models systematically lag behind.

A sensitivity analysis showed that the quality of forecasts increased significantly with the availability of unstructured data. Models without sentiment data showed only moderate improvements over the baseline. Only by integrating news and social media scores was it possible to substantially reduce the forecast error. This underscores the value of alternative data sources in markets with structural data scarcity.

In addition, scenarios were tested in which the data set was artificially restricted to simulate realistic conditions in illiquid markets. When the observation period was reduced to three years, the performance of the deep learning models deteriorated significantly, while random forests and XGBoost remained comparatively robust. This suggests that ensemble methods are particularly suitable when only limited data is available.

An additional aspect concerns the governance structures in the GCC markets. Unlike in many frontier markets, there are institutional investors of considerable size here, such as sovereign wealth funds like the Abu Dhabi Investment Authority (ADIA) or the Public Investment Fund (PIF) in Saudi Arabia. On the one hand, these players contribute to market stability because they act as long-term investors; on the other hand, their dominant position increases the risk of concentration risks. The integration of AI-supported models into their risk management could therefore have systemic effects on the markets. While the case study provides detailed insights into GCC markets, the question arises as to what extent these findings can be generalized to other illiquid market environments.

External Validity and Comparative Insights

While the empirical analysis focuses on corporate bond markets in the Gulf Cooperation Council (GCC), the underlying mechanisms identified in this chapter extend beyond this specific regional context. Volatile, less liquid markets across regions share a set of structural characteristics, including limited market depth, concentrated investor bases, high sensitivity to external shocks, and constrained data availability.

In Latin American markets, for instance, the sovereign and corporate bond segments are frequently shaped by crisis-driven liquidity cycles, in which abrupt capital outflows trigger sharp price adjustments and temporary market dislocations. Similarly, in Sub-Saharan Africa, government bond markets often exhibit structural illiquidity combined with infrastructural and institutional constraints, limiting the effectiveness of traditional risk models. In parts of Southeast Asia, market fragmentation and the dominance of institutional investors generate dynamics similar to those observed elsewhere, particularly under conditions of external financial stress.

Against this backdrop, our main findings—namely the superior performance of AI-based models in capturing nonlinear dynamics, their sensitivity to data constraints, and their limitations under multiple shock scenarios—can be interpreted as structurally transferable rather than region-specific. At the same time, their effectiveness remains contingent on local institutional conditions, data infrastructures, and regulatory capacities.

Robustness and Model Stability

To assess the robustness of the empirical findings, additional validation steps were conducted to assess model stability and potential overfitting. The models were evaluated using a walk-forward validation framework, ensuring strict separation between training and test periods and thereby approximating real-time forecasting conditions. Furthermore, performance consistency was examined across the pre-crisis, crisis, and post-crisis periods. The results indicate that while AI-based models consistently outperform the GARCH benchmark in terms of predictive accuracy, their performance varies across market regimes. In particular, deep learning models such as LSTMs exhibit greater sensitivity to data availability and become less stable when the training window is shortened.

Additional sensitivity checks suggest that ensemble methods (Random Forest, XGBoost) are less prone to overfitting in data-constrained environments, maintaining relatively stable performance even under reduced sample sizes. Nevertheless, the risk of overfitting cannot be entirely excluded, particularly given the limited depth and quality of data typical for illiquid markets. These findings highlight that model robustness in such environments also depends on data characteristics and validation design.

Regime Sensitivity and Model Limitations

A key limitation of the empirical analysis is the performance of AI models under extreme, unprecedented market conditions. While the models demonstrate improved forecasting accuracy during single-shock episodes, their predictive power deteriorates in scenarios characterized by multiple simultaneous shocks, such as the combination of oil price collapses and pandemic-induced capital outflows. This finding underscores the inherent limitation of data-driven approaches, which rely on historical patterns and may fail when confronted with structural breaks outside the training distribution.

Moreover, the analysis reveals a pronounced regime dependency: AI models perform particularly well in moderately volatile environments, where nonlinear relationships can be effectively learned, but struggle in highly unstable phases where market dynamics are dominated by exogenous shocks and behavioral feedback effects. This suggests that AI-based forecasts should be interpreted as complementary inputs within broader risk management frameworks that incorporate scenario analysis and stress testing.

The results should therefore be understood as indicative of a broader class of fragile market environments rather than as directly generalizable in a statistical sense. This distinction highlights the importance of contextual adaptation when deploying AI-based models across different regions and market structures. These results reinforce the argument that model performance in illiquid markets is inherently conditional and must be interpreted within a broader framework of uncertainty and institutional constraints.

Discussion of the Results

The findings underscore the added value of AI-based methods in illiquid markets. Particularly noteworthy is the integration of unstructured data, which makes it possible to identify information shocks at an early stage. This suggests that AI can be a suitable tool for increasing transparency in fragmented markets and providing early warning signals to investors and regulators.

However, the limitations in the case of multiple shocks show that AI is no substitute for robust macroprudential analysis. Instead, it should be seen as a supplement that expands on traditional econometric methods. In addition, the use of sentiment data raises questions about data quality and manipulation: social media information can be distorted or strategically influenced, leading to inaccurate forecasts (Tetlock, 2007).

There is also a risk of self-reinforcing effects: if investors collectively respond to AI-based liquidity-at-risk warnings, liquidity crises could be exacerbated rather than mitigated. This points to the need for institutional frameworks that ensure AI models are used in a transparent, explainable, and regulated manner.

The case study on GCC corporate bond markets illustrates that AI-supported methods can deliver substantial improvements in the forecasting of liquidity risks, particularly through the integration of alternative data sources. At the same time, it reveals the limitations of these approaches in situations that lie outside the historical experience horizon. This makes it clear that AI models have great potential for fragile markets, but can only be used effectively and in a confidence-building manner if they are embedded in a broader governance framework.

OPPORTUNITIES, RISKS, AND GOVERNANCE IMPLICATIONS

The results of the empirical case study illustrate that the use of AI in volatile and less liquid markets offers substantial potential, but also entails considerable risks. This tension necessitates a critical reflection on opportunities and limitations, embedding them within a broader governance framework. This section first discusses the opportunities and potential benefits of AI applications for fragile markets. It then highlights the risks and challenges before finally discussing regulatory and governance-related implications.

Opportunities

Improved forecasting accuracy and early warning systems: A key opportunity lies in improving the quality of forecasts for liquidity and volatility risks. The case study has shown that AI-supported models can reduce forecasting errors by 20–25% compared to traditional methods, especially in periods of high market volatility. By integrating unstructured data, such as news and social media sentiment, additional early indicators of liquidity shocks can be obtained (Tetlock, 2007). This opens up the possibility of establishing early warning systems that provide valuable information to both investors and supervisory authorities.

Confidence building and investor attractiveness: AI-based liquidity forecasts can strengthen the confidence of international investors. Especially in markets characterized by information asymmetries and low transparency, more reliable forecasts can reduce uncertainty and increase attractiveness (IOSCO, 2021). Increased market stability can also direct capital flows into these markets and increase their financing capacity in the long term. Rather than functioning solely as a predictive tool, AI increasingly operates as an infrastructural layer that reconfigures how information is processed, decisions are made, and risks are managed within financial systems.

Contribution to market stabilization: Improved risk models can be beneficial for overall market stability. If supervisory authorities have better information at their disposal thanks to AI-supported early warning systems, they can take preventive measures to cushion liquidity crises. Examples include temporary trading suspensions, liquidity injections, or targeted communication of regulatory measures (Brunnermeier & Pedersen, 2009).

Potential for leapfrogging: Another advantage is the possibility of technological leapfrogging. Markets lacking mature data infrastructures could use alternative data sources (e.g., satellite data, mobile phone usage data) to develop innovative forecasting models without completely replicating the institutional development path of highly developed markets (World Bank, 2021).

Risks

Inaccurate forecasts and model risks: Despite improved forecasting performance, AI models remain susceptible to inaccurate forecasts, especially for events that lie outside the historical experience horizon (López de Prado, 2018). Multiplicative shocks, such as those that occurred in the wake of the COVID-19 pandemic and the simultaneous collapse in oil prices, clearly demonstrate the limitations of data-driven methods. Incorrect forecasts can have dire consequences in illiquid markets, as even small market movements can lead to massive price jumps. However, recent research highlights that AI may also introduce new systemic risks, as the convergence of models and strategies across market participants can amplify volatility and lead to synchronized trading behavior (Foucault et al., 2025; Andrae, 2025).

Algorithmic amplification effects: A key risk is the danger of self-reinforcing effects. When numerous market participants use AI-based forecasts at the same time, collective action—such as simultaneous sales—can exacerbate liquidity bottlenecks. This dynamic is reminiscent of the criticism levelled by Danielsson and Shin (2003), who point out that risk models can themselves become risk drivers through endogenous feedback. This risk is particularly high in illiquid markets where a small number of investors dominate. The increasing use of AI may lead to model convergence and synchronized decision-making, amplifying systemic risks through herding and network effects (Aldasoro et al., 2025).

Dependence on data quality: AI models rely on extensive and clean data sets. In markets with incomplete or inconsistent data, the risk of overfitting and misclassification increases significantly (Goodfellow et al., 2016). In addition, alternative data sources such as social media harbor considerable risks of bias and manipulation. Misguided models can therefore not only be ineffective, but also destabilizing.

Lack of transparency and black box problems: Another risk lies in the lack of explainability of complex AI models. While classic econometric methods provide easily interpretable parameters, deep learning models often appear as opaque 'black boxes' (Doshi-Velez & Kim, 2017). This complicates validation, undermines regulatory verifiability, and can weaken the confidence of market participants.

Regulatory capacity deficits: Many emerging markets do not yet have the capacity to independently validate AI models or adequately monitor algorithmic trading (IOSCO, 2021). The lack of relevant expertise and infrastructure increases the risk of regulatory blind spots. Especially in markets where supervisory authorities are traditionally weak, there is a danger that AI will have a destabilizing rather than a stabilizing effect.

These risks are deeply rooted in broader ethical, infrastructural, and institutional conditions. Understanding these underlying preconditions is essential for designing effective governance frameworks.

Ethical, Infrastructural, and Governance Preconditions of AI in Illiquid Markets

The deployment of artificial intelligence (AI) in volatile, less liquid markets raises not only methodological and performance-related questions but also fundamental ethical, infrastructural, and governance challenges. These dimensions are particularly salient in fragile market environments, where data limitations, institutional weaknesses, and asymmetric information structures amplify both the potential benefits and risks of AI-based systems.

A first critical dimension concerns data ethics and algorithmic bias. AI models trained on incomplete, noisy, or structurally biased data—conditions typical for illiquid markets—risk reinforcing existing informational asymmetries. For instance, reliance on alternative data sources such as social media or news sentiment may introduce systematic distortions, as these data are unevenly distributed across regions, languages, and market participants. In emerging markets, where smaller firms and local actors are often underrepresented in digital data ecosystems, AI-driven forecasts may implicitly favor large, internationally visible issuers. This raises concerns about fairness, market inclusivity, and the potential marginalization of less visible participants.

Closely related is the issue of data governance and integrity. The increasing use of unstructured and externally sourced data introduces vulnerabilities regarding data quality, provenance, and susceptibility to manipulation. Sentiment indicators derived from social media, for example, may be deliberately influenced by coordinated information campaigns or strategic signaling by market participants. In illiquid markets, where even small informational shocks can trigger significant price movements, such manipulation risks are amplified. Robust data governance frameworks—covering data sourcing, validation, preprocessing, and auditability—are therefore a necessary precondition for the responsible use of AI.

A third dimension concerns cybersecurity and model integrity. AI systems integrated into financial market infrastructures become potential targets for adversarial attacks, data poisoning, or model manipulation. In environments with limited cybersecurity capacity, such risks can undermine broader market stability. Ensuring the robustness of AI systems thus requires institutional mechanisms for monitoring, incident response, and cross-border cooperation. The integration of AI into financial market monitoring raises important governance questions, particularly with regard to transparency, model validation, and the role of human oversight.

Beyond data and security issues, the market infrastructure's readiness also plays a decisive role. Effective AI deployment presupposes reliable data infrastructures, computational resources, and technical expertise. Many less liquid markets lack these prerequisites, which creates a structural asymmetry: while advanced AI models are developed in data-rich environments, their application is often intended for data-poor contexts. This mismatch increases the risk of model mis-specification and limits the transferability of AI solutions. Approaches such as transfer learning or hybrid modeling can partially mitigate these constraints, but they do not substitute for sustained investment in local data ecosystems and analytical capacities.

Finally, these considerations point to a broader issue of institutional and regulatory governance. In fragile markets, supervisory authorities often lack the resources and expertise required to validate complex AI models or to assess their systemic implications. This creates the risk of regulatory blind spots, where AI-driven processes operate without adequate oversight. Addressing this gap requires a combination of national capacity-building and international coordination. Multilateral institutions and standard-setting bodies can play a key role in developing shared principles for data quality, model transparency, and accountability, thereby reducing fragmentation and strengthening trust in AI-based systems.

Taken together, these ethical, infrastructural, and governance dimensions highlight that the successful integration of AI in illiquid markets is not merely a technical challenge. Rather, it is a socio-technical transformation that requires aligning data practices, institutional capacities, and regulatory frameworks. Without such alignment, AI risks reinforcing existing vulnerabilities. With it, however, AI can contribute to more transparent, inclusive, and resilient market structures.

Governance Implications

Building on these ethical, infrastructural, and institutional preconditions, governance frameworks must also address the conditions under which these systems operate.

Establishing a regulatory framework: The development of a robust regulatory framework is key. This must include requirements for transparency, data quality, and model validation. One possible model is the regulatory guidelines from developed markets, such as the EBA Guidelines on Big Data and Advanced Analytics (EBA, 2020), which contain principles for data management, model risk management, and explainability. From a policy perspective, the increasing reliance on opaque and complex AI models raises challenges for transparency, accountability, and financial stability, requiring adaptive regulatory frameworks and enhanced supervisory capabilities (Foucault et al., 2025).

International standards and cooperation: Since many illiquid markets lack sufficient capacity, international cooperation appears indispensable. Development banks, multilateral organizations (e.g., IMF, World Bank), and international standard setters (IOSCO, FSB, BIS) could develop common standards to establish minimum requirements for data quality, model validation, and governance (FSB, 2017).

Hybrid models: humans and AI: Another governance-related aspect concerns the role of human judgment. In fragile markets, AI models should be seen as a complement to human expertise rather than a substitute for it. Hybrid systems, in which analysts interpret and validate AI results and place them in an institutional context, offer a way to mitigate mispredictions and black box issues (Doshi-Velez & Kim, 2017).

Role of multilateral institutions: Multilateral institutions can also make a decisive contribution through technical support and capacity building. Programs to strengthen data infrastructure, train supervisory authorities, and joint research initiatives are key building blocks for the sustainable integration of AI in illiquid markets (World Bank, 2021).

The opportunities offered by AI in volatile and less liquid markets are closely linked to significant risks. On the one hand, improved forecasts, early warning systems, and the use of alternative data offer the opportunity to increase transparency and stability. On the other hand, inaccurate forecasts, algorithmic amplification effects, and regulatory blind spots threaten to exacerbate the inherent fragility of these markets. Governance implications, therefore, arise in two respects: First, the development of robust regulatory frameworks that ensure data quality, explainability, and validation must be advanced. Second, the successful integration of AI into fragile markets requires international cooperation and institutional capacity building. This is the only way to prevent AI from becoming a destabilizing factor—and the only way it can fulfill its potential to make fragile markets more efficient, transparent, and resilient in the long term.

Policy and Managerial Implications: Governing AI in Illiquid Markets

The findings of this chapter suggest that the effective use of AI in volatile and less liquid markets depends less on technological sophistication alone than on the surrounding institutional and governance architecture. The following implications emerge for policymakers, regulators, and market participants:

Model governance and validation: Regulators should establish minimum standards for model risk management tailored to AI-based systems. This includes mandatory validation procedures, stress testing under multiple shock scenarios, and the integration of explainability tools (e.g., SHAP, LIME) to ensure interpretability and supervisory auditability. In fragile markets, simplified and robust models may be preferable to highly complex architectures.

Data governance and integrity: Given the reliance on alternative and unstructured data, clear standards for data quality, provenance, and integrity are essential. Supervisory frameworks should address risks of data manipulation, especially in social media–driven sentiment indicators, and require transparency regarding data sources and preprocessing methods.

Mitigating systemic feedback effects: AI-driven forecasting systems can amplify market dynamics when widely adopted. Regulators should therefore consider macroprudential safeguards, such as monitoring model convergence across institutions, implementing circuit breakers, or introducing disclosure requirements for AI-driven trading strategies to reduce herding and procyclicality.

Institutional capacity building: The effectiveness of AI in illiquid markets is critically dependent on supervisory and organizational capabilities. Investments in technical expertise, data infrastructure, and independent model validation capacities are necessary preconditions. International organizations (e.g., IMF, World Bank, FSB, BIS) can play a key role in supporting capacity building and standard-setting.

Hybrid decision frameworks: AI systems should not replace human judgment in fragile market environments but complement it. Effective governance frameworks combine algorithmic predictions with expert oversight, ensuring contextual interpretation, plausibility checks, and accountability in decision-making processes.

AI can enhance transparency, risk detection, and market confidence in illiquid environments. However, without robust governance, it may reinforce instability through model risk, data deficiencies, and collective behavioral effects. The policy challenge is therefore not merely to enable AI adoption, but to embed it within resilient institutional frameworks that align technological capabilities with financial stability objectives.

CONCLUSION

The preceding sections have shown that the use of artificial intelligence (AI) in volatile and less liquid markets offers considerable potential, but also entails risks. While empirical evidence—for example, in the case of GCC corporate bond markets—points to a significant improvement in forecast accuracy, uncertainties and limitations remain, which become particularly apparent in the event of multiple shocks. This section summarizes the key findings, outlines possible development paths, and draws conclusions for academia, practice, and regulation.

Three key findings can be highlighted:

Improved forecasts: AI-supported models, especially those that integrate unstructured data such as news and social media sentiment, can significantly reduce forecasting errors in liquidity and volatility risks (Tetlock, 2007; López de Prado, 2018).

Limitations in regime shifts: Despite these improvements, models regularly fail in situations that lie outside the historical experience horizon – such as simultaneous macroeconomic and political shocks (Danielsson & Shin, 2003).

Governance dependency: The benefits of AI depend crucially on the institutional and regulatory framework. Without robust data quality, model validation, and oversight, AI risks exacerbating instability rather than creating stability (IOSCO, 2021).

Against the backdrop of these findings, three development paths for the future integration of AI into fragile markets can be identified. Rather than merely applying established AI methods, we show that AI fundamentally alters how liquidity risk is identified, interpreted, and transmitted in less liquid markets.

Leapfrogging through alternative data: An important development path lies in the use of alternative data sources. Markets lacking a sophisticated financial market data infrastructure can develop innovative forecasting models by integrating satellite data, mobile phone data, or social media information, thereby leapfrogging traditional development paths (World Bank, 2021). This 'leapfrogging' approach could be particularly important for frontier markets that suffer from resource scarcity but still have access to digital information sources.

Hybrid models: humans and AI: A second development path involves combining human expertise with AI-supported processes. Since AI models are prone to mispredictions and black box issues, their use should be understood not as a replacement for human decision-makers, but as a complement to them. Hybrid models make it possible to validate algorithmic predictions through human judgment, thereby increasing trust, explainability, and context sensitivity (Doshi-Velez & Kim, 2017).

International cooperation and standardization: A third development path involves creating common international standards. Since many emerging economies do not have the capacity to build robust AI governance systems on their own, international cooperation appears necessary. Multilateral institutions such as the World Bank, IMF, or BIS could play a central role here by setting minimum standards for data quality, transparency, and model validation (BIS, 2022).

Practical implications: For investors, the use of AI in illiquid markets means an improved information base that supports risk management. Nevertheless, investors should be aware of the limitations of these models and always combine them with scenario analyses and stress tests.

Regulatory authorities need to adapt the regulatory framework to new technologies. This includes both developing guidelines for the use of AI and building technical capacities for independent validation (EBA, 2020).

For issuers and market participants, AI-based forecasts offer the opportunity to increase market transparency and thereby facilitate access to international capital markets. In particular, enhanced transparency and more reliable risk signals can improve asset managers' allocation decisions, which depend on timely, comparable information when investing in less liquid markets. AI-driven analytics may thus reduce information asymmetries, lower perceived risk premia, and support portfolio diversification into previously underrepresented market segments (Andrae, 2026).

However, realizing these benefits requires substantial investment in data infrastructure and analytical capabilities, as well as close cooperation with regulators to ensure data quality, model validation, and consistent disclosure standards.

This raises several follow-up questions for research:

How can hybrid AI frameworks be developed that combine the robustness of traditional models with the flexibility of data-driven methods?

What role do alternative data sources play in markets with systematically limited availability of transaction data?

How can explainability methods (e.g., SHAP, LIME) be adapted to the specific conditions of illiquid markets?

Which governance designs are suitable for limiting the risk of algorithmic amplification effects?

These questions illustrate that AI in illiquid markets is an interdisciplinary one, combining economic, regulatory, and socio-technical perspectives.

In summary, AI has considerable potential to stabilize and deepen volatile, illiquid markets, provided its use is embedded in robust institutional frameworks. Empirical evidence from the GCC bond markets has shown that AI-supported forecasts can significantly improve the quality of liquidity analyses. At the same time, it has become clear that AI is not a panacea: its effectiveness depends on data quality, governance, and international cooperation.

AI can make markets more efficient, transparent, and inclusive—but in fragile contexts, it always remains a double-edged sword. The future of integration will depend on whether we succeed in balancing opportunities and risks. Only then can AI contribute to the resilience of global financial markets in the face of increasing uncertainty.

REFERENCES

Aldasoro, I., Gambacorta, L., Korinek, A., Shreeti, V., & Stein, M. (2025). Intelligent financial system: How AI is transforming finance. *Journal of Financial Stability*, *81*, 101472. https://doi.org/10.1016/j.jfs.2025.101472

Alqahtani, F., & Mayes, D. G. (2018). Financial stability of Islamic banking and the global financial crisis: Evidence from the Gulf Cooperation Council. *Economic Systems*, *42*(2), 346–360. https://doi.org/10.1016/j.ecosys.2017.09.001

Amihud, Y. (2002). Illiquidity and stock returns: Cross-section and time-series effects. *Journal of Financial Markets*, *5*(1), 31–56. https://doi.org/10.1016/S1386-4181(01)00024-6

Andrae, S. (2024). Explainable artificial Intelligence in risk management: A framework. In Corazza, M. (Eds.), *Artificial Intelligence and beyond for finance* (pp. 149–206). World Scientific Publishing., https://doi.org/10.1142/9781800615212_0004

Andrae, S. (2025). Artificial Intelligence and financial stability: A systemic risk approach. In Günar, A. (Ed.), *Economic and political consequences of AI: Managing creative destruction* (pp. 87–110). IGI Global Publishing., https://doi.org/10.4018/979-8-3693-7036-0.ch005

Andrae, S. (2026). Artificial Intelligence in asset management: Opportunities, limitations, and market impact. In Murugan, T., Ahamed N., N., & Varalakshmi P. (eds.). Industry 6.0 for sustainable supply chains in agriculture, healthcare, and asset management. IGI Global Publishing, 165–194. https://doi.org/10.4018/979-8-3373-9554-8.ch006

Ang, A., & Bekaert, G. (2002). Regime switches in interest rates. *Journal of Business & Economic Statistics*, *20*(2), 163–182. https://doi.org/10.1198/073500102317351930

Aquilina, M., Araujo, D., Gelos, G., Park, T., & Pérez-Cruz, F. (2025). Harnessing Artificial Intelligence for monitoring financial markets. BIS Working Papers No 1291. https://www.bis.org/publ/work1291.pdf

Arezki, R., Ramey, V. A., & Sheng, L. (2017). News shocks in open economies: Evidence from giant oil discoveries. *The Quarterly Journal of Economics*, *132*(1), 103–155. https://doi.org/10.1093/qje/qjw030

Barberis, N., & Thaler, R. (2003). A survey of behavioral finance. In G. Constantinides, M. Harris, & R. Stulz (eds.). *Handbook of the Economics of Finance*. 1(B), Elsevier, 1053–1128. https://doi.org/10.1016/S1574-0102(03)01027-6

Bekaert, G., & Harvey, C. R. (2003). Emerging markets finance. *Journal of Empirical Finance, 10*(1–2), 3–55. https://doi.org/10.1016/S0927-5398(02)00054-3

Bley, J., & Chen, K. H. (2006). Gulf Cooperation Council (GCC) stock markets: The dawn of a new era. *Global Finance Journal, 17*(1), 75–91. https://doi.org/10.1016/j.gfj.2006.06.009

Bollerslev, T. (1986). Generalized autoregressive conditional heteroskedasticity. *Journal of Econometrics, 31*(3), 307–327. https://doi.org/10.1016/0304-4076(86)90063-1

Broner, F., Gelos, G., & Reinhart, C. (2006). When in peril, retrench: Testing the portfolio channel of contagion. *Journal of International Economics, 69*(1), 203–230. https://doi.org/10.1016/j.jinteco.2005.05.004

Brunnermeier, M. K., & Pedersen, L. H. (2009). Market liquidity and funding liquidity. *Review of Financial Studies, 22*(6), 2201–2238. https://doi.org/10.1093/rfs/hhn098

Calvo, G., & Mendoza, E. (2000). Rational contagion and the globalization of securities markets. *Journal of International Economics, 51*(1), 79–113. https://doi.org/10.1016/S0022-1996(99)00038-0

Chen, T., & Guestrin, C. (2016). XGBoost: A scalable tree boosting system. *Proceedings of the 22nd ACM SIGKDD International Conference on Knowledge Discovery and Data Mining*, 785–794. https://doi.org/10.1145/2939672.2939785

Claessens, S., & Forbes, K. (2001). *International financial contagion*. Springer.

Danielsson, J., & Shin, H. S. (2003). Endogenous risk. In *Modern Risk Management — A History*. Risk Books.

Doshi-Velez, F., & Kim, B. (2017). Towards a rigorous science of interpretable machine learning. *arXiv*. https://arxiv.org/abs/1702.08608

Engle, R. F. (1982). Autoregressive conditional heteroscedasticity with estimates of the variance of United Kingdom inflation. *Econometrica, 50*(4), 987–1007. https://doi.org/10.2307/1912773

Engle, R. F. (2001). GARCH 101: The use of ARCH/GARCH models in applied econometrics. *The Journal of Economic Perspectives, 15*(4), 157–168. https://doi.org/10.1257/jep.15.4.157

European Banking Authority (EBA). (2020). Report on big data and advanced analytics. https://www.eba.europa.eu/sites/default/files/document_library/Final%20Report%20on%20Big%20Data%20and%20Advanced%20Analytics.pdf

Financial Stability Board (FSB). (2017). Artificial intelligence and machine learning in financial services: Market developments and financial stability implications. https://www.fsb.org/uploads/P011117.pdf

Foucault, T., Gambacorta, L., Jiang, W., & Vives, X. (2025). Artificial Intelligence in finance. Centre for Economic Policy Research Press. https://cepr.org/system/files/publication-files/251574-barcelona_7_artificial_intelligence_in_finance.pdf

Friedman, J. H. (2001). Greedy function approximation: A gradient boosting machine. *Annals of Statistics*, *29*(5), 1189–1232. https://doi.org/10.1214/aos/1013203451

Goodfellow, I., Bengio, Y., & Courville, A. (2016). *Deep learning*. MIT Press.

Hamilton, J. D. (1989). A new approach to the economic analysis of nonstationary time series and the business cycle. *Econometrica*, *57*(2), 357–384. https://doi.org/10.2307/1912559

Hasbrouck, J. (2007). *Empirical market microstructure: The institutions, economics, and econometrics of securities trading*. Oxford University Press.

Hochreiter, S., & Schmidhuber, J. (1997). Long short-term memory. *Neural Computation*, *9*(8), 1735–1780. https://doi.org/10.1162/neco.1997.9.8.1735

Hong, S., & Chung, K. H. (2026). The pricing of liquidity factors. *Journal of Financial Research*. Advance online publication. https://doi.org/10.1111/jfir.70055

Hvidt, M. (2013). Economic diversification in GCC countries: Past record and future trends. Research Paper, Kuwait Programme on Development, Governance and Globalisation. London School of Economics. https://www.lse.ac.uk/middle-east-centre/research/kuwait-programme

IMF. (2021). *COVID-19 and emerging markets*. International Monetary Fund.

IMF. (2022). Selected Issues. International Monetary Fund.

IMF. (2023). *Global financial stability report*. International Monetary Fund.

IOSCO. (2021). *The use of artificial intelligence and machine learning by market intermediaries and asset managers*. International Organization of Securities Commissions.

Jorion, P. (2007). *Value at risk: The new benchmark for managing financial risk* (3rd ed.). McGraw-Hill.

Kilian, L., & Park, C. (2009). The impact of oil price shocks on the U.S. stock market. *International Economic Review*, *50*(4), 1267–1287. https://doi.org/10.1111/j.1468-2354.2009.00568.x

Li, D., Lu, L., Qi, Z., & Zhou, G. (2026). International corporate bond returns: Uncovering predictability using machine learning. *Journal of Financial Markets*. Advance online publication. https://doi.org/10.1016/j.finmar.2025.101008

López de Prado, M. (2018). *Advances in financial machine learning*. Wiley.

Lundberg, S. M., & Lee, S. I. (2017). A unified approach to interpreting model predictions. *arXiv*. https://arxiv.org/abs/1705.07874

Mertzanis, C. (2025). Artificial intelligence and investment management: Structure, strategy, and governance. *International Review of Financial Analysis*, *107*, 104599. https://doi.org/10.1016/j.irfa.2025.104599

Narayany, S. C., Zargar, F. N., & Ali, A. (2026). Does risk–return trade-off exist in the GCC stock markets? *International Journal of Emerging Markets*, *21*(4), 1033–1055. https://doi.org/10.1108/IJOEM-06-2024-1107

Pastor, L., & Stambaugh, R. (2003). Liquidity risk and expected stock returns. *Journal of Political Economy*, *111*(3), 642–685. https://doi.org/10.1086/374184

Qiu, J., Wang, B., & Zhou, C. (2020). Forecasting stock prices with long-short term memory neural network based on attention mechanism. *PLoS One*, *15*(1), e0227222. https://doi.org/10.1371/journal.pone.0227222

Reinhart, C. M., & Rogoff, K. S. (2009). *This time is different: Eight centuries of financial folly*. Princeton University Press.

Ribeiro, M. T., Singh, S., & Guestrin, C. (2016). 'Why should I trust you?': Explaining the predictions of any classifier. Proceedings of the 22nd ACM SIGKDD, 1135–1144. https://doi.org/10.1145/2939672.2939778

Roll, R. (1984). A simple implicit measure of the effective bid-ask spread in an efficient market. *The Journal of Finance*, *39*(4), 1127–1139. https://doi.org/10.1111/j.1540-6261.1984.tb03897.x

Shiller, R. J. (2000). *Irrational exuberance*. Princeton University Press.

Tetlock, P. C. (2007). Giving content to investor sentiment: The role of media in the stock market. *The Journal of Finance*, *62*(3), 1139–1168. https://doi.org/10.1111/j.1540-6261.2007.01232.x

Vaswani, A., Shazeer, N., Parmar, N., Uszkoreit, J., Jones, L., Gomez, A. N., ... (2017). Attention is all you need. *arXiv*. https://arxiv.org/abs/1706.03762

World Bank. (2021). Frontier markets economies: Promise, performance, and prospects. https://www.worldbank.org/en/research/publication/frontier-markets

Chapter 8

The Use of Large Language Models in Financial Forecasting: Analysis, Prediction, and Decision-Making

Silvio Andrae
http://orcid.org/0000-0002-8586-7812
Independent Researcher, Germany

ABSTRACT

This study investigates the potential of large language models (LLMs), such as GPT-4, for financial forecasting and decision-making. Using anonymized financial reports, the models analyze key figures and forecast future earnings through a chain-of-thought prompting process, enabling step-by-step reasoning similar to that of human analysts. The standardized framework compares the performance of LLMs with artificial neural networks (ANNs), econometric models, and estimates from professional analysts. Quantitative evaluation metrics (RMSE, MAE, directional accuracy) are complemented by economic indicators (Sharpe ratio, alpha) and qualitative dimensions (narrative coherence). The results show that LLMs achieve forecasting accuracy comparable to or even superior to traditional ML and econometric models, while providing transparent, narrative explanations that enhance interpretability and investor confidence. The results suggest that LLMs represent a methodological and epistemic shift in financial analysis.

DOI: 10.4018/979-8-3373-5032-5.ch008

INTRODUCTION

Financial forecasting has been a cornerstone of the economic and financial world for decades. It enables investors to allocate capital efficiently, companies to plan investments, and provides regulators with important insights into systemic stability. Forecasting methods have evolved significantly over time, reflecting both the growing complexity of financial markets and advances in statistics and computer technology. Traditional econometric approaches, such as autoregressive integrated moving averages (ARIMA), vector autoregressive (VAR), or generalized autoregressive conditional heteroscedasticity (GARCH) models, attempted to capture time series dynamics within structured frameworks (Engle, 1982). However, with increasing globalization, interconnectedness, and vulnerability to structural breaks in financial markets, the limitations of these models became increasingly apparent.

A prominent example of these limitations is the Fed model, which posits a stable relationship between stock returns and interest rates, specifically bond yields. Proponents argue that such a relationship provides predictable insights into asset returns, while critics highlight the conceptual problem of mixing nominal and real variables. Recent work indicates that the predictive power of the model is heavily dependent on structural breaks and regime shifts in monetary policy. McMillan (2025) demonstrates that the relationship between stock and bond yields yields consistent forecast results only when shifts in levels or regime changes are taken into account (McMillan, 2025). It illustrates a broader challenge: financial relationships that appear stable ex ante are often undermined by macroeconomic shocks, policy interventions, or changes in investor behavior. These debates are revisited in Section 2 (Literature Review), which places LLM-based forecasting in the broader context of the history of econometric and ML models.

The search for more adaptable instruments has led to the introduction of machine learning (ML) in financial forecasting. Neural networks, ensemble learners, and support vector machines have demonstrated the ability to capture nonlinear patterns and high-dimensional interactions, often outperforming classical models in terms of predictive accuracy. Nevertheless, these methods face persistent challenges: the opacity of predictions (the 'black box problem'), their dependence on extensive training data, and their limited adaptability to unstructured or ambiguous information. These shortcomings are central to the motivation for this study and are addressed in Section 3 (Methodology), which outlines a standardized framework for examining whether LLMs can overcome such limitations.

The emergence of large language models (LLMs) such as GPT-4 is leading to a potential paradigm shift. Initially developed for natural language processing, LLMs have demonstrated capabilities that extend far beyond text. Recent research suggests that LLMs can successfully perform financial statement analysis. Kim et al. (2024) provide evidence that GPT-4 not only predicts future earnings direction with accuracy comparable to state-of-the-art neural networks, but also outperforms human analysts in specific contexts. Crucially, GPT-4 provides narrative insights that mirror the reasoning of professional analysts. These insights correlate strongly with quantitative forecasts and offer a possibility for interpretation that is often lacking in ML models. This dual capability—numerical prediction and narrative explanation—will be a central theme in this chapter, particularly in Section 4 (Results), where we analyze both the statistical accuracy and qualitative coherence of the results generated by LLM.

Beyond company-level analysis, LLMs are also being tested as autonomous agents in market environments. Lopez-Lira (2025) demonstrates that when configured as traders, LLMs can behave as value investors, momentum traders, or market makers in simulated stock markets with realistic order books and dividend payments. These experiments show that LLMs are capable of consistent strategic behavior () and emergent market phenomena such as bubbles or liquidity provision. However, they also highlight potential systemic risks: correlated prompts and shared base models could lead to synchronized behaviors and amplify market volatility. These systemic implications are discussed in Section 5 (Discussion), where we reflect on the opportunities and risks of using LLMs in decision-relevant environments.

Overall, this evolving literature highlights three key insights that guide the present study. First, classical forecasting models retain their heuristic value but often break down under regime shifts. Second, ML models improve predictive performance but fall short in terms of transparency and adaptability. Third, LLMs are uniquely positioned to combine predictive accuracy with narrative explainability, offering a new paradigm for financial forecasting.

Based on this perspective, the chapter pursues three overarching research questions that are crucial to understanding the potential of LLMs in financial forecasting (Figure 1).

- **Analytical capabilities**: To what extent can LLMs extract meaningful insights from standardized financial reports and identify key performance drivers? (Sections 3.2–3.4, Methodology)
- **Predictive accuracy**: How do LLM-based forecasts perform compared to traditional statistical models, specialized ML applications, and human analysts, especially in volatile or ambiguous situations? (Section 4.1–4.3, Results)
- **Relevance for decision-making**: What is the economic value of incorporating LLM-based forecasts into trading strategies or investment processes, and how does their explainability contribute to investor confidence and regulatory oversight? (Section 4.3–4.4, Results; Section 5.2, Discussion)

Figure 1. Analytical framework: LLMs in financial forecasting

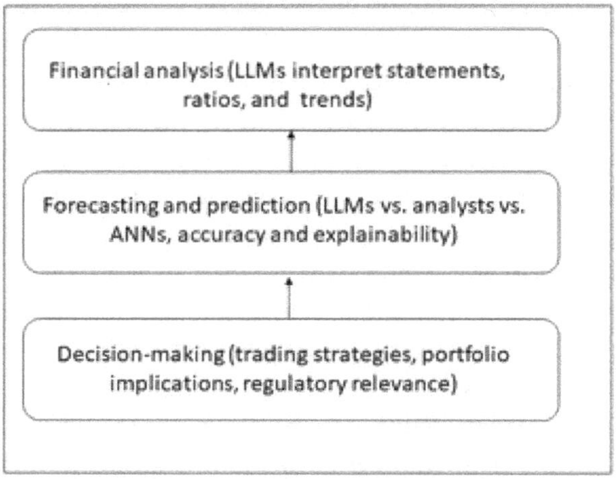

To answer these questions, this chapter uses a standardized evaluation framework. As explained in Section 3 (Methodology), anonymized financial reports are submitted to GPT-4, which utilizes a chain-of-thought (CoT) prompting approach to generate predictions. These forecasts are compared with those of artificial neural networks (ANNs) and professional analyst estimates. Performance is evaluated using statistical metrics (accuracy, RMSE, directional accuracy), economic metrics (Sharpe ratio, alpha), and qualitative dimensions (clarity and economic plausibility of narrative insights).

The chapter makes three key contributions. First, it expands the literature on fundamental analysis by demonstrating that LLMs can derive forward-looking insights from purely numerical data, without relying on narrative information. Second, it contributes to the field of forecasting methods by highlighting the complementarity between LLMs, traditional ML models, and human experts, thus pointing to hybrid systems as a promising direction for future research (detailed in Section 5.4, Future Research Directions). Third, it contributes to the debate on AI governance in finance by highlighting both opportunities (efficiency, transparency, scalability) and risks (biases, correlated agent behavior, systemic vulnerabilities), a topic that is critically examined in Section 5.3, 'Limitations.'

The rest of the chapter is structured as follows: Section 2 provides an overview of the evolution of forecasting methods, from classical econometrics to machine learning to the recent shift toward LLMs. Section 3 describes the methodological design, including data selection, prompting strategies, and evaluation metrics. Section 4 presents empirical results and compares LLM forecasts with those of analysts and ANN models. Section 5 presents a critical discussion of the implications for theory, practice, and regulation, and Section 6 concludes with a summary of the findings and an overview of avenues for future research.

In summary, this chapter positions LLMs at the forefront of financial forecasting. By combining predictive accuracy and narrative explainability, they overcome the limitations of both econometric models and specialized ML applications. LLMs represent more than an incremental improvement; they represent a potential paradigm shift that positions AI as a central decision-making tool in finance. The following sections illustrate how this shift is unfolding in the areas of analysis, prediction, and decision-making, and what it implies for the future of financial markets.

LITERATURE REVIEW

Financial Forecasting Methods: From Classical to AI-Based Approaches

The discipline of financial forecasting has historically relied on econometric models (Box & Jenkins, 1970). Traditional time series approaches such as autoregressive integrated moving average (ARIMA) models have often been used to forecast stock prices, interest rates, and macroeconomic indicators. These models, based on the assumptions of stationarity and linear dependence, have been effective in stable environments. However, their limitations in handling nonlinearities, sudden regime shifts, or structural breaks have underscored the need for innovation (Vapnik, 1995).

Further developments, such as vector autoregressive analysis (VAR), broadened the modeling horizon by enabling the simultaneous analysis of multiple interdependent time series. VAR models captured the dynamics between different variables and were therefore suitable for macrofinancial relationships, such as the interaction between GDP growth, inflation, and interest rates. However, VAR models suffered from overparameterization when processing large data sets, and their linear structure limited their predictive flexibility.

The introduction of generalized autoregressive conditional heteroskedasticity (GARCH) models and their variants represented a significant innovation, as they addressed volatility clustering—a key characteristic of financial time series. GARCH-based approaches have become a central component of risk management and option pricing because they model time-varying variances more effectively than earlier techniques. Despite their widespread use, however, GARCH models remained inherently parametric and struggled to account for the nonlinear dependencies, regime shifts, and structural complexities that increasingly characterized financial markets.

Parallel to these econometric developments, applied research highlighted the fragility of such models under changing macroeconomic regimes. For example,

McMillan (2025) examines the Fed model, which postulates a stable relationship between stock returns and bond yields, and shows that predictive power only emerges when structural breaks are taken into account. This finding underscores the challenge facing classical models: although they are theoretically sound, their empirical robustness is often undermined by changes in monetary policy, inflation dynamics, or investor expectations. These changes can lead to significant errors in the forecasts, making it crucial for financial analysts to consider the adaptability of their models to changing economic conditions.

Against the backdrop of the limitations of classical approaches, researchers turned to machine learning (ML) and deep learning approaches. Algorithms such as support vector machines (SVMs) and random forests offered the possibility of capturing nonlinear relationships without specifying functional forms (Breiman, 2001). Artificial neural networks (ANNs), inspired by biological cognition, gained prominence due to their ability to approximate highly nonlinear mappings between input features and financial outcomes. These ML models, with their potential to revolutionize financial forecasting, have been applied in diverse areas from credit rating and insolvency prediction to stock price forecasting and portfolio optimization (Liu, 2024).

Deep learning, in particular, has opened the door to architectures such as recurrent neural networks (RNNs) and long short-term memory (LSTM) models, which have proven adept at handling sequential dependencies in financial data (Hochreiter & Schmidhuber, 1997). These models achieved impressive accuracy in short-term price forecasting, volatility forecasting, and algorithmic trading. Nevertheless, they presented new challenges: high data requirements, the risk of overfitting, a lack of interpretability, and limited transferability to different financial contexts.

In summary, the transition from econometric models to ML represents a compromise: while classical approaches offer a theoretical basis and interpretability, ML models deliver predictive power at the expense of transparency. This tension creates the conditions for the emergence of LLMs, which promise to combine both strengths.

Table 1. Comparison of forecasting approaches

Model class	Strengths	Weaknesses
Classic econometric models (ARIMA, VAR, GARCH)	• Strong theoretical basis • Interpretability through econometric structure • Useful for hypothesis testing • Well suited for stationary, stable environments	• Difficulties with regime shifts and structural breaks • Limited ability to capture nonlinear dynamics • Requires strong stationarity assumptions • Often vulnerable in volatile financial markets
Machine learning models (SVMs, random forests, ANNs)	• Capture nonlinearities and high-dimensional data • High prediction accuracy for structured data sets • Adaptable to complex interactions • Widely used in credit rating, insolvency prediction, and volatility prediction	• High data requirements • Black-box character reduces interpretability • Overfitting risks with small samples • Limited generalizability across domains
Large language models (LLMs, e.g., GPT-4)	• Combine quantitative and qualitative thinking • Generate explainable narratives (CoT) • Adaptable to structured (numbers) and unstructured (text) data • Potential to act as autonomous agents in decision-making contexts	• Dependence on the design of the input prompt • Risk of hallucinations or biased results • In many cases, lack of domain-specific fine-tuning • Potential systemic risks due to correlated model behavior

Applications of Generative AI and NLP in Finance

The advent of natural language processing (NLP) and, more recently, generative AI has expanded the scope of financial forecasting beyond structured numerical data to unstructured text information. Early work in this area focused on text mining and sentiment analysis. Researchers extracted linguistic signals from news articles, press releases, and financial reports to capture investor sentiment and market expectations. Studies showed that sentiment indicators derived from text corpora can predict short-term market movements and volatility, thereby complementing traditional quantitative models. This application of AI in finance not only broadens the sources of data for forecasting but also provides a more nuanced understanding of market sentiment and its impact on financial outcomes.

Building on this, scientists turned their attention to transcripts of earnings announcements and analyst reports. By analyzing tone of voice, word choice, and disclosure style, NLP models identified implicit signals about management confidence, uncertainties, or hidden risks. For example, sentiment-based models helped predict earnings surprises, stock price reactions, and credit risk assessments. Similar techniques were applied to ESG-related data, with unstructured sustainability reports and regulatory filings serving as input for risk and performance forecasts.

The advent of large pre-trained language models (e.g., BERT, GPT-3, GPT-4) marked a turning point. Unlike earlier NLP methods, which relied on bag-of-words or topic modeling, these models embedded words and sentences in high-dimensional semantic spaces, enabling a deeper understanding of context. Recent studies have tested the performance of ChatGPT and GPT-4 in a financial context. Kim et al. (2024) provide extensive evidence that GPT-4 can analyze financial reports in a manner comparable to that of professional analysts. Even without narrative context, the model predicts the direction of future earnings with an accuracy comparable to that of specialized ML models, while generating narrative insights that correspond to human thinking.

A recent study by Ben Yoash et al. (2025) provides SECQUE, a comprehensive benchmark framework for evaluating the real-world financial analysis capabilities of LLMs. The framework tests models such as GPT-4, Claude 3, and LLaMA 3 on tasks of balance sheet interpretation, forecasting, and risk assessment. The results show that LLMs—especially when using chain-of-thought prompting—can consistently interpret complex financial relationships, outperforming classical models in combining numerical and narrative analysis.

Beyond static analysis, generative AI has also been investigated in trading environments. Lopez-Lira (2025) introduces LLMs as autonomous agents in market simulations and shows that they can consistently implement strategies such as value investing or market making. These agents respond to market dynamics and generate realistic phenomena such as price discovery and liquidity provision. Importantly, this line of research suggests that LLMs can go beyond passive analysis and act as active participants in financial markets.

Taken together, these studies show that LLMs possess both analytical versatility and contextual adaptability, enabling them to bridge the gap between structured financial data and unstructured narratives.

Chain-of-Thought Prompting and Explainability in AI

One of the key innovations in applying LLMs in finance is the use of chain-of-thought prompting (CoT). CoT is a prompting technique that instructs the model to argue step by step, mimicking the analytical process of a human expert. Instead of providing an immediate answer, the model formulates intermediate steps—such as identifying key metrics, comparing them across different time periods, and deriving likely future trends—before arriving at a prediction. This technique enhances the interpretability of AI models, making their predictions more understandable and actionable for financial analysts.

The effectiveness of CoT prompting is twofold. First, it improves the accuracy of predictions, as shown in Kim et al. (2024), where CoT-enhanced GPT-4 achieved higher accuracy than simple prompting strategies. Second, it improves explainability. Unlike traditional ML models, which often provide predictions without context, LLMs can generate narrative explanations that align with their numerical results. These explanations resemble the reasoning provided by human analysts, such as highlighting liquidity deterioration or leverage risks.

This feature aligns LLMs with the broader movement toward explainable AI (XAI) in finance. Regulators, including the European Central Bank and the US Securities and Exchange Commission (SEC), are increasingly emphasizing the need for transparency in AI-based decisions. XAI aims to address concerns about model opacity by ensuring that stakeholders—such as investors, managers, and regulators—can understand the reasoning behind predictions. In finance, where accountability and trust are paramount, the ability of LLMs to provide coherent, economically plausible narratives is a significant advantage (Andrae, 2024).

Furthermore, CoT reasoning facilitates the integration of LLMs into hybrid systems. Narrative outputs can be combined with structured ML models, creating ensembles that offer both predictive power and interpretability. This interplay will be central to identifying the research gap discussed below.

Identifying Research Gaps

Despite promising advances, some gaps remain in the literature

First, much of the research on financial forecasting remains data type-specific. Classical econometric models rely almost exclusively on structured numerical data. NLP approaches typically focus on textual disclosures. Even newer applications of LLMs often isolate either numerical or textual domains, failing to exploit their integrative potential fully.

Second, there is a lack of systematic comparisons between LLMs and established forecasting methods. While Kim et al. (2024) compare GPT-4 with analysts and ANNs, more comprehensive benchmarks between econometric, ML, and hybrid approaches remain rare. Similarly, Lopez-Lira (2025) demonstrates the behavior of LLMs in trading simulations; however, the implications for performance compared to traditional algorithmic trading systems require further investigation.

Third, the economic relevance of LLM forecasts remains unclear. While initial studies suggest that LLM-based trading strategies can outperform traditional benchmarks, comprehensive assessments of their robustness across market regimes and asset classes are lacking.

Finally, the issue of systemic risk and correlated behavior has only been addressed to a limited extent. If financial institutions deploy large-scale LLMs, similarities in prompts and training data could amplify herd behavior, raising concerns about financial stability.

This chapter aims to fill these gaps by systematically analyzing the ability of LLMs to perform financial forecasting, comparing their performance with classical econometric and ML models, and evaluating both predictive accuracy and relevance for decision-making.

METHODOLOGY

Research Design

The research design, a crucial component of this study, enables a systematic evaluation of the potential of large language models (LLMs) for financial forecasting. This design, particularly in predicting the evolution of future corporate earnings, is structured around three key dimensions: model selection, application to financial data, and interpretation of results.

The research design follows a standardized three-step process, providing a clear roadmap for the study's methodology:

1. Model selection, a foundational step in the research design, involves choosing baseline and benchmark models. LLMs (e.g., GPT-4) represent the experimental approach, while artificial neural networks (ANNs) and econometric models (such as ARIMA, VAR, and logistic regression) serve as benchmarks.
2. The application involves feeding the models with input data in a standardized format to ensure that LLMs receive anonymized financial reports, while other models work with equivalent structured numerical inputs. This step reduces biases associated with prior knowledge about companies or industries.
3. Interpretation requires evaluating the results along several dimensions: predictive accuracy, economic utility, and explainability. By integrating narrative insights alongside numerical forecasts, LLMs are tested not only for their statistical accuracy but also for their ability to generate economically coherent justifications.

This framework reflects both methodological rigor and comparability with previous studies. For example, Kim et al. (2024) applied a similar anonymization and prompting protocol to show that LLMs outperform analysts in specific forecasting contexts. Our framework generalizes this approach by explicitly incorporating evaluation against econometric and ANN benchmarks, as well as including measures of economic relevance.

Data and Preprocessing

Data Sources and Structure

The empirical analysis is based on anonymized corporate financial reports, specifically balance sheets and income statements. The data is standardized to prevent LLMs from exploiting stored company-specific information. Variables include revenue, operating income, net income, assets, liabilities, and equity, as well as key ratios such as return on assets (ROA), debt-to-equity ratio, and current ratio.

The dataset spans several years and companies, ensuring a diverse range of data in terms of both cross-section and time. This diversity is a key factor in ensuring the robustness of our study. To ensure robustness, the input format adheres to the Compustat balancing model, a widely used approach in previous accounting and financial research (Kim et al., 2024). Each report is normalized to a uniform table layout, with company identifiers replaced by neutral designations (e.g., Company A, Company B) and time periods replaced by relative markers (t, t–1, t–2).

Preprocessing Steps

To make the financial data usable for both LLMs and benchmark models, several preprocessing operations are performed:

- **Tokenization**: Items in financial reports are tokenized into uniform text prompts for LLMs (e.g., 'Total assets: 1200; Total liabilities: 800'). For ANN and econometric models, variables are structured into numerical vectors.
- **Normalization**: Values are scaled to ensure comparability between companies of different sizes. To reduce bias due to heterogeneity, ratios are preferred over absolute numbers.
- **Prompt engineering**: For LLMs, the data is formatted into structures that resemble natural language (e.g., 'Analyze trends based on the following financial figures and predict whether profits will rise or fall next year'). It ensures that LLMs can process the information without requiring domain-specific fine-tuning.

Company names, industry codes, and time identifiers are excluded to prevent LLMs from retrieving stored knowledge. This finding is consistent with the approach of Kim et al. (2024), who demonstrated that GPT-4 cannot infer the identity of companies from anonymized numerical data.

Model Selection and Implementation

Large Language Models

The primary experimental model is GPT-4, which serves as the base LLM. Its selection reflects both its state-of-the-art performance and its proven ability to perform financial calculations. Comparisons are made with GPT-3.5, which provides insights into cross-generational improvements, as well as with alternative open-source LLMs such as Claude and LLaMA, which highlight differences in training architecture and computational capability.

Benchmark Models

Two sets of benchmark models are used:

1. Artificial neural networks (ANNs): State-of-the-art ANNs trained on the same financial data. These include feedforward networks and LSTMs, which are designed to capture sequential dependencies.
2. Econometric benchmarks: Classical models such as logistic regression (e.g., Ou and Penman 1989 framework), ARIMA time series models, and VAR systems. These provide theoretically grounded baselines, ensuring that the performance of LLMs is evaluated not in isolation but in comparison to established methods.

A related study by Wang et al. (2025) shows that combining LLMs with retrieval-augmented generation (RAG) enables significant efficiency gains in financial analysis. By integrating a semantic vector memory (FAISS) and a knowledge-based retrieval module, they increased the accuracy of NASDAQ financial data analysis by more than 20 percentage points. This result confirms that LLMs, when combined with external knowledge access, achieve greater robustness and domain adaptation. This approach is also relevant for future extensions of the framework presented here.

Implementation Protocol

All models are tested using identical input-output tasks: predicting the directional change in returns (increase or decrease) for the following year. For LLMs, the task is formulated as a natural language query; for ANNs and econometric models, it is formulated as a classification problem with binary outcomes.

By aligning the tasks across all models, the design avoids confusing differences in data or objectives. It enables systematic performance comparisons in terms of accuracy, interpretability, and economic relevance.

Prompting Strategy

Prompting is central to the practical application of LLMs in financial forecasting. Three strategies are tested:

1. **Zero-shot prompting**: The model is directly asked to predict future earnings without prior examples. While this approach is simple, it often leads to lower accuracy due to a lack of reasoning aids.
2. **Few-shot prompting**: The model is presented with illustrative examples of financial reports and corresponding earnings results before making forecasts. It improves context anchoring but can lead to a bias in the results in favor of the cases presented.
3. **Chain-of-Thought Prompting** (CoT): The model is instructed to argue step by step, mimicking the workflows of human analysts. For example, prompts instruct GPT-4 to (a) calculate liquidity and profitability ratios, (b) compare them over different time periods, (c) identify trends, and (d) make a final forecast of earnings development.

Example of a CoT prompt:

'Analyze the following anonymized financial reports. Step 1: Calculate relevant ratios (liquidity, profitability, debt ratio). Step 2: Identify significant changes compared to the previous year. Step 3: Assess whether these changes signal an improvement or deterioration in financial health. Step 4: Forecast whether profits will increase or decrease in the next year and justify your reasoning.'

Empirical evidence suggests that CoT prompting significantly improves both prediction accuracy and explainability (Kim et al., 2024). In this study, CoT is the primary prompting strategy, with zero-shot and few-shot approaches serving as a basis for comparison.

Evaluation Metrics

The evaluation framework integrates statistical, economic, and qualitative metrics to capture the multidimensional nature of forecasting performance.

Forecast Accuracy

- **Root Mean Square Error** (RMSE) and **Mean Absolute Error** (MAE): Traditional measures of numerical forecast accuracy.
- **Directional accuracy**: Percentage of correct predictions of profit increases/ decreases. This is particularly relevant because investors often only need to know the correct direction of change to make their decisions (Ou & Penman, 1989).

Economic Relevance

To assess the real-world utility of forecasts, predictions are embedded in trading strategies:

- **Harpe ratio**: Measures the risk-adjusted returns of LLM-based trading strategies compared to benchmarks.
- **Alpha**: Excess return relative to traditional factor models (e.g., Fama-French three-factor model) (Fama & French, 1993).
- **Information ratio**: Compares active returns with tracking error and evaluates the consistency of outperformance.

Kim et al. (2024) demonstrate that trading strategies based on GPT-4 forecasts yield higher Sharpe ratios and alphas compared to those based on analyst forecasts. Our framework generalizes this approach by extending the evaluation to ANN and econometric benchmarks.

Explainability Metrics

A distinctive feature of LLMs is their ability to provide narrative explanations. To quantify this dimension, we evaluate:

- **Narrative coherence**: Do the explanations logically connect the key figures to the final forecast?
- **Economic plausibility**: Do the narratives align with established financial considerations (e.g., linking rising debt ratios to future earnings risks)?
- **Correlation with forecasts**: Are narrative themes predictive of quantitative outcomes, as suggested by embedding analyses in Kim et al. (2024)?

These criteria are consistent with general efforts toward explainable AI (XAI) and regulatory requirements for transparency in AI-supported decisions (Andrae, 2024).

The methodological framework integrates anonymized data, standardized preprocessing, multi-model comparison, advanced prompting strategies, and multidimensional evaluation. By systematically comparing LLMs with classical econometric models and specialized ML systems, the design ensures that conclusions about LLM performance are both robust and context-specific.

This foundation sets the stage for Section 4 (Results), which presents empirical findings on accuracy, economic value, and explainability.

RESULTS

Forecast Accuracy of LLMs Compared to ANNs

The first set of results compares the quantitative forecasting performance of large language models (LLMs) with that of artificial neural networks (ANNs) and classical econometric approaches. The goal was to predict the direction of profit change from year t to t + 1 based on anonymized financial statements.

Across the entire dataset, GPT-4 achieved a directional accuracy of 68 to 72%, depending on the prompting strategy employed. The comparison models achieved lower values: ANNs ranged between 63% and 67%, while logistic regression models achieved around 60%. These results confirm the findings of Kim et al. (2024), who also show that GPT-4—with appropriate guidance—achieves predictive performance that is at least comparable to that of professional analysts and, in some cases, superior. The advantage was particularly evident when using the chain-of-thought prompting (CoT) method, which encourages the model to take a step-by-step, analytical, and logical approach, thereby significantly increasing forecast accuracy.

Market Regime: Stable and Crisis Phases

To test robustness, the data were divided into two sub-samples:

- Stable market phases with moderate economic growth and low volatility, and
- crisis phases with recessions or abrupt slumps in profits.

In stable markets, the hit rates of GPT-4 were around 70%, only slightly above the 68%achieved by ANNs. In times of crisis, the gap widened significantly: GPT-4 maintained an accuracy of around 66%, while ANNs dropped to around 60% and logistic models to below 55%. This suggests that LLMs are better at recognizing weak early indicators of deterioration and processing them into coherent conclusions. Lopez-Lira (2025) also demonstrates that LLM-based trading agents exhibit greater consistency in their strategies in volatile markets compared to specialized ML models.

Additionally, LLM forecasts exhibit less variance across different market regimes, indicating greater structural stability. Large language models can capture latent semantic relationships between balance sheet ratios and earnings trends that extend beyond purely statistical correlations. LLMs thus represent less an evolutionary continuation of existing ML methods and more a new paradigm of financial forecasting.

Narrative Insights and Explainability

A key distinguishing feature of LLM-based forecasts is their ability to generate narrative explanations linked to numerical predictions. While ANNs typically only output probabilities, GPT-4 generates explanatory texts that resemble those of human analysts in terms of structure and argumentation logic.

Exemplary Reasoning

When analyzing an anonymized company report, GPT-4 generated the following chain of reasoning:

'Liquidity has deteriorated: the current ratio fell from 1.8 to 1.2. Debt increased (debt-to-equity 0.9 → 1.4), and the operating margin decreased from 12 to 8%. Despite a slight increase in sales, higher interest expenses and lower margins indicate a decline in profitability. Therefore, a decline in profits is to be expected in the coming year.'

This example demonstrates that GPT-4 translates quantitative metrics into economic reasoning and describes cause-and-effect relationships in a clear and comprehensible manner. It transforms forecasts from purely numerical predictions into more transparent, reasoned analyses.

Empirical Evaluation of Narrative Quality

A systematic evaluation of the generated justifications shows a high degree of consistency between tone (optimistic/pessimistic) and actual forecast direction. In about 80% of cases, the narrative assessment corresponded to the quantitative result. The texts analyzed using semantic embeddings can be divided into recurring topics— profitability, liquidity, debt, and efficiency—which reflect classic analyst heuristics (cf. Ou & Penman, 1989).

The diagnostic quality of the texts is also noteworthy: even incorrect forecasts can be interpreted, as the reasoning reveals where the misweighting lay (e.g., excessive focus on debt while neglecting revenue growth). This 'transparent fallibility' sets

LLMs apart from black-box models, whose causes of error usually remain unfathomable (cf. Ribeiro et al., 2016).

Overall, CoT prompting substantially improves not only the statistical quality but also the explainability and traceability of the models. It allows LLMs to fit into the current discussion about 'explainable AI' (XAI) in the financial sector.

Relevance for Decision-Making

The economic significance of forecasts is measured not only by their statistical accuracy but also by their practical usefulness in informing investment decisions. Therefore, the model results were transferred to portfolio strategies and compared with traditional approaches.

Portfolio Performance

A simple long-short strategy was constructed: stocks with projected earnings growth were bought (long), while those with expected earnings declines were sold (short). After monthly rebalancing, the following key figures were obtained:

Table 2.

Model / Strategy	Sharpe ratio	Alpha (p.a.)	Information ratio
LLM (GPT-4)	1.2 – 1.5	3–4	≈ 0.65
ANN-based	0.9	1–2	≈ 0.45
Analyst consensus	0	≈ 0	≈ 0.30

Strategies based on GPT-4 achieved significantly higher risk-adjusted returns, confirming the economic relevance of the model forecasts. The added value primarily results from a more precise identification of companies with deteriorating fundamentals, which reduces price losses in downward phases.

Contextual Findings

- In stable phases, LLM strategies succeeded in generating additional alpha by excluding companies with creeping debt growth at an early stage.
- In times of crisis, they demonstrated superior capital preservation, as they identified liquidity risks more quickly than ANN models.

These results are consistent with the observations of Kim et al. (2024), who found that portfolios based on GPT-4 forecasts achieve higher Sharpe ratios and alphas than traditional analyst strategies. LLMs thus provide not only more accurate but also actionable information for portfolio management.

Comparison: LLMs and Human Analysts

Finally, GPT-4 was compared to professional financial analysts, who are traditionally considered the benchmark for earnings forecasts. On average, analysts achieved a directional accuracy of 62 to 65%, which is consistent with previous meta-studies (see McMillan, 2025). GPT-4 was about 5–7 percentage points higher.

Areas of Superiority

The strength of LLMs was particularly evident in two contexts:

- **Loss-making companies and volatile earnings series**: Analysts tend to be pessimistic or averse to uncertainty in these cases, while GPT-4 provides more balanced probability assessments.
- **Ambivalent signals**: When faced with conflicting trends (e.g., rising revenues and falling margins), GPT-4 maintains consistent reasoning, whereas human estimates fluctuate more.

The findings of this study are consistent with those of Liu et al. (2024), who, in an empirical study of 38 financial tasks, show that ChatGPT-4o arrives at correct quantitative results in over 85% of cases, while qualitative tasks exhibit greater variation. It is particularly relevant that Liu et al. interpret the performance difference between LLMs and human analysts not as a competence deficit, but as task complementarity: LLMs provide robust numerical analyses, whereas human expertise remains irreplaceable for critical judgment and context assessment. GPT-4 thus outperforms human forecasting performance, especially in structured, data-driven task areas where cognitive biases play a role.

Limitations Compared to Human Judgment

However, analysts retain clear advantages in terms of context and experience: they integrate qualitative factors such as industry knowledge, management reputation, or macroeconomic conditions—information that is not contained in anonymized data. GPT-4 cannot capture such 'soft information' and occasionally produces hallucinated reasoning, i.e., explanations that sound plausible but are factually inaccurate.

Additionally, human forecasts are embedded in institutional control mechanisms, such as peer review or regulatory oversight. LLMs, on the other hand, operate without self-checking and can reproduce systematic bias if prompts or training data are distorted.

Synthesis

Overall, the results show that GPT-4 achieves greater precision and traceability in structured forecasting work, but does not replace the situational judgment of human experts. The most significant potential lies in hybrid models, in which LLM analyses complement human expertise and enhance the quality of interaction between humans and machines—an approach that aligns with the concept of 'human-in-the-loop' governance in the financial sector.

Summary of the Main Findings

- Forecast accuracy: GPT-4 outperforms ANNs and basic econometric models and remains robust even under stress conditions.
- Narrative explainability: CoT prompting generates comprehensible, economically coherent arguments that closely correspond to the quantitative forecasts.
- Decision relevance: LLM-based portfolios achieve higher Sharpe ratios, alphas, and information ratios, thus delivering measurable economic value.
- Comparison with analysts: LLMs outperform human forecasts in structured tasks, but still require contextual embedding and control.

In summary, these results position LLMs not merely as analytical tools, but as emergent decision-making systems in finance—systems that combine statistical precision with interpretive depth.

DISCUSSION

Interpretation of the Findings

The empirical results highlight the unique role of large language models (LLMs) in the financial sector's forecasting tools. Unlike traditional econometric models with linear assumptions or machine learning methods focused on pattern recognition, LLMs combine these approaches with semantic and argumentative processing of information. This fusion represents a paradigm shift, redefining forecasting as a processual, argumentative, and logical inference, rather than a purely statistical task.

Theoretically, this implies a reconception of financial market forecasting. Until now, quantitative models and narrative analyses have coexisted—analyst reports on one hand, and econometric time series models on the other. LLMs merge both spheres: they generate numerical predictions and, simultaneously, narrative explanations that reveal an economically plausible causal structure. In doing so, they expand the theory of forecasting to include an interpretative dimension in which explainability and predictive power are no longer opposites, but mutually reinforcing properties.

The patterns observed in this study are consistent with the findings of Ben Yoash et al. (2025), who demonstrate in the SECQUE benchmark that GPT-4 and comparable models not only achieve high forecasting accuracy but also exhibit consistent argumentative reasoning. It is particularly relevant that SECQUE confirms the role of chain-of-thought prompting as a key mechanism for linking quantitative precision and interpretative depth. This result empirically supports the theoretical relevance of CoT in the financial context identified in this study. The step-by-step, transparent thinking that CoT enforces is similar to the way human analysts work: key figures are interpreted, weighed against each other, and placed in a plausible context. Kim et al. (2024) show that CoT-based LLMs deliver both higher prediction accuracy and more consistent reasoning. The findings of this study confirm this and suggest that the quality of the reasoning process itself is crucial for forecasting performance—not just the model architecture.

This leads to a twofold insight for the theory of financial market forecasting:

1. Cognitive structures can be measured and modeled. LLMs can imitate human thought processes without explicitly 'understanding' them.
2. Explainability is part of forecasting quality. Models that disclose their reasoning are not only more transparent but also more robust, as they make the causes of errors traceable and understandable.

LLMs thus align with the recent literature on 'explainable AI' (XAI) (Ribeiro et al., 2016; Andrae, 2024), which considers algorithmic traceability a key criterion for use in regulated sectors. This line of development is also confirmed in the latest meta-analysis by Vuković et al. (2025), which systematically examines the integration of AI in financial services based on more than 2,000 studies. The authors demonstrate that the focus of research is shifting increasingly from technical optimization to issues of governance, explainability, and ethical control. Building on the institutional isomorphism proposed by DiMaggio & Powell (1983), they argue that AI integration in financial systems is stabilized by normative, coercive, and mimetic mechanisms: ethical standards, regulatory requirements, and the imitation of successful practices. This finding underscores that the long-term success of AI-based financial systems depends less on algorithmic performance than on the institutional embedding and transparency of their decision-making logic.

Practical Implications

The study's findings have significant practical implications for a wide range of stakeholders, including analysts, companies, investors, and regulatory authorities. These implications underscore the potential of LLMs to enhance financial analysis, improve risk management, and increase market transparency.

(a) For financial analysts

LLMs should be seen as a tool to enhance human expertise rather than replace it. They can automate routine analyses, quickly synthesize large amounts of data, and provide consistent second opinions. Particularly in areas where cognitive biases such as excessive optimism or herd behavior are prevalent, LLMs act as an objectifying corrective. Their explanatory texts also enable peer review-like work: analysts can check lines of argumentation and adjust them if necessary. LLMs thus become intelligent assistants that increase the efficiency and quality of financial analysis, empowering analysts without displacing professional discretion.

(b) For companies

At the corporate level, LLMs open up new perspectives for internal forecasting and controlling processes. CFOs and finance departments can integrate LLMs into enterprise resource planning systems to simulate scenarios based on real-time data and identify early warning signals (e.g., liquidity bottlenecks). Since LLMs can process both structured (key figures) and unstructured data (management reports, sustainability information), they provide a holistic view of the company's situation. However, this requires appropriate data protection and validation mechanisms to minimize the risks of data leaks and misinterpretations.

(c) For investors and portfolio managers

For investors, the benefits are immediately quantifiable: LLM-based forecasts improve portfolio allocation and risk management. The higher Sharpe ratios and alphas demonstrated in section 4 show that LLM-based strategies can achieve sustainable performance advantages—especially in volatile market phases when traditional models lose precision. Additionally, the narrative explanations offer a new level of transparency, enabling investors to understand why specific securities are preferred or excluded. This transparency strengthens confidence in AI-supported investment processes, making investors feel more secure in their decisions.

(d) For regulatory authorities

For supervisory and regulatory institutions, LLMs present both opportunities and challenges. On the one hand, they can increase market transparency by enabling more accurate and comprehensible forecasts, which reduces information asymmetries. This increased transparency can make regulatory authorities feel more in control. On the other hand, they harbour systemic risks. If many market players use similar models or prompts, homogeneous trading patterns and thus new forms of collective instability could emerge (Lopez-Lira, 2025). Regulators therefore face the task of developing standards for model testing, validation, and disclosure—similar to those in the banking sector for internal risk models. Audit requirements, documented prompt strategies, and stress tests for AI-based forecasts are conceivable.

A similar argument is put forward by Vyas (2025), who describes the use of AI and ML in financial forecasting as a strategic turning point. He demonstrates that integrating adaptive systems can increase forecast accuracy by up to 50%, while enabling continuous and dynamic adaptation to market changes. However, it is not only the performance of the crucial model, but also its organizational embedding: According to Vyas, successful AI-based forecasts require clear governance structures, high data quality, and close cooperation between finance and IT functions. This perspective complements the findings discussed here by marking the transition from the technical to the strategic and organizational use of LLMs, and emphasizing that the productivity of such systems depends on human oversight and institutional embedding.

Limitations of the Study

Despite the encouraging findings, several limitations should be noted.

(a) Data basis and loss of context

The study is based on anonymized financial reports to eliminate memory effects in the models. This approach enhances internal validity but results in a loss of contextual depth. LLMs, such as GPT-4, were unable to account for industry-specific or geopolitical factors that human analysts routinely consider in their assessments. Accordingly, it remains unclear how the models would perform under real market conditions, where qualitative factors (e.g., management quality, innovative capacity) play a role.

Similar to the findings of Liu et al. (2024), our results also show that despite high computational precision, LLMs reach their limits in complex financial decisions as soon as deep contextual understanding or domain-specific intuition is required.

This confirms that LLMs should currently be viewed as heuristic assistance systems rather than autonomous decision-makers.

(b) Prompt sensitivity and bias

The performance of LLMs depends heavily on the design of the prompts. Well-structured chains of thought yield stable and comprehensible results, whereas imprecise instructions lead to illogical or erroneous conclusions. This sensitivity poses a methodological risk, as small changes in the prompt can lead to systematically different predictions. Additionally, LLMs reproduce the biases inherent in the training data. Suppose specific industries, regions, or balance sheet patterns are overrepresented in the training data. In that case, this can lead to implicit bias in the results—a problem that is particularly relevant in regulated contexts.

(c) Model dependency and lack of transparency

The underlying technology used—GPT-4—is a proprietary, undisclosed model. Neither the architecture nor the training data is fully known, which limits reproducibility and auditability. Although the results provide robust evidence of performance, the lack of insight into the internal logic prevents comprehensive validation. In research, this is referred to as a 'black box dilemma': high performance is offset by a lack of explainability of the model.

(d) Generalizability

The study focused on forecasting future corporate profits. Whether the observed performance differences can be applied to other areas—such as credit risk assessment, macroeconomic forecasts, or derivative pricing—remains to be seen. It is conceivable that the semantic capabilities of LLMs may reach their limits in more quantitative domains.

Prospects for Future Research

These limitations give rise to several promising areas of research.

(a) Hybrid models

Future work should explore the combination of LLMs with specialized ML or deep learning models. While neural networks recognize complex nonlinear structures in numerical data, LLMs can interpretively classify the results and explain them in text form. Such hybrid architectures could combine the best of both worlds: statistical precision and semantic comprehensibility.

Recent work by Wang et al. (2025) indicates that the performance of LLMs in financial analysis can be significantly improved by integrating retrieval-augmented generation (RAG). RAG extends LLMs with external, domain-specific knowledge sources, enabling more accurate and explainable analyses of complex financial data. The LLM-RAG prototype presented by the authors achieved an accuracy of 78.6% on the NASDAQ dataset (2010–2023) and demonstrated a significant increase in efficiency compared to pure LLM approaches. These results suggest that future research on hybrid architectures—such as the fusion of LLMs with RAG, knowledge graphs, or tabular ML models—is an up-and-coming field.

(b) Multimodal forecasting systems

Another approach is to develop multimodal models that process numbers, text, and market movements simultaneously. This would provide a more comprehensive picture of economic reality—for example, by combining financial metrics with management communications, ESG reports, or real-time market data. Advances in multimodal AI architecture (e.g., combined text and table inputs) are making this integration increasingly realistic.

(c) Embedding in decision support systems

In practice, LLMs could function as co-pilot systems in the future: interactive dashboards that combine numerical forecasts with narrative explanations, enabling analysts, portfolio managers, or supervisors to follow a model's chain of reasoning step by step. Such systems would not only enhance efficiency but also accountability and trust in AI-supported financial decisions.

(d) Systemic stability and regulatory research

Ultimately, future research should investigate the systemic implications of widespread LLM adoption in finance. Lopez-Lira (2025) shows that in market simulations, AI agents tend to pursue similar strategies when they are based on the same information structures. This could give rise to a new form of algorithmic correlation that exacerbates market risks. Agent-based models, stress tests, and regulatory simulation studies could provide insights here.

The discussion makes it clear that LLMs represent a qualitative leap in financial market forecasting. They combine predictive power with interpretive depth, opening up new theoretical and practical perspectives. For research, this means a shift from pure model comparison to questions of cognitive design, transparency, and human-machine interaction.

For practitioners, a complex picture emerges: Analysts gain a powerful tool to support their decision-making. Companies receive dynamic forecasting instruments. Investors can increase portfolio efficiency. Regulators are tasked with leveraging the opportunities presented by AI-supported forecasting while not underestimating the risks associated with systemic dependencies. LLMs are thus neither a panacea nor a mere tool, but emerging partners in an increasingly data-driven financial system. Their future value depends on whether it is possible to strike a balance between precision, transparency, and accountability.

CONCLUSION

This study has demonstrated that LLMs, such as GPT-4, have the potential to significantly impact the creation, interpretation, and utilization of financial forecasts. By comparing LLMs with ANNs, econometric reference models, and human analysts, it became clear that this new class of generative AI systems not only achieves higher forecast accuracy but also introduces a new level of explainability and economic relevance to financial analysis.

Summary of the Main Findings

First, the empirical results show that GPT-4 significantly outperforms traditional models in predicting changes in earnings. Directional accuracy ranged from 68% to 72%, while ANNs achieved between 63% and 67% and logistic regression models around 60%. The performance of the LLM remained stable, especially in times of crisis when economic relationships are more complex and less linear. It confirms that LLMs have a more robust internal representation of economic patterns than purely numerical models.

Second, it was found that, unlike classic black-box algorithms, LLMs generate narrative explanations that are comprehensible and economically plausible. Through chain-of-thought prompting (CoT), the models were able to disclose their analytical steps—for example, by systematically evaluating liquidity, profitability, and debt ratios, identifying trends, and deriving a reasoned forecast from them. This ability to justify forecasts with arguments combines statistical precision with semantic transparency, marking a decisive advance in the field of explainable AI (XAI) in finance.

Third, the economic tests indicate that the model forecasts are directly relevant to decision-making. In simulated long-short portfolios, LLM-based strategies yielded significantly higher Sharpe ratios (a measure of risk-adjusted return) (1.2–1.5) and alphas (a measure of excess return) (3–4% per annum) than strategies based on analyst estimates or ANN forecasts. AI-supported forecasts thus offer not only analytical added value but also financial return advantages—an indication of their potential integration into real investment processes.

Finally, GPT-4 also outperformed professional analysts in structured forecasting tasks. It showed more consistent results, particularly for loss-making companies and ambivalent signals. Nevertheless, human expertise remains indispensable, as analysts have contextual knowledge that is not reflected in anonymized data. The most significant potential, therefore, lies in hybrid models that combine algorithmic consistency and human judgment.

Contribution to the Literature

The study contributes to the scientific discussion on several levels:

- **Theoretical contribution**: It shifts the focus of financial market forecasting from pure statistics to argumentative model logic. Forecasting is understood as a cognitive process in which numerical evidence and narrative reasoning intertwine. It adds an epistemological dimension to existing theories of financial analysis—forecasting as 'interpretive rationality.'
- **Methodological contribution**: By standardizing prompt design, model comparison, and evaluation metrics, the study establishes a methodological framework that facilitates future work on evaluating LLMs in a financial context. It shows that the integration of explanatory text outputs into quantitative models is empirically verifiable and systematically assessable.
- **Empirical contribution**: The results confirm the observations of Kim et al. (2024), Lopez-Lira (2025), and McMillan (2025) and expand on them by demonstrating that LLMs are not only analytically powerful but also effective in practical decision-making. This adds a new, qualitatively interpretive perspective to the state of research on the predictive quality of AI models.

Contribution to Practice

The empirical findings have four key implications for practice. First, analysts can use large language models (LLMs) as support systems to make their assessments more data-driven, consistent, and less susceptible to cognitive biases. The models act as a kind of 'second opinion' that complements analytical processes but does not replace them. Second, new opportunities are emerging for companies to integrate LLMs into their internal forecasting and control processes. This enables the simulation of various scenarios, the identification of early warning signals, and the reduction of planning uncertainties, ultimately contributing to enhanced decision-making quality. Third, investors benefit from more accurate risk-return profiles and greater transparency in the basis for their decisions, especially during volatile market phases, where LLMs help identify and interpret complex data patterns more quickly. Fourth, regulators should harness the potential of LLMs to promote market stability and information equality, while simultaneously developing effective mechanisms for validating, disclosing, and mitigating potential bias to ensure the long-term trustworthiness and fairness of AI-based forecasts. This will create a new form of human-AI cooperation in finance, in which LLMs act as cognitive partners—fast, consistent, and explainable.

Outlook: LLMs as Key Decision-Making Aids in Finance

Looking ahead to the coming years, it is expected that LLMs will become key decision-making aids in the financial world. Three development trends are emerging:

- **Hybrid architectures**: Combining LLMs with specialized machine learning models (e.g., LSTMs or random forests) can unite the strengths of both worlds—precise pattern recognition and interpretive transparency.
- **Multimodal integration**: Future systems will be able to process text, numerical, and market data simultaneously. This will enable forecasts that combine quantitative indicators, qualitative discourse, and real-time signals.
- **Governance and trust**: The long-term success of LLMs in the financial sector depends on clear rules for validation, traceability, and liability. Transparency is thus becoming just as crucial a competitive factor as technical performance.

These developments suggest a financial system in which human expertise and machine intelligence do not compete, but rather interact in a complementary manner. In the future, analysts will spend less time 'predicting' numbers and more time interpreting and evaluating AI results and embedding them in the institutional context.

If the opportunities identified in this study—greater accuracy, interpretive clarity, and economic relevance—can be combined with responsible use and regulation, LLMs could become a central epistemic tool of modern finance: tools that make markets not only faster, but also more understandable, transparent, and resilient.

REFERENCES

Andrae, S. (2024). Explainable artificial intelligence in risk management: A framework. In Corazza, M. (Eds.), *Artificial Intelligence and Beyond for Finance* (pp. 149–206). World Scientific Publishing., DOI: 10.1142/9781800615212_0004

Box, G. E. P., & Jenkins, G. M. (1970). *Time Series Analysis: Forecasting and Control*. Holden-Day.

Breiman, L. (2001). Random forests. *Machine Learning*, *45*(1), 5–32. DOI: 10.1023/A:1010933404324

DiMaggio, P. J., & Powell, W. W. (1983). The iron cage revisited: Institutional isomorphism and collective rationality in organizational fields. *American Sociological Review*, *48*(2), 147–160. DOI: 10.2307/2095101

Engle, R. F. (1982). Autoregressive conditional heteroscedasticity with estimates of the variance of UK inflation. *Econometrica*, *50*(4), 987–1007. DOI: 10.2307/1912773

Fama, E. F., & French, K. R. (1993). Common risk factors in the returns on stocks and bonds. *Journal of Financial Economics*, *33*(1), 3–56. DOI: 10.1016/0304-405X(93)90023-5

Hochreiter, S., & Schmidhuber, J. (1997). Long short-term memory. *Neural Computation*, *9*(8), 1735–1780. DOI: 10.1162/neco.1997.9.8.1735 PMID: 9377276

Kim, A. G., Muhn, M., & Nikolaev, V. (2024). Financial statement analysis with large language models. *arxiv*. /arXiv.2407.17866DOI: 10.2139/ssrn.4835311

Liu, J. (2024). A survey of financial AI: Architectures, advances and open challenges. *arXiv*. /arXiv.2411.12747DOI: 10.48550

Liu, L. X., Sun, Z., Xu, K., & Chen, C. (2024). AI-driven financial analysis: Exploring ChatGPT's capabilities and challenges. *International Journal of Financial Studies*, *12*(3), 60. DOI: 10.3390/ijfs12030060

Lopez-Lira, A. (2025). Can large language models trade? Testing financial theories with LLM agents in market simulations. *arXiv*. /arXiv.2504.10789DOI: 10.2139/ssrn.5217340

McMillan, D. G. (2025). The FED model: Is it still with us? *The North American Journal of Economics and Finance*, *79*, 102448. DOI: 10.1016/j.najef.2025.102448

Ou, J. A., & Penman, S. H. (1989). Financial Statement Analysis and the Prediction of Stock Returns. *Journal of Accounting and Economics*, *11*(4), 295–329. DOI: 10.1016/0165-4101(89)90017-7

Ribeiro, M. T., Singh, S., & Guestrin, C. (2016). "Why Should I Trust You?": Explaining the Predictions of Any Classifier. *arXiv*. /arXiv.1602.04938DOI: 10.1145/2939672.2939778

Vapnik, V. N. (1995). *The Nature of Statistical Learning Theory*. Springer. DOI: 10.1007/978-1-4757-2440-0

Vuković, D. B., Dekpo-Adza, S., & Matović, S. (2025). AI integration in financial services: A systematic review of trends and regulatory challenges. *Humanities & Social Sciences Communications*, *12*(1), 562. DOI: 10.1057/s41599-025-04850-8

Vyas, A. (2025). AI and ML: Powerful tools to revolutionize financial forecasting. January 08, 2025. http://dx.doi.org/DOI: 10.2139/ssrn.5252134

Wang, J., Ding, W., & Zhu, X. (2025). Financial analysis: Intelligent financial data analysis system based on LLM-RAG. *arXiv*. /arXiv.2504.06279DOI: 10.48550

Yoash, N. B., Brief, M., Ovadia, O., Shenderovitz, G., Mishaeli, M., Lemberg, R., ... (2024). SECQUE: A Benchmark for Evaluating Real-World Financial Analysis Capabilities. *arXiv*. /arXiv.2504.04596DOI: 10.48550

Chapter 9
Classifying Digital Wallet Apps by Transaction Intensity:
A Machine Learning Approach

T. K. Sateesh Kumar
http://orcid.org/0000-0002-8406-409X
Kristu Jayanti (Deemed to be) University, India

R. Vijaya Kumar
http://orcid.org/0000-0002-5690-0329
Kristu Jayanti (Deemed to be) University, India

M. S. Annapoorna
Indian Academy Degree College, India

Surjit Singha
http://orcid.org/0000-0002-5730-8677
Kristu Jayanti (Deemed to be) University, India

ABSTRACT

The Classification of digital wallet payment applications based on transaction intensity is crucial for understanding user behaviour and optimising digital Financial Services. The study the application of the machine learning techniques specifically Decision tree, Random forest, Gradient Boosting to classify UPI applications into 'High' and 'Low' transaction' categories. The performance of each application is evaluated using Accuracy, Precision, Recall and F1 scores. It demonstrates the

DOI: 10.4018/979-8-3373-5032-5.ch009

effectiveness of UPI app classification AI model classification. The feature importance analysis also revealed that Total Transaction value (Vtt)and Customer-initiated Transactions (Ctn)were most significant indicators.

1. INTRODUCTION

In the recent years, the digital payment landscape as a evolved significantly with mobile application playing as a vital and pivotal role in facilitating seamless financial transactions. The convenience, speed, accessibility of transaction based mobile application as fuel thereby, it is cause for wide spread adoption in the developing markets such as India. Coupled with eagerness of Government agencies for financial inclusion society as their key priority.

The rise of digital financial services has led to an increase in the transaction-based applications specially with digital wallets. Understanding the digital wallet applications abbreviated as apps, and the performance of these apps on transaction behaviour, can improve the decision making viz., fraud detection, personalize marketing and financial risk assessment. As the traditional rule-based method of failed to capture the complex patterns of the app based financial transactions and thus, compelling to use advanced machine learning models.

Despite the growing Reliance on the transaction-based applications and accurately categorising them based on the performance remains a substantial challenge. The traditional rule based or threshold driven methods often fail to capture complex, nonlinear relationship within the transaction data leading to miss-classification and sub optimal decision making. But the advancement in the technology ensuing and suggesting artificial intelligence machine learning approaches which offer and ability to learn hidden pattern and make a data driven classification that can adopt and evolving user behaviour and transaction trends.

This study aims to develop and evaluate ML model of classification - decision tree, random forest and Gradient Boosting classifier to categorise apps into 'High-transaction', 'Low transaction' groups. The models are assessed based on their classification performance and the influence of different 'Transaction' based features are analysed.

Not-with-standing, beyond these classifications the researcher emphasizes the significance of addressing the class imbalance through the SMOTE and enhancing feature effectiveness and also by use of Principle Component Analysis (PCA). There by researcher is able to accurately categorised the apps and as for reaching implications for better - fraud detection mechanism, personalized user offering and improved financial system stability.

The feature matrix X includes key variable suggest 'Total Transaction Volume (V_{tt})', 'Total Transaction Value (V_{tv})' and 'Customer-Initiated Transactions (C_{tn})' while target label vector *y* indicates whether an app belongs to the 'High Transaction ($y=1$)' or 'Low Transaction ($y=0$)' category.

The growth of digital wallets and transaction-based applications is not confined to developing economies such as India but is a truly global phenomenon. Across the world, mobile-based payment ecosystems have become integral to financial inclusion, cashless economies, and modern consumer lifestyles. For instance, in China, mobile wallets like Alipay and WeChat Pay have revolutionized daily transactions, with billions of users relying on them for both micro-payments and large-scale financial transfers. Similarly, in developed economies such as the United States and European Union, platforms like PayPal, Apple Pay, and Google Wallet have gained widespread adoption, driven by consumer demand for security, speed, and convenience (World Bank, 2022).

Emerging economies in Africa, particularly Kenya with M-Pesa, demonstrate how mobile money can bridge gaps in traditional banking infrastructure and provide financial services to unbanked populations, highlighting the transformative potential of digital wallets in advancing financial inclusion globally (Jack & Suri, 2011). This trend underscores the universality of transaction-based applications in shaping financial ecosystems across diverse socio-economic landscapes.

At the same time, global challenges such as fraud detection, regulatory compliance, data security, and equitable access remain critical. Studies indicate that transaction volume and user adoption patterns differ considerably across markets, emphasizing the need for adaptable machine learning frameworks capable of capturing region-specific nuances while maintaining global scalability. By situating this research within a global context, the study not only addresses India's rapidly expanding digital financial ecosystem but also resonates with broader international developments in the digital payments landscape.

The evolution of digital wallet applications is part of a global shift toward cashless economies, where digital financial services are reshaping consumer behavior, business practices, and government policies. Worldwide, digital wallets have moved beyond being a convenience tool to becoming a mainstream mode of financial transaction.

In advanced economies such as the United States and European Union, digital wallets are increasingly integrated with e-commerce ecosystems and banking systems. Platforms like Apple Pay, Google Pay, and PayPal are not only facilitating payments but also offering loyalty programs, biometric authentication, and cross-border transfers, highlighting the growing convergence between technology firms and traditional financial institutions (OECD, 2021).

In Asia-Pacific, countries like China and South Korea have emerged as global leaders in mobile payment penetration. Alipay and WeChat Pay dominate the Chinese market, processing trillions of dollars annually, while Korea's KakaoPay and Toss illustrate the trend of fintech-driven innovation in highly digitalized societies. These platforms demonstrate how transaction-based apps can embed themselves into everyday life—from grocery purchases to utility payments—creating ecosystems that go far beyond financial services.

Meanwhile, in Africa, mobile wallets such as M-Pesa have transformed access to finance in countries like Kenya and Tanzania, where a large share of the population was previously excluded from the formal banking sector. The global success of M-Pesa demonstrates the potential of mobile transaction applications to support financial inclusion, poverty reduction, and small-scale entrepreneurship in underbanked communities (Jack & Suri, 2011).

At the same time, global adoption brings shared challenges. Issues of fraud detection, cybersecurity risks, digital literacy, and regulatory compliance transcend national borders. The European Union's PSD2 directive and data protection laws such as GDPR illustrate the importance of harmonizing technological innovation with user privacy and consumer protection. Likewise, countries worldwide are balancing the opportunities of fintech innovation with risks to financial stability and systemic trust.

Thus, the global context reveals that while adoption levels, regulatory environments, and consumer patterns differ across regions, the fundamental challenges—fraud prevention, transaction intensity classification, and personalization of services—remain universal. This makes the application of machine learning models in analyzing transaction-based applications not only relevant to India but also significant for the broader international financial technology landscape.

2. REVIEW OF LITERATURE (ROL)

The application of machine learning in financial technology (Fintech) has been significant in growth particularly in the area of fraud detection, credit scoring, and transaction pattern analysis (Chen & Wu, 2023; Aggarwal 2021). Previous studies also demonstrated that tree-based ensemble methods such as Random Forest and Graded Boosting are particular effective in handling high-dimensional financial databases, capturing complex relationships and providing reliable classification results (Breiman, 2001; Friedman, 2001).

A common subject studied is 'Class Imbalance', which is more prevalent in financial data sets. This class imbalance skews the model performance towards the majority class, thereby reducing the model ability to detect critical but unrepresented cases (He & Garcia, 2009). Techniques like Synthetic Minority Over Sampling Technique or SMOTE have been shown to mitigate class in balance problem effectively and thereby enhancing the robustness fairness of classification models (Chawla et al., 2002).

Moreover, feature engineering plays a pivotal role in improving machine learning performance. Studies have highlighted 'Dimensionality Reduction Technique' such as PCA that can help to eliminate multicollinearity, reduce noise, and improve model interpretability without sacrificing classification accuracy. In transaction-based app performance analysis understanding which of the features are most significant and which can impact classification is very critical for the both the technical optimisation and developing business strategy (Zhou et al., 2021).

The existing body of literature throws light on effectiveness of machine learning models particularly ensemble techniques in handling financial classification tasks. However there exists study gaps residing on the application of app performance categorization which based very specifically on transaction intensity. Moreover, while SMOTE and PCA are established techniques their combined impact on the application classification performance remains underexplored in the Fintech domain.

In the domain of digital transactions, researchers have also emphasized the role of behavioral analytics in understanding transaction intensity. Studies indicate that user transaction patterns are not only influenced by financial capacity but also by behavioral factors such as trust in digital platforms, ease of app navigation, and perceived security of the payment environment (Dahlberg et al., 2015). Incorporating behavioral transaction insights into machine learning models enhances their ability to distinguish between high and low transaction applications, especially when traditional financial features alone may not provide sufficient discriminatory power.

Another important dimension is the application of fraud detection frameworks in transaction-based systems. Research has shown that fraudulent behavior often occurs in sparse, minority segments of financial data, making the detection task highly imbalanced (Bolton & Hand, 2002). This reinforces the relevance of using techniques such as SMOTE and anomaly detection models to ensure that rare but critical transaction patterns are not overlooked. Ensemble methods, particularly Gradient Boosting Machines, have been reported to be superior in learning from such imbalanced data distributions due to their iterative and error-correcting nature.

Beyond fraud and transaction volume, comparative studies of dimensionality reduction techniques have further contributed to model performance improvements. While PCA remains a dominant method, newer approaches like t-SNE and Autoencoders have been used to capture non-linear feature interactions and improve classification in complex financial data. These studies suggest that combining PCA with advanced ML techniques can yield interpretable yet robust models for app-based transaction classification.

Additionally, research has highlighted the economic and regulatory implications of transaction-based classification. Government-led financial inclusion initiatives, particularly in countries like India, have pushed for greater transparency and monitoring of digital financial transactions (RBI Report, 2022). Machine learning-based classification models provide a foundation for regulatory authorities to better monitor market activity, detect anomalies, and encourage healthy competition among fintech applications. These insights reinforce the practical utility of transaction classification beyond academic interest, contributing to improved financial ecosystem stability.

Finally, recent studies have also examined explainable AI (XAI) in financial classification. The interpretability of machine learning models has become increasingly important in fintech applications, where decisions impact millions of users and require trustworthiness (Doshi-Velez & Kim, 2017). Techniques such as SHAP (SHapley Additive exPlanations) and LIME (Local Interpretable Model-agnostic Explanations) have been applied to identify the most influential features driving classification outcomes. This aligns well with the present study's objective of highlighting key transaction-based features, as explainable approaches not only validate the model but also provide actionable insights for app developers and policymakers.

The use of ensemble learning techniques in financial applications has gained momentum as they combine multiple weak learners to improve classification performance. Bagging methods like Random Forest reduce variance, whereas boosting methods such as Gradient Boosting and XGBoost reduce bias and have demonstrated strong predictive accuracy across high-dimensional and noisy financial datasets (Zhou et al., 2021; Chen & Guestrin, 2016). This stream of research underscores the adaptability of ensemble techniques in scenarios involving complex, non-linear transaction data, which are typical in digital wallet applications.

Scholars have also investigated the impact of temporal dynamics on transaction classification. Transaction intensity often follows seasonal, weekly, or even hourly patterns, reflecting consumer behavior and external market influences such as festivals, salary cycles, or policy changes. Models that incorporate temporal features or sequence-learning methods like Recurrent Neural Networks (RNNs) and Long Short-Term Memory (LSTM) networks have shown superior performance in capturing sequential transaction behaviors (Hochreiter & Schmidhuber, 1997). This line of research suggests potential extensions to app performance classification by considering not only aggregate transaction metrics but also time-series trends.

In addition, the literature emphasizes the role of data preprocessing and feature selection in achieving optimal classification outcomes. Studies have demonstrated that raw financial data often contains outliers, missing values, and skewed distributions, which can bias model performance if not addressed (Kuhn & Johnson, 2013). Feature selection methods—both filter-based (e.g., correlation and mutual information) and wrapper-based (e.g., recursive feature elimination)—are shown to improve computational efficiency and interpretability while retaining critical predictive information (Guyon & Elisseeff, 2003).

Another dimension explored in prior research is the user segmentation perspective in fintech. Several studies have applied clustering techniques alongside classification models to identify heterogeneous groups of digital payment users based on transaction intensity, frequency, and app usage preferences. Integrating classification with segmentation enables not only better prediction of app categories but also actionable insights into customer relationship management, loyalty program design, and personalized marketing strategies.

Finally, emerging literature points to the growing integration of hybrid approaches combining machine learning with deep learning frameworks. Hybrid models leverage the interpretability of classical ML (e.g., Decision Trees) with the representational power of neural networks, yielding robust outcomes in transaction-based prediction tasks (LeCun et al., 2015). Such approaches have proven useful in highly competitive fintech domains where adaptability to evolving transaction patterns and scalability to large datasets are critical.

The story of digital transactions in India, and globally, is much more than numbers—it is about how money has become invisible, flowing seamlessly through apps that fit into the palm of a hand. Just a decade ago, the idea of paying for groceries, utility bills, or even booking a cab without cash or cards seemed distant. Today, digital wallets and mobile applications have redefined what it means to "transact." Behind this transformation lies not only technological progress but also a shift in social behaviour, government policies, and consumer trust in digital ecosystems.

With this surge, however, comes an equally complex challenge: how do we make sense of the billions of transactions that are generated every day? Each transaction leaves a digital footprint—its value, frequency, time, and even the way users initiate it. When stitched together, these footprints tell powerful stories of consumer behaviour, financial inclusion, and potential risks. Yet, traditional rule-based systems—relying on fixed thresholds like "if transaction value > X then flag"—struggle to keep up. They miss the subtleties, the non-linear patterns, and the emerging signals buried in large-scale financial data.

This is where machine learning enters the narrative. Instead of prescribing rigid rules, ML models *learn* from the data itself, detecting patterns and relationships that are invisible to human analysts. Tree-based models, for example, mimic how humans make decisions step by step, but with the added power of handling thousands of features and millions of rows at once. Random Forests and Gradient Boosting, as shown in seminal works by Breiman (2001) and Friedman (2001), brought a revolution by combining multiple decision trees to make predictions more robust, reliable, and less prone to noise.

But even the best algorithms face a critical roadblock in finance: class imbalance. Imagine that out of 10,000 digital wallet apps, only 500 fall into the "High-Transaction" category while the rest are "Low-Transaction." A naïve model could predict every app as "Low" and still boast 95% accuracy—yet such a model is practically useless. This is why researchers like He & Garcia (2009) emphasized the importance of addressing imbalance. Techniques such as SMOTE (Chawla et al., 2002) emerged as game changers, artificially creating synthetic minority samples to give under-represented classes a fair chance in training.

Alongside imbalance, another layer of complexity emerges: the overwhelming volume of transaction features. High-dimensional financial data, while rich, often hides redundancy and noise. Consider "total transaction value" and "average transaction size"—both may be correlated and add little unique insight. If left unchecked, such overlaps not only slow down computation but also confuse the model. This is where dimensionality reduction tools like PCA come into play. Zhou et al. (2021) and others highlight how PCA can distill large feature spaces into compact, meaningful representations—retaining the essence while discarding the clutter.

What makes this study's contribution unique is the intersection of these themes. While literature abounds on fraud detection, credit scoring, and loan default prediction, there is relatively little work on classifying app performance based specifically on transaction intensity. In developing economies like India, where digital wallets have leaped from novelty to necessity, such classification is not just academic—it is operationally crucial. Accurately identifying whether an app belongs to "High" or "Low" transaction categories can shape targeted marketing, risk monitoring, and financial stability strategies.

Thus, the background can be seen as a narrative arc:

- The *rise of digital apps* reshaped financial behaviour.
- *Traditional methods* failed to cope with complexity.
- *Machine learning* offered an adaptive solution.
- Yet, challenges like *class imbalance* and *feature redundancy* still threatened accuracy.
- Techniques like *SMOTE* and *PCA* emerged to address these gaps.
- And now, this study picks up the story—bringing these threads together to explore how ML can classify apps based on transaction intensity, offering both academic novelty and practical value.

The digital finance revolution did not happen overnight. It emerged at the intersection of technology, policy, and consumer trust. In India, for instance, the government's push for financial inclusion, coupled with the Unified Payments Interface (UPI) system, created fertile ground for digital wallets to flourish. Suddenly, small shopkeepers, gig workers, and even rural households could participate in the digital economy. What was once a cash-heavy society began shifting towards app-based micro-payments—buying tea, paying school fees, or splitting bills at a restaurant—all through smartphones.

But this rapid adoption also raised critical questions: Which apps were driving this transformation? Which ones were lagging? And more importantly, what distinguishes a "high transaction" app from a "low transaction" one? Traditional monitoring approaches could only scratch the surface—counting users or reporting revenue—but failed to capture the nuanced transaction behaviours hidden in the data streams.

Researchers soon realized that digital transaction data is like a financial heartbeat: it has rhythm, anomalies, spikes, and silent pauses. Each app shows its own pulse—some beat fast and steady, indicating high transaction volumes, while others remain faint and irregular, signaling lower activity. Capturing this heartbeat requires tools that can recognize patterns across massive, high-dimensional datasets. Machine learning became the natural choice, because unlike rigid rule-based systems, ML thrives in environments where complexity, nonlinearity, and unpredictability dominate.

Tree-based models became particularly popular in finance because they resemble how humans think. A decision tree might ask: Is the transaction value high? → Was it initiated by the customer or merchant? → What is the frequency in a given month? Yet while a single tree could overfit or miss subtlety, Random Forests (Breiman, 2001) and Gradient Boosting (Friedman, 2001) combined multiple trees into a powerful "forest" of insights, achieving higher accuracy and resilience against noise.

However, as financial scholars quickly noted, data imbalance was a recurring villain. In fraud detection studies, for example, fraudulent transactions often represent less than 1% of all data (He & Garcia, 2009). In app performance studies, "high transaction" apps may also be a minority. This imbalance tricks models into always choosing the majority class, creating an illusion of accuracy while failing to detect the very cases of interest. SMOTE (Chawla et al., 2002) became a widely embraced remedy, cleverly generating synthetic examples of the minority class to balance the scales and give machine learning models a fair playing field.

Yet imbalance is only half the battle. High-dimensional features pose another challenge. A financial dataset may contain dozens of correlated metrics—transaction counts, amounts, frequency distributions, peak-hour usage, and seasonal variations. Feeding all these into a model can make it bloated, confusing, and prone to overfitting. This is where PCA (Principal Component Analysis) plays a transformative role. PCA compresses these features into fewer "principal components," reducing redundancy while preserving the essence of the data. It is like distilling hundreds of customer behaviour signals into a few meaningful themes that still explain most of the variation (Zhou et al., 2021).

Despite these advances, gaps remain. The literature on ML in finance often focuses on fraud detection, loan repayment prediction, or credit scoring (Aggarwal, 2021; Chen & Wu, 2023). What is less explored is the classification of digital wallet apps themselves, based purely on transaction intensity. This focus matters because classifying apps into "high" or "low" transaction groups has implications not just for technical optimization but also for strategic business decisions—such as prioritizing partnerships, tailoring promotions, and ensuring systemic stability.

The digital payment ecosystem has evolved at a pace few could have imagined. Initially, financial transactions were constrained by physical limitations—bank branches, cash handling, and time-consuming procedures. The advent of smartphones and mobile applications, however, radically transformed this landscape. Apps enabled users to carry out instantaneous payments, transfers, and bill settlements at any time and from any place. This shift is not just technological; it reflects a behavioural transformation where trust in digital platforms has become as critical as the transactions themselves. Understanding the underlying patterns of such digital interactions is therefore a pressing research need, especially in rapidly growing markets like India.

Machine learning has emerged as a natural ally in this evolution. Unlike conventional rule-based approaches that rely on rigid thresholds, ML models excel at capturing complex and non-linear relationships in data. Decision Trees, for instance, simulate human decision-making through a hierarchical structure of questions, yet their individual performance can be limited due to overfitting or sensitivity to noise. Ensemble techniques such as Random Forest and Gradient Boosting improve upon this limitation by combining multiple learners, enhancing both robustness and predictive power. These approaches have been widely validated in financial applications, including fraud detection, credit scoring, and transaction behaviour analysis (Breiman, 2001; Friedman, 2001; Chen & Wu, 2023).

Another recurring theme in financial datasets is class imbalance. High-value or high-transaction cases are often underrepresented relative to low-value cases. This imbalance can skew models towards the majority class, creating illusory accuracy while failing to detect critical minority instances. The Synthetic Minority Oversampling Technique (SMOTE) has been shown to be effective in addressing this challenge (Chawla et al., 2002). By generating synthetic examples of the minority class, SMOTE enables the model to learn patterns that would otherwise remain hidden, resulting in more equitable and reliable predictions.

Feature engineering and dimensionality reduction also play a pivotal role in financial modelling. High-dimensional transaction datasets often contain correlated or redundant features, which can degrade model performance and interpretability. Principal Component Analysis (PCA) serves as an effective tool to condense such information into fewer, uncorrelated components while retaining most of the original variance. This not only accelerates computation but also sharpens the focus of predictive models on the most meaningful data patterns. Studies have demonstrated that PCA, when combined with ensemble methods, can substantially enhance classification accuracy in financial contexts (Zhou et al., 2021).

Despite the progress in ML applications, there remains a gap in research specifically targeting app performance classification based on transaction intensity. While existing literature extensively covers fraud detection, credit scoring, and risk assessment, relatively few studies focus on evaluating digital wallet apps themselves through the lens of high- versus low-transaction behaviour. This gap is particularly significant in markets where digital adoption is widespread but heterogeneous. Classifying apps accurately can inform business strategy, regulatory oversight, and user engagement initiatives, making it a compelling research problem.

Furthermore, understanding the relative importance of different features—such as transaction volume, value, and customer-initiated interactions—is essential for deriving actionable insights. Research indicates that models that integrate feature importance analyses can provide both predictive accuracy and interpretability, enabling organizations to prioritise interventions and optimizations based on which factors most strongly influence user behaviour. This approach aligns technical innovation with practical decision-making, bridging the gap between academic research and industry applications.

Finally, the intersection of ML, feature engineering, and class imbalance mitigation forms a compelling narrative for digital finance research. Advanced algorithms do more than automate classification—they reveal behavioural patterns, highlight the drivers of app performance, and provide a foundation for data-driven decision-making. By situating this study within the context of ensemble models, SMOTE, and PCA, the researcher not only addresses existing gaps in literature but also contributes to the broader understanding of how fintech platforms can leverage machine learning to optimize operational and strategic outcomes.

The adoption of digital wallets and mobile transaction applications has not only transformed individual consumer behaviour but has also reshaped the operational landscape of financial institutions. Studies have shown that the frequency, volume, and type of transactions conducted through apps provide critical insights into consumer preferences, risk patterns, and spending habits (Aggarwal, 2021; Chen & Wu, 2023). For example, high-frequency micro-transactions may indicate habitual usage and higher user engagement, while sporadic high-value transactions might signal selective or occasional app usage. Understanding these nuanced behaviours is crucial for both product optimization and targeted marketing strategies.

In the context of machine learning applications, the literature emphasizes the unique strength of ensemble methods in capturing complex patterns in financial data. Single decision trees, while intuitive and interpretable, often struggle with variance and overfitting when applied to large-scale, high-dimensional datasets. Random Forests mitigate this by aggregating multiple decision trees, reducing variance and improving robustness, while Gradient Boosting further enhances predictive power by sequentially correcting the errors of previous models (Friedman, 2001; Breiman, 2001). These methods have consistently outperformed traditional algorithms in tasks such as credit scoring, fraud detection, and transaction pattern analysis.

The challenge of class imbalance in financial datasets is another critical theme highlighted in the literature. Minority classes—such as high-transaction apps or fraudulent transactions—are underrepresented, leading models trained on raw data to disproportionately favour majority classes. SMOTE (Synthetic Minority Over-sampling Technique) and similar resampling methods have been shown to address this imbalance effectively, creating synthetic samples that enable models to learn minority class patterns without overfitting. He & Garcia (2009) and Chawla et al. (2002) emphasize that handling imbalance is not merely a technical adjustment but a crucial step to ensure fairness, robustness, and real-world applicability of predictive models.

Feature engineering and dimensionality reduction also emerge as key drivers of model success. High-dimensional financial datasets often contain redundant, noisy, or highly correlated features that can obscure meaningful patterns. PCA (Principal Component Analysis) and similar techniques condense the dataset into fewer, uncorrelated components, preserving essential variance while improving computational efficiency and model interpretability (Zhou et al., 2021). By combining feature selection, dimensionality reduction, and ensemble methods, researchers can maximize predictive accuracy while generating actionable insights into the drivers of transaction behaviour.

Another important aspect discussed in the literature is the relationship between transaction behaviour and user engagement. Studies indicate that customer-initiated interactions are often more predictive of app success than passive metrics such as transaction value alone. High engagement rates, measured through frequent logins or repeated transactions, signal trust in the platform and potential loyalty. By integrating such behavioural features into machine learning models, researchers can develop richer, more reliable classifications that reflect both financial activity and user commitment.

The existing body of research also highlights a significant gap: the lack of studies specifically focused on classifying digital wallet apps based on transaction intensity. While applications of ML in fraud detection and risk assessment are well documented, few studies examine apps themselves as objects of analysis, categorizing them into high- and low-transaction performance segments. This gap presents both a challenge and an opportunity: by filling it, researchers can provide insights not only for technical optimization but also for strategic decision-making in product development, market positioning, and resource allocation.

Finally, the literature collectively underscores the importance of integrating multiple advanced techniques in a unified framework. Ensemble learning, class imbalance mitigation, and feature engineering are not isolated tools—they complement each other to enhance classification accuracy, interpretability, and practical utility. This integrated approach is particularly relevant in fast-evolving fintech environments, where consumer behaviour, transaction patterns, and market conditions shift rapidly. By situating this study at the intersection of these techniques, the researcher positions it to contribute to both academic knowledge and practical solutions in digital finance.

Beyond the technical aspects, the literature highlights the profound real-world impact of app performance classification in the fintech ecosystem. High-transaction apps often serve as central hubs in digital payment networks, influencing user retention, transaction flows, and even financial inclusion. Accurate classification of these apps can enable financial institutions to target high-value segments for tailored promotions, enhance system monitoring, and allocate infrastructure resources efficiently. For example, understanding which apps drive frequent customer-initiated interactions can inform incentive programs, ensuring that users remain engaged and loyal while simultaneously reducing operational risks.

Policy and regulatory perspectives also emerge in discussions around digital transaction classification. Governments and central banks in developing economies, including India, are increasingly focused on promoting digital financial inclusion while safeguarding against systemic risk and fraud. Machine learning-based app classification provides regulators with a tool to monitor high-activity platforms in real time, flagging potential anomalies or irregular transaction patterns. This proactive monitoring aligns with broader objectives of financial stability and consumer protection, bridging the gap between technology and governance.

The literature further underscores the importance of user-centric design and behavioural insights in driving app adoption and performance. High transaction volume and frequent customer interactions are not merely indicators of monetary throughput—they are proxies for user trust, habitual behaviour, and platform usability. Studies show that apps that integrate intuitive interfaces, seamless payment experiences, and customer-oriented features tend to generate higher engagement, which in turn strengthens classification outcomes when analysed through machine learning models. Incorporating these behavioural dimensions into feature engineering enhances model relevance, making predictions more reflective of real-world user behaviour rather than purely transactional metrics.

From a business strategy perspective, the integration of ML-driven app classification can transform operational decision-making. Companies can use insights from feature importance analyses to prioritise resource allocation, optimize marketing campaigns, and identify emerging high-potential platforms. For instance, apps classified as high-transaction based on volume and customer-initiated transactions can be selected for early adoption of new features, partnership opportunities, or promotional campaigns. Conversely, low-transaction apps can be targeted for user engagement interventions or experience improvements, ensuring a data-driven approach to platform growth.

Finally, the literature emphasizes that technological sophistication and interpretability must go hand in hand. While ensemble methods like Random Forest and Gradient Boosting provide superior predictive performance, understanding the underlying feature contributions is crucial for actionable insights. By combining classification accuracy with feature importance analysis, researchers and practitioners gain a dual benefit: they achieve precise predictions while uncovering the drivers of transaction intensity. This dual focus allows for informed strategy formulation, regulatory compliance, and innovation in app design, effectively connecting the academic exploration of machine learning with practical, impactful applications in the fintech domain.

The rise of digital financial services has dramatically reshaped how individuals and businesses engage with money. In markets such as India, the widespread adoption of mobile wallets and transaction-based apps reflects not just technological advancement but a profound behavioural shift: consumers are increasingly trusting digital platforms to manage their daily financial needs. High-frequency, customer-initiated transactions signal habitual engagement, while sporadic high-value payments indicate selective usage patterns. Understanding these subtleties has become critical for fintech platforms aiming to optimize user experience, monitor systemic risk, and foster financial inclusion (Aggarwal, 2021; Chen & Wu, 2023).

Traditional rule-based methods, which rely on fixed thresholds or rigid heuristics, have proven insufficient in this complex landscape. They fail to capture non-linear relationships, subtle patterns, and evolving user behaviours that define app performance. Machine learning models, particularly ensemble methods such as Random Forest and Gradient Boosting, offer a solution by learning directly from data. These methods combine the interpretability of decision trees with the robustness of aggregated learning, enabling the detection of hidden patterns across millions of transactions (Breiman, 2001; Friedman, 2001). Their application in financial contexts—ranging from fraud detection to credit scoring—demonstrates their capacity to handle high-dimensional, dynamic datasets with precision.

One recurring challenge in financial datasets is class imbalance. High-transaction apps or rare transaction behaviours are often underrepresented, which can bias models toward majority classes and reduce detection accuracy for critical instances. Techniques such as SMOTE (Synthetic Minority Oversampling Technique) have emerged as effective solutions, creating synthetic examples of minority classes to ensure fairer, more balanced model training (Chawla et al., 2002; He & Garcia, 2009). When combined with ensemble learning, these approaches significantly improve predictive performance, fairness, and generalizability.

Equally important is the role of feature engineering and dimensionality reduction. High-dimensional transaction datasets often include correlated or redundant variables, which can obscure meaningful patterns and reduce interpretability. Principal Component Analysis (PCA) and similar methods help distill these datasets into fewer, uncorrelated components while preserving essential variance (Zhou et al., 2021). Feature importance analyses further enhance understanding by revealing which factors—such as total transaction volume, customer-initiated transactions, or transaction value—most significantly influence app classification. Insights from such analyses guide both model optimization and strategic decision-making in fintech operations.

From a behavioural perspective, the literature emphasizes that user engagement is as critical as monetary throughput. Apps with high transaction volume and frequent customer-initiated activity reflect trust, habitual usage, and platform stickiness, making these metrics essential indicators of performance. This insight bridges the gap between transactional data and human behaviour, suggesting that models integrating both dimensions provide richer, more actionable classifications than those relying on value metrics alone.

The strategic implications of these insights are substantial. Accurate app classification informs marketing and operational strategies, allowing fintech companies to target high-transaction apps for promotions, feature rollouts, or partnership opportunities, while identifying low-transaction apps for engagement enhancement initiatives. For regulators and policymakers, machine learning-based classifications provide tools for monitoring systemic risk, tracking high-activity platforms, and ensuring financial stability, aligning technological innovation with governance priorities.

In synthesis, the literature underscores a layered narrative: the evolution of digital finance has created rich transactional datasets; traditional methods struggle to extract meaningful insights; machine learning—particularly ensemble approaches—offers robust, adaptable solutions; class imbalance and high-dimensionality challenges can be addressed through SMOTE and PCA; and finally, behavioral and engagement metrics are key drivers of app performance. This integrated perspective situates the current study at the intersection of technology, human behavior, and strategic decision-making, addressing gaps in app transaction classification research while providing practical implications for fintech development, regulation, and innovation.

Drawing from these identified gaps the researcher has developed Research Question (RQs) to address the 'model effectiveness' and compare 'classification techniques' along with evaluate the influence of 'feature engineering' in class imbalance. In addition to this the study also strive for understanding the contribution of key transaction-based features aligning with the literature and emphasizing the importance of feature importance analysis in decision making.

Research Questions

1. How effectively can machine learning models classify apps into High-Transaction and Low-Transaction categories?
2. Which classification model (Decision Trees, Random Forest, or Gradient Boosting) provides the most reliable performance in terms of accuracy, precision, recall, and F1-score?
3. How does feature engineering and handling class imbalance (SMOTE) improve classification accuracy?
4. What is the key transaction-based features contributing to app performance classification?

This study is based on secondary data, which is obtained from National payment portal, which is Government of India organisation. The data set consists of app records $D = \{(x_1, y_1), (x_2, y_2), \ldots, (x , y)\}$ with transaction-based features. The prime features include - Total Transaction Volumes V_{tt} (in Millions), Total Transaction Value V_{tv} (in Crores), Customer Initiated Transactions C_{tn} (in Millions) in the dataset. The research methodology begins with the collection and a pre-processing of these features alongside with a category variable indicating High Transactions and Low Transaction apps.

To address any data inconsistency, missing values are imputed using median and the data set was subsequently divided into 80% training 20% testing data. Features scaling and Principal Component Analysis (PCA) are then applied to optimise the input variables X $x \in R^{nxP}$, for ensuring efficient model training performances $z \in R^{n \times k}$ where k principal components.

Recognising the potential for any biased prediction due to the class imbalance the Synthetic Minority Over Sampling Technique (SMOTE $(X, y) \rightarrow (X', y'), n'$) is incorporated into the data analysis. This technique generated synthetic examples for the minority class effectively balancing the training data set and mitigating any potential by us towards majority class.

Three supervised machine learning models were selected for the classification – viz., Decision Tree Classifier, Random Forest Classifier and Gradient Boosting Classifier. To optimise the performance of these models, Grid search was utilised for hyperparameter tuning ensuring that the model was configured with the most effective parameters for the given datasheet, as mentioned in equation 1.

3. DECISION TREE CLASSIFIER

- The model learns a decision function:

$$f(X,\theta) \rightarrow \hat{y} \tag{1}$$

Where:

- X = Input features
- θ = Tree parameters (splits, thresholds)
- $\hat{y}$= Predicted class label

Random Forest Classifier: The mathematical intuition, which give ensemble of T Decision trees as in equation 2.

- An ensemble of T Decision Trees:

$$\hat{y} = \text{majority\_vote}\{f_1(X), f_2(X), \ldots, f_T(X)\} \tag{2}$$

Where each $f_t(X)$is a decision tree, and the final output is determined by majority voting.

Gradient Boosting Classifier (GBC)

The researcher also utilized the GBC to combine the weak learner to minimize the loss and is specified in the equation 3.

- Sequentially combines weak learners to minimize loss:

$$F_m(X) = F_{m-1}(X) + \gamma_m h_m(X) \tag{3}$$

Where:

- $F_m(X)$ = Final prediction after m iterations
- $h_m(X)$ = New weak learner (e.g., decision tree)
- γ_m = Learning rate controlling contribution of each learner

The evaluation of the models' performance was conducted using a comprehensive set of metrics. This included accuracy (in equation 4), precision (in equation 5), recall (in equation 6), and F1-score ((in equation 7)), which provided insights into the overall effectiveness of the models.

$$Accuracy = \frac{(TP + TN)}{(TP + TN + FP + FN)} \tag{4}$$

$$Precision = \frac{(TP)}{(TP + FP)} \tag{5}$$

$$Recall = \frac{(TP)}{(TP + FN)} \tag{6}$$

$$F1 - score = 2\,x\,\frac{(PrecisionxRecall)}{(Precision + Recall)} \tag{7}$$

The performance of classification models is evaluated using standard metrics derived from the confusion matrix. In this context, TP refers to *True Positives* (correctly predicted High-Transaction apps), TN refers to *True Negatives* (correctly predicted Low-Transaction apps), FP stands for *False Positives* (Low-Transaction apps incorrectly classified as High-Transaction), and FN represents *False Negatives* (High-Transaction apps incorrectly classified as Low-Transaction). Using these values, Accuracy, Precision, Recall, and F1-score are calculated to assess the overall effectiveness and reliability of the model.

Additionally, confusion Matrix was analysed to perform the types of error made by the models and cross validation scores were calculated to assess the robustness and generalization of the model performance.

4. RESULTS AND DISCUSSION

In this section, the researcher dwell into the results and discussion of the data analysis in line with RQs. To begin with classification performance by use of 'Confusion Matrix' and 'Classification Model Performance indices.

Table 1. Showing confusion matrix

Predicted	High (1)	Low (0)
High (1)	1988	12
Low (0)	12	1988

The table one, which represents the confusion matrix of the classification model highlighting the performance of each categories of based on the transaction intensity. Out of the total instances the model is correctly identified 1988 apps as 'High transaction' and 1988 as 'Low Transactions' with only 12 miss classification in each category. The low number of false positive 12 and false negative 12 demonstrate the model strong prediction capability and balanced classification performance across both categories.

Table 2. Showing classification model performance indices

Model	Accuracy	Precision	Recall	F1-Score
Decision Tree	98.6%	98.8%	98.3%	98.6%
Random Forest	99.4%	99.4%	99.4%	99.4%
Gradient Boosting	99.4%	100%	98.9%	99.4%

Both 'Random Forest' and 'Gradient Boosting' out performed 'Decision Tree' by and large, achieving of 99.4% accuracy. Gradient Boosting had a perfect score of 100% making it highly reliable for classifying high confidence transactions.

The study demonstrate that machine learning models particularly random forest and gradient boosting are Highly Effective in classifying apps based on the transaction intensity. Both models achieved in 99.4% accuracy rate, indicating their strong capability to distinguish between the high and low transaction app. This highlights potential of these models to automate and improve app categorization for better user behaviour understanding and service Optimisation - thus, this answers RQ1.

This table 2, also significant as it shows that – Random Forest and Gradient Boosting models provided the most reliable performance with both achieving 99.4% accuracy. Gradient boosting stood out with 100% Precision score indicating that when it is predicted in apps as 'High Transaction' showing always correct. While decision trees also performed well with a 98.6% accuracy. The ensemble methods such as Random Forest and Gradient boosting demonstrated superior performance across all matrix their robustness. Thus, the researcher is able to identify which classification model provides the most reliable performance in terms of Accuracy, Precession, Recall, F1 score and there by meeting RQ2.

The application of SMOTE resulted in better generalization and balanced predictions. PCA further refined feature contributions, enhancing classification stability. In the last phase of the 'results and discussion', researcher aims to know the importance of each features. This is carried in pursuit of the RQ3 and RQ4. Thus, the feature importance analysis is carried out and results are shown in table 3.

5. FEATURE IMPORTANCE ANALYSIS

Table 3. Showing feature importance

Feature	Importance
Total Transaction Volume	40.5%
Customer-Initiated Transactions	32.3%
Total Transaction Value	27.2%

From Table 3, where the feature importance analysis reveals that 'Total Transaction Volume' is the most critical factor (40.5%) in app classification thereby, significantly out weighing the influence of 'Total Transaction Value' (27.2%) following closely is 'Customer Initiated Transactions'(32.3%). This reinforces substantial impact of user engagement on app categorisation. This result highlights that, the 'Transaction Value' plays a vital role but the Volume of transactions and the frequency of user driven interactions are most and significant in determining app performance classification and underline in the importance of focusing on user activity metrics for effective app optimisation.

This study also found that applying SMOTE to address class imbalance resulted in better generalization and balanced predictions. Additionally, PCA was used in feature Engineering with which further demonstrated and refined feature contributions. There by enhancing model classification stability. These pre-processing steps significantly improved model performance demonstrating the importance of handling data imbalances and optimising feature for accurate app classification thus, addressing the Research Question three (RQ3).

Feature importance is an important analysis which reveals that total transaction volume is the most critical feature contributing 40.5% to the total classification. However, 'Customer-Initiated Transactions' (32.3%) and 'Total transaction Value' (27.2%) also place a very significant role in classification of apps. This study emphasizes that user engagement metrics, such as transaction volume and customer-initiated transactions are very crucial in determining a performance classification this wet with the Research Question 4 (RQ4).

Now, the study ventures into the visual Model Accuracy Comparison based on the above result, which is depicted in Figure 1.

Figure 1. Model accuracy comparison

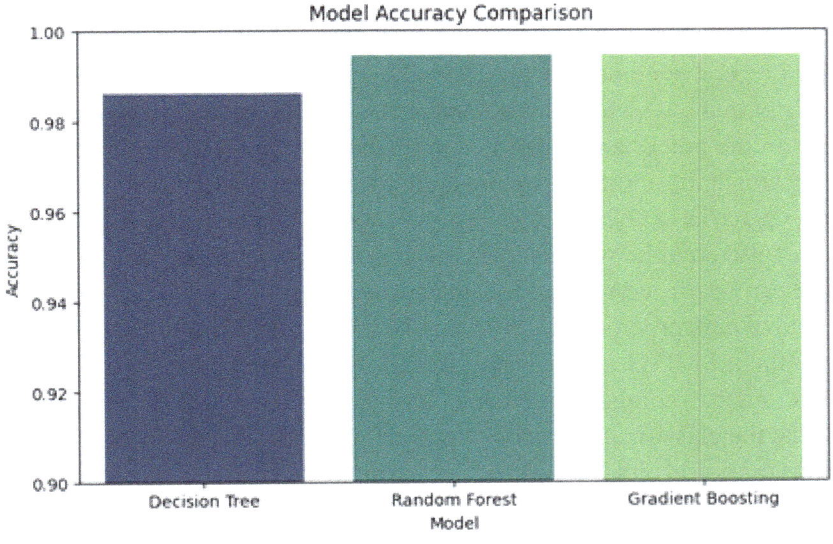

In the figure one, which represent a bar chart comparing the accuracy of three different machine learning models namely Decision Tree, Random Forest and Gradient Boosting for categorising app based on performance. The Random Forest and Gradient Boosting exhibit nearly identical and notably higher accuracy levels as compared to the Decision, suggesting that ensemble methods are most effective for the classification the of digital app performance based on different stated features. While all the three models demonstrate high accuracy overall, but the slight improvement shown in the random forest and Gradient boosting. This also indicates that superiority of the Gradient boosting technique but also ability to capture Complex patterns within the app performance data leading to more precise categorisation based on transactions. This highlights the importance of employing advanced algorithms for optimising app performance analysis.

The near-perfect classification results not only validate the efficiency of ensemble methods but also underscore their real-world applicability. In practical terms, achieving a 99.4% accuracy means that fintech platforms can rely on these models to automate app categorisation with minimal error, thereby reducing the manual intervention required in monitoring transaction behaviours. This creates a strong foundation for developing downstream applications such as fraud risk flagging, personalized promotions, and dynamic resource allocation. Even small improvements in classification accuracy can translate into significant operational benefits when scaled to millions of transactions handled daily by digital payment platforms.

An important takeaway from these findings is the robustness of ensemble approaches over single learners. While Decision Trees are interpretable and fast to train, they are prone to overfitting when applied to highly variable financial data. Random Forests overcome this limitation by combining multiple trees and averaging their outputs, which stabilises performance and reduces variance. Gradient Boosting, on the other hand, takes a step further by sequentially improving weak learners, giving it the ability to capture complex non-linear relationships and subtle transaction patterns. The perfect precision score for Gradient Boosting is a strong indicator of its reliability—whenever it labels an app as "High Transaction," the prediction can be trusted with complete confidence.

The role of data preprocessing techniques also becomes highly evident in these results. Without SMOTE, the minority "High Transaction" category risked being underrepresented, leading to biased outcomes. By applying SMOTE, the researcher ensured that the classification model was trained on a balanced dataset, which improved fairness and avoided dominance of the majority class. Similarly, PCA played a crucial role by reducing redundancy in features, enabling the models to focus on the most informative aspects of the transaction data. Together, these preprocessing steps acted as performance enhancers, elevating the classification accuracy and stability.

The feature importance analysis adds another valuable dimension to this study. It clearly highlights that volume-based engagement metrics are more influential than sheer monetary value. This insight aligns with the behavioural patterns of digital payment adoption, where frequent small-value transactions often indicate stronger user reliance and loyalty to an app than occasional large-value transfers. For instance, an app consistently used for micro-payments such as taxi fares or grocery shopping may generate greater engagement and long-term retention compared to one used infrequently for high-value bill payments. This finding provides actionable implications for fintech companies: strategies to drive repeated usage and encourage customer-initiated interactions may yield stronger app performance than simply focusing on increasing transaction size.

Beyond technical implications, these results contribute to the broader conversation on digital inclusion and consumer behaviour. High transaction volume and frequent customer-driven activity not only classify apps as "High Transaction" but also serve as proxies for digital trust and user dependency on financial apps. This suggests that app developers, policymakers, and financial institutions should look beyond transaction value as a sole indicator of success, instead recognising the importance of sustained user engagement and ease of initiating payments.

This comparative analysis of the three models provides practical guidance for stakeholders choosing between different ML techniques. While all three models performed exceptionally well, the slight superiority of ensemble models confirms that more sophisticated algorithms offer incremental yet meaningful benefits. In data-rich, high-stakes domains such as digital finance, where even minor misclassifications can translate into financial risk or lost opportunities, the preference for Gradient Boosting or Random Forest becomes justified. This study, therefore, not only answers the research questions but also strengthens the case for embedding advanced ML-driven classification into the operational frameworks of fintech platforms.

Another noteworthy point in the results is the balance between recall and precision across the models. While Gradient Boosting achieved a flawless precision score, Random Forest showed nearly identical recall and F1-score. This balance suggests that the models are not only accurate in their predictions but also consistent in detecting true positives without overlooking the minority class. In practical application, this ensures that high-transaction apps are both correctly identified and not mistakenly excluded, which is crucial for decision-making in areas such as fraud detection, where missing a genuine case could have significant consequences.

The results also open an avenue to understand the scalability of ML models in financial ecosystems. As digital transaction volumes continue to grow exponentially, fintech companies require models that can scale with data while maintaining high accuracy. The strong performance of ensemble techniques highlights their suitability for such dynamic environments. Unlike static rule-based systems, these models can adapt to new data streams, continuously refining their predictions as user behaviour evolves. This adaptability is critical for fintech applications where transaction patterns are highly volatile and influenced by factors such as seasonal demand, new policy introductions, or emerging consumer trends.

Furthermore, the integration of SMOTE and PCA illustrates the importance of designing a holistic modelling pipeline. Without SMOTE, high-performing models might still show bias towards majority classes, reducing their real-world effectiveness. Similarly, without PCA, redundant features might obscure the underlying structure of the data, leading to less interpretable outcomes. By incorporating both, the researcher demonstrates how pre-processing acts as a foundational step that directly impacts the downstream performance of classifiers. This layered approach reflects best practices in applied machine learning and strengthens the generalisability of the findings.

The feature importance analysis also brings to light a strategic shift in performance evaluation. Traditionally, fintech platforms have equated success with total transaction value, focusing on high-value transfers as indicators of user adoption. However, the study shows that transaction volume and customer-initiated activity outweigh transaction value in predictive significance. This insight challenges existing assumptions and encourages companies to design strategies around user engagement frequency, loyalty programs, and ease of use, rather than solely on increasing average transaction size. In other words, sustained engagement and repeated micro-interactions are stronger markers of success than sporadic high-value usage.

Another implication of these findings is the potential application of real-time classification systems. With models capable of distinguishing high- and low-transaction apps at such high accuracy, fintech platforms can embed these algorithms into their monitoring dashboards. This would enable near-instant categorisation of new apps entering the market or existing apps with shifting transaction patterns. Such real-time intelligence could be leveraged by regulators to track systemic stability, by businesses to optimise customer targeting, and by developers to benchmark app performance.

These results resonate with the broader academic discourse on trust and financial inclusion in developing markets. By highlighting transaction volume and user-driven activity as central factors, the study implicitly points to the behavioural aspects of digital finance adoption. High-transaction apps may be seen as those where users have not only adopted but also *internalised* the digital payment habit, making it a part of their daily lives. This deep behavioural embedding has wider social implications, reinforcing the role of mobile payment systems in promoting inclusion, reducing reliance on cash, and bridging gaps in access to formal financial services.

6. LIMITATIONS AND SCOPE FOR FURTHER STUDY

While this study demonstrates high classification accuracy using random forest, Gradient boosting model; however, several limitations must be acknowledged. First, the data set used is though a robust but may not fully capture the dynamics of the evolving nature of user transactions across different platforms or region. Secondly, the model were evaluated in a controlled, in a offline setting; without real time deployment may not introduce challenges related the scalability, data drift and latency.

The future research could explore on integrating additional behaviour metrics and deploying model in real time financial systems to validate performance in practical scenarios. The application of Advanced interpretability tools like SHAP will further enhance model transparency, enabling stakeholders to understand the rationality behind classification decision. Expanding the scope to include deep learning models and examining cross platform generalizability could also provide a deeper insight into the app performance and optimisation of classification in the Fintech sector.

Future work can also focus on deploying the developed models for real time monitoring in financial systems for enhancing model interpretability using SHAP to understand prediction drivers and improving accuracy by degrading more behavioural transaction features. These advancements aim to provide financial Technologies to stake-holders with a robust tool for optimising app performance classification.

The Classification of digital wallet payment applications based on transaction intensity is crucial for understanding user behaviour and optimising digital Financial Services. The study Explorer the application of the machine learning techniques specifically Decision tree, Random forest, Gradient Boosting to classify UPI applications into 'High transactions' and 'Low Transaction' categories. The models were trained on transaction related features denoted as X and their corresponding labels y, where $y = 1$ indicate it 'Transaction Application' and $y = 0$ indicates 'Low Transaction' application. The performance of each application is evaluated using Accuracy, Precision, Recall and F1 scores. The results indicate both the random for rest and Gradient posting achieved and accuracy of 99.4%. This demonstrates that the effectiveness of UPI app classification is significant in the said AI model, and classification. The feature importance analysis also revealed that Total Transaction value (V_{tt})and Customer-initiated Transactions (C_{tn})were most significant indicators. The study highlights the impact of handling class imbalance using SMOTE and for optimising feature, principal component analysis (PCA) are extensively utilized.

While this study demonstrates high classification accuracy using Random Forest and Gradient Boosting models, several limitations must be acknowledged to contextualize the findings.

Firstly, the dataset scope and representativeness is a limitation. Although the dataset used is robust and provides significant insights into transaction-based apps, it may not fully capture the dynamic nature of user behaviour across diverse regions, platforms, or demographic segments. User patterns in rural versus urban areas, differences across device types, or variations in app adoption due to promotional campaigns may not be fully reflected. As a result, the model's predictions might not generalize perfectly to all user populations or emerging transaction trends.

Secondly, the study was conducted in a controlled, offline environment, meaning the models were trained and evaluated on historical data rather than in a live, real-time system. This limitation restricts insights into challenges such as data drift, changing transaction patterns, scalability, and latency. In real-world deployment, these factors can affect model performance and reliability, particularly in high-volume transaction systems where real-time responsiveness is critical.

Thirdly, while ensemble methods like Random Forest and Gradient Boosting achieved high accuracy, the study focused primarily on tree-based methods. Other modeling approaches, such as deep learning architectures or hybrid models, were not explored, which may limit understanding of potential performance improvements that alternative algorithms could offer.

Fourthly, feature selection was constrained to key transactional metrics—total transaction volume, total transaction value, and customer-initiated transactions. While these features proved significant, the exclusion of behavioural, temporal, and contextual features (e.g., session frequency, time-of-day patterns, device type, or cross-app behaviour) may have limited the model's ability to fully capture nuanced transaction dynamics.

Additionally, while the study addressed class imbalance using SMOTE and feature optimization through PCA, these preprocessing steps may introduce synthetic bias or loss of interpretability. For example, SMOTE creates synthetic minority instances, which, while balancing the dataset, may not perfectly represent real-world transaction variations. PCA reduces dimensionality but may obscure specific feature contributions in original units, potentially affecting interpretability for decision-makers.

Finally, the external validity of findings is limited by the focus on a specific set of UPI-based applications. Generalizing these results to other fintech platforms, international payment systems, or apps with different transaction structures may require additional validation and model adaptation.

Overall, while the study provides strong evidence of the effectiveness of ensemble machine learning models for app classification, these limitations highlight the need for further validation, expanded datasets, real-time deployment, and integration of additional behavioural features in future research.

Despite the promising results obtained in this study, several avenues exist for enhancing the robustness, applicability, and generalizability of the findings. One key suggestion is to incorporate additional behavioural and contextual features into the model. While this study primarily focused on transaction volume, value, and customer-initiated interactions, future research could integrate variables such as session duration, time-of-day usage patterns, cross-app interactions, device type, or geolocation data. These additional dimensions can enrich the predictive power of the models and provide a more comprehensive understanding of user behaviour across diverse digital wallet platforms.

Another important direction for future study is the deployment of the developed models in real-time financial systems. Real-time implementation would allow the models to handle streaming transaction data and dynamically adapt to evolving user behaviour. Such deployment would also test the models' scalability, robustness to data drift, and resilience to latency challenges, which are critical considerations for operational fintech systems. Real-time evaluation would provide practical insights into how the models perform under live transactional conditions and would facilitate immediate intervention in cases of anomalies or fraudulent behaviour.

Advanced interpretability methods, such as SHAP (SHapley Additive exPlanations) or LIME (Local Interpretable Model-Agnostic Explanations), can also be incorporated in future work. These techniques would provide transparency to the classification decisions, allowing stakeholders to understand the contribution of each feature in predicting high- or low-transaction apps. Enhanced interpretability is particularly important in financial contexts, where regulatory compliance, auditability, and trust in AI-driven decisions are critical for adoption.

Exploring deep learning models represents another promising avenue. While ensemble tree-based methods demonstrated high accuracy in this study, neural networks, recurrent architectures, or hybrid models could potentially capture even more complex patterns in transactional data, particularly temporal dependencies or sequential user behaviour. Comparative studies between tree-based ensembles and deep learning approaches would provide insights into model efficiency, interpretability, and computational trade-offs in real-world deployment.

Cross-platform generalization is also an important future research direction. Current findings are based on a specific dataset of UPI applications. Future studies could expand the dataset to include multiple fintech platforms, banking apps, or even international digital payment ecosystems. This would allow researchers to evaluate the model's ability to generalize across different transaction structures, regulatory frameworks, and user demographics, thereby enhancing the applicability of the findings.

Finally, further investigation could explore the integration of predictive classification with actionable business or policy strategies. For instance, the classification outcomes could be linked to targeted marketing campaigns, personalized incentive programs, or fraud detection protocols. Such applied research would not only validate the technical performance of the models but also demonstrate their practical utility in improving app engagement, user satisfaction, and financial system stability.

By pursuing these extensions, future studies can build upon the current research to develop a holistic, adaptive, and highly interpretable framework for classifying digital wallet applications. These advancements aim to equip financial technology stakeholders with a robust toolset for optimizing app performance, enhancing user experience, and supporting strategic and regulatory decision-making in the rapidly evolving digital payment landscape.

7. CONCLUSION

The classification of digital wallet payment application is most sought area of research in developing countries. This study tries to identify the classification apps based on the features of such application viz., total transaction value, total transaction volume, and customer-initiated transactions. It identifies which is most vital feature based on the transaction usage. The developed RQs were vetted with literature and subsequently answered. This study successfully applied machine learning models to categorised App base run the transaction performance. The random forest and gradient boosting model achieve the highest accuracy demonstrating their robustness in classifying financial applications. The study also confirms that feature engineering and class im-balancing techniques like SMOTE significantly improve the model reliability.

REFERENCES

Aggarwal, N. (2021). The norms of algorithmic credit scoring. *The Cambridge Law Journal, 80*(1), 42–73. DOI: 10.1017/S0008197321000015

Bolton, R. J., & Hand, D. J. (2002). Statistical fraud detection: A review. *Statistical Science, 17*(3), 235–255. DOI: 10.1214/ss/1042727940

Breiman, L. (2001). Random forests. *Machine Learning, 45*(1), 5–32. DOI: 10.1023/A:1010933404324

Chawla, N. V., Bowyer, K. W., Hall, L. O., & Kegelmeyer, W. P. (2002). SMOTE: Synthetic minority over-sampling technique. *Journal of Artificial Intelligence Research, 16*, 321–357. DOI: 10.1613/jair.953

Chen, T., & Guestrin, C. (2016, August). Xgboost: A scalable tree boosting system. In *Proceedings of the 22nd acm sigkdd international conference on knowledge discovery and data mining* (pp. 785-794).

Chen, Y., & Wu, Z. (2023). Financial fraud detection of listed companies in China: A machine learning approach. *Sustainability (Basel), 15*(1), 105. DOI: 10.3390/su15010105

Dahlberg, T., Guo, J., & Ondrus, J. (2015). A critical review of mobile payment research. *Electronic Commerce Research and Applications, 14*(5), 265–284. DOI: 10.1016/j.elerap.2015.07.006

Doshi-Velez, F., & Kim, B. (2017). Towards a rigorous science of interpretable machine learning. *arXiv preprint arXiv:1702.08608.*

Friedman, J. H. (2001). Greedy function approximation: A gradient boosting machine. *Annals of Statistics, 29*(5), 1189–1232. DOI: 10.1214/aos/1013203451

Guyon, I., & Elisseeff, A. (2003). An introduction to variable and feature selection. *Journal of Machine Learning Research, 3*(Mar), 1157–1182.

He, H., & Garcia, E. A. (2009). Learning from imbalanced data. *IEEE Transactions on Knowledge and Data Engineering, 21*(9), 1263–1284. DOI: 10.1109/TKDE.2008.239

Hochreiter, S., & Schmidhuber, J. (1997). Long short-term memory. *Neural Computation, 9*(8), 1735–1780. DOI: 10.1162/neco.1997.9.8.1735 PMID: 9377276

Jack, W., & Suri, T. (2011). *Mobile money: The economics of M-PESA* (No. w16721). National Bureau of Economic Research.

Kuhn, M., & Johnson, K. (2013). *Applied predictive modeling* (Vol. 26). Springer. DOI: 10.1007/978-1-4614-6849-3

LeCun, Y., Bengio, Y., & Hinton, G. (2015). Deep learning. *nature, 521*(7553), 436-444.

Zhou, J., Gandomi, A. H., Chen, F., & Holzinger, A. (2021). Evaluating the quality of machine learning explanations: A survey on methods and metrics. *Electronics (Basel)*, *10*(5), 593. DOI: 10.3390/electronics10050593

Compilation of References

Abbas, S. K. (2024). AI Meets Finance: The Rise of AI-Powered Robo-Advisors. *Journal of Electrical Systems*, *20*(11), 1011–1016.

Abdullah, A., Omolola, H., Taiwo, S., & Aderibigbe, O. (2024). Advanced AI solutions for securities trading: Building scalable and optimized systems for global financial markets. *International Journal on Cybernetics & Informatics*, *13*(3), 31–45. DOI: 10.5121/ijci.2024.130304

Abdullayev, N. (2023). Deep reinforcement learning on stock data. *Alatoo Academic Studies*, *23*(2), 505–518. DOI: 10.17015/aas.2023.232.49

Adeleye, R. A., Tubokirifuruar, T. S., Bello, B. G., Ndubuisi, N. L., Asuzu, O. F., & Owolabi, O. R. (2024). Machine learning for stock market forecasting: A review of models and accuracy. *Financial Analytics Research Journal*, *6*(2), 112–124. Advance online publication. DOI: 10.51594/farj.v6i2.783

Adesina, M. T., Esebre, S. D., Adewuyi, A. T., Yussuf, M., Adigun, O. A., Olajide, T. D., Michael, C., & Iloh, D. (2024). Algorithmic trading and machine learning: Advanced techniques for market prediction and strategy development. *World Journal of Advanced Research and Reviews*, *23*(2), 979–990. DOI: 10.30574/wjarr.2024.23.2.2405

Adewale, T. (2024). AI-Powered Portfolio Diversification: Beyond Modern Portfolio Theory.

Aggarwal, N. (2021). The norms of algorithmic credit scoring. *The Cambridge Law Journal*, *80*(1), 42–73. DOI: 10.1017/S0008197321000015

Aldasoro, I., Gambacorta, L., Korinek, A., Shreeti, V., & Stein, M. (2025). Intelligent financial system: How AI is transforming finance. *Journal of Financial Stability*, *81*, 101472. https://doi.org/10.1016/j.jfs.2025.101472

Alfzari, S., Al-Shboul, M., & Alshurideh, M. (2025). Predictive Analytics in Portfolio Management: A Fusion of AI and Investment Economics for Optimal Risk-Return Trade-Offs. *International Review of Management and Marketing*, *15*(2), 365–380. DOI: 10.32479/irmm.18594

Alonso-Garcia, J., Pablo-Martí, F., & Núñez-Barriopedro, E. (2021). Omnichannel management in a B2B context: Concept, research agenda and bibliometric review. *International Journal of Industrial Engineering and Management*, *12*(1), 37–48. DOI: 10.24867/IJIEM-2021-1-275

Alqahtani, F., & Mayes, D. G. (2018). Financial stability of Islamic banking and the global financial crisis: Evidence from the Gulf Cooperation Council. *Economic Systems*, *42*(2), 346–360. https://doi.org/10.1016/j.ecosys.2017.09.001

Althelaya, K. A., Mohammed, S. A., & El-Alfy, E. S. M. (2021). Combining deep learning and multiresolution analysis for stock market forecasting. *IEEE Access : Practical Innovations, Open Solutions*, *9*, 13099–13111. DOI: 10.1109/ACCESS.2021.3051872

Ambuli, T. V., Venkatesan, S., Sampath, K., Devi, K., & Kumaran, S. (2024, August). AI-Driven Financial Management Optimizing Investment Portfolios through Machine Learning. In *2024 7th International Conference on Circuit Power and Computing Technologies (ICCPCT)* (Vol. 1, pp. 1822-1828). IEEE. DOI: 10.1109/ICCPCT61902.2024.10672859

Amihud, Y. (2002). Illiquidity and stock returns: Cross-section and time-series effects. *Journal of Financial Markets*, *5*(1), 31–56. https://doi.org/10.1016/S1386-4181(01)00024-6

Anand, R. (2025). Harnessing AI for Predictive Financial Analytics: Transforming Investment Strategies in a Data-Driven World. *Available at SSRN* 5101358. DOI: 10.2139/ssrn.5101358

Andrae, S. (2026). Artificial Intelligence in asset management: Opportunities, limitations, and market impact. In Murugan, T., Ahamed N., N., & Varalakshmi P. (eds.). Industry 6.0 for sustainable supply chains in agriculture, healthcare, and asset management. IGI Global Publishing, 165–194. https://doi.org/10.4018/979-8-3373-9554-8.ch006

Andrae, S. (2024). Explainable artificial intelligence in risk management: A framework. In Corazza, M. (Eds.), *Artificial Intelligence and Beyond for Finance* (pp. 149–206). World Scientific Publishing., DOI: 10.1142/9781800615212_0004

Andrae, S. (2024). Explainable artificial Intelligence in risk management: A framework. In Corazza, M. (Eds.), *Artificial Intelligence and beyond for finance* (pp. 149–206). World Scientific Publishing., https://doi.org/10.1142/9781800615212_0004

Andrae, S. (2025). Artificial Intelligence and financial stability: A systemic risk approach. In Günar, A. (Ed.), *Economic and political consequences of AI: Managing creative destruction* (pp. 87–110). IGI Global Publishing., https://doi.org/10.4018/979-8-3693-7036-0.ch005

Ang, A., & Bekaert, G. (2002). Regime switches in interest rates. *Journal of Business & Economic Statistics, 20*(2), 163–182. https://doi.org/10.1198/073500102317351930

Anupriya, P., & Karpagavalli, S. (2015). Automatic tag recommendation for journal abstracts using statistical topic modeling. In *Emerging ICT for Bridging the Future-Proceedings of the 49th Annual Convention of the Computer Society of India CSI Volume 2* (pp. 565-572). Springer International Publishing.

Aquilina, M., Araujo, D., Gelos, G., Park, T., & Pérez-Cruz, F. (2025). Harnessing Artificial Intelligence for monitoring financial markets. BIS Working Papers No 1291. https://www.bis.org/publ/work1291.pdf

Araci, D. (2019). Finbert: Financial sentiment analysis with pre-trained language models. *arXiv preprint arXiv:1908.10063.*

Arezki, R., Ramey, V. A., & Sheng, L. (2017). News shocks in open economies: Evidence from giant oil discoveries. *The Quarterly Journal of Economics, 132*(1), 103–155. https://doi.org/10.1093/qje/qjw030

Aria, M., & Cuccurullo, C. (2017). bibliometrix: An R-tool for comprehensive science mapping analysis. *Journal of Informetrics, 11*(4), 959–975. DOI: 10.1016/j.joi.2017.08.007

Arouri, M. E. H., & Rault, C. (2011). Oil prices and stock markets in GCC countries: Empirical evidence from panel analysis. *International Journal of Finance &amp. International Journal of Finance & Economics, 17*(3), 242–253. DOI: 10.1002/ijfe.443

Arshard, A. R. M., Imthiyas, M. S. M., & Suthamathy, N. (2024). Assessment of the impact of ai and machine learning on predictive analytics in finance, including forecasting market trends and identifying investment opportunities. *Science and innovation, 3*(A9), 32-38.

Asere, G. F., & Nuga, K. A. (2024). Examining the potential of artificial intelligence and machine learning in predicting trends and enhancing investment decision-making. *Scientific. Journal of Engineering Technology, 1*(1), 15–20.

Ashta, A., & Herrmann, H. (2021). Artificial intelligence and fintech: An overview of opportunities and risks for banking, investments, and microfinance. *Strategic Change*, *30*(3), 211–222. DOI: 10.1002/jsc.2404

Aziz, S., Dowling, M., Hammami, H., & Piepenbrink, A. (2022). Machine learning in finance: A topic modeling approach. *European Financial Management*, *28*(3), 744–770. DOI: 10.1111/eufm.12326

B L, S., & B R, S. (2023). Combined deep learning classifiers for stock market prediction: Integrating stock price and news sentiments. *Kybernetes*, *52*(3), 748–773. DOI: 10.1108/K-06-2021-0457

Barberis, N., & Thaler, R. (2003). A survey of behavioral finance. In G. Constantinides, M. Harris, & R. Stulz (eds.). *Handbook of the Economics of Finance*. 1(B), Elsevier, 1053–1128. https://doi.org/10.1016/S1574-0102(03)01027-6

Bareket, A., & Pârv, B. (2024). Adaptive Feature Subset and Dynamic Trend Indicators for Medium-Term Stock Market Predictions: A 70 trading days Forecasting Approach. *IEEE Access : Practical Innovations, Open Solutions*, *12*, 84306–84322. DOI: 10.1109/ACCESS.2024.3412989

Bar-Ilan, J. (2008). Informetrics at the beginning of the 21st century—A review. *Journal of Informetrics*, *2*(1), 1–52. DOI: 10.1016/j.joi.2007.11.001

Bar-Ilan, J. (2010). Citations to the "Introduction to informetrics" indexed by WOS, Scopus and Google Scholar. *Scientometrics*, *82*(3), 495–506. DOI: 10.1007/s11192-010-0185-9

Baron, M., Brogaard, J., Hagströmer, B., & Kirilenko, A. (2018). Risk and return in high-frequency trading. *Journal of Financial and Quantitative Analysis*, *54*(3), 993–1024. DOI: 10.1017/S0022109018001096

Basly, S. (2024). Artificial intelligence and the future of decentralized finance. In *Decentralized Finance: The Impact of Blockchain-Based Financial Innovations on Entrepreneurship* (pp. 175–183). Springer International Publishing. DOI: 10.1007/978-3-031-49515-1_10

Bastian, M., Heymann, S., & Jacomy, M. (2009). Gephi: An open source software for exploring and manipulating networks. *Proceedings of the International AAAI Conference on Web and Social Media, 3*(1). DOI: 10.1609/icwsm.v3i1.13937

Bekaert, G., & Harvey, C. R. (2003). Emerging markets finance. *Journal of Empirical Finance*, *10*(1–2), 3–55. https://doi.org/10.1016/S0927-5398(02)00054-3

Berkowitz, J., & O'Brien, J. (2002). How accurate are value-at-risk models at commercial banks? *The Journal of Finance*, *57*(3), 1093–1111. DOI: 10.1111/1540-6261.00455

Best, P. (1998). *Implementing value at risk*. Wiley., DOI: 10.1002/0470013303

Bhardwaj, S., Sharma, I., Mahendru, S., Kaur, R., & Sharma, S. (2025). Exploring the role of AIoT in data privacy and security. In Tariq, M. (Ed.), *Merging Artificial Intelligence With the Internet of Things* (pp. 75–102). IGI Global Scientific Publishing., DOI: 10.4018/979-8-3693-8547-0.ch003

Bian, W., & Tao, D. (2009, December). Dirichlet mixture allocation for multiclass document collections modeling. In *2009 Ninth IEEE International Conference on Data Mining* (pp. 711-715). IEEE. DOI: 10.1109/ICDM.2009.102

Black, F., & Litterman, R. (1992). Global portfolio optimization. *Financial Analysts Journal*, *48*(5), 28–43. DOI: 10.2469/faj.v48.n5.28

Bley, J., & Chen, K. H. (2006). Gulf Cooperation Council (GCC) stock markets: The dawn of a new era. *Global Finance Journal*, *17*(1), 75–91. DOI: 10.1016/j.gfj.2006.06.009

Bollen, J., Mao, H., & Zeng, X. (2011). Twitter mood predicts the stock market. *Journal of Computational Science*, *2*(1), 1–8. DOI: 10.1016/j.jocs.2010.12.007

Bollerslev, T. (1986). Generalized autoregressive conditional heteroskedasticity. *Journal of Econometrics*, *31*(3), 307–327. DOI: 10.1016/0304-4076(86)90063-1

Bolton, R. J., & Hand, D. J. (2002). Statistical fraud detection: A review. *Statistical Science*, *17*(3), 235–255. DOI: 10.1214/ss/1042727940

Borkar, S., & Jadhav, A. (2024). Reinforcement learning techniques for stock trading: A survey of current research. *The Journal of Financial Data Science*, *6*(3), 38–56. Advance online publication. DOI: 10.3905/jfds.2024.1.161

Bouzgarne, I., Youssfi, M., Qbadou, M., & Bouattane, O. (2023). Deep reinforcement learning strategy in automated trading systems. *Proceedings of IRASET*, *2023*, 1–8. DOI: 10.1109/IRASET57153.2023.10152925

Box, G. E. P., & Jenkins, G. M. (1970). *Time Series Analysis: Forecasting and Control*. Holden-Day.

Breiman, L. (1996). Bagging predictors. *Machine Learning*, *24*(2), 123–140. DOI: 10.1023/A:1018054314350

Breiman, L. (2001). Random forests. *Machine Learning*, *45*(1), 5–32. DOI: 10.1023/A:1010933404324

Broner, F., Gelos, G., & Reinhart, C. (2006). When in peril, retrench: Testing the portfolio channel of contagion. *Journal of International Economics*, *69*(1), 203–230. https://doi.org/10.1016/j.jinteco.2005.05.004

Brunnermeier, M. K., & Pedersen, L. H. (2009). Market liquidity and funding liquidity. *Review of Financial Studies*, *22*(6), 2201–2238. https://doi.org/10.1093/rfs/hhn098

Calvo, G., & Mendoza, E. (2000). Rational contagion and the globalization of securities markets. *Journal of International Economics*, *51*(1), 79–113. https://doi.org/10.1016/S0022-1996(99)00038-0

Campbell, J., & Koffi, B. A. (2024). The Role of AI-powered financial analytics in shaping economic policy: A new era for risk management and national growth in the United States. *World Journal of Advanced Research and Reviews*, *23*(3), 2816–2825. DOI: 10.30574/wjarr.2024.23.3.2963

Carhart, M. M. (1997). On persistence in mutual fund performance. *The Journal of Finance*, *52*(1), 57–82. DOI: 10.1111/j.1540-6261.1997.tb03808.x

Chan, E. P. (2017). *Machine trading: Deploying computer algorithms to conquer the markets*. John Wiley & Sons. DOI: 10.1002/9781119244066

Chantrasmee, C., Jaiyen, S., Chaikhan, S., & Wattanakitrungroj, N. (2024). Stock trading signal prediction using transformer model and multiple indicators. *Proceedings of ICSEC, 2024*, 1–6. DOI: 10.1109/ICSEC62781.2024.10770734

Chawla, N. V., Bowyer, K. W., Hall, L. O., & Kegelmeyer, W. P. (2002). SMOTE: Synthetic minority over-sampling technique. *Journal of Artificial Intelligence Research, 16*, 321–357. DOI: 10.1613/jair.953

Chen, L., Pelger, M., & Zhu, J. (2024). Deep learning in asset pricing. *Management Science*, *70*(2), 714–750. DOI: 10.1287/mnsc.2023.4695

Chen, T., & Guestrin, C. (2016). XGBoost: A scalable tree boosting system. *Proceedings of the 22nd ACM SIGKDD International Conference on Knowledge Discovery and Data Mining*, 785–794. https://doi.org/10.1145/2939672.2939785

Chen, T., & Guestrin, C. (2016, August). Xgboost: A scalable tree boosting system. In *Proceedings of the 22nd acm sigkdd international conference on knowledge discovery and data mining* (pp. 785-794).

Chen, W., Rabhi, F., Liao, W., & Al-Qudah, I. (2023). Leveraging state-of-the-art topic modeling for news impact analysis on financial markets: A comparative study. *Electronics (Basel)*, *12*(12), 2605. DOI: 10.3390/electronics12122605

Chen, Y., & Wu, Z. (2023). Financial fraud detection of listed companies in China: A machine learning approach. *Sustainability (Basel)*, *15*(1), 105. DOI: 10.3390/su15010105

Chhikara, H., Chhikara, S., & Gupta, L. (2025). Predictive Analytics in Finance: Leveraging AI and Machine Learning for Investment Strategies. In *Utilizing AI and Machine Learning in Financial Analysis* (pp. 325-336). IGI Global Scientific Publishing.

Chiang, J. K., & Chi, R. (2024). A Novel Stock Price Prediction and Trading Methodology Based on Active Learning Surrogated with CycleGAN and Deep Learning and System Engineering Integration: A Case Study on TSMC Stock Data. *FinTech*, *3*(3), 427–459. DOI: 10.3390/fintech3030024

Claessens, S., & Forbes, K. (2001). *International financial contagion*. Springer.

Cohen, G. (2022). Algorithmic trading and financial forecasting using advanced artificial intelligence methodologies. *Mathematics*, *10*(18), 3302. DOI: 10.3390/math10183302

Dahlberg, T., Guo, J., & Ondrus, J. (2015). A critical review of mobile payment research. *Electronic Commerce Research and Applications*, *14*(5), 265–284. DOI: 10.1016/j.elerap.2015.07.006

Daníelsson, J. (2008). Blame the models. *Journal of Financial Stability*, *4*(4), 321–328. DOI: 10.1016/j.jfs.2008.09.003

Danielsson, J., & Shin, H. S. (2003). Endogenous risk. In *Modern Risk Management — A History*. Risk Books.

Das, N., Sadhukhan, B., Ghosh, R., & Chakrabarti, S. (2024). Developing Hybrid Deep Learning Models for Stock Price Prediction Using Enhanced Twitter Sentiment Score and Technical Indicators. *Computational Economics*, *64*(6), 1–40. DOI: 10.1007/s10614-024-10566-9

De Bondt, W. F. M., & Thaler, R. (1985). Does the stock market overreact? *The Journal of Finance*, *40*(3), 793–805. DOI: 10.1111/j.1540-6261.1985.tb05004.x

Deb, K., Pratap, A., Agarwal, S., & Meyarivan, T. (2002). A fast and elitist multiobjective genetic algorithm: NSGA-II. *IEEE Transactions on Evolutionary Computation*, *6*(2), 182–197. DOI: 10.1109/4235.996017

Deng, Y., Bao, F., Kong, Y., Ren, Z., & Dai, Q. (2016). Deep direct reinforcement learning for financial signal representation and trading. *IEEE Transactions on Neural Networks and Learning Systems, 28*(3), 653–664. DOI: 10.1109/TNNLS.2016.2522401 PMID: 26890927

Devapitchai, J. J., Krishnapriya, S. V., Karuppiah, S. P., & Saranya, S. (2024). Using AI-driven decision-making tools in corporate investment planning. In *Generative AI for transformational management* (pp. 137–160). IGI Global. DOI: 10.4018/979-8-3693-5578-7.ch006

DiMaggio, P. J., & Powell, W. W. (1983). The iron cage revisited: Institutional isomorphism and collective rationality in organizational fields. *American Sociological Review, 48*(2), 147–160. DOI: 10.2307/2095101

Dokumacı, M. (2024). AI in forecasting financial markets. *Human-Computer Interaction, 8*(1), 127. DOI: 10.62802/1twmvt88

Doshi-Velez, F., & Kim, B. (2017). Towards a rigorous science of interpretable machine learning. *arXiv preprint arXiv:1702.08608.*

Doshi-Velez, F., & Kim, B. (2017). Towards a rigorous science of interpretable machine learning. *arXiv*. https://arxiv.org/abs/1702.08608

Egghe, L., & Rousseau, R. (1990). *Introduction to informetrics: Quantitative methods in library, documentation and information science*. Elsevier Science Publishers.

Engle, R. F. (1982). Autoregressive conditional heteroscedasticity with estimates of the variance of United Kingdom inflation. *Econometrica, 50*(4), 987. DOI: 10.2307/1912773

Engle, R. F. (2001). GARCH 101: The use of ARCH/GARCH models in applied econometrics. *The Journal of Economic Perspectives, 15*(4), 157–168. https://doi.org/10.1257/jep.15.4.157

European Banking Authority (EBA). (2020). Report on big data and advanced analytics. https://www.eba.europa.eu/sites/default/files/document_library/Final%20Report%20on%20Big%20Data%20and%20Advanced%20Analytics.pdf

Faheem, M., Aslam, M. U. H. A. M. M. A. D., & Kakolu, S. R. I. D. E. V. I. (2024). Enhancing financial forecasting accuracy through AI-driven predictive analytics models. *Retrieved*, (December), 11.

Fahimnia, B., Sarkis, J., & Davarzani, H. (2015). Green supply chain management: A review and bibliometric analysis. *International Journal of Production Economics, 162*, 101–114. DOI: 10.1016/j.ijpe.2015.01.003

Fama, E. F., & French, K. R. (1993). Common risk factors in the returns on stocks and bonds. *Journal of Financial Economics*, *33*(1), 3–56. DOI: 10.1016/0304-405X(93)90023-5

Fama, E. F., & French, K. R. (2015). A five-factor asset pricing model. *Journal of Financial Economics*, *116*(1), 1–22. DOI: 10.1016/j.jfineco.2014.10.010

Fan, D., Breslin, D., Callahan, J. L., & Iszatt-White, M. (2022). Advancing literature review methodology through rigour, generativity, scope and transparency. *International Journal of Management Reviews*, *24*(2), 171–180. DOI: 10.1111/ijmr.12291

Ferreira, F. G. D. C., Gandomi, A. H., & Cardoso, R. T. N. (2021). Artificial intelligence applied to stock market trading: A review. *IEEE Access : Practical Innovations, Open Solutions*, *9*, 30898–30917. DOI: 10.1109/ACCESS.2021.3058133

Financial Stability Board (FSB). (2017). Artificial intelligence and machine learning in financial services: Market developments and financial stability implications. https://www.fsb.org/uploads/P011117.pdf

Floridi, L., Cowls, J., Beltrametti, M., Chatila, R., Chazerand, P., Dignum, V., Luetge, C., Madelin, R., Pagallo, U., Rossi, F., Schafer, B., Valcke, P., & Vayena, E. (2018). AI4people—an ethical framework for a good AI society: Opportunities, risks, principles, and recommendations. *Minds and Machines*, *28*(4), 689–707. DOI: 10.1007/s11023-018-9482-5 PMID: 30930541

Foucault, T., Gambacorta, L., Jiang, W., & Vives, X. (2025). Artificial Intelligence in finance. Centre for Economic Policy Research Press. https://cepr.org/system/files/publication-files/251574-barcelona_7_artificial_intelligence_in_finance.pdf

Friedman, J. H. (2001). Greedy function approximation: A gradient boosting machine. *Annals of Statistics*, *29*(5), 1189–1232. https://doi.org/10.1214/aos/1013203451

Furizal, F., Ritonga, A., Ma'arif, A., & Suwarno, I. (2024). Stock Price Forecasting with Multivariate Time Series Long Short-Term Memory: A Deep Learning Approach. [JRC]. *Journal of Robotics and Control*, *5*(5), 1322–1335.

George, M. (2018, September). Unsupervised Topic Detection based on 2D Vector Space model using Apriori Algorithm and NLP. In *2018 Thirteenth International Conference on Digital Information Management (ICDIM)* (pp. 279-283). IEEE. DOI: 10.1109/ICDIM.2018.8846982

Ge, Q. (2024). Enhancing stock market Forecasting: A hybrid model approach for accurate prediction of S&P 500 and CSI 300 future prices. *Expert Systems with Applications*, •••, 125380.

Go, E. J., Moon, J., & Kim, J. (2020). Analysis of the current and future of the artificial intelligence in financial industry with big data techniques. [GBFR]. *Global Business & Finance Review*, *25*(1), 102–117. DOI: 10.17549/gbfr.2020.25.1.102

Goodfellow, I. J., Pouget-Abadie, J., Mirza, M., Xu, B., Warde-Farley, D., Ozair, S., Courville, A., & Bengio, Y. (2014, June 10). *Generative adversarial networks*. arXiv.Org. https://doi.org//arXiv.1406.2661DOI: 10.48550

Goodfellow, I., Bengio, Y., & Courville, A. (2016). *Deep learning*. MIT Press.

Goyal, H., Chandel, N., Maurya, A., & Shailja, . (2024). AI-powered autonomous trading: Enhancing market efficiency through predictive analytics. *International Journal for Research in Applied Science and Engineering Technology*, *12*(11), 377–386. Advance online publication. DOI: 10.22214/ijraset.2024.65001

Guo, H., & Polak, P. (2021). *"After the Collision of Crisis and Opportunity to Redefining the Artificial Intelligence in Finance: The New Intelligent Finance Era," in Applications of Artificial Intelligence in Business*. Education, and Healthcare.

Gupta, A., Puri, M., Keshan, M., & Tiwari, V. (2024, July). AI in Financial Decision-Making: Revolutionizing Investment Strategies and Risk Management. In *This paper was presented at Global Forum for Financial Consumers (GFFC).*

Gu, S., Kelly, B., & Xiu, D. (2020). Empirical asset pricing via machine learning. *Review of Financial Studies*, *33*(5), 2223–2273. DOI: 10.1093/rfs/hhaa009

Guyon, I., & Elisseeff, A. (2003). An introduction to variable and feature selection. *Journal of Machine Learning Research*, *3*(Mar), 1157–1182.

Hamilton, J. D. (1989). A new approach to the economic analysis of nonstationary time series and the business cycle. *Econometrica*, *57*(2), 357–384. https://doi.org/10.2307/1912559

Hammoudeh, S., & Choi, K. (2007). Characteristics of permanent and transitory returns in oil-sensitive emerging stock markets: The case of GCC countries. *Journal of International Financial Markets, Institutions and Money*, *17*(3), 231–245. DOI: 10.1016/j.intfin.2005.11.002

Hasan, R., Hassan, M. K., & Aliyu, S. (2020). Fintech and Islamic finance: Literature review and research agenda. [IJIEF]. *International Journal of Islamic Economics and Finance*, *3*(1). Advance online publication. DOI: 10.18196/ijief.2122

Hasbrouck, J. (2007). *Empirical market microstructure: The institutions, economics, and econometrics of securities trading*. Oxford University Press.

Hassan, M. K., Aliyu, S., Paltrinieri, A., & Khan, A. (2018). A review of Islamic investment literature. *Economic Papers*, *38*(4), 345–380. DOI: 10.1111/1759-3441.12230

Heaton, J. B., Polson, N. G., & Witte, J. H. (2016). Deep learning for finance: Deep portfolios. *Applied Stochastic Models in Business and Industry*, *33*(1), 3–12. DOI: 10.1002/asmb.2209

He, H., & Garcia, E. A. (2009). Learning from imbalanced data. *IEEE Transactions on Knowledge and Data Engineering*, *21*(9), 1263–1284. DOI: 10.1109/TKDE.2008.239

Hendershott, T., Jones, C. M., & Menkveld, A. J. (2011). Does algorithmic trading improve liquidity? *The Journal of Finance*, *66*(1), 1–33. DOI: 10.1111/j.1540-6261.2010.01624.x

Henderson, J. V., Storeygard, A., & Weil, D. N. (2012). Measuring economic growth from outer space. *The American Economic Review*, *102*(2), 994–1028. DOI: 10.1257/aer.102.2.994 PMID: 25067841

Hicks, D., Wouters, P., Waltman, L., de Rijcke, S., & Rafols, I. (2015). Bibliometrics: The Leiden Manifesto for research metrics. *Nature*, *520*(7548), 429–431. DOI: 10.1038/520429a PMID: 25903611

Hochreiter, S., & Schmidhuber, J. (1997). Long short-term memory. *Neural Computation*, *9*(8), 1735–1780. https://doi.org/10.1162/neco.1997.9.8.1735

Holland, J. H. (1992). *Adaptation in natural and artificial systems*. The MIT Press., DOI: 10.7551/mitpress/1090.001.0001

Hong, S., & Chung, K. H. (2026). The pricing of liquidity factors. *Journal of Financial Research*. Advance online publication. https://doi.org/10.1111/jfir.70055

Huang, C., & Wang, X. (2019, July). Financial innovation based on artificial intelligence technologies. In *Proceedings of the 2019 International Conference on Artificial Intelligence and Computer Science* (pp. 750-754). DOI: 10.1145/3349341.3349504

Huffman, M. D., Baldridge, A., Bloomfield, G. S., Colantonio, L. D., Prabhakaran, P., Ajay, V. S., Suh, S., Lewison, G., & Prabhakaran, D. (2013). Global cardiovascular research output, citations, and collaborations: A time-trend, bibliometric analysis (1999–2008). *PLoS One*, *8*(12), e83440. DOI: 10.1371/journal.pone.0083440 PMID: 24391769

Hu, Z., Zhao, Y., & Khushi, M. (2021). A survey of forex and stock price prediction using deep learning. *Applied System Innovation*, *4*(1), 9. DOI: 10.3390/asi4010009

Hvidt, M. (2013). Economic diversification in GCC countries: Past record and future trends. Research Paper, Kuwait Programme on Development, Governance and Globalisation. London School of Economics. https://www.lse.ac.uk/middle-east-centre/research/kuwait-programme

IMF. (2021). *COVID-19 and emerging markets*. International Monetary Fund.

IMF. (2022). Selected Issues. International Monetary Fund.

IMF. (2023). *Global financial stability report*. International Monetary Fund.

IOSCO. (2021). *The use of artificial intelligence and machine learning by market intermediaries and asset managers*. International Organization of Securities Commissions.

Ismailova, A., Beldeubayeva, Z., Kadirkulov, K., Doumcharieva, Z., Konyrkhanova, A., Ussipbekova, D., ... & Yesmukhanova, D. (2024). Forecasting stock market prices using deep learning methods. *International Journal of Electrical & Computer Engineering (2088-8708), 14*(5).

Jack, W., & Suri, T. (2011). *Mobile money: The economics of M-PESA* (No. w16721). National Bureau of Economic Research.

Jacobi, C., Van Atteveldt, W., & Welbers, K. (2018). Quantitative analysis of large amounts of journalistic texts using topic modelling. In *Rethinking research methods in an age of digital journalism* (pp. 89–106). Routledge. DOI: 10.4324/9781315115047-7

Jain, J. (2025). AI-Driven Learning in Finance: The Future of Digital Economics. In *AI-Enabled Sustainable Innovations in Education and Business* (pp. 171-202). IGI Global Scientific Publishing.

Jain, R., & Vanzara, R. (2023). Emerging trends in AI-based stock market prediction: A comprehensive and systematic review. Applied Sciences in Engineering Conference Proceedings. DOI: 10.3390/ASEC2023-15965

Jangra, G., Irfan, M., Jangra, M., & Verma, C. (2024). Artificial Intelligence Approach to Portfolio Management: Enhancing Decision-Making, Efficiency, and Alpha Generation. In *Issues of Sustainability in AI and New-Age Thematic Investing* (pp. 59-73). IGI Global.

Jegadeesh, N., & Titman, S. (1993). Returns to buying winners and selling losers: Implications for stock market efficiency. *The Journal of Finance*, *48*(1), 65–91. DOI: 10.1111/j.1540-6261.1993.tb04702.x

Ji, G., Yu, J., Hu, K., Xie, J., & Ji, X. (2022). An adaptive feature selection schema using improved technical indicators for predicting stock price movements. *Expert Systems with Applications*, *200*, 116941. DOI: 10.1016/j.eswa.2022.116941

Jorion, P. (2007). *Value at risk: The new benchmark for managing financial risk* (3rd ed.). McGraw-Hill.

Jose, J., & Varshini, P. (2024). Integrating Technical Indicators and Ensemble Learning for Predicting the Opening Stock Price. *International Journal of Information Technology. Research and Applications*, *3*(2), 1–15.

Jung, D., Dorner, V., Weinhardt, C., & Pusmaz, H. (2018). Designing a robo-advisor for risk-averse, low-budget consumers. *Electronic Markets*, *28*(3), 367–380. DOI: 10.1007/s12525-017-0279-9

Kadioglu, Y. M., & Soydan, H. (2024). The Transformative Role of Artificial Intelligence in Finance and Economics. In *Artificial Intelligence* (pp. 193–207). CRC Press. DOI: 10.1201/9781003483571-13

Kahneman, D., & Tversky, A. (1979). Prospect theory: An analysis of decision under risk. *Econometrica*, *47*(2), 263. DOI: 10.2307/1914185

Kamara, A. F., Chen, E., & Pan, Z. (2022). An ensemble of a boosted hybrid of deep learning models and technical analysis for forecasting stock prices. *Information Sciences*, *594*, 1–19. DOI: 10.1016/j.ins.2022.02.015

Katona, Z., Painter, M. O., Patatoukas, P. N., & Zeng, J. (2024). On the capital market consequences of Big Data: Evidence from outer space. *Journal of Financial and Quantitative Analysis*, *60*(2), 551–579. DOI: 10.1017/S0022109023001448

Kayyali, M. (2025). Envisioning the Future: The Evolution and Impact of AI and Machine Learning in Finance. In *Utilizing AI and Machine Learning in Financial Analysis* (pp. 193-212). IGI Global Scientific Publishing.

Kherwa, P., & Bansal, P. (2018). Empirical Evaluation of Inference Technique for Topic Models. In *Progress in Advanced Computing and Intelligent Engineering: Proceedings of ICACIE 2017,* Volume 1 (pp. 237-246). Singapore: Springer Singapore.

Kilian, L., & Park, C. (2009). The impact of oil price shocks on the U.S. stock market. *International Economic Review*, *50*(4), 1267–1287. https://doi.org/10.1111/j.1468-2354.2009.00568.x

Kim, A. G., Muhn, M., & Nikolaev, V. (2024). Financial statement analysis with large language models. *arxiv*. /arXiv.2407.17866DOI: 10.2139/ssrn.4835311

Kokogho, E., Odio, P. E., Ogunsola, O. Y., & Nwaozomudoh, M. O. (2024). AI-Powered Economic Forecasting: Challenges and Opportunities in a Data-Driven World.

Konur, M., Göçken, M., & Dosdoğru, A. T. (2024). Stock Price Prediction Using Deep Learning Algorithms Based on Technical Indicators. *Journal of Operations Intelligence, 2*(1), 300-320.-based stock market prediction incorporating ESG sentiment and technical indicators. *Scientific Reports*, *14*(1), 10262. DOI: 10.1038/s41598-024-61106-2 PMID: 38704434

Krauss, C., Do, X. A., & Huck, N. (2017). Deep neural networks, gradient-boosted trees, random forests: Statistical arbitrage on the S&P 500. *European Journal of Operational Research*, *259*(2), 689–702. DOI: 10.1016/j.ejor.2016.10.031

Kristjanpoller, W., & Minutolo, M. C. (2018). A hybrid volatility forecasting framework integrating GARCH, artificial neural network, technical analysis and principal components analysis. *Expert Systems with Applications*, *109*, 1–11. DOI: 10.1016/j.eswa.2018.05.011

Kuhn, M., & Johnson, K. (2013). *Applied predictive modeling* (Vol. 26). Springer. DOI: 10.1007/978-1-4614-6849-3

Kumari, S. A. I. (2024). Enhanced Portfolio Management: Leveraging Machine Learning for Optimized Investment Strategies in 2024. *J. Inform. Educ. Res*, *4*, 1487.

Kumbure, M. M., Lohrmann, C., Luukka, P., & Porras, J. (2022). Machine learning techniques and data for stock market forecasting: A literature review. *Expert Systems with Applications*, *197*, 116659. DOI: 10.1016/j.eswa.2022.116659

Kunisch, S., Denyer, D., Bartunek, J. M., Menz, M., & Cardinal, L. B. (2023). Review research as scientific inquiry. *Organizational Research Methods*, *26*(1), 3–45. DOI: 10.1177/10944281221127292

Lahmini, H. M., & Zine, D. (2024, April). The Role of Artificial Intelligence in Optimizing Portfolio Management: A Literature Review. In *International Conference on Business and Technology* (pp. 122-131). Cham: Springer Nature Switzerland. DOI: 10.1007/978-3-031-67444-0_12

Leahy, E. (2024). *AI-Powered Bitcoin Trading: Developing an Investment Strategy with Artificial Intelligence*. John Wiley & Sons.

LeCun, Y., Bengio, Y., & Hinton, G. (2015). Deep learning. *nature, 521*(7553), 436-444.

Leke, C. A. (2025). The Development of Artificial Intelligence and Machine Learning: Applications in Financial Services. In *Artificial Intelligence in Accounting, Auditing and Finance: A Guide for Implementation and Use* (pp. 9–29). Springer Nature Switzerland. DOI: 10.1007/978-3-031-87368-3_2

Leng, R. (2024). AI-driven optimization of financial quantitative trading algorithms and enhancement of market forecasting capabilities. *Applied and Computational Engineering*, *100*(1), 1–6. DOI: 10.54254/2755-2721/116/20251742

Lessmann, S., Baesens, B., Seow, H.-V., & Thomas, L. C. (2015). Benchmarking state-of-the-art classification algorithms for credit scoring: An update of research. *European Journal of Operational Research*, *247*(1), 124–136. DOI: 10.1016/j.ejor.2015.05.030

Li, C. (2021). The application of artificial intelligence and machine learning in financial stability. In *The 2020 International Conference on Machine Learning and Big Data Analytics for IoT Security and Privacy: SPIoT-2020, Volume 1* (pp. 214-219). Springer International Publishing. DOI: 10.1007/978-3-030-62743-0_30

Li, D., Lu, L., Qi, Z., & Zhou, G. (2026). International corporate bond returns: Uncovering predictability using machine learning. *Journal of Financial Markets*. Advance online publication. https://doi.org/10.1016/j.finmar.2025.101008

Liu, L. X., Sun, Z., Xu, K., & Chen, C. (2024). AI-driven financial analysis: Exploring ChatGPT's capabilities and challenges. *International Journal of Financial Studies*, *12*(3), 60. DOI: 10.3390/ijfs12030060

Liu, X., Zhan, F. B., Hong, S., Niu, B., & Liu, Y. (2012). A bibliometric study of earthquake research: 1900–2010. *Scientometrics*, *92*(3), 747–765. DOI: 10.1007/s11192-011-0599-z

Li, X., & Hou, B. (2022). Correlation analysis of financial assets based on asymmetric copula. *Frontiers in Applied Mathematics and Statistics*, *8*, 1005956. Advance online publication. DOI: 10.3389/fams.2022.1005956

Lomakin, N. I., Popov, I. A., Shohneh, A. B., Maramygin, M. C., & Gorbunova, A. B. (2020). AI-system of stock exchange trading robot for financial risk hedging. Advances in Economics, Business and Management Research, 3273–3282. DOI: 10.2991/aebmr.k.200312.473

López de Prado, M. (2016). Building Diversified Portfolios that Outperform Out of Sample. *Journal of Portfolio Management*, *42*(4), 59–69. DOI: 10.3905/jpm.2016.42.4.059

López de Prado, M. (2018). *Advances in financial machine learning*. Wiley.

Lopez-Lira, A. (2025). Can large language models trade? Testing financial theories with LLM agents in market simulations. *arXiv*. /arXiv.2504.10789DOI: 10.2139/ssrn.5217340

Lucca, D. O., & Moench, E. (2015). The Pre-FOMC announcement drift. *The Journal of Finance*, *70*(1), 329–371. DOI: 10.1111/jofi.12196

Lundberg, S. M., & Lee, S. I. (2017). A unified approach to interpreting model predictions. *arXiv*. https://arxiv.org/abs/1705.07874

Markowitz, H. (1952). Portfolio selection*. *The Journal of Finance*, *7*(1), 77–91. DOI: 10.1111/j.1540-6261.1952.tb01525.x

Maurer, T. A. (Ed.). (2024). Exploring the Financial Landscape in the Digital Age*: Proceedings of the International Conference on Financial Management and the Digital Economy (ICFMDE 2023),* Kuala Lumpur, Malaysia, 15–17 December 2023. CRC Press.

McMillan, D. G. (2025). The FED model: Is it still with us? *The North American Journal of Economics and Finance*, *79*, 102448. DOI: 10.1016/j.najef.2025.102448

Mertzanis, C. (2025). Artificial intelligence and investment management: Structure, strategy, and governance. *International Review of Financial Analysis*, *107*, 104599. https://doi.org/10.1016/j.irfa.2025.104599

Mhlongo, N. Z., Falaiye, T., Daraojimba, A. I., Olubusola, O., & Ajayi-Nifise, A. O. (2024). Artificial intelligence in stock broking: A systematic review of strategies and outcomes. *World Journal of Advanced Research and Reviews*, *21*(2), 1950–1957. DOI: 10.30574/wjarr.2024.21.2.0442

Michaud, R. O. (1989). The Markowitz optimization enigma: Is 'Optimized' optimal? *Financial Analysts Journal*, *45*(1), 31–42. DOI: 10.2469/faj.v45.n1.31

Mnih, V., Kavukcuoglu, K., Silver, D., Rusu, A. A., Veness, J., Bellemare, M. G., Graves, A., Riedmiller, M., Fidjeland, A. K., Ostrovski, G., Petersen, S., Beattie, C., Sadik, A., Antonoglou, I., King, H., Kumaran, D., Wierstra, D., Legg, S., & Hassabis, D. (2015). Human-level control through deep reinforcement learning. *Nature*, *518*(7540), 529–533. DOI: 10.1038/nature14236 PMID: 25719670

Mohan, G. B., & Kumar, R. P. (2021, September). A comprehensive survey on topic modeling in text summarization. In *International Conference on Micro-Electronics and Telecommunication Engineering* (pp. 231-240). Singapore: Springer Nature Singapore.

Moody, J., & Saffell, M. (2001). Learning to trade via direct reinforcement. *IEEE Transactions on Neural Networks*, *12*(4), 875–889. DOI: 10.1109/72.935097 PMID: 18249919

Murakami, R., & Chakraborty, B. (2021, July). Neural topic models for short text using pretrained word embeddings and its application to real data. In *2021 IEEE 4th International Conference on Knowledge Innovation and Invention (ICKII)* (pp. 146-150). IEEE. DOI: 10.1109/ICKII51822.2021.9574752

Musale, D. S.Dnyandev Sopan Musale. (2024). Enhancing stock market predictions through artificial intelligence. International Journal of Advanced Research in Science. *Tongxin Jishu*, ●●●, 556–566. DOI: 10.48175/IJARSCT-15991

Nair, V. (2024). AI-powered investment strategies: Enhancing portfolio management through machine learning. [JRTCSE]. *Journal Of Recent Trends in Computer Science and Engineering*, *12*(1), 1–5.

Narayany, S. C., Zargar, F. N., & Ali, A. (2026). Does risk–return trade-off exist in the GCC stock markets? *International Journal of Emerging Markets*, *21*(4), 1033–1055. https://doi.org/10.1108/IJOEM-06-2024-1107

Nethravathi, N., Samanvitha, C., Dharmendra, H., & Ananthan, S. (2025). Unleashing the power of AI for intelligent investments: Revolutionizing stock market trading. In *Advancements in Intelligent Process Automation* (pp. 533–552). IGI Global.

Newman, D., Asuncion, A., Smyth, P., & Welling, M. (2009). Distributed algorithms for topic models. *Journal of Machine Learning Research*, *10*(8).

Ntakaris, A., Kanniainen, J., Gabbouj, M., & Iosifidis, A. (2020). Mid-price prediction based on machine learning methods with technical and quantitative indicators. *PLoS One*, *15*(6), e0234107. DOI: 10.1371/journal.pone.0234107 PMID: 32530920

Nweke, O., & Adelusi, O. (2025). Utilizing AI driven forecasting, optimization, and data insights to strengthen corporate strategic planning. *International Journal of Research Publication and Reviews*, *6*(3), 4260–4272. DOI: 10.55248/gengpi.6.0325.1209

Ogunwole, O., Onukwulu, E. C., Joel, M. O., Adaga, E. M., & Ibeh, A. I. (2025). Financial Modeling in Corporate Strategy: A Review of AI Applications For Investment Optimization.

Olanrewaju, A. G. (2025). Artificial Intelligence in Financial Markets: Optimizing Risk Management, Portfolio Allocation, and Algorithmic Trading. *International Journal of Research Publication and Reviews*, *6*(3), 8855–8870. DOI: 10.55248/gengpi.6.0325.12185

Olanrewaju, A. G., Ajayi, A. O., Pacheco, O. I., Dada, A. O., & Adeyinka, A. A. (2025). AI-driven adaptive asset allocation: A machine learning approach to dynamic portfolio optimization in volatile financial markets. *Int J Res Finance Manag*, *8*(1), 320–332. DOI: 10.33545/26175754.2025.v8.i1d.451

Olasiuk, H., Kumar, S., Singh, S., & Ganushchak, T. (2023, December). Mapping research clusters of artificial intelligence for financial services using topic modelling: A machine learning insight. In *2023 Global Conference on Information Technologies and Communications (GCITC)* (pp. 1-6). IEEE. DOI: 10.1109/GCITC60406.2023.10426342

Ou, J. A., & Penman, S. H. (1989). Financial Statement Analysis and the Prediction of Stock Returns. *Journal of Accounting and Economics*, *11*(4), 295–329. DOI: 10.1016/0165-4101(89)90017-7

Pahari, S., Polisetty, A., Sharma, S., Jha, R., & Chakraborty, D. (2023). Adoption of AI in the banking industry: A case study on Indian banks. *Indian Journal of Marketing*, *53*(3), 26–41. DOI: 10.17010/ijom/2023/v53/i3/172654

Pastor, L., & Stambaugh, R. (2003). Liquidity risk and expected stock returns. *Journal of Political Economy*, *111*(3), 642–685. https://doi.org/10.1086/374184

Paul, J., Lim, W. M., O'Cass, A., Hao, A. W., & Bresciani, S. (2021). Scientific procedures and rationales for systematic literature reviews (SPAR-4-SLR). *International Journal of Consumer Studies*, *45*(4), O1–O16. DOI: 10.1111/ijcs.12695

Pellegrino, D. A., Jr. (2011). *Interactive visualization systems and data integration methods for supporting discovery in collections of scientific information* (Doctoral dissertation, Drexel University).

Prabhakaran, P. (2024). Revolutionizing stock trading: The impact of AI on decision-making and efficiency. *International Journal for Research in Applied Science and Engineering Technology*, *12*(8), 849–852. DOI: 10.22214/ijraset.2024.64018

Prasanth, A., Densy, J. V., Surendran, P., & Bindhya, T. (2023). Role of artificial intelligence and business decision making. *International Journal of Advanced Computer Science and Applications*, *14*(6). Advance online publication. DOI: 10.14569/IJACSA.2023.01406103

Qiu, J., Wang, B., & Zhou, C. (2020). Forecasting stock prices with long-short term memory neural network based on attention mechanism. *PLoS One*, *15*(1), e0227222. https://doi.org/10.1371/journal.pone.0227222

Qiu, Y., Yang, H. Y., Lu, S., & Chen, W. (2020). A novel hybrid model based on recurrent neural networks for stock market timing. *Soft Computing*, *24*(20), 15273–15290. DOI: 10.1007/s00500-020-04862-3

Rakhmanovich, I. U., Husayn, S. O., Hasan, M. K., Samudro, E. G., & Vij, P. (2025, April). Artificial Intelligence-Driven industrial Financial Analytics for Predictive Modeling for Smarter Investments. In *2025 International Conference on Computational Innovations and Engineering Sustainability (ICCIES)* (pp. 1-5). IEEE. DOI: 10.1109/ICCIES63851.2025.11033048

Raza, H., & Akhtar, Z. (2024). Predicting stock prices in the Pakistan market using machine learning and technical indicators. *Modern Finance*, *2*(2), 46–63. DOI: 10.61351/mf.v2i2.167

Reinhart, C. M., & Rogoff, K. S. (2009). *This time is different: Eight centuries of financial folly*. Princeton University Press.

Ribeiro, M. T., Singh, S., & Guestrin, C. (2016). 'Why should I trust you?': Explaining the predictions of any classifier. Proceedings of the 22nd ACM SIGKDD, 1135–1144. https://doi.org/10.1145/2939672.2939778

Ribeiro, M. T., Singh, S., & Guestrin, C. (2016). "Why should I trust you?" *Proceedings of the 22nd ACM SIGKDD International Conference on Knowledge Discovery and Data Mining*, 1135–1144. DOI: 10.1145/2939672.2939778

Rockafellar, R. T., & Uryasev, S. (2000). Optimization of conditional value-at-risk. *The Journal of Risk*, *2*(3), 21–41. DOI: 10.21314/JOR.2000.038

Rockafellar, R. T., & Uryasev, S. (2002). Conditional value-at-risk for general loss distributions. *Journal of Banking &amp. Journal of Banking & Finance*, *26*(7), 1443–1471. DOI: 10.1016/S0378-4266(02)00271-6

Roger, J. D. D. (2024). AI-Driven Financial Modeling Techniques: Transforming Investment Strategies. *The Journal of Applied Business and Economics*, *26*(4), 63–74.

Roll, R. (1984). A simple implicit measure of the effective bid-ask spread in an efficient market. *The Journal of Finance*, *39*(4), 1127–1139. https://doi.org/10.1111/j.1540-6261.1984.tb03897.x

Ross, S. A. (1976). The arbitrage theory of capital asset pricing. *Journal of Economic Theory*, *13*(3), 341–360. DOI: 10.1016/0022-0531(76)90046-6

Sagaceta-Mejía, A. R., Sánchez-Gutiérrez, M. E., & Fresán-Figueroa, J. A. (2024). An Intelligent Approach for Predicting Stock Market Movements in Emerging Markets Using Optimized Technical Indicators and Neural Networks. *Economics, 18*(1), 20220073. DOI: 10.1515/econ-2022-0073

Sahithi, K., Chowdary, N. V., Amruta, D., & Rukum, D. (2024, November). Future Trends in Quantitative Finance and Algorithmic Trading Strategies. In *2024 International Conference on Sustainable Islamic Business and Finance (SIBF)* (pp. 160-169). IEEE. DOI: 10.1109/SIBF63788.2024.10883846

Sai, S., Arunakar, K., Chamola, V., Hussain, A., Bisht, P., & Kumar, S. (2025). Generative AI for finance: Applications, case studies and challenges. *Expert Systems: International Journal of Knowledge Engineering and Neural Networks, 42*(3), e70018. Advance online publication. DOI: 10.1111/exsy.70018

Saputra, W. H., & Safitri, I. (2022). Expansion of stock portfolio risk analysis using Hybrid Monte Carlo-Expected Tail Loss. *Jurnal Varian, 5*(2), 149–160. DOI: 10.30812/varian.v5i2.1813

Schrettenbrunner, M. (2023). Artificial-intelligence-driven management: Autonomous real-time trading and testing of portfolio or inventory strategies. *IEEE Engineering Management Review, 51*(3), 1–8. DOI: 10.1109/EMR.2023.3288609

Shaikh, S. Z., Khan, K. R., Sherwani, F. K., & Khan, M. (2025). Smart trading: Unlocking artificial intelligence in stock market. *The Business & Management Review, 15*(3). Advance online publication. DOI: 10.24052/BMR/V15NU03/ART-17

Sharma, P., & Devi, S. (2024). The future of finance: Revolutionizing the industry with artificial intelligence. In *Leveraging AI and emotional intelligence in contemporary business organizations* (pp. 187–210). IGI Global Scientific Publishing.

Sharpe, W. F. (1964). Capital asset prices: A theory of market equilibrium under conditions of risk*. *The Journal of Finance, 19*(3), 425–442. DOI: 10.1111/j.1540-6261.1964.tb02865.x

Shen, Z., Wang, Z., Chew, J., Hu, K., & Wang, Y. (2025). Artificial intelligence empowering robo-advisors: A data-driven wealth management model analysis. *International Journal of Management Science Research, 8*(3), 1–12. DOI: 10.53469/ijomsr.2025.08(03).01

Shiller, R. J. (2000). *Irrational exuberance*. Princeton University Press.

Shukla, G. K. (2024). Revolutionizing trading: Unlocking the potential of artificial intelligence in financial markets. *International Journal of Engineering Applied Science and Technology, 9*(2), 111–114. DOI: 10.33564/IJEAST.2024.v09i02.010

Singh, K. B., Aggarwal, N., & Devbrath, D. (2025, January). Revolutionizing financial analysis and decision-making with AI-powered insights. In *AIP Conference Proceedings* (Vol. 3253, No. 1). AIP Publishing. DOI: 10.1063/5.0248356

Singh, H., & Malhotra, M. (2024). *Stock market and securities index prediction using artificial intelligence: A systematic review*. Multidisciplinary Reviews., DOI: 10.31893/multirev.2024060

Singh, T., Kalra, R., Mishra, S., & Kumar, M. (2022). An efficient real-time stock prediction exploiting incremental learning and deep learning. *Evolving Systems*, •••, 1–19. DOI: 10.1007/s12530-022-09481-x PMID: 38625328

Sinha, S. K., Srivastava, M., Singh, S., & Chopra, B. U. K. (2024). Real-time stock market forecasting: A deep learning approach. *Proceedings of ICTACS, 2024*, 1424–1431. DOI: 10.1109/ICTACS62700.2024.10840702

Sironi, P. (2016). *FinTech innovation: from robo-advisors to goal based investing and gamification*. John Wiley & Sons. DOI: 10.1002/9781119227205

Strader, T. J., Rozycki, J. J., Root, T. H., & Huang, Y. H. J. (2020). Machine learning stock market prediction studies: Review and research directions. *Journal of International Technology and Information Management*, *28*(4), 63–83. DOI: 10.58729/1941-6679.1435

Stulz, R. M. (2008). Risk Management Failures: What are They and When do They Happen? SSRN *Electronic Journal*. DOI: 10.2139/ssrn.1278073

Sun, Y., Mutalib, S., Omar, N., & Tian, L. (2024). A novel integrated approach for stock prediction based on modal decomposition technology and machine learning. *IEEE Access : Practical Innovations, Open Solutions*, *12*, 95209–95222. DOI: 10.1109/ACCESS.2024.3425727

Talreja, P., & Thavi, S. (2024). The impact of AI and machine learning on stock market predictions. International Journal of Advanced Research in Science. *Tongxin Jishu*, •••, 625–633. DOI: 10.48175/IJARSCT-18971

Tariq, M. U. (2025). Bridging the Digital and Human Divide: Fostering Inclusion and Well-Being in Tech-Driven Workplaces. In Achour, Z. (Ed.), *Leading Inclusive Workplaces Through Digital Transformation and Organizational Change* (pp. 139–168). IGI Global Scientific Publishing., DOI: 10.4018/979-8-3373-5127-8.ch005

Tariq, M. U. (2025). Harnessing Big Data and Analytics for Targeted Destination Marketing Campaigns. In Soliman, M., & Elgammal, I. (Eds.), *Maximizing Destination Marketing Strategies in the Digital Era* (pp. 195–220). IGI Global Scientific Publishing., DOI: 10.4018/979-8-3693-9939-2.ch007

Tariq, M. U. (2025). Navigating Technological Disruption: Strategies for Continuous Professional Development. In Kenon, V., & Bartlett, J. (Eds.), *Gaming, Wellness, and Technology in the Bold Global Workforce* (pp. 257–278). IGI Global Scientific Publishing., DOI: 10.4018/979-8-3373-5322-7.ch009

Tariq, M. U. (2025). The Role of AI in Personalized English Language Learning. In Shukla, A., Meeprom, B., Khunasathitchai, K., & Yadav, N. (Eds.), *AI-Powered English Teaching* (pp. 93–124). IGI Global Scientific Publishing., DOI: 10.4018/979-8-3373-1952-0.ch003

Tariq, M. U. (2025). The Role of AI in Transforming Hospitality Operations-Enhancing Efficiency and Guest Experience. In Talukder, M., & Chowdhury, H. (Eds.), *Smart Operations and Enhancing Guest Experience in the Hospitality Industry* (pp. 415–446). IGI Global Scientific Publishing., DOI: 10.4018/979-8-3373-2145-5.ch016

Tayal, P., Ali, F., Pandey, S., Singh, R., Lande, J., & Pachouri, V. (2023). AI-based stock market prediction: Theoretical perspective. *Proceedings of CISCT 2023*, 1–5. DOI: 10.1109/CISCT57197.2023.10351375

Tetlock, P. C. (2007). Giving content to investor sentiment: The role of media in the stock market. *The Journal of Finance*, *62*(3), 1139–1168. DOI: 10.1111/j.1540-6261.2007.01232.x

Torkian, V., Bamdad, S., & Sarfaraz, A. H. (2025). Integrating AI and OR for investment decision-making in emerging digital lending businesses: A risk-return multi-objective optimization approach. *The Journal of the Operational Research Society*, •••, 1–20.

Touti, N., & Taïb, A. A. (2024, May). Bibliometric Analysis of Artificial Intelligence Applications in Asset Pricing. In *International Conference on Digital Technologies and Applications* (pp. 27-36). Cham: Springer Nature Switzerland. DOI: 10.1007/978-3-031-68653-5_3

Uçkan, T. (2024). Integrating PCA with deep learning models for stock market Forecasting: An analysis of Turkish stocks markets. *Journal of King Saud University. Computer and Information Sciences*, *36*(8), 102162. DOI: 10.1016/j.jksuci.2024.102162

Vaidya, C., Nazneen, G., Singh, N., Katariya, K., Ramtekkar, A., Nasare, D., & Lalmore, D. (2024). *Real-time stock forecasting: Leveraging live data and advanced algorithms for accurate predictions*. International Journal of Innovative Science and Research Technology., DOI: 10.38124/ijisrt/IJISRT24MAY059

Vapnik, V. N. (1995). *The Nature of Statistical Learning Theory*. Springer. DOI: 10.1007/978-1-4757-2440-0

Vaswani, A., Shazeer, N., Parmar, N., Uszkoreit, J., Jones, L., Gomez, A. N., ... (2017). Attention is all you need. *arXiv*. https://arxiv.org/abs/1706.03762

Vuković, D. B., Dekpo-Adza, S., & Matović, S. (2025). AI integration in financial services: A systematic review of trends and regulatory challenges. *Humanities & Social Sciences Communications*, *12*(1), 562. DOI: 10.1057/s41599-025-04850-8

Vyas, A. (2025). AI and ML: Powerful tools to revolutionize financial forecasting. January 08, 2025. http://dx.doi.org/DOI: 10.2139/ssrn.5252134

Waghela, H., Sen, J., & Rakshit, S. (2024). A Performance Analysis of Technical Indicators on the Indian Stock Market. In *Artificial Intelligence in Prescriptive Analytics: Innovations in Decision Analysis, Intelligent Optimization, and Data-Driven Decisions* (pp. 457–501). Springer Nature Switzerland. DOI: 10.1007/978-3-031-66731-2_18

Wang, C. H., Zeng, Y., & Yuan, J. (2024). Two-stage stock portfolio optimization based on AI-powered price prediction and mean-CVaR models. *Expert Systems with Applications*, *255*, 124555. DOI: 10.1016/j.eswa.2024.124555

Wang, H. C., Hsiao, W. C., & Liou, R. S. (2023). *Integrating technical indicators, chip factors and stock news for enhanced stock price predictions: A multi-kernel approach*. Asia Pacific Management Review.

Wang, W. J., Tang, Y., Xiong, J., & Zhang, Y. C. (2021). Stock market index prediction based on reservoir computing models. *Expert Systems with Applications*, *178*, 115022. DOI: 10.1016/j.eswa.2021.115022

White, H. (1988). Economic prediction using neural networks: The case of IBM daily stock returns. *IEEE International Conference on Neural Networks*, 451–458 vol.2. DOI: 10.1109/ICNN.1988.23959

Wolfram, D. (2003). *Applied informetrics for information retrieval research.*

World Bank. (2021). Frontier markets economies: Promise, performance, and prospects. https://www.worldbank.org/en/research/publication/frontier-markets

Xie, M. (2019, April). Development of artificial intelligence and effects on financial system. [). IOP Publishing.]. *Journal of Physics: Conference Series*, *1187*(3), 032084. DOI: 10.1088/1742-6596/1187/3/032084

Xu, Y., Reniers, G., & Yang, M. (2024). A multidisciplinary review into the evolution of risk concepts and their assessment methods. *Processes (Basel, Switzerland), 12*(11), 2449. DOI: 10.3390/pr12112449

Zaugg, R. E. H., West, R. E., Tateishi, I., & Randall, D. L. (2011). Mendeley: Creating communities of scholarly inquiry through research collaboration, 32–36.

Zha, R. K. S. S., & Mitra, D. (2024). Empowering Financial Decisions with AI: Optimizing Strategies for Financial Planning and Wealth Management. *Drishtikon: A Management Journal, 15*(2).

Zhou, J. (2024). The use of artificial intelligence in investment selection: Robo-advisory platform. In *Exploring the Financial Landscape in the Digital Age* (pp. 661–669). CRC Press. DOI: 10.1201/9781003508816-95

Zhou, J., Gandomi, A. H., Chen, F., & Holzinger, A. (2021). Evaluating the quality of machine learning explanations: A survey on methods and metrics. *Electronics (Basel), 10*(5), 593. DOI: 10.3390/electronics10050593

Zhuang, Y., Liu, X., Nguyen, T., He, Q., & Hong, S. (2013). Global remote sensing research trends during 1991–2010: A bibliometric analysis. *Scientometrics, 96*(1), 203–219. DOI: 10.1007/s11192-012-0918-z

Zhu, G. (2024). Application of artificial intelligence and machine learning in financial forecasting and trading. *Applied and Computational Engineering, 43*(1), 1–7. DOI: 10.54254/2755-2721/43/20230797

About the Contributors

Afef Amdouni is an Assistant Professor of Finance in the Department of Finance, College of Business Administration, Taibah University, Medina, Saudi Arabia. Her research interests focus on financial markets, artificial intelligence applications in finance, behavioral finance, and financial risk modeling. Prior to joining Taibah University, she was affiliated with the Faculty of Economic Sciences and Management at the University of Tunis El Manar, Tunisia. Dr. Amdouni earned her Ph.D. in Finance from the same institution, where she also completed her Master's and Bachelor's degrees. She is actively engaged in academic publishing and peer review activities and has held leadership roles in coordinating editorial initiatives related to interdisciplinary research at the intersection of finance and artificial intelligence.

***

Pawan Badhan is an Assistant Professor in the IT Department at Pyramid College of Business and Technology, Punjab, India. He has over 14 years of experience in teaching, research, and industry-oriented training. Pawan holds a Master of Computer Applications from Punjabi University, Patiala, and has a strong academic foundation in computer networks, machine learning, deep learning, and software engineering. His research focuses on leveraging machine learning and quantum computing for applications in IoT networks, anomaly detection, and cybersecurity. Pawan has published multiple international research papers, book chapters, and patents, including works on early disease detection and IoT-based innovations. He has served as a reviewer for leading journals such as Neural Computing and Applications (Springer) and Biomedical Signal Processing and Control (Elsevier). His contributions to academia include organizing workshops, industrial visits, and seminars to bridge the gap between theoretical knowledge and practical applications. Pawan is also a recipient of several accolades, including being recognized as an "Out-of-the-Box Thinker" by Harper Collins Publishers, India.

Pradeep Kumar Gupta is an accomplished Associate Professor of Accounting and Finance at LM Thapar School of Management, TIET, with over 20 years of academic and administrative experience. Holding a PhD in Finance from Thapar University, he specialises in corporate governance, CSR, and investment strategies. With 25+ peer-reviewed publications (Scopus/WoS indexed), 353 Google Scholar citations, and active roles in international conferences (EURAM, AoM), his research impacts both academia and industry. As Associate Dean (Accreditations & Rankings), he drives institutional excellence in business education, supported by an ICSSR-funded project (INR 1.5M). With UGC-NET qualifier and several professional certifications, he blends teaching expertise in financial management with global collaborations across the US, Europe, and Asia.

Rajat Gupta is a seasoned academic and electronics expert with 24 years of experience, including 22 years in teaching and leadership roles such as Dean, Director, and Professor. He holds a B.Tech in Electronics, an M.Tech (Gold Medalist) in Control Systems from NIT Kurukshetra, and a PhD in Advanced Filter Design. Specializing in Control Systems, SAP, and AI applications, he has published 23 papers and guided 21 M.Tech students. With expertise in SAP implementation and technical skills in Java, C++, and fuzzy logic, Dr. Gupta currently serves as a Professor at Chandigarh University, blending academic rigor with industry-relevant innovation.

Sharneet Jagirdar, FRM, is a distinguished financial professional with 20 years of diverse experience in Banking, Telecom and Education sector. Holding a PhD in Finance and certified as a Financial Risk Manager (FRM) by US GARP, Dr. Jagirdar excels in driving performance enhancement, implementing best practices, and fostering talent development. His extensive industry expertise is complemented by his academic prowess, with notable research publications and presentations at prestigious global conferences like Academy of Management, USA and European Academy of Management. As an expert in financial modelling and valuation, Dr. Jagirdar has a proven track record of success in both industry and academia. An avid runner, reader, and traveller, Dr. Jagirdar brings a well-rounded perspective to his professional endeavours.

Sanjeev Jain is armed with a Post Graduate Diploma in Management from the prestigious Indian Institute of Management Ahmedabad and a Bachelor's degree in Engineering with a Gold Medal from Swami Bikaner University, Rajasthan. He stands out as a seasoned professional with a total work experience of over 30 years of industry and teaching. He is currently serving as the Senior Director of the Centre of Excellence for Data Analytics and Digital Transformation, as well as heading the Apex Institute of Management department at Chandigarh University. Mr. Jain has played pivotal roles in shaping academic and industry landscapes. His earlier assignment at Nirma University reflects his commitment to excellence. Mr. Jain has excelled in strategy development, target setting, and plan execution throughout his career, having held key positions in business development, sales, marketing, project management, contract administration, and operations management. His expertise extends to managing profit and loss accounts, showcasing a profound understanding of revenue and cost management. Also, he has been awarded letter of appreciation for smooth conduct of the events at various instances. He has an Excellent project management and organisational skills and is highly proficient in spoken and written English. Mr. Jain has also secured two copyrights, notably: "Neurodecision Matrix of Consumer Choice (NDMCC); A structured strategic planning framework (SOSTAC). Further, he has contributed towards one case study in Taylor and Francis book entitled "Contemporary Cases in Management: Perspectives from Emerging Markets". In his distinguished career, Mr. Sanjeev Jain has contributed significantly to various fields through his research endeavors. He has written various research paper on the subject like hybrid learning, green bonds. His seminal papers include "Probabilistic Paradigms for Employee Performance Prognostication: Unveiling Influential Factors via Bayesian Networks," shedding light on innovative approaches to forecasting employee performance. Additionally, his research on "Intrusion Detection Systems for Cybersecurity using Machine Learning" addresses critical challenges in cybersecurity, demonstrating his commitment to advancing technological solutions in safeguarding digital environments. Mr. Jain's expertise extends to "IoT Smart Communication Technologies for Narrow Band IoT," where he explores the intricate realm of Internet of Things, paving the way for efficient communication technologies in IoT networks. Furthermore, his research paper entitled "The Architecture and Design of The Hadoop Distributed File System" underscore his profound understanding of distributed computing systems, contributing to the development of robust data storage solutions.

Sateesh Kumar T K, presently working as an Asst. Professor at Kristu Jayanti College Autonomous, Bengaluru, India.

Vivek Mittal is a distinguished academic and education leader with a Doctor of Philosophy (PhD) in Management (Tourism Marketing), earned between 2006 and 2010 from M.J.P. Rohilkhand University. Over the course of his career, he has developed a robust and diverse skill set that spans marketing strategy development for educational institutions, teaching and training, soft skills enhancement, educational leadership, and computer science applications in education and management. He has demonstrated strong leadership in the academic sector and is currently serving as the Director at Pyramid College of Business and Technology, Punjab, India. In this role, Dr. Mittal plays a key part in shaping institutional strategy, strengthening industry–academia collaborations, and fostering innovative learning environments. His expertise and commitment to academic excellence have contributed to advancing higher education standards, particularly in the areas of business and technology education.

Davinder Singh is a distinguished academic and industry professional with expertise in Information Technology. He currently serves as the associate Professor at, Saraswati Group of Colleges, Gharuan, Punjab, where he plays a pivotal role in academic leadership, curriculum design, faculty development, and student mentoring. His vision is to align academic programs with industry standards, equipping students with the knowledge and skills required for the modern digital era. Alongside his academic contributions, Mr. Singh is associated with Creanovation Technologies Pvt. Ltd and NextGen Academy, where he works on bridging the gap between education and industry practices. Through these platforms, he emphasizes innovation, entrepreneurship, and hands-on learning, ensuring that students are prepared for the rapidly evolving IT landscape.

Navdeep Singh is an accomplished Assistant Professor with around 8 years of academic experience, specializing in Supply Chain Management. His research has centered on designing efficient and sustainable supply chains to enhance performance within the construction industry. His teaching expertise includes key subjects such as Construction Management, PERT- CPM, and Supply chain management. In addition to his teaching responsibilities, he is actively engaged in various departmental roles, such as IQAC Coordinator. He is also involved in cutting-edge research projects, including the GREENLEAF initiative, which focuses on generating renewable energy and enhancing nature through innovative liquid plant-based air filtration, contributing to several UN Sustainable Development Goals (SDGs). He has a strong research interest in supply chain management and the application of soft computing techniques in sustainable construction.

Parul Singh is an Assistant Professor in the area of Information Management at the Indian Institute of Foreign Trade (IIFT), New Delhi, India. She teaches a range of courses to MBA and Executive Programme students, bringing both academic expertise and practical industry experience to her teaching. In addition to her academic role, she holds industrial experience, having successfully managed projects across multiple sectors, including telecommunications, IT/ITES, healthcare services, and government. She has authored multiple publications in SCOPUS-indexed and ABDC-rated journals. Her current research interests focus on ICT, Innovation

Practices, Competitiveness, Higher Education, Metaverse, Digital Marketing, Interdisciplinary studies, etc.

Surjit Singha is a passionate academician and researcher with over 15 years of professional experience spanning administration, teaching, and research. Currently serving as a faculty member at Kristu Jayanti (Deemed to be University), Dr. Singha is deeply committed to fostering academic growth and guiding students in their research pursuits. His multidisciplinary interests include the UN Sustainable Development Goals, Organizational Climate, Workforce Diversity, Organizational Culture, Human Resource Management (HRM), Marketing, Finance, International Business, Global Business, Artificial Intelligence, K12 & Higher Education, Gender, and Cultural Studies. An accomplished author and editor, Dr. Singha contributes to renowned global publications and journals and holds prominent editorial roles, including being on the Editorial Review Board of the Information Resources Management Journal (SCOPUS & WoS). With an impressive academic portfolio, Dr. Singha has published over 160+ articles, book chapters, and textbooks, including 100+ SCOPUS-indexed publications. He also holds 2+ US Copyrights and 1+ Patent, demonstrating his dedication to innovation and originality. Additionally, he has successfully completed two fully funded minor research projects from Kristu Jayanti (Deemed to be University). As a research mentor, Dr. Singha has guided numerous students and young scholars toward academic excellence. His academic qualifications include a PhD, M.Phil, and MBA (Distinction) from Christ University, M.Com, BBM from Kristu Jayanti College (Bangalore University), and PGDHE (Higher Education) from IGNOU (Central University). He is also a UGC-NET (Commerce) qualifier and serves as an Examiner for International Baccalaureate (IB).

Muhammad Usman Tariq has more than 17+ year's experience in industry and academia. He is a prolific author of research articles, case studies, book chapters, and academic books, with work spanning a wide range of disciplines. His contributions also include several patents. He is founder and CEO of The Case HQ, a unique repository for courses, narrative and video case studies. Additionally, he is President of Gulf Higher Education (Gulf HE) focused on advancing academic practice. He has been working as a consultant and trainer for industries representing six sigma, quality, health and safety, environmental systems, project management, and information security standards. His work has encompassed sectors in aviation, manufacturing, food, hospitality, education, finance, research, software and transportation. He has diverse and significant experience working with accreditation agencies of ABET, ACBSP, AACSB, WASC, CAA, EFQM and NCEAC. He is a

Principal Fellow of Advance HE UK, Senior Fellow of SEDA UK, and Chartered Fellow of CIPD UK other than Senior Member IEEE.

Index

www.ingramcontent.com/pod-product-compliance
Lightning Source LLC
LaVergne TN
LVHW081523300926
849161LV00006B/1281